D0786801

The Power of the Zoot

AMERICAN CROSSROADS

Edited by Earl Lewis, George Lipsitz, Peggy Pascoe, George Sánchez, and Dana Takagi

The Power of the Zoot

Youth Culture and Resistance during World War II

Luis Alvarez

UNIVERSITY OF CALIFORNIA PRESS
Berkeley   Los Angeles   London

University of California Press, one of the most distinguished university presses in the United States, enriches lives around the world by advancing scholarship in the humanities, social sciences, and natural sciences. Its activities are supported by the UC Press Foundation and by philanthropic contributions from individuals and institutions. For more information, visit www.ucpress.edu.

Chapter 5 contains revised material originally published as "Zoot Violence on the Home Front: Race, Riots, and Youth Culture during World War II," in Maggie Rivas-Rodriguez, editor, *Mexican Americans and World War II* (Austin: University of Texas Press, 2005). The epilogue contains revised material originally published as "From Zoot Suits to Hip Hop: Towards a Relational Chicana/o Studies," *Latino Studies* 5 (2007): 53–75.

University of California Press
Berkeley and Los Angeles, California

University of California Press, Ltd.
London, England

Library of Congress Cataloging-in-Publication Data

Alvarez, Luis, 1972–.
    The power of the zoot : youth culture and resistance during World War II / Luis Alvarez.
        p.   cm. — (American crossroads ; 24)
    Includes bibliographical references and index.
    ISBN 978-0-520-25301-8 (cloth : alk. paper)
    1. Popular culture—United States—History—20th century.   2. Youth—United States—Social life and customs—20th century.   3. Minority youth—United States—Social life and customs—20th century.
    4. Fashion—United States—History—20th century.
    5. United States—Social life and customs—1918–1945.   6. United States—Social conditions—20th century.   7. United States—Race relations.   8. World War, 1939–1945—Social aspects—United States.
    9. Sleepy Lagoon Trial, Los Angeles, 1942–1943.
    10. Zoot Suit Riots, Los Angeles, Calif., 1943.   I. Title.

E169.A45   2008
306.0973—dc22   2007033316

Manufactured in the United States of America

17   16   15   14   13   12   11   10   09   08
10   9   8   7   6   5   4   3   2   1

This book is printed on Natures Book, which contains 50% post-consumer waste and meets the minimum requirements of ANSI/NISO Z39.48–1992 (R 1997) (*Permanence of Paper*).

The publisher gratefully acknowledges the generous
contribution to this book provided by the Lisa See
Endowment Fund in Southern California History
of the University of California Press Foundation.

Contents

Illustrations

Acknowledgments
and Dedication

The Power of the Zoot would never have been if not for the generosity, support, and assistance of many people. I would like to thank, first and foremost, everyone who took the time to share with me their personal histories and recollections of the early 1940s. These former zoot suiters and their families provided the inspiration for this project. I am particularly grateful in this regard to my great uncle, Antonio Alvarez. He not only introduced me to the zoot when I first interviewed him for an undergraduate research paper many years ago, but always showed me it was possible to live with style and dignity. I dedicate this book to him.

Certain of the interviewees preferred not to have their names used. I have chosen to respect their wishes by referring to them with pseudonyms.

During my time as a graduate student at the University of Texas at Austin (UT), as a faculty member in the history departments of the University of Houston (UH) and the University of California, San Diego (UCSD), and in my travels between these institutions, this project benefited from the many friends and colleagues who shared their time, constructive criticism, and ideas on how to make it better. I thank them all. At UT, I learned a great deal from David Montejano, Toyin Falola, Neil Foley, Ted Gordon, Jose Limon, Gunther Peck, and my fellow graduate students, especially those in the Advanced Seminar in Postcolonial Borderlands and the Advanced Seminar in Chicana/o Research. At UH, Raul Ramos, Monica Perales, and Joe Glatthaar helped make the adjustment to my first job much easier, and it was a joy to work with John Hart, Sue Kellogg, Marty Melosi, Tatcho Mindiola, Steve Mintz, Joe Pratt, Lupe San Miguel, Landon Storrs, and the graduate students in my Chicana/o and ethnic studies seminars. Also at UH, Jimmy Patino provided valuable research assistance. At UCSD, I have been warmly welcomed into a rich and engaging intellectual community by each of my new colleagues in the history department and by many others across campus. In this regard, and in many cases, for their deep engagement with my work, I am particularly thankful to Jody Blanco, Fatima El-Tayeb, Yen Le Espiritu, Tak Fujitani, David Gutiérrez, Ramón Gutiérrez, Sara Johnson, Lisa Lowe, Curtis Marez, Natalia Molina, Nayan Shah, Shelley Streeby, Danny Widener, and Lisa Yoneyama. As it developed, this project also benefited greatly from my discussions and interchanges with Steve Azcona, Manuel Callahan, Ed Escobar, Judith Halberstam, Lisa Lowe, Vicki Ruiz, Sonia Saldivar Hull, Maggie Rivas-Rodriguez, George Sánchez, Chela Sandoval, Paul Spickard, Zaragosa Vargas, Victor Viesca, and Diego Vigil. I am especially grateful to Ed Escobar and Diego Vigil for generously sharing their expertise in pertinent archives and for identifying interviewees, respectively. Two other individuals, David Gutierrez and George Lipsitz, have my utmost appreciation for their unflagging support of and engagement with this work since its inception.

At the University of California Press, Niels Hooper was a wonderful editor from beginning to end, and I thank him for helping make this a better book. Ed Escobar and Vicki Ruiz provided the sort of incisive, thoughtful, and extensive reviews of the manuscript that every author should be so fortunate to have.

My family not only supported me from the beginning of this project but eagerly discussed it, attended conference presentations, read different parts of the book as it developed, and provided comfort and home-cooked meals along the research trail. I would not have enjoyed working on this book nearly as much as I did if not for the time it enabled me to spend with Sylvia Alvarez, Corey and Lankford Jackson, Vanessa and Chris Wright, and Denna and Sadys Espitia. My parents, Robert and Karen, and my sister, Amalia, are always there for me in any way I might ever ask and, at the same time, ask the hard questions that make me think about why my work is important. Marilyn Espitia lived with this project from its earliest stages as a dissertation proposal, sat through so many hours of practice job talks and conference presentations that she could have delivered the presentations herself, and, no matter my own frustrations, always believed in me.

This book was also made possible with financial assistance from the Graduate Opportunity Program, Office of Graduate Studies, and the UT history department; the history department, College of Liberal Arts and Social Sciences, and Center for Mexican American Studies at UH; dissertation and postdoctoral fellowships from the Ford Foundation; and a President's Postdoctoral Fellowship from the University of California.

Research for the book benefited greatly from the kindness of many librarians and archivists and their willingness to share their time and expertise. I especially appreciate aid from the staffs at the Perry Castañeda Library and the Nettie Lee Benson Library at UT; the Department of Special Collections at the University of California, Los Angeles; the Southern California Library for Social Studies and Research; the Huntington Library and Art Gallery; the Department of Special Collections at California State University, Long Beach; the Department of Special Collections at Stanford University; the Municipal Archives in New York City; the Schomburg Center for Black Research; and the National Archives and Records Administration, Pacific Region (Laguna Niguel).

Introduction

In his autobiography, Malcolm X recalls venturing into his local New York army recruitment office during the early years of World War II. He describes entering the armed forces depot "costumed like an actor. With my wild zoot suit I wore the yellow knob-toe shoes, and I frizzled my hair up into a reddish bush of conk. I went in, skipping and tipping, and I thrust my tattered greetings at that reception desk's white soldier— 'Crazy-o, daddy-o, get me moving. I can't wait to get in . . .'—very likely that soldier hasn't recovered from me yet." Shortly following this initial encounter, Malcolm was sent to the army psychiatrist, where he said, " 'Daddy-o, now you and me, we're from up North here, so don't you tell nobody . . . I want to get sent down South. Organize them nigger soldiers, you dig? Steal us some guns and kill up crackers!' That psychiatrist's blue pencil dropped and his professional manner fell off in all directions. He stared at me as if I were a snake's egg hatching, fumbling for his red pencil. I knew I had him . . ." Malcolm was not surprised when he soon received his 4-f card in the mail excusing him from the army.[1]

Around the same time, Alfred Barela, a young Mexican American zoot suiter from Los Angeles, wrote to a municipal court judge who had "bawled him out" for disturbing the peace. In his letter, Barela claimed,

> Ever since I can remember I've been pushed around and called names because I'm a Mexican. I was born in this country. Like you said I should have the same rights and privileges of other Americans. . . . Pretty soon I

guess I'll be in the Army and I'll be glad to go. But I want to be treated like
everybody else. We're tired of being pushed around. We're tired of being
told we can't go to this show or that dance hall because we're Mexican or
that we better not be seen on the beach front, or that we can't wear draped
pants or have our hair cut the way we want to.[2]

Unlike Malcolm's strategic use of his zoot suit to alienate himself from
the mainstream and evade the draft, Barela's comments suggest that *his*
zoot style did not preclude him from willingly joining the service in an
effort to assimilate in the United States during the war.

This book investigates the multiple meanings and immense popularity of zoot suit culture during World War II. In virtually every city from
coast to coast, young men "dressed to the nines" in a full zoot suit—with
its signature broad-rimmed hat, drape pants that ballooned out at the
knee and were closely tapered at the ankle, oversized jacket, and on
occasion, gold or silver watch chain hanging from the pocket. Young
women also crafted their own zoot style by wearing short skirts, heavy
makeup, and the same fingertip-length coats as their male counterparts.
The zoot, however, was about much more than the suit of clothes or
even the jazz music or jitterbug dancing that were such important parts
of the social scene. As a popular cultural phenomenon that captured the
attention of much of the U.S. home front, the zoot serves as a window
on what urban authorities, social reformers, the media, older generations of Americans, and zoot suiters themselves thought about whom
and what was considered American. Whether eliciting sympathy for
their struggles to adjust to the shifting wartime economy and political
climate, jealousy for their extravagant style and valuing of leisure, or
disgust for their alleged association with crime, danger, and a general
threat to the home front, zoot suiters were a lightning rod for popular
conversations about the success or failure of the war effort and, ultimately, the boundaries of the wartime national polity.

The rising tide of wartime xenophobia among Americans, which grew
as a response to overseas battles against fascism; increased migration of
African Americans, Mexican immigrants, and poor whites to big cities;
and related feelings of being left out of the wartime economic boom,
helped lead many to conflate the zoot suit with juvenile delinquency and
home front instability. In a 1943 exposé on zoot suiters, the *Washington
Post* underscored the alleged subversive tendencies of zoot suiters:

The outfit is very expensive, costing 100$ or more, has pronounced swank
and goes into infinite details. Chief features are the broad felt hat, the long
key chain, the pocket knife of certain size and shape, worn in the vest

pocket by boys, in the stocking by girls, the whiskey flask of peculiar shape to fit into the girl's bosom, the men's haircut of increasing density and length at the neck—all of which paraphernalia has symbolic and secret meanings for the initiates. In some places the wearing of the uniform by the whole gang is a danger signal, indicating a predetermined plan for concerted action and attack.[3]

Big-city newspapers and local authorities across the country similarly associated the zoot's high cost and alleged connections to violence, drinking, premarital sex, and other immoral behavior with danger and the threat of attack, characteristics that carried powerfully negative connotations in the post–Pearl Harbor wartime United States. Despite the presence of many zoot suiters in the armed services and in war industry jobs, zoot style came to represent what was morally and politically deficient with the home front.

Yet in conducting research for this book, a number of former zoot suiters I interviewed went to great lengths to explain how their fashion and style meant something very different. In the face of increasingly negative depictions of themselves in the popular media and larger society, zoot suiters' style and attitude often accentuated their own positive affirmation of one another. One former zoot suiter, a Mexican American woman named Maria who grew up in Los Angeles during the war, explained why she and her girlfriends wore their zoot style: "I felt good dressing like that. I think it's because . . . you felt like people were kind of looking down on you. You didn't feel like you belonged. But it didn't bother me, but I know a lot of people it did. They wanted to belong to a certain group, so we formed our own little group."[4]

Perry, a black youth of West Indian parents who grew up in Harlem during the early war years, similarly attested that the zoot was fundamentally about self-valorization. It was, he stated, part of "a whole mentality about looking good. The colors you saw, those peg pants, I mean, man, . . . that was it! . . . The mentality among many of the people there [in Harlem] was looking good and so the clothes and everything had a really high priority."[5] Perry's insistence that the zoot was all about "looking good" and Maria's that it made her "feel good" are not the simple propositions they might seem. Amidst growing concerns among the mainstream media, city officials, and the general public that zoot suiters undermined the war effort with their outrageous costumes and makeup, sexually loose and violent behavior, and general lack of respect for authority, "feeling good" and "looking good" were no trivial matter. For Maria, Perry, and others the zoot was more than just cloth cut and stitched together. It was also part of an outlook on and approach to life that helped them claim dignity in a society that routinely dehumanized them. Zoot suiters' fashion choices, along with their valuing of jazz music, dancing, and recreation, often entailed a critical stance toward authority that rendered back to society the aggression it practiced during wartime, while they also opened spaces of autonomy and independence for many of the youth involved.[6]

RACE, GENDER, GENERATION, AND THE ZOOT

When he was in his late teens and early twenties, during the last years of the Great Depression, my great uncle Antonio spent most of his days working in Los Angeles for the Civilian Conservation Corps, part of President Franklin Roosevelt's New Deal. He was introduced to zoot style by friends during his weekends off in East L.A., where he wore his one and only brown zoot on Fridays, Saturdays, and Sundays while attending dances or big band concerts and frequenting pool halls, malt shops, and cafés. Whenever he visited his hometown of San Diego just a few hours away, however, Antonio was always careful to never wear his zoot suit for fear his mother would "kill" him.[7] He was deeply worried about what his mother might think, say, or do if she were to find out he was a zoot suiter, because she viewed the style as disrespectful and a waste of his time and money. My great uncle Antonio's testimony underscores the generational and cultural uniqueness of the zoot in the years just before and during World War II. Antonio's experience suggests that, at a time when many Americans adhered to calls for wartime unity and conformity as the primary means to achieve economic success, social mobility, and more effective political representation, zoot suiters—at least when they weren't fearful of their parents' wrath—often highlighted their race and gender and their cultural differences from the rest of U.S. society.

The multiracial character of the zoot—evident in its popularity among Mexican Americans, African Americans, Asian Americans, and white youth—reveals that zoot suiters drew from a wide range of cultural influences that often extended far beyond their most immediate familial, neighborhood, and even "traditional" cultural worlds.[8] The predominantly working-class youth at the center of debates over the place of the zoot in home-front culture based their identities as young people in the United States at least in part on their many shared experiences with others.[9] African American, Mexican American, Asian

American, and white zoot suiters shared fashion trends, listened to the latest jazz and big band music, and danced the jitterbug or Lindy Hop together. By sharing a style and public spaces, including dance halls, movie theaters, and street corners, they not only showed that different races in the wartime United States sometimes lived, worked, or played together but also challenged the segregated sensibilities of 1940s America.

The social practices and behavior of zoot suiters also often conflicted with gender norms regarding how young men and women should act.[10] Because of popular doubts about their active commitment to the war effort, the masculinity of male zoot suiters, in particular, was often construed as an affront to the heroic masculinity of white sailors and soldiers. Nor was masculinity the property solely of men or femininity solely that of women. Male zoot suiters were often labeled by urban authorities, the media, and the general public as overly feminine for their constant attention to appearance, and female zoot suiters as too masculine for what was perceived as bold and very public behavior. The subversive gender dynamics of the zoot were also apparent in the way zoot suiters struggled among themselves for ownership of style, neighborhood turf, and sexual companionship. When young women fended off unwanted sexual advances, young men and women sometimes violently fought one another. When zooters engaged in sexual behavior with one another, intrazoot gender dynamics sometimes challenged social taboos against interracial dating and miscegenation and assumptions about how young people should act in public.

The multiracial, gendered, and transregional nature of the zoot suggests that zoot suiters were part of a much broader network of wartime popular cultural production and consumption, social relationships, and political struggles. Consequently, as much as this study highlights the life experiences of zoot suiters, it also examines nonzoot youth, parents and older generations of nonwhite communities, local authorities, and journalists, all of whom had much to say about zoot suits and those who wore them. While this book's primary focus is zoot suiters, it also considers how their wartime experiences resonated and conflicted with those of defense workers, military personnel, and countless others on the home front. For each of these groups, the zoot suit, whether viewed in a positive or negative light, was an important part of home-front culture. Many nonzoot youth saw zoot suiters as "clowns" or "hoodlums," much as many local officials and journalists considered the zoot a symbol of juvenile delinquency. Like my great uncle Antonio's mother, older members of nonwhite communities often looked on the zoot with disdain for its alleged affiliation with gangs, crime, drugs, and prostitution—activities seen as undermining the wartime efforts of African Americans and Mexican Americans to assimilate into U.S. society. In the end, this book examines how a diverse group of Americans made sense of the zoot and understood it as critical to wartime debates over the makeup of U.S. identity and the nation. While some have labeled those who lived through World War II the "greatest generation" for winning the war and launching the United States into the role of global superpower, the history of the zoot illustrates that the wartime generation was not a monolith, that home-front politics were contested, and that young people played a critical role in the fate of the nation at war. If nothing else, zoot suiters revealed the plurality in American identity and illuminated the wide range of social relationships possible on the home front.[11]

THE POWER OF THE ZOOT

Zoot suiters elicited commentary from a number of critics both during and after the war. In the 1940s, for example, Carey McWilliams, Beatrice Griffith, and Octavio Paz offered widely varying interpretations of the zoot as emblematic of Mexican Americans' cultural struggle to be accepted in U.S. society.[12] During the Civil Rights Movement, the growth of Chicana/o and African American studies helped elevate the zoot as an icon of historical resistance against assimilation and struggle for the cultural autonomy of nonwhites. Since then, following the first book-length study of the zoot, by Mauricio Mazón in the 1980s, historians Edward Escobar and Eduardo Pagan have illuminated the ways zoot culture reflected government policy and society's attitudes toward racial minorities and the ways the nonwhite middle class struggled for acceptance during the war.[13] An even younger generation of scholars has continued to explore more deeply the gender, sexual, and ethnic character of the zoot as a means to better understand the identity and agency of young Mexican Americans and African Americans.[14]

This book builds on these works by telling the story of the zoot with the youth themselves as central figures. Highlighting the perspective of zoot suiters reveals the race, gender, and regional differences among them, their connections with other Americans during World War II, and a narrative in which they aren't simply victims to forces outside their control. *The Power of the Zoot* departs from previous studies that characterize zoot suiters predominantly as objects of middle-class social reform concerned with wartime juvenile delinquency, as targets of state-sanctioned violence at the hands of city police and white military personnel, or as ethnic studies icons of resistance. Zoot suiters were not simply metaphors for the political agendas of others; rather they practiced their own cultural politics that, if examined carefully, can teach us a great deal about how seemingly powerless populations craft their own identities and claim dignity. Moreover, by investigating zoot suiters in both Los Angeles and New York, the two urban areas where the zoot was most a part of the cultural landscape, I demonstrate how zoot suiters' experiences in specific places were linked to broader flows of culture, economy, and politics. Rather than view the zoot as a singularly ethnic, strictly male, or regional cultural experience, in other words, I understand it as a multiracial, gendered, and national phenomenon.

In too many historical studies of U.S. youth culture the youth themselves are rendered invisible, perhaps in part because, as cultural critic and historian George Lipsitz asserts, "public records most often reflect the concerns of those in power and only rarely contain evidence of the thoughts, action, or aspirations of teenagers and young adults unless those groups are seen as some kind of threat to people with power."[15] Examining the history of zoot suiters thus requires taking seriously the experiences and meanings of youth during World War II.[16] Because "youth" were increasingly considered a critical part of the nation's ultimate success or failure during the war, they were expected to contribute to the war effort as sailors, soldiers, or defense workers. At the same time, the war increased unsupervised leisure time for youth, allowed them to cultivate a sense of independence and responsibility for their own decision making, and led to their emergence as a distinct consumer market. While many zoot suiters participated in the war effort, they were also regularly linked to juvenile delinquency and home-front instability. The range of zoot suiter experiences thus suggests that their youthfulness was determined not just by their age but also by the unique experiences that stemmed from the liminal position they occupied between child and adult during wartime.[17]

Treating zoot suiters as serious historical actors also mandates looking beyond formal political venues such as labor organizations and elections to more fully understand the history of marginalized populations. People's everyday cultural practices, including fashion, music, and dance, are often among the most common resources they use to garner strength, make their lives better, and shape the society in which they live. Indeed, as the African American author and cultural critic Ralph Ellison remarked in 1943, "perhaps the zoot suit conceals profound political meaning; perhaps the symmetrical frenzy of the Lindy Hop conceals clues to great potential power."[18]

Heeding Ellison's observation, this book makes dignity a key feature in the history of zoot suiters.[19] More than the static quality of being worthy, honored, or esteemed, dignity encompasses the variety of ways zoot suiters struggled to make sense of the world around them and navigate the poverty many of them faced on a daily basis. Their cultural practices, including choices in fashion, music, and dance, both claimed dignity and challenged the denial of their dignity by others in wartime society. The struggle for dignity by zoot suiters was thus a politics of refusal: a refusal to accept humiliation, a refusal to quietly endure dehumanization, and a refusal to conform. As historian Stuart Cosgrove suggests, the zoot was a cultural gesture signifying the refusal "to concede to the manners of subservience."[20]

Dignity, of course, may very well have meant something different for zoot suiters of different races, genders, and regions. Dignity for a black male zoot suiter in New York, in other words, was often not the same as dignity for a Mexican American female zoot suiter in Los Angeles. Some claimed dignity by voicing displeasure with second-class citizenship. Others claimed it by joining the military or simply being the best jitterbug dancer at a night club. Zoot suiters' claims to dignity, furthermore, often contradicted, or even hampered, the struggles for dignity by others, including fellow zoot suiters. Many male zoot suiters, for example, reinforced submissive female gender roles by expecting women zoot suiters to submit to their sexual desires. The money spent on fashion, music, movies, and other forms of recreation served only to oil the gears of the wartime capitalist boom that helped alienate many of the youth to begin with. Part of what this book investigates, consequently, is how the zoot functioned as a form of opposition at the same that it reinforced wartime hierarchies of race, gender, and class power. In a more theoretical context, literary critic Ross Chambers similarly notes that some acts of resistance directly challenge unequal access to resources and power while others simply create "room to maneuver" by subtly undermining status quo relationships while often reinforcing larger structures of domination.[21]

If dignity helps provide a fresh vocabulary for understanding the history of zoot suiters during World War II, it also illuminates the terrain on which their efforts to navigate the wartime United States unfolded.

The most prominent sites explored in the chapters that follow are the physical and discursive bodies of zoot suiters, along with the public spaces they inhabited. Zoot bodies were targets of practices designed to subject them to the authority of others and home to practices that subverted such authority.[22] Public space—including cafés and restaurants, places of entertainment, and city streets—similarly functioned as sites where zoot suiters both claimed dignity and encountered the discipline and disapproval of local officials and the general public. While zoot suiters were denied dignity when their bodies were discursively constructed by city authorities and journalists as dangerous, criminal, and threatening to the war effort, or were physically beaten by police, renegade civilians, or servicemen, they employed a "body politics of dignity" to confront such dehumanizing rhetoric and practices.[23] While many zoot suiters' struggles for dignity may not always, or even often, have directly challenged the racism or sexism of the state, middle-class social reformers, or the wartime political economy, they did at times subvert dominant race and gender relations and thus make them unworkable in the everyday circles of youth.

The stories of Malcolm X and Alfred Barela with which this introduction begins underscore the complex history of the zoot. The experiences of both young men demonstrate how nonwhite youth simultaneously experienced social alienation and struggled for national belonging, used their own bodies and public space to craft a politics of opposition and accommodation, and challenged notions of race, gender, and nation as fundamentally white at the same time that they reinforced their own marginalization. Malcolm X's use of his body as the vehicle for his outrageous suit of clothes; for his "skipping," "tipping," and "thrusting" in the face of authority; and for his proclamation to organize southern African Americans marked it as a site of struggle against the presumably white, uniformed, and patriotic soldier. Malcolm X's zoot performance expressed displeasure with the seemingly contradictory expectation that he serve in the armed forces even though he and other African Americans were denied some of the privileges of U.S. democracy at home. Alfred Barela's willingness to place himself on the front lines similarly identified his body as the critical terrain on which his manhood and identity as an American depended. Unlike Malcolm X, however, Barela eagerly sought to prove his worthiness for U.S. citizenship and national belonging by volunteering for military duty.[24] Although Malcolm X and Barela expressed opposing objectives, their testimonies together suggest that hep cats (as African American zoot suiters were often called), pachucos (as Mexican American zoot suiters were referred to), and others who donned the zoot during World War II practiced a complicated and sometimes contradictory cultural politics in which they did not simply assimilate into wartime society or rebel against it.[25] Whether rejecting or embracing the expectation that they contribute to the war effort, zoot suiters sought dignity in the face of dehumanization and often difficult life circumstances.

The rest of this book is organized into three parts. Part I, "Dignity Denied: Youth in the Early War Years," discusses the political and economic context of the United States in the early 1940s, when the zoot suit style grew in popularity. In chapters 1 and 2, I explore how the wartime political economy fostered discrimination and segregation in employment, housing, education, and law enforcement. Focusing on the two largest urban areas of zoot activity, Los Angeles and New York, these chapters focus on how and why the zoot suit came to be a symbol of unpatriotic and subversive behavior. I also examine the efforts of middle-class white and nonwhite social reformers who, albeit unwittingly and with noble intentions, used the zoot as a vehicle for pushing their Americanization agendas. For nonwhites in particular, the method of performing normative race and gender identities to secure equality identified zoot suiters as alien and disruptive. Drawing from the archives of local officials in Los Angeles and New York, the records of Mexican American and African American reformers, and the mainstream press in both cities, part I shows the different ways nonwhite youth were racialized during the early war years and ways their dignity was denied on the home front, and argues that nonwhite middle-class activists were complicit in the dehumanization of nonwhite working-class youth.

Part II, "The Struggle for Dignity: Zoot Culture during World War II," turns to how zoot suiters created their own style that challenged dominant ideas about U.S. identity and the nation, explored the style's possibilities, and claimed dignity. Chapters 3 and 4 shed light on the intricacies of zoot fashion, speech, music, and dance and reveal how zoot suiters mobilized their own bodies and occupied public spaces in the face of their dehumanization. While distinguishing between Mexican American and African American male zoot styles, part II also explores more fully the gendered dimensions of zoot culture, including the vibrant style of women zoot suiters. The race and class injuries suffered by nonwhite youth detailed in part I were often experienced as insults to their gender identity. This, in turn, led them to create new masculine and feminine identities in an effort to restore their dignity. In struggling for dignity on the terrain of gender, however, some male zoot suiters injured the dignity of women. While this section of the book highlights the resistance of zoot suiters to Jim Crow segregation and constrictive gender roles, it also demonstrates that the relationship among zoot suiters reinforced gender roles and that zoot suiter consumption fueled the wartime economy that helped alienate them to begin with. Chapters 3 and 4 rely heavily on interviews of former zoot suiters. These oral histories highlight the perspective of zoot suiters and help provide "thick description" of their cultural performance. Although offering perspectives not available from other sources, oral history also entails the challenge of accounting for the inaccuracies of historical memory, including contradictions in the meaning, timing, and importance of events, people, and ideas. Throughout part II, I strive to corroborate the stories, dates, and names conveyed in oral histories with other sources.[26] While part II does not offer a comprehensive account of wartime youth culture, it does provide a race, gender, and regional analysis of zoot style as one contribution to mapping the intersections between the cultural histories of Mexican Americans, African Americans, and to a lesser extent, Japanese Americans and Filipina/o Americans.

Part III, "Violence and National Belonging on the Home Front," examines how the series of race riots on the home front quashed the cultural politics and claims to dignity by zoot suiters and other nonwhites. Focusing on June of 1943, chapter 5 probes the so-called Zoot Suit Riots in Los Angeles by rereading the records of city politicians, activists, and military personnel, as well as incorporating the testimonies of nonwhite youth who lived through the violence. Chapter 6 connects the riots in Los Angeles with violence against zoot suiters in other urban areas, as well as labor and race riots in Detroit, Harlem, and the South during the same summer of 1943. While most previous scholarship treats these riots as separate episodes caused by increasing local hysteria concerning wartime consensus, part III highlights the riots as a national trend toward vigilante violence as a mechanism of social control. These chapters view the efforts of zoot suiters to achieve cultural autonomy and of nonwhite workers to improve employment opportunities as two sides of the same coin. Both types of self-activity challenged dominant ideas about race and gender and, as a result, sparked violent reactions. Violence thus emerges in part III as an important arena in which the boundaries of U.S. identity were physically debated.

The epilogue briefly considers youth cultural production in the United States since World War II. While zoot suiters were politicized for their insurgent behavior, it was the postwar youth cultural workers who more directly confronted structural inequality. The cultural politics and imaginative social possibilities practiced by zoot suiters in the 1940s, in other words, served as something of a dress rehearsal for more overtly politicized social movements in later years. Rather than trace the zoot suit through the postwar decades as a commodity or icon, therefore, I end *The Power of the Zoot* by speculating about the shifting cultural relationships and struggles for dignity by African American and Mexican American youth during the civil rights era and in more recent times, paying particular attention to their literary and musical production. Throughout this book my goal is to listen to what zoot suiters have to tell us about the United States during World War II. In doing so, my intension is to illuminate not only what happened in the past but also what *might* have happened and how such possibilities might help us make sense of the present and imagine a different future.

PART ONE

Dignity Denied

Youth in the Early War Years

CHAPTER I

Race and Political Economy

During the early years of World War II, William Dickerson became the first African American to complete the training course in aircraft metalworking at Bakersfield Junior College in south-central California. At a time when few African Americans even enrolled in such courses, let alone graduated, Dickerson's confidence and pride were at an all-time high when he subsequently sent his application for employment to the Consolidated Aircraft Company of San Diego. Although the company had secured millions of dollars in wartime federal contracts and advertised that it would hire all youths who had completed appropriate training, its response was a simple and blunt: "No Negroes Accepted." While Dickerson did what he thought necessary to be in a position to contribute to the U.S. war effort and improve his own standard of living, his efforts, according to the investigative report on his case of discrimination by the National Negro Congress (NNC), were rewarded with "all the stinging, insulting impact of a slap in the face."[1]

The discouragement and frustration Dickerson must have felt after his rejection reflects the paradoxical place of many African Americans in the U.S. political economy during the early 1940s. On the one hand, most young, able-bodied African Americans, along with their Mexican American counterparts, were expected to support the war effort at home or serve in the armed forces overseas as part of the grand plan to defeat fascism. On the other hand, many of these same individuals were excluded from discourses of patriotism and national belonging because of their race or ethnicity. African Americans and Mexican Americans were simultaneously viewed as much needed participants in the war effort and as marginal to the national polity.[2]

The paradoxical position of nonwhites on the home front not only denied them their dignity but also pushed race relations to the forefront of domestic political debate. As U.S. involvement in the conflict overseas intensified, so did discussions about the role of African Americans, Mexican Americans, and Asian Americans in the war effort and concerns about whether they posed threats to the stability of the home front. Race discrimination in war industry employment and in the policing of nonwhite communities emerged as critical political issues. The wartime political economy hindered the full inclusion of many African Americans and Mexican Americans in the war effort and, as a result, denied them equal membership in U.S. society. Race discrimination and police violence denied dignity to nonwhite Americans and made nonwhite youth in particular an increasingly important focus of home-front politics. Discrimination and police violence revealed the limited access to wartime resources and placed limits on freedom of movement and personal expression. By juxtaposing the wartime experiences of African Americans and Mexican Americans in Los Angeles and New York City, this chapter illustrates the national scope of wartime race relations and the extent of dignity's denial.

Entry into the war increased employment and political opportunities for many African Americans, Mexican Americans, and women.[3] While rejections like William Dickerson's were more the norm at the beginning of war, the desperate need for labor led to more success stories in following years. The number of women in the workforce, for example, increased from 12 to 18 million between 1940 and 1945.[4] In her seminal work on seasonal cannery workers in California, historian Vicki Ruiz details how a number of Mexican American women left for more stable and higher-paying positions in defense industry plants as the war unfolded.[5] Similarly, African Americans constituted 8 percent of all war workers in 1945, up from 3 percent in 1942, and, while virtually no Mexican Americans were employed in Los Angeles area shipyards in 1941, 17,000 worked there by 1944.[6] The explosion of wartime manufacturing not only helped lift the nation from the doldrums of the Great Depression but also enabled millions of marginalized and previously underemployed populations to partake in the long-awaited and much needed economic growth by taking jobs and earning wages previously held mainly by white men.

Following the bombing of Pearl Harbor and throughout U.S. involvement in the war, thousands of young African Americans and Mexican Americans also joined the armed forces to help defend U.S. democracy in Europe, the Pacific, and elsewhere.[7] More than 3 million African Americans registered under the Selective Service Act of 1940, and despite a rejection rate more than twice that for white applicants, approximately 1 million African Americans served during World War II.[8] Once enlisted in the army or navy, African Americans still faced daily segregation in their units, eating and sleeping arrangements, and occupational assignments. African Americans were still prohibited from joining the Marines.[9] Mexican Americans did not experience segregation in the military to the extent African Americans did. More than 350,000 served in the armed forces during World War II, many of them engaging in combat on the front lines and earning numerous military honors.[10] Through their active participation in the war effort, whether as factory workers or soldiers, many African Americans, Mexican Americans, and women implicitly made the case for their full inclusion and assimilation into U.S. society.

As historian Gary Gerstle argues, however, "if World War II was a 'good war,' it was also a 'race war.'"[11] Citizenship and national belonging were often defined by participation in the war effort, which was in turn routinely restricted, or at least segregated, by race and conflated with whiteness. The demand for more employees and servicemen on the part of corporate employers and government officials did not ease longstanding principles of Jim Crow segregation or enhance socioeconomic mobility for African Americans and Mexican Americans. Like Dickerson, some were still refused war industry jobs outright because of their race or ethnicity. Of the many African Americans and Mexican Americans who did secure employment in the aircraft factories and shipyards of California, the Pacific Northwest, the Atlantic seaboard, the Gulf coast, and elsewhere, most were often relegated to the lowest-paid positions with little hope of promotion. Even though the rhetoric of home-front unity offered African American, Mexican American, and women citizens the chance to demonstrate their patriotism, the boundaries of national identity were also marked in racial and gendered terms. While World War II is often considered a turning point in the integration of nonwhites and women into U.S. society, the period also underscored their status as second-class citizens.

Segregation and systematic discrimination based on race were imposed by local officials, often enthusiastically reinforced by the mainstream press and general public, and resulted in everyday discrimination in housing, education, and public services against nonwhites. In areas with large numbers of African Americans and Mexican Americans, it was not unusual for them to be barred from restaurants, public swimming pools, parks, theaters, and schools. In many places, nonwhites were allowed to visit public pools or parks only on a certain day of the week. Signs that read, "Tuesday's reserved for Negroes and Mexicans" were not uncommon.[12] In many retail businesses where African Americans and Mexican Americans were allowed, separate-seating arrangements relegated them to balconies or other less desirable sections. Schools were often segregated by locale, language, or race, leaving African American and Mexican American youth with less qualified instructors, inadequate educational supplies, and the worst facilities for learning.[13] Historian David Montejano points to the similar Jim Crow experiences of Mexican Americans and African Americans in Texas, arguing that "there was no constitutionally sanctioned 'separate but equal' provision for Mexicans as there was for blacks. . . . But in political and sociological terms, blacks and Mexicans were basically seen as different aspects of the same race problem."[14]

Although where in a movie theater one could sit or which day of the week one could swim at a local pool may not seem vitally important, such segregation and race discrimination helped police the boundaries of U.S. cultural citizenship.[15] For their African American and Mexican American targets, these policies and attitudes were a dehumanizing experience that underscored their inferior status. While discrimination and segregation translated into a materially measurable loss of opportunity and resources for nonwhites, they also stripped many of the less tangible right to live with dignity.

Focusing on Los Angeles and New York, two of the nation's centers of war production, this chapter investigates how race discrimination and police violence limited the social mobility of African Americans and Mexican Americans, marked their physical and discursive bodies as threats to the stability of the home front, and dehumanized them, often in public view.[16] Despite the increase in the number of war industry jobs for nonwhites following the bombing of Pearl Harbor, employers continued to limit access to jobs for African Americans and Mexican Americans, stunted their upward mobility, and characterized them as inferior workers. Big-city law enforcement viewed them as criminal and dangerous — perceptions that led to increasing use of violence as a method of social and political control. The lives of many nonwhites in

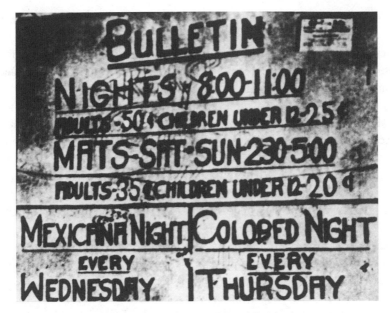

Figure 1. Wartime segregation in a Los Angeles theater, ca. 1942.
Alice McGrath Papers, 1490 b2 f11 18, Department of Special
Collections, Charles E. Young Research Library, University of
California, Los Angeles (UCLA).

the early 1940s were thus defined in part by the denial of their dignity by
forces borne of the wartime political economy.

WARTIME IN THE CITY OF ANGELS

Perhaps more than any other region in the United States, the West experienced an industrial boom during World War II. Driven by such traditional war industries as aircraft construction and shipbuilding, along with the production of large amounts of raw materials including steel, aluminum, and oil, the western economy sustained remarkable growth. During the war years, the region attracted upwards of $40 billion in funds from the federal government, and a lion's share of this money was funneled into California factories producing war materials.[17] New factories and service industries stimulated extensive networks of military and science centers in Los Angeles and San Diego, creating a desperate need for workers all along the Pacific Coast.[18]

The prospect of employment increased the flow of migrants into Southern California. California's population grew by nearly 4 million people in the 1940s, equaling almost half of all migrants from east of the Mississippi River.[19] The growth of ship and aircraft construction industries helped fuel the continuation of the Great Migration, which included more than a quarter of a million African Americans from the Deep South, as well as the immigration of more than 500,000 Mexicans from south of the border.[20] In 1940, on the eve of U.S. entry into World War II, Los Angeles was home to 64,000 African Americans and at least 220,000 ethnic Mexicans, of whom more than 65,000 were Mexican immigrants.[21]

Despite the growth of war industries in Southern California, however, many recent arrivals found it difficult to secure employment during the initial war years. Very few African Americans, in particular, worked for the major military contractors when the United States entered the war. In 1941, for example, Douglas Aircraft Corporation employed only 10 African Americans out of more than 30,000 employees, North American Aviation, Inc., employed 8 African Americans out of 12,500 employees, Lockheed-Vega employed 54 black workers out of 48,000 employees, and out of nearly 3,000 employees, Bethlehem Shipbuilding employed only 2 African Americans. Mexican Americans were employed in war industry jobs in larger numbers, as evident in their making up nearly 10 percent of Bethlehem employees.

Although the Mexican American population was nearly four times that of African Americans in the Los Angeles area, Mexican Americans entered the job market at a lower rate. Employer arguments against hiring Mexican Americans included beliefs that "the average Mexican doesn't seem to be in the market for jobs," "they [Mexicans] probably expect to get agricultural work, or construction labor," or "they do not have confidence in themselves or in the Employment Service."[22] The line between Mexican Americans and Mexican nationals was often blurred, as both groups were excluded from the war effort because of their ethnicity, language, or, in the case of Mexican immigrants, nationality. Both groups were also often considered incapable of adequately performing skilled labor, acquiring the education needed for higher-level jobs, or simply satisfying the cultural expectations of war workers to be suitably "American." The special committee on Mexican relations of the 1942 Los Angeles County Grand Jury, for example, argued in a letter to the U.S. secretary of war that even U.S.-born Mexican Americans were often suspected of being undocumented noncitizens and, along with their Mexican national counterparts, often denied war industry jobs at the same time they were freely drafted into the armed forces.[23] On the other hand, as historian Neil Foley has argued, compared to most African American workers, the growing Mexican American middle class was able to more effectively declare a white racial identity, in what would emerge as a common strategy for many Mexican Americans to demand equal citizenship.[24]

The largest corporations in California denied violating Executive Order 8802, whereby the president prohibited race discrimination in employment. In fact, however, a number of them did rely on racist hiring practices, particularly when it came to African American applicants. North American Aviation, for example, circulated public statements throughout 1941 that African Americans would be hired only as janitors and that it did not want African Americans working for the company who were "too light, too smart or too young." The owner of Paulsen and Nardon Company of Los Angeles similarly declared that he "would not hire Negroes if he could help it, that he didn't see any need to employ Negroes when he could get sufficient good white help." Ironically, however, many of these same companies, including Douglas Aircraft, North American Aviation, Bethlehem Shipbuilding, and Consolidated Aircraft Corporation, claimed there was no evidence of racial bias in their hiring process. The Vultee Aircraft Company in the Los Angeles area even argued that the fact that the company had never hired an African American did not prove discrimination.[25] Historian Josh Sides concludes that "both within and outside the workplace, African Americans encountered disheartening and capricious restrictions that made economic parity with whites virtually impossible."[26] On the whole, the track record for defense corporations in Southern California during the early war years shows that they only reluctantly hired nonwhite workers and relegated those they did hire to the lowest-paid positions regardless of skill and denied them opportunity for upward mobility, unionization, or long-term job security.

Given the challenges many African Americans and Mexican Americans faced in securing defense industry jobs in the area, a number of Los Angeles–based organizations pressed for enlarging the role of nonwhites in the war effort. Following the lead of national efforts to desegregate the armed forces and the domestic workplace, including those of the National Association for the Advancement of Colored People (NAACP) and A. Philip Randolph's March on Washington, several social reform groups in Los Angeles—among them the Young Men's Christian Association (YMCA), the Citizens Committee for Latin American Youth (CCLAY), and an organization of area high school staff and teachers—advocated the hiring of Mexican American and African American youth in defense jobs. Heeding calls by local officials and the general public to help defend the country, many Mexican American and African American community leaders considered employment as a welder, woodworker, sheet metal worker, or riveter in shipbuilding and aircraft construction as prized opportunities to contribute to the war effort. Many groups sponsored programs in "war emergency and defense" devoted to strengthening public morality in wartime, training workers for war industry jobs, and even providing free lodging and food for youth arriving from outside the Los Angeles area in search of employment.[27] To meet their goal of integrating African Americans and Mexican Americans into the wartime economy, however, many community-based organizations were forced to recognize that systemic race discrimination continued to exclude many of their constituents from full participation. The Los Angeles council of the National Negro Congress (NNC), for example, argued that the discrimination against African Americans in defense industries was of the same ilk as other Jim Crow policies aimed at limiting the upward mobility of black communities.[28] For many African Americans and Mexican Americans, participation in wartime employment was a way to improve one's socioeconomic position and demonstrate national loyalty by performing normative U.S. identities in a time of crisis.

Those concerned with the plight of nonwhite workers often argued that race discrimination in war industries was counterproductive because it limited the number of able-bodied Americans contributing to the war effort. In a speech in March 1943 Charlotta Bass, owner of the African American newspaper the *California Eagle* and first black member of the Los Angeles County Grand Jury, determined that racial discrimination greatly hampered the manufacturing of airplanes and ships in Los Angeles. She emphasized that African American women, in particular, were often discharged from low-level positions at aircraft plants for little or no reason, that employers prevented promotion of qualified black workers, and that in workplaces where the American Federation of Labor (AFL) had a strong presence, most nonwhite workers were refused skilled positions. African American and Mexican American women who did obtain lower-end positions, Bass pointed out, were exploited by poor wages, exclusion from unions, and lack of upward mobility. Bass claimed that these undemocratic practices not only limited production but, ultimately, endangered the lives of men fighting on the front lines.[29]

Because of increasing labor shortages and thanks to the work of Bass, the CCLAY, and other like-minded Angelinos, the numbers of African Americans and Mexican Americans employed in war industry jobs rose dramatically as U.S. involvement in the war deepened. By early 1943, the numbers of African American workers in the aircraft construction industry rose to 2,000 employees at Douglas Aircraft, 2,500 at North American Aviation, 1,700 at Lockheed-Vega, and 800 at Vultee Consolidated. The shipyards also saw the number of African American workers rise by 1943, with 1,200 employed by California Shipping, 400 by Western Pipe and Steel, 300 by Bethlehem, 300 by Consolidated, 200 by Los Angeles Dry Dock, and 150 by Haagson. By 1944, nearly 15 percent of shipyard workers in Los Angeles were Mexican American, including over 1,300 at California Shipping alone.[30]

While the intensifying labor shortage led to more jobs for African Americans and Mexican Americans, and thus more workplace interaction between the two groups, inequality between them and white workers persisted. Most nonwhite workers were hired for positions requiring the lowest skill, leaving them at the bottom of company payrolls and with fewer benefits than white workers. Access to higher-paying jobs with better chances of promotion was particularly restricted for African American workers, who did not fare as well as Mexican Americans in securing war industry employment during the war's initial years. African American workers were also denied consistent protection of organized labor. In fact, although the Congress of Industrial Organizations (CIO) began recruiting blacks once the United States entered the war, most unions would not admit African Americans. Some unions, including several made up of Los Angeles shipbuilding workers, advocated "white only" admissions. Others allowed Mexicans, Filipinos, and Chinese, but refused African Americans.[31]

The segregation and racist treatment experienced by African American shipyard workers is chronicled in the brilliant 1940s novel *If He Hollers Let Him Go* by Chester Himes. Himes's main character in the novel, Bob Jones, arrives in Los Angeles from Cleveland in the fall of 1941 in search of a job. Jones describes his search when he says, "it wasn't being refused employment in the plants so much. When I got here practically the only job a Negro could get was service in the white folks' kitchens. But it wasn't that so much. It was the look on the people's faces when you asked them about a job." Throughout the novel, Jones, who secures a job as a foreman in a shipbuilding plant, describes the daily racial tension between blacks and whites, the refusal of whites to work with blacks, and his own frustration, which eventually leads to his demotion.[32]

Residential patterns and policies also segregated most African Americans and Mexican Americans from native-born whites and left them in close proximity to other nonwhites and immigrants. By the early 1940s, most Mexican Americans were concentrated on the LA's east side, in such areas as Boyle Heights and Belvedere, barrios marked by poverty, poor schooling, and limited growth potential. Although such neighborhoods were home to the majority of the city's Mexican Americans, they were by no means ethnically exclusive. Historian George Sánchez has found that, "in almost every section of Los Angeles where Mexicans lived, they shared neighborhoods with other ethnic groups," including Chinese, Japanese, Filipino, Jewish, and African Americans, as well as recent European immigrants.[33]

Carey McWilliams, chief of the Division of Immigration and Housing in California, and future chair of the Sleepy Lagoon Defense Committee, described one typical Mexican American barrio of nearly a thousand people in Los Angeles. He noted leaking roofs, doors and windows in need of repair, few kitchen sinks, hardly any modern plumbing or flush toilets, and much evidence of overcrowding. According to McWilliams, such conditions were easy to find in Mexican barrios throughout Southern California. Such poor housing, he noted, "narrows the range of employment opportunities; reduces the opportunities for cultural adjustment, both for groups and individuals, and also makes for discrimination. It would be folly indeed to deny that Mexicans are victimized by race-prejudice in Los Angeles County, and, for that matter, in many other areas."[34] McWilliams cited living conditions in the Hick's neighborhood in the El Monte area as a case in point. The ethnic Mexican residents there experienced high rates of disease, malnutrition, and infant mortality; lacked refrigeration and indoor plumbing; and averaged less than three rooms total in a dwelling housing almost six people. The entire Hick's camp was found to have only one bathtub, owned by an African American originally from Virginia who was married to a Mexican woman.[35]

Although different ethnic groups intermingled and shared residential districts, black settlement in Los Angeles was concentrated in a few locations. During the early war years, these areas included a corridor of city blocks stretching south of downtown along Central Avenue and through Little Tokyo, left vacant after the Japanese American internment. The growth of the Central Avenue district, which by 1940 was home to half of the city's black population, stemmed from restrictive covenants and block restrictions enforced during the first decades of the twentieth century. By the outbreak of World War II, African Americans made up more than 4 percent of the city's population, and Central Avenue served as the center of black living and business. When thousands of African Americans arrived in Los Angeles looking for employment in war industries, most prior patterns of segregation held firm, and many found it difficult to find homes outside the blocks surrounding Central Avenue or Little Tokyo.[36] In both areas, African American residents often occupied small, subdivided single-family apartments designed to maximize tenant occupancy. As more people settled in these areas, many moving in with relatives on arrival in the city, living conditions deteriorated. Historian Josh Sides characterizes the available housing in Little Tokyo—a community designed for roughly 30,000 people that was home to more than 80,000 in the early 1940s—as "grossly substandard, commonly characterized by flimsy partitioning, dangerous overcrowding, and inadequate plumbing and sewer problems."[37]

The continued immigration of African Americans and Mexicans into Los Angeles led to the growth of ethnic neighborhoods and multi-ethnic interaction in the workplace, and forced area leaders to deal head-on with segregation and race discrimination. While African American and Mexican American activists pushed for full inclusion in U.S. society (see chapter 2), city authorities were not always so progressive in their thinking about race. Race discrimination in employment worked in tandem with residential segregation to concentrate African American and Mexican American populations in certain sections of the city—and also made it easier for city officials to police nonwhite communities and address any potential problems of crime or disruptive behavior in these areas.

Following U.S. entry into the war in late 1941, tension grew between city law enforcement and nonwhite communities. Historian Edward Escobar argues that the Los Angeles Police Department (LAPD) was allowed newfound autonomy by city leaders in hiring, training, and performance practices. This professionalization of the LAPD coincided with increasing public fear of the alleged criminality and immorality of nonwhite youth, popular perceptions exacerbated by wartime migration, employment, and settlement patterns. The result was an LAPD crackdown on crime accompanied by verbal and physical abuse against African Americans and Mexican Americans, reflecting a view of nonwhites as dangerous threats to the peace and stability of the U.S. home front. By harassing and arresting nonwhite youth for everything from walking in the wrong (i.e., white) part of town or driving too nice a car, the police rendered the physical bodies of African American and Mexican

American youth important sites on which the boundaries of the national polity were enforced.[38]

From late 1941 to late 1943, the relationship between the LAPD and Mexican American Los Angeles was hostile and explosive. Harassment of Mexican American youth was evident on city streets; in theaters, restaurants, and nightclubs; and even on playgrounds. Officers of the Hollenbeck police precinct, in particular, were among the most feared in Los Angeles. In a series of incidents beginning in November of 1941, at least five Mexican American boys between the ages of fifteen and nineteen were removed from the Evergreen Playground in East Los Angeles only to be kicked, cursed, and beaten by Hollenbeck officers.[39]

In another incident involving Hollenbeck officers, in mid-1942, eighteen-year-old Aurora Maldinado was walking with several of her friends to the local market just a few blocks from her East Los Angeles home. As they rounded a corner, Aurora saw her brother Pete approaching on the opposite side of the street. Before they had a chance to meet up with one another, an LAPD patrol car pulled over, stopped Pete, and began to question him. After Pete told the white officer who had gotten out of the car that he was visiting home while on furlough from Camp Berkeley, Texas, where he was stationed in the army, the officer allowed him to continue on his way. Then, according to Aurora, the patrol car left, only to make a U-turn and circle back to stop Pete a second time. This time, a Mexican American officer got out of the car, asked Pete for his furlough papers, and ordered him into the backseat. When Pete asked why, the Mexican American officer began to hit him in the face and stomach. As a gathering crowd from the neighborhood was held back by more police arriving in squad cars, Aurora ran to get her mother. When Mrs. Maldinado arrived and protested her son being beaten and arrested, officers pushed her to the ground. Pete passed out in the backseat, and "the next thing I remember," he later recounted, "I was in a little room at Hollenbeck Police Station. I was all cut up on my head and blood was coming down my head and back. I could just see black, but couldn't see nothing real cause my face was so beat up. I just heard the cops calling me "marijuana." Every time they slapped me they called me "marijuana." I tried to get up, but every time I got up I fell down. The last blow I remember was when I got hit over the eye. I don't know from there who hit me."[40] Pete Maldinado's beating at the hands of the LAPD forces us to recognize that the physical bodies of Pete and his mother served as sites on which the police, as agents of the state, exercised their authority.

The beating of Pete Maldinado reflects the chronic tension that existed between the Mexican American community and the LAPD. It also raises important questions about the politics of youth and intra-ethnic class conflict in the early war years. For example, how did the behavior of Mexican American and African American youth become an important part of the debate about the stability of the home front and the fate of the nation at war? Pete's service in the armed forces did little to stem his abuse at the hands of the LAPD. In fact, his army service might have exacerbated the situation. The idea of poor Mexican American youth fighting for U.S. freedom overseas contradicted their characterization as delinquent hoodlums. Just as membership in the armed forces signaled national belonging, a brutal beating at the hands of city police marked nonwhite youth's public performance of their racial identity as threatening to white hegemony. Moreover, while we cannot be certain why the Mexican American officer apparently initiated the violence (perhaps to win his white partner's approval?), his behavior highlights the conflict between working-class Mexican Americans and the LAPD, as well as a deeper, class conflict within the Mexican American community itself.

While young African American and Mexican American men were the most consistent targets of police harassment, young women were not spared. One incident began after Esther Guerrero and Sara Chavez, two teens from Los Angeles, chose the best seats available at their local movie theater and sat down to enjoy the show. Before they could get comfortable, however, they were asked to move by an usher who told them they were sitting in a section where "persons of Mexican extraction" were not allowed. When Chavez and Guerrero refused to move, protesting that no one else was sitting in the area, the manager of the theater was summoned. The confrontation escalated, and police officers were called to remove the young women from their seats. In front of the parents of one of the girls, who were also in the audience and began to argue with management, the police embarrassed and intimidated the girls until they were frightened enough to change their seats rather than be kicked out of the theater.[41]

Segments of the Mexican American community responded to such police behavior by demanding equal protection of the laws, a position that was well intentioned but also served to further alienate many working-class nonwhite youth. The Citizens Committee for Latin American Youth protested the LAPD's treatment of Mexican American boys, who they claimed were all of good character, in a letter to the Hollenbeck

Police Station. "We do not believe that vicious youngsters should be mollycuddled [*sic*]," CCLAY wrote. "It is our position that a police officer should be possessed of an innate sense of proportion to enable him to distinguish between the vicious juvenile and the good juvenile. If the officer places them both in the same category the inevitable result will create disrespect for the law on the part of those upon whom this Citizens Committee is depending to assist the Police Department in its program to curb juvenile delinquency."[42] By insisting that police officers be required to distinguish between "vicious" and "good" juveniles, CCLAY exposed the LAPD's practice of "calling a Mexican a Mexican" regardless of whether any law was broken and irrespective of nationality or class status. At the same time, however, in response to valid concerns about intra-ethnic violence and crime among Mexican Americans, CCLAY did not protest LAPD officers' aggressive approach toward those nonwhite youth who may have been guilty of such behavior. The CCLAY conformed its indictment of police violence to complement a broader wartime political agenda that stressed assimilation and patriotism and valued "good" Mexican Americans who obeyed police officers despite their often racist and violent practices. Despite forcefully claiming that LAPD abuse was disproportionately directed at Mexican American and African American youth, CCLAY left unexamined the assumption that "bad" nonwhite youth threatened home-front society and subverted the war effort through crime, drugs, and street violence.

Segregation, race discrimination in war industry employment, and police violence in Los Angeles were fueled in part by the long-standing perceptions of city leaders and residents that the region had a "Mexican problem." Ever since congressional debates over the admission of Mexicans to the United States in the 1920s, the coerced repatriation of more than 500,000 ethnic Mexicans in the early 1930s, and institution of the Bracero program to import Mexican workers during and after the war, Mexicans and Mexican Americans in the city had often been viewed as either an obstacle to progress or people to be exploited for their labor.[43] Such negative views of Mexican Americans and Mexicans in particular and nonwhites more generally—exacerbated by growing numbers of African Americans and first-generation U.S.-born children of Mexican immigrants—elicited aggressive attempts to strengthen citywide segregation and discrimination. Throughout the early years of World War II, fear spread among whites that African Americans and Mexican Americans were invading the city, siphoning wartime opportunities from white citizens, and eroding the city's wartime stability. More than a chronicle

of injustice and inequality, race discrimination in war industry employment, segregation and settlement patterns, and police violence constituted a dehumanizing assault on the dignity of the area's African
American and Mexican American populations.

WARTIME IN NEW YORK CITY

In a letter written from Europe during the fall of 1942, Private Sal
Thomas, a black soldier from New York City, illustrated the contradiction of fighting for democracy overseas while civil rights were not fully
protected on the home front. Noting the similarities between southern
whites and "Hitler's Aryan race," Thomas wrote, "I wonder how come
those people preach similar doctrines of lust and false superiority and
yet are opposed on the battlefield of this war? Is it that the crackers
don't want Hitler to tell them how to run their Negroes? I hope the cen-
sor will pardon my idiotic babble and realize I am just a simple 'ex-
Harlem' fool who probably couldn't last as long as a white man if we
were both struck in the heart with a bullet. Ha ha, aren't I a scream?"[44]
Thomas's indictment of U.S. racism from abroad underscores the fact
that service in the army or navy did not necessarily curtail discrimination in the military or workplace or in everyday life on the home front.

Although industrial growth in the Northeast did not match that in
the U.S. West, New Yorkers expected young African Americans to follow Thomas's lead and toil for the war effort. Early on in the war, the
state of New York had more consumer industries than military or other
government-funded manufacturers. In 1940 and 1941 New York ranked
seventh among states in per-capita value of military contracts. Of the
war jobs that were available, the number of African American hires
were paltry in 1941: as only 5 percent of war employee trainees were
black; one of fifty African Americans who completed training programs
were placed by the U.S. Employment Service; and African Americans
held only 142 of the more than 29,000 war industry jobs in ten New
York factories.[45] Over 40 percent of New York City's African American
population was on some form of government relief, and many still
worked on Works Progress Administration jobs. A year later, in 1942,
unemployment rates for African Americans in the city were higher than
they had been at the end of the Great Depression in 1939. Historian
Dominic J. Capeci Jr. argues that "everyone except black people benefited from the immediate prosperity the war brought."[46]

Few war jobs were available to the large numbers of blacks in the city. Although New York City did not attract as many African American migrants during the war years as other cities did, it had been a popular destination for blacks from around the country throughout the Great Depression. Like the young Malcolm X, who came to New York from the Midwest via Detroit and Boston, nearly 150,000 blacks flocked to New York in the 1930s in search of better economic opportunity. By 1940 more than 450,000 African Americans lived in New York.

As the war unfolded, however, the number of defense-related jobs in New York rose sharply, and so did black employment. In 1942 the city saw a 40 percent increase in the number of industrial jobs available, and in 1943 New York received 12 percent of all navy contracts.[47] Employment opportunities for African Americans in war production increased dramatically between 1940 and 1944 because of the growing demand for labor, the larger number of defense contracts awarded in the city, the success of the Double V campaign to achieve victory abroad against fascism and at home for civil rights, the national publicity that African American–led protests like the March on Washington attracted, the pressure such activism placed on President Roosevelt to address discrimination, and subsequent local efforts in New York and other urban areas to secure positions in aviation and other war-related businesses. Nevertheless, such jobs remained difficult for African Americans to obtain due to discriminatory hiring practices. When hired, moreover, black workers were largely placed in the most menial positions with little chance for advancement.

Due in part to the size of New York's African American community, efforts to integrate African Americans in New York into national defense operations drew much attention. Politicians and civil rights activists alike participated in conferences, forums, and study groups encouraging African Americans, particularly black youth, to support U.S. victory in the war.[48] Prior to establishment of the federal Fair Employment Practices Committee, Mayor Fiorello La Guardia, known since his response to the Harlem Riot in 1935 as friendly to African American New York, participated with other national leaders on a committee for "Negro Americans in Defense Industries." The New York governor's office also requested state legislation prohibiting discrimination in businesses that affected the public interest and created a governor's committee on discrimination in employment to deal specifically with hiring practices in defense industries. In a 1941 memorandum entitled "American Negro in National Defense Industries," La Guardia argued that the participation of African American residents of the city in the war effort went hand in hand with democracy.[49] Similarly, in a memo to "all holders of defense contracts," Sidney Hillman, director of the Office of Production Management in Washington, D.C., urged the hiring of black workers and "every available source of labor capable of producing defense materials . . . in the present emergency."[50]

All along the eastern seaboard, African American political leaders argued that supporting the Allied war effort and defeating fascism abroad was the most effective strategy in securing improved civil rights and equality at home. These patriotic sentiments were championed by African American political organizations, many of which emphasized the role of black youth in current struggles for freedom. In its 1942 Fourth of July Declaration for Negro Youth, for instance, the Southern Negro Youth Congress (SNYC) trumpeted:

> Up from the fields of cotton and corn, out of the pits and mills and factories, from the schools, churches, and club rooms, in the armed forces and naval stations, amid the shot and shell of the battle front, Negro Americans will come forth to the celebration of the Fourth of July. On this day we will pledge our strength, our talents, our lives to the cause of Victory in this war against the Hitler-Axis enemies of our country and all mankind. We Negro youth love our country and the high principles of Freedom, Equality, and Opportunity and the dignity of man upon which America was founded.[51]

Less than a year later, in April of 1943, Edward Strong, the national secretary of the National Negro Congress stressed that "it is essential to realize that freedom of all people will be determined by the outcome of the world-wide struggle now in progress against fascism." In his address to the Eastern Seaboard Conference on the Problems of the War and the Negro People, Strong noted that if the reactionary coalition of Hitler, his partners in Tokyo and Rome, and his American colleagues succeeded in vanquishing the Allied powers, an era of darkness unprecedented in human history would ensue. "Consequently," continued Strong, "the liberation struggle for any oppressed people at this crucial hour in world history must be based upon the self-evident, fundamental and decisive truth that all people who would be free will advance their cause by joining the anti-fascist coalition of the thirty United Nations."[52] The conference heralded the four freedoms pronounced by President Roosevelt—freedom of speech and worship, and freedom from want and from fear—and stressed the full use of manpower, protection of democratic rights, and improvement in wartime living standards, including the use of price and rent controls.

Strong, the SNYC, and many other advocates of African American equality were careful to couch any claims to national belonging and equality in the anti-fascist rhetoric of the wartime United States. The New York City conference that Strong addressed was well attended by representatives from a variety of circles. The labor movement, for example, was represented by members of the National Maritime Union; the Automobile Workers of America; the United Electrical, Radio, and Machine workers; and various segments of the AFL. The audience's diversity led Strong to conclude his speech by saying that all the attendees had come "because they are firmly convinced that such a coalition has been proved to be the soundest strategy in fighting for common aims and in opposing those common enemies who are out to destroy labor, the Negro, the Jew, and the foreign born."[53]

Despite calls for the employment of African Americans, it remained difficult for African Americans to find work in war production plants. Despite denials to the contrary, most corporate employers on the East Coast, like their western counterparts, commonly discriminated in hiring. Most excluded African Americans from the most skilled positions. In separate letters to Mayor La Guardia, three of the largest aircraft companies in the state of New York—Brewster Aeronautical Corporation, Grumman Aircraft Engineering Corporation, and Republic Aviation Corporation—claimed that the minimal presence of African Americans in the aviation industry was due only to their late start in the business, not to discrimination.[54] Responding to pressures from both federal and local governments, some employers did attempt to address their poor records of hiring African Americans. Efforts to diversify employee ranks, however, translated into tokenism at best and a confirmation of racist hiring and workplace behavior at worst. At Republic Aviation, for example, a program to hire more African American employees consisted of training one African American for skilled work and training more only if the "experiment" was successful.[55]

Employers denials of racism and the lack of any systematic policy to encourage the hiring of nonwhites had a dire impact on the lives of African Americans in New York City. As in Los Angeles, enrolling in job training programs and securing employment were often unpleasant and dehumanizing experiences for black applicants. In its pamphlet "Growing up in Harlem," the board of directors of the West Harlem Council of Social Agencies declared the situation particularly acute for young blacks. In many African American communities of New York City, claimed the council, youthful residents faced such limited opportunities for jobs in public utilities, defense plants, and other industrial and mercantile establishments that many had to rely on at least some form of public assistance.[56]

Throughout the early war years, the mayor's office was flooded with letters from concerned African Americans, Puerto Ricans, Italians, Jews, and other minority constituencies struggling to secure employment.[57] La Guardia, a leader well known for showing sympathy for the needs of New York's African American community, received an especially large number of complaints from black residents. One typical letter told the story of African American Harrold Lindo, who, despite a college education, ten years' experience as a clerk, and a high score on the entrance exam, was passed over no fewer than twelve times for both junior- and senior-level positions as a typist in the United States Civil Service Commission. Lindo objected not only to open racial discrimination by governmental agencies but also to the lack of any recourse to protest such treatment.[58] His experience differed little from those of Rebecca Elliot, George Sclier, Pearl Cotton, and countless other individuals seeking defense jobs who wrote letters to the mayor and were often "told very frankly that firms do not desire to employ colored people."[59] One Harlem resident asserted that the city's African Americans were frustrated that their "sincerest and most earnest efforts to become part of the defense program have met with evasion and even forthright rejection."[60]

By the beginning of America's involvement in the war, most African Americans who had migrated to New York in search of employment were concentrated in predominantly poor neighborhoods. In 1940 some 107,000 African Americans resided in Brooklyn, and another 52,000 in the Bronx and Queens. But Harlem, home to over 60 percent of the city's black population, was the center of African American cultural and political life.[61] Covering nearly four hundred square blocks in northern Manhattan, Harlem ran south to north from 110th to 155th Street and east to west from 3rd Avenue to Amsterdam Avenue. As the city' population grew, so did Harlem, and its geographic boundaries were stretched to include an increasingly diverse population, including Italian, Puerto Rican, and even Irish communities.

Like stable jobs in war industries, quality housing in other areas of New York was difficult to come by because of overt discrimination.[62] One African American woman, Mercedes Owens endured humiliation in securing an apartment in an uptown neighborhood near 145th Street. After inquiring with several housing agencies about available properties, she was told, among other things, "We don't rent to colored people, only white." When Owens complained to housing authorities that she deserved better treatment, one responded, "We don't have colored people upsetting our houses. You can make any complaints you want to, it don't mean a thing." Following her experiences, and in the spirit of the Double V campaign, Owens noted that racial intolerance in New York City, especially where housing was concerned, formed the very essence of Nazi ideology.[63] After relating her story to Mayor La Guardia in a lengthy letter, Owens received little sympathy or aid. The mayor's office responded by highlighting La Guardia's record against discrimination and noting that there is "no provision of law which prevents the owner of a multiple dwelling from renting apartments to tenants whom he considers desirable."[64] Such limited housing options left African Americans concentrated in Harlem, Bedford Stuyvesant, and other largely black neighborhoods throughout the city.[65] Moreover, despite its predominantly working-class character, Harlem suffered from higher rents and food prices than most other sections of the city.

As in other areas of the country, the use of force by city police in New York helped maintain a racial hierarchy in which white trumped black. Amidst wartime rhetoric demanding a stable and secure home front, city authorities sought to control any semblance of racial unrest. In New York, as in Detroit, Philadelphia, and elsewhere, African Americans faced seemingly routine police violence. By 1942 the New York Police Department (NYPD) increasingly employed methods of aggressive social control, providing further evidence that popular calls for national unity were accompanied by volatile, often violent, race relations on the home front.

Much of the African American community in New York viewed the NYPD as guilty of racist conduct. The black press, including the NAACP's the *People's Voice* and the *Amsterdam News,* regularly focused on incidents that illustrated the explosive relationship between the NYPD and African American New York. One case that sparked citywide debate over police brutality involved Wallace Armstrong, a young African American who was killed in Harlem by white police officer Harold Reidman in May of 1942. The mentally unbalanced Armstrong was to have been committed to the mental institute of Bellevue Hospital by his father, who had requested the aid of police in transporting his son. When Armstrong rebelled at the idea of being manhandled by the police, a scuffle ensued. According to eyewitnesses, Reidman beat Armstrong heavily on the head before the youth produced a pocket knife to defend himself. Although Armstrong did not attempt to use the knife, Reidman drew his pistol and threatened to shoot the young man. Armstrong then stumbled and, in a stupor, began to amble aimlessly down the block, Reidman following with his pistol drawn. After the two traveled several blocks, backup squad cars arrived to find a gathering crowd of angry Harlemites. Armstrong, still bloody and disoriented from the initial assault, was beaten again with nightclubs by at least four officers. When they finally stopped, Officer Reidman stepped back and said he'd "like to shoot this fellow." When another cop answered, "Go ahead and do it," Reidman obliged and fired twice at Armstrong until his body slumped to the pavement. As mounted police officers attempted to disperse the crowd, an ambulance arrived to transport Wallace to Harlem Hospital. He was announced dead on arrival.[66]

The same month Wallace Armstrong was killed, high-profile clashes between African American citizens and white police officers spread from Manhattan to suburban Long Island. Although relations between the NYPD and African Americans had been tense in several Long Island neighborhoods since the 1940 beating of a young black teenager named Tets Park for resisting arrest, the increasing frequency of police beatings and killings pushed the African American residents of Hempstead Town to strike back. The conflict began after two young African American soldiers who had been involved in an argument at a local nightspot were subsequently accosted by white NYPD officers. Witnesses later claimed that the officers' methods were "somewhat drastic and totally uncalled for." According to the bystanders, at least two officers beat one of the soldiers over the head with a pistol and dragged him along the street toward their squad car in order to take him to the police station less than three blocks away. Before the evening was over, black residents of Hempstead Town converged on South Franklin Street where the beating had occurred to throw bricks and rocks at NYPD officers and break patrol car windshields. The NYPD responded to the melee, which lasted for over half an hour.[67] It is no coincidence that black soldiers were the targets of police violence in this and other instances. African American and other nonwhite servicemen embodied the contradiction of fighting for democracy overseas when such freedoms were not readily available at home, and their physical bodies often became the sites of struggle in which police, the public, and the youth themselves expressed claims to national belonging or sought to patrol its boundaries.

While the Armstrong and Hempstead Town cases might be extreme examples of police brutality, they were not isolated incidents. As U.S.

involvement in the war deepened and calls for home-front unity grew louder, the use of force against black youth by the NYPD seemed to increase. The *People's Voice* valiantly publicized such police violence. The newspaper reported in April 1943, for example, that NYPD officers patrolling Harlem kicked African Americans Cecil Harris, Steve Dubois, and Alonzo Green in the stomach and groin until the youth were wet with their own urine. Arrested, they were spat on by officers at the police station.[68] In another incident in June of the same year, the *People's Voice* reported, Fred Brown of Harlem was beaten with an iron bar and framed for disorderly conduct by a plain-clothes police officer.[69] In part because of the efforts of NAACP-sponsored journalism, police violence against black youth in the early war years emerged as a critical issue on the agendas of many African American religious and political leaders who wanted African Americans to be equal participants in the nation's effort to win the war.

Although young men suffered the brunt of police violence, young women were also targeted. In April of 1943, for example, Ethelen Burnett, a fifteen-year-old high school sophomore who had grown up in Harlem, was beaten by a subway policeman without provocation in the men's room of the 207th Street station. Like the Wallace Armstrong and Hempstead Town incidents, the attack on Burnett mobilized the Harlem community to protest the mistreatment of African American youth by law enforcement. Immediately following the Burnett beating, parents organized a mass meeting at the Golden Gate Ballroom to protest police aggression in Harlem. The event included addresses by Councilman Adam Clayton Powell and several other high-profile African American political figures.[70]

The growing use of police force against African American youth in the city further politicized the Harlem community. A collection of more than two hundred black and white New Yorkers, for instance, formed the City-Wide Citizens Committee on Harlem (CCCH) in late 1941. Aimed at improving life in Harlem, the CCCH battled juvenile delinquency and discrimination, fought for child care and employment opportunities, and served as an important political force in the community.

Much of New York's African American population struggled to join the U.S. war machine. The message from city leaders and wartime propaganda was clear that African Americans should be active participants in war production, yet blacks were also increasingly the targets of race discrimination in hiring practices and police violence. *New York Age* columnist Ludlow W. Werner captured the contradictions and frustrations of many African American New Yorkers when he wrote the following lines in May of 1943:

> I am an American, but if I live in New York City, I pay higher rents and live in more squalid quarters than other citizens.
> I am an American, but if I live in New York, I may not be employed . . . except as porter, elevator operator or in a menial capacity for the most part . . .
> I am an American, but if I live in New York City, I may take out membership only in the Negro Y.M.C.A.'s.
> I am an American, but if I am a skilled worker, I may not become a member of the A.F. of L. Union except in a few rare instances.
> I am an American, but if I am accused of a crime in the North, I am always guilty before I am tried.
> I am an American, but if I am accused of a crime in the South, I may not even face trial—I may be lynched. . . .
> I am an American, but I am a Negro.[71]

THE POLITICS OF RACE IN THE WARTIME UNITED STATES

The volatile race relations in Los Angeles and New York were local manifestations of national patterns of segregation, discrimination, and police violence. Virtually every urban center, including Philadelphia, Detroit, Chicago, and Houston, experienced similar conditions that resulted in limited participation for nonwhites in the war effort. While New York and Los Angeles exemplified the increasingly tense relationship between employers, police, and nonwhite groups, the role of nonwhites in wartime society emerged as an important issue for the federal government as well.

For its part, the federal government addressed U.S. race relations by monitoring hiring practices in war industries and discouraging race discrimination. Spurred by the national attention focused on racism by A. Philip Randolph's proposed March on Washington and other instances of political activism, perhaps the most important of these efforts was a series of reports by the President's Committee on Fair Employment Practice (FEPC), which found discrimination against prospective African Americans and other nonwhite employees to be common practice. The FEPC was formed to implement Executive Order 8802, which outlawed discrimination in defense industry and federal hiring based on race, creed, color, or national origin. In its initial research and investigative reports, completed in October of 1941, the FEPC announced that race discrimination was indeed widespread in defense industries. The reports

highlighted numerous employer practices that ran afoul of Executive
Order 8802, including requiring statements of race or religion on applications, barring nonwhite workers from participating in unions, and
hiring nonwhite workers in custodial work in disingenuous attempts to
adhere to the federal law.[72] Moreover, the FEPC claimed employers
must do more to reverse discriminatory hiring policies than simply issu-
ing a statement of nondiscriminatory employment.

The results of FEPC efforts were mixed. The committee did contribute to some positive results for nonwhite hiring in war industries.
Industrial jobs held by African Americans increased 13 percent between
1940 and 1944, training programs for African American students doubled in the same period, and African Americans made up 8 percent of all
war workers by 1944, up from three percent in 1942.[73] As historian
Alan Winkler argues, however, the FEPC "was never wholly effective"
in addressing the problem of race discrimination, at least in part because
"it was underfunded and understaffed from the beginning."[74] Moreover,
while it did recognize the prevalence of discrimination, the FEPC also
claimed that the low number of nonwhite employees was due simply to
a scarcity of African American and Mexican American applications.
Despite its findings, the FEPC ultimately blamed the low numbers of
nonwhite citizens in defense industries on African American and Mexican American communities themselves. In a 1942 report, for instance,
the committee argued that "Mexicans and Negroes tend to make an
unjustifiable issue of any failure to secure jobs." In a December 1942
conference, over a year after the FEPC found glaring violations of
Executive Order 8802, the U.S. Employment Service maintained that
"when whites are not successful in securing jobs, they take it as a matter
of course, but if Negroes fail, half of them will say it is because they are
black." African Americans and Mexican Americans were further falsely
accused of not adequately seeking defense training because they feared
traveling to white communities to attend classes.[75] Of course, it was
rarely questioned why so few such classes were available in nonwhite
areas of town.

Business and political leaders issued a range of responses to the FEPC
findings. Some claimed that to get jobs, nonwhites need only upgrade
their training for more skilled positions. Others, like the Georgia state
director of vocational training, argued flatly against incorporating
African Americans into defense jobs. "The need for these men [African
Americans] as workers has not been established." he claimed. "It would
be a waste of public money to train them, and I would hate to be a party

to that waste." Many African Americans and Mexican Americans believed the FEPC did little more than provide token employment and could have done much more to provide training in more skilled technical fields.[76] In the end, the resources, power, and foresight behind the FEPC were inadequate to addressing the problems of race discrimination in defense industry employment. Still, while the FEPC was unable to cure the nation's deep-seated problems of race discrimination, it did, as historian Merl E. Reed suggests, spark debate and open political avenues for civil rights advocates that would widen in the years following World War II.[77]

Despite their limitations, Executive Order 8802 and the FEPC were at least intended to help incorporate nonwhites into the war effort. Another executive order, initiated under the guise of national security, however, directly assaulted the dignity of a specific nonwhite group in the United States. Japanese Americans, not African Americans or Mexican Americans, were the primary target of Executive Order 9066. Following the Japanese attack on Pearl Harbor in December 1941, xenophobia and fear of further enemy incursions on U.S. soil grew, resulting in great public animosity toward Japanese Americans living on the West Coast. Concerns that Japanese Americans would work in concert with the Japanese as fifth-column saboteurs spread wildly in the press and among government officials, ultimately leading President Roosevelt to sign the executive order that authorized the incarceration of nearly 120,000 Japanese Americans living in the United States, at least two-thirds of whom were citizens. In the spring of 1942, in what was deemed by U.S. authorities a military necessity because of Pearl Harbor and Japanese military victories throughout Southeast Asia, both Issei (immigrants born in Japan) and Nisei (their U.S.-born, American citizen children), were banned from the West Coast. The U.S. War Relocation Authority directed them to leave their homes, bringing only what they could carry on their backs, and report to assembly centers all along the West Coast.

By the end of the summer, the bank accounts and property assets of Issei, who were barred from becoming U.S. citizens, had been liquidated, and virtually all West Coast Japanese Americans had been shipped by train to internment camps in the interior of the country. Surrounded by barbed wire and armed guards from the U.S. military, these camps were located in remote, desolate areas such as Heart Mountain, Wyoming; Topaz, Utah; Amache, Colorado; Jerome, Arkansas; and Manzanar and Tule Lake, California. Although a few thousand internees were released within a year, most remained incarcerated for several years, with the last not being released until March 1946.[78] In addition to being imprisoned against their will and forced to leave real and personal property behind, internees of military age were soon drafted into the U.S. armed forces, a development that led several hundred young Japanese Americans to resist the draft. Ultimately, as legal scholar and historian Eric Muller suggests, the Japanese and Japanese Americans' "crime was their ethnicity, and the government had made them pay for it with their livelihoods, their possessions, their liberty, and their dignity."[79] The internment of Japanese Americans during World War II represents the starkest of reminders that race relations on the home front were tense, often violent, and were intertwined with ideas of national security and belonging, and involved the dignity of those caught in the middle of such politics.

While African Americans and Mexican Americans did not endure the horrors of internment, they did face formidable obstacles in striving to participate in the war effort and join a unified home front. Finding a place in the wartime United States meant having to deal with race discrimination and police violence—common experiences that were not simply the result of individual decisions and behavior but were, as indicated by the federal government's systematic effort to address such problems, deeply rooted in structural and institutional conditions of the U.S. political economy. More than just the misguided abuse of power by a few overly aggressive police officers or employers, the physical abuse of nonwhite youth and the reluctance to hire them in war industry jobs were part of an unwritten policy among city police departments, corporate America, and the general public to bar African Americans and Mexican Americans from full participation in U.S. society.

CONCLUSION

When the United States entered World War II after the bombing of Pearl Harbor, the tension in race relations on the home front became more acute. Despite the eventual increase in the number of nonwhites hired in defense industries, many African Americans and Mexican Americans continued to be pushed to the margins of the war effort and the national polity. In the process, through discrimination and violence, their dignity was denied. The range of African American and Mexican American experiences in Los Angeles and New York illustrates that the contradictions between race, the political economy, and national belonging were national patterns that affected a diverse group of people. Bob Jones, Chester Himes's African American protagonist in *If He Hollers Let Him*

Go, further underscores the racial dimensions of life on the home front when he claims, "I was the same colour as the Japanese and I couldn't tell the difference. 'A yeller-bellied Jap' coulda meant me too. I could always feel race trouble, serious trouble, never more than two feet off."[80]

In New York, Los Angeles, and other parts of the country, the explosiveness of race relations and the maltreatment of African American and Mexican American youth provoked a range of political responses. As juvenile delinquency came to be viewed in racial terms and as purported crime waves among young nonwhites came to be viewed as threats to wartime unity, the activities of African American and Mexican American youth were increasingly monitored by their own communities, city police, and powerful politicians. As the racialization of juvenile delinquency intensified, many Americans sought to shape the discourse and perceptions about African American and Mexican American youth in the United States, but only by speaking for them rather than listening to them. Chapter 2 turns to civic conversations about race, class, and juvenile delinquency that burgeoned in Los Angeles and New York during World War II.

Class Politics
and Juvenile Delinquency

In July of 1944 the *Los Angeles Times* published an article entitled "Youthful Gang Secrets Exposed." Subtitled "Young Hoodlums Smoke 'Reefers,' Tattoo Girls, and Plot Robberies," the article claimed that recent statements made by Mexican American juvenile delinquents in Los Angeles Superior Court detailed the lifestyle of young gangsters in the city. The article alleged that young Mexican American gangsters were addicted to narcotics and routinely concealed weapons, robbed pedestrians, spoke a strange and unintelligible argot, performed sadistic mutilations on unwilling neophytes, and smoked marijuana, or "yiska," costing five dollars a cigarette. Claiming to uncover the inner workings of juvenile gangs that had been growing since the war began, the article explained how young women were recruited into gangs against their will under the threat of violence, forced to mutilate themselves by tattooing gang symbols on their bodies, and made to use their high pompadours to hide knives or fingernail files for boyfriends to use as weapons in street fights. Each gang was said to have its own club hangout where members gathered for dancing, drinking, having orgies, and planning schemes to obtain illegal drugs and liquor. What was more, the article suggested, Mexican American male gang members were taught upon initiation to hate servicemen, young women gangsters were prohibited from having any contact with servicemen, and most gangsters carried rubber hoses containing stones or metal with which to beat servicemen.[1]

The sensational reporting by the *Times,* reflecting a pattern seen in many mainstream newspapers in Los Angeles and other big cities during the first years of World War II, demonized Mexican American and African American youth as violent, criminal, hypersexual, and animal-like. Articles of this kind strongly suggested that, whereas white youth played the patriotic and dutiful role of serviceman, Mexican American and African American youth posed a dangerous threat to the political and moral stability of the home front. Big-city newspapers thus placed nonwhite youth outside the bounds of wartime nationalism.

Journalism of this sort was only part of a much broader pattern between 1942 and 1944 in which concerns over wartime juvenile delinquency dominated civic debate across the country. One consequence of the wartime political economy discussed in chapter 1 was that the role of young people in the war effort was an increasingly critical issue for many Americans. As the war unfolded, more Americans realized that the country's future lay in the hands of its youth, whether in defending its democratic principles on battlefields around the world or in contributing to the home-front production necessary for victory. Any youth behavior that did not serve these purposes was deemed a catastrophic drain on the war effort.

As evident in the *Times* article cited above, juvenile delinquency was increasingly viewed as a race problem, and such dehumanizing rhetoric painted nonwhite youth as undesirable, a sentiment that reflected the exclusivity of the U.S. nation-state.[2] Popular discourse characterizing nonwhite youth as animal-like, hypersexual, and criminal marked their bodies as "other" and, when coming from city officials and the press, served to help construct for the public a social meaning of African American and Mexican American youth. In these ways, the physical and discursive bodies of nonwhite youth were the sites upon which their dignity was denied. Just as police violence and race discrimination denied them equal participation in home-front democracy, their depiction in such a negative light marked them as alien. Once the United States was fully engaged in the war, nonwhite youth became a much talked-about public enemy on the home front, second only perhaps to Japanese Americans.

By the time the *Los Angeles Daily News* published its article exposing the secrets of gang lifestyle in the summer of 1944, African American and Mexican American youth in Los Angeles were commonly thought of as "gangsters" or "zoot suiting punks." Their African American counterparts in New York were similarly labeled "hoodlums" and "gangsters." Despite the uproar over the purported rise in delinquency among nonwhite youth, however, such trends are difficult to document. Several fact-finding missions in Los Angeles, for example, discovered that juvenile delinquency among white youth, both male and female, had risen more sharply than that of Mexican American or African American youth in 1941 and 1942.[3] It was juvenile delinquency among nonwhites, however, that much of the public thought to negatively influence white youth, posing dangers of race mixing, unlawful behavior, and immoral activity.

In response to the rising concern over juvenile delinquency, a number of African American and Mexican American leaders worked diligently to include nonwhite youth in the war effort and limit youth crime. These efforts complemented broader calls for equality of nonwhites on the home front and highlighted African American and Mexican American performances of normative social, cultural, and political (and sometimes racial) identities as a central strategy in the battle for wartime inclusion.[4] In addition to championing the creation of more war industry jobs for young nonwhites, African American and Mexican American leaders created numerous programs to increase adult supervision, after-school activities, and extracurricular events intended to keep nonwhite youth off the streets and engaged in productive behavior. Most of these social reformers sought to assimilate nonwhite youth into the fabric of U.S. society by getting them involved in the war effort and emphasizing their similarity to white youth. Though African American and Mexican American activists intended to counter the dehumanization of nonwhite youth and combat crime and violence in their own communities, ultimately their ideology further denied the dignity of African American and Mexican American youth by funneling them into preconceived programs for assimilation.[5]

This chapter traces how municipal governments and the mainstream press in Los Angeles and New York racialized juvenile delinquency following U.S. entry into the war. It pays particular attention to the bodies of nonwhite youth as a primary battlefield on which their dignity was denied. The chapter also shows how middle-class African Americans and Mexican Americans and a variety of social reformers, including labor and communist party organizers, mobilized politically around the growing debate over juvenile delinquency. City authorities, the press, and social reformers consistently cast the growing crisis of juvenile delinquency as a "race problem," a position that more often than not placed nonwhite youth on the outside of the national imaginary.

THE RACIALIZATION OF JUVENILE DELINQUENCY IN WARTIME LOS ANGELES

The debate over juvenile delinquency intensified in Los Angeles following the infamous Sleepy Lagoon incident in August 1942. The trouble began when twenty-two-year-old José Díaz was found bleeding to death after a house party at a ranch near the Sleepy Lagoon, a popular swimming hole and hangout for Mexican American youth on the outskirts of the city. After the discovery of Díaz's body, the LAPD swept through Mexican American neighborhoods in the city, rounding up more than six hundred Mexican American youth. Despite a lack of evidence, twenty-two individuals between the ages of seventeen and twenty-four, all affiliated with the so-called 38th Street Gang, were arrested, charged with murder and assault, and tried. According to many observers, the trial, presided over by Judge Charles Fricke, was "grimy with prejudice, inside and outside the courtroom."[6] The defendants were denied their constitutional right to a fair trial: they were not permitted to consult with their attorneys during the trial or change clothes or cut their hair to improve their appearance before the jury, and the judge admitted prejudicial evidence offered by the prosecution.[7] Furthermore, Judge Fricke consistently referred to the defendants as members of a gang, and allowed the prosecuting attorney to argue in his closing statement that there was a "smidgeon of truth" in the proposition that all Mexicans were cowards and did not fight fair.[8] Nineteen of the defendants were convicted, including three of first-degree murder and two for assault with a deadly weapon.[9] In the end, more than ten of the boys were sent to San Quentin prison despite evidence of their innocence. In addition, a number of the young girls affiliated with the 38th Street Gang were taken from the custody of their parents and placed in the Ventura School for Girls, a notorious reform school, until they turned twenty-one.

Because it was a grave injustice to the individual defendants, the Sleepy Lagoon case also had a wide-ranging political impact in Los Angeles and beyond. It intensified the growing concern over juvenile delinquency and demanded a response by city, county, and state authorities. From late 1942 into 1943, a growing number of California legislative committees, organizations, and media outlets identified the problem of juvenile delinquency among nonwhites as a crucial issue in domestic politics. The political attention focused on African American and, particularly, Mexican American youth resulted in a variety of local- and state-financed programs designed to address juvenile delinquency,

Figure 2. The Sleepy Lagoon defendants, 1942. *Los Angeles Times*, photograph by *Times* staff photographer. Department of Special Collections, Charles E. Young Research Library, UCLA.

including the Citizens Committee on Youth in Wartime (part of the California State War Council), the Los Angeles Youth Project, and several special investigations of youth gang activity.

Perhaps the most visible of all the government-sanctioned inquiries into juvenile delinquency was the 1942 Los Angeles County Grand Jury, initiated in October only a few weeks after the death of José Díaz. Charged with reporting on the problems of youth across the county, the grand jury affected area policy involving youth for several years.[10] The offices of Los Angeles mayor Fletcher Bowron and County Supervisor John Anson Ford closely monitored the findings of the grand jury and considered its perspectives in their governing.[11]

Of the many policemen, politicians, and other public figures who spoke to the grand jury, Lieutenant Edward Duran Ayres of the Los Angeles County Sheriff's Department most blatantly characterized juvenile delinquency as a race problem. Ayres blamed much of the city's crime and violence on young African Americans and Mexican Americans. In his testimony Ayres portrayed nonwhite youth as so vile and dangerous as to suggest they shouldered sole responsibility for wartime crime, gang warfare, and unpatriotic behavior. Although Ayres acknowledged that nonwhite youth faced structural disadvantages such as higher rates of underemployment, lower wages, discrimination, and segregation, his testimony relied on biological reasoning to explain how African Ameri-

cans and Mexican Americans maintained a "lower perspective of responsibility and citizenship" than white Americans. Using animal imagery,
Ayres claimed that nonwhite youth were inferior and "naturally"
inclined to commit violent crimes. "Although a wild cat and a domestic
cat are of the same family," he argued, "they have certain biological
characteristics so different that while one may be domesticated the other
would have to be caged to be kept in captivity; and there is practically as
much difference between the races of man."[12] For Ayres, of course, it
was African American and Mexican American youth who needed to be
caged because of their disregard for the value of human life. For Mexican
Americans, at least, this characteristic stemmed from their Aztec heri-
tage and history of "heathen altars" on which "bodies [were] ripped
opened by stone knives, and their hearts torn out while still beating."[13]

   The Ayres report, as his grand jury testimony came to be known, was
not alone in characterizing the race and masculinity of Mexican
American youth as uncontrollable, wild, and inhumane. A Los Angeles
Superior Court judge, for example, admonished one Mexican American
youth, "It's absolutely necessary that fellows like you be taken out of
circulation. You must learn that you cannot endanger lives by running
around in wolf packs together and starting fights on the public streets."[14]
Such discourse portrayed nonwhite youth, like wolves or wild cats in
need of being caged, as a predatory threat to home-front unity and a
dangerous source of crime, violence, and immorality.

   According to Ayres, the violence committed by nonwhite youth was
much worse than that of white youth. He testified that the differences
could be seen, for example, in the divergent strategies of fighting that
different youth employed. "The Caucasian, especially the Anglo-Saxon,
when engaged in fighting, particularly among youths," argued Ayres,
"resort to fisticuff [sic] and may at times kick each other, which is considered unsportive, but this Mexican element considers all that to be a
sign of weakness, and all he knows and feels is a desire to use a knife or
some lethal weapon. In other words, his desire is to kill, or at least to let
blood."[15] Ayres's portrayal of Mexican American youth as genetically
prone to violence enabled him to blame them for the purported rise in
juvenile delinquency.

   To contain the threat posed by juvenile delinquency and remedy the
alleged lack of control exercised by Mexican American and African
American families over their children, Ayres proposed a heavy-handed
policy based on force. "It is just as essential," Ayres declared, "to incarcerate every member of a particular gang, whether there be 10 or 50, as

it is to incarcerate one or two of the ring leaders. In other words—take them out of circulation until they realize that the authorities will not tolerate gangsterism."[16] Although mass roundups, arrests, and purges in African American and Mexican American neighborhoods or the finger-printing of every youth interrogated by police was illegal, Ayres argued, these practices should be made legal and employed if the city hoped to deter crime. Ayres painted a picture of nonwhite youth in Los Angeles as the primary culprits of hooliganism and as perpetrators of un-American-ness. At a time when U.S. forces were fighting overseas for democracy, Ayres characterized nonwhite youth as disrupting and eroding demo-cratic practices at home. The irony, of course, is that African American and Mexican American youth could legitimately have accused Ayres of doing the same.

Ayres further illuminated his theory of the link between delinquency and biology in his final comments to the grand jury. Such biological con-nections, he asserted, explained the similarities in poor behavior between Mexican Americans and Filipinos, thus effectively "orientalizing" both groups.[17] Conflating race, ethnicity, nation, and geography, he con-cluded his testimony:

> Representatives of the Mexican colony will [be] loathe to admit that it is in any way biological, . . . but the fact remains that the same factors, discrimi-nation, lack of recreation facilities, economics, etc, have also always applied to the Chinese and Japanese in California, yet they have always been law abiding and have never given our authorities trouble except in that of opium among the Chinese, and that of gambling among both the Chinese and Japanese, but such acts of violence as now are in evidence among the young Mexicans has been entirely unknown among these two Oriental peoples. On the other hand, among the Filipinos crime and violence in proportion to their population is quite prevalent, and practically all of it over women. This is due to the fact that there are so few Filipino women here, and also the biological aspect enters into it, as the Filipino is a Malay, and ethnologists trace the Malayan people to the American Indian, ranging from the south-western part of the United States down through Mexico, Central America and into South America. The Malay is even more vicious than the Mongolian, to which race the Japanese and Chinese, of course belong. In fact, the Malay seems to have all the bad qualities of the Mongolian and none of the good qualities. As for the Negro, we also have a biological aspect, to which the contributing factors are the same as in respect to the Mexican—which only aggravates the condition, as to the two races.[18]

Ayres's pseudo-anthropological rant not only vilified Mexican Ameri-can and African American youth and discursively marked their bodies as monstrous but also reflected the thinking of many other city and county officials. Ayres's superior, Los Angeles County sheriff E. W. Biscailuz, supported his lieutenant's position. Writing to the grand jury shortly after Ayres testified, Sheriff Biscailuz noted that "the statistics and data embodied in the report read before your body by Lt. Edward Duran Ayres of my Foreign Relations Bureau, . . . together with the statements submitted by the Los Angeles Police Department, I believe fully cover the situation."[19]

Los Angeles chief of police C. B. Horrall similarly supported Ayres's brand of scientific racism in his own presentations to the grand jury.[20] Horrall characterized Ayres's performance before the grand jury as "an intelligent statement of the psychology of the Mexican people, particularly the youths." Horrall echoed Ayres in his own descriptions of the criminal nature of the Mexican American community. He argued that the city's gangsters were predominantly second-generation Mexicans who came from a poor class of people who first arrived in the United States prior to 1920 and were unable to acquire or accept the standard of living in the United States. Horrall further maintained that young Mexican American gangsters had no respect for their parents, and in turn, Mexican American parents were unable to control their kids.[21]

Several LAPD officers also blamed juvenile delinquency on Mexican Americans during the grand jury investigation. Their comments referred to the reputed biological inferiority of Mexican Americans, the proliferation of Mexican American gangs at recreation centers around the city, and criticism of county courts for being too lenient on Mexican American delinquents. To address the perceived crisis, many officers favored crackdowns on all suspected Mexican American youth regardless of whether sufficient evidence was present to link them to any crime.[22] Captain Vernon Rasmussen, head of the Homicide Subversive Bureau of the LAPD, urged that the Mexican American gang situation "must be dealt with firmly and without sympathy for the individuals."[23] The alleged criminality of nonwhite youth, reasoned the LAPD, justified and required the use of force—a practice that helped entrench discrimination by law enforcement.

Mayor Fletcher Bowron supported the LAPD's approach to the crisis of juvenile delinquency and demanded increased police protection against Mexican American gangs. In numerous letters to fellow city and state officials in 1942 and 1943, Bowron highlighted one primary cause of juvenile delinquency: the lack of parental responsibility and communal control exhibited by older generations of Mexican Americans and African Americans.[24] In his defense of the LAPD, Bowron accused

African Americans and Mexican Americans in the city of "a widespread prejudice against police officers."[25]

In addition to using animal imagery and criminal terminology to describe Mexican American and African American youth, city and county authorities conflated nonwhite bodies and communities with disease.[26] Amidst the massive migration of African Americans to industrial centers, for example, black settlements and neighborhoods were characterized as health threats to others around them. While the dilapidated living conditions in black neighborhoods may well have posed a high risk of cultivating sickness and certainly justified attention from authorities, officials often blamed the social and sexual practices of black people for undermining the health of the city at large. It was no great leap from citing black areas of town as being run down to attributing dirtiness, unhealthiness, and contagion to black bodies and spaces. In a letter to the U.S. surgeon general in October of 1943, for instance, Mayor Bowron, in his zeal to keep LA healthy, emphatically denounced the health dangers posed by African American migrants to the Central Avenue area of the city. Citing a lack of adequate housing and the spread of prostitution and venereal disease in black communities, Bowron claimed that Los Angeles faced a "very serious situation . . . from increase of our colored population."[27] The office of County Supervisor Ford similarly noted that the area's Mexican American population made little effort to alleviate the poor living conditions in their neighborhoods that led to bad health.[28] Certain parts of town, such as the Alpine, Flats, and Happy Valley barrios in East Los Angeles, thus came to be identified with the alleged sickly and contagious character of their residents.

Not only the neighborhoods inhabited by Mexican Americans and African Americans were marked as vile threats, but also their physical bodies and behavior. Civilian and military authorities' specific concerns about venereal disease implied that the "dirty bodies" of young dark-skinned women could contaminate the "clean bodies" of servicemen on leave. The portrayal of many young Mexican American women, in particular, as sexually loose or even as prostitutes identified them as subverting the family reproduction and economic growth considered vital to the war effort and overlooked the labor they contributed both in- and outside the home. Public health discourse thus equated young nonwhite female bodies with difference, bad conduct, and danger.[29] The popular belief linking health and sexuality to the collective well-being of the nation-state marginalized these young women. Despite their growing employment in some defense industry jobs, they found it difficult to fully embody the "Rosie" or "Rosita the riveter" image, because their race, gender, and class composition resulted in exclusion and demonization. Ultimately, the allegedly malignant bodies of African American and Mexican American youth were considered foreign to the national American body.

Concern about the racial aspect of juvenile delinquency grew also at the level of county politics as the war unfolded. When County Supervisor Ford addressed youth problems in a series of letters to county probation and other youth officials in 1939, he was not particularly concerned with nonwhite youth. In fact, the policies he outlined to curb delinquency, including increased activity of the Boy Scouts and other supervised extracurricular activities, were directed as much at white youth as at African Americans, Mexican Americans, or Asian Americans.[30] By 1942, however, in the midst of the growing craze over Mexican gangs and the racial nature of youth crime, Ford and others he worked with on the issue, including the chief deputy probation officer of Los Angeles County, Karl Holton, singled out African American and Mexican American youth as the city's major deviants.[31] Thus, while Ford and others may have proffered a more liberal and philanthropic approach to aiding the plight of nonwhite youth in the city, they still framed the problem of juvenile delinquency in racial terms.

Vocal opposition to the overtly racialist and biologically based analyses of men like Ayres, Horrall, and Biscailuz did arise. For example, Carey McWilliams, chief of the California Division of Immigration and Housing, and an outspoken lawyer-activist for the rights of the state's ethnic Mexicans, argued that stressing biological factors was misguided because juvenile delinquency was a wartime problem in virtually all U.S. cities, regardless of ethnic or racial composition. In his own testimony to the Los Angeles County Grand Jury, McWilliams went so far as to suggest that the wartime "Good Neighbor" policy toward Latin America advocated by President Roosevelt was threatened by the maltreatment of Mexicans and Mexican Americans in the United States.[32] Eduardo Quevedo, chairman of the Citizens Committee for Latin American Youth, and county chief probation officer Karl Holton similarly argued that associating Mexican American youth with lawlessness was often based on unfounded discriminatory assumptions rather than statistical evidence.[33]

Guy T. Nunn, a field representative of the Minority Groups Service of the War Manpower Commission, a body charged with investigating the employment problems of Spanish-speaking men and women, echoed McWilliams's testimony. Nunn told the grand jury that "delinquency is not a monopoly of any racial or national group; it is a monopoly of poverty, excessive housing concentration, social and economic discrimination. These, far more than juvenile delinquency, characterize our Spanish-speaking minority."[34] Challenging the policy of the LAPD, Nunn went on to suggest that "strong arm tactics, especially when applied indiscriminately to all youth of Mexican extraction, will not eliminate delinquency."[35] Mexican consul Manuel Aguilar offered another alternative voice in the grand jury investigations, stressing in his testimony that human beings are not born delinquents, but are socially conditioned by home influences, education, and poverty. For Aguilar, as for McWilliams and Nunn, juvenile delinquency was not defined by ethnicity or race, but encompassed a broad spectrum of U.S. as well as international society.[36]

In its concluding "Report on Special Committee on Problems of Mexican Youth," the grand jury sided with the likes of McWilliams, Nunn, and Aguilar. Skeptical of the reasoning of Ayres and others like him, the grand jury noted a variety of "handicaps suffered by the young people of Mexican ancestry," disadvantages that had nothing to do with their supposed cultural or biological inferiority. The report pointed out that "such things as bad housing, segregation, unfortunate publicity attending many of their activities, seasonal employment, the small number of the older generation who have become naturalized American citizens, low income, lack of opportunity for technical training, were emphasized as being responsible for the attitude of mind on the part of the young people concerned, which had resulted in much unsocial conduct on their part."[37] Although it endorsed the LAPD's efforts to stem the rise of juvenile delinquency, the grand jury was also convinced that "young people of Mexican ancestry have been more sinned against than sinning, in the discriminations and limitations that have been placed on them and their families."[38]

Despite its findings, the actual process of the grand jury may have, in fact, enhanced the racialization of juvenile delinquency. In addition to providing a public stage on which local officials could exaggerate the criminal activity of African American and Mexican American youth, the grand jury unwittingly characterized those youth as the taproot of delinquency by framing its inquiry in terms of a "Mexican problem" and a "race problem." No matter how eloquent McWilliams, Nunn, or Consul Aguilar were in their critiques of Ayres, the mayor, or the tactics of the

LAPD, they were forced to respond to the allegations of those who presumed that juvenile delinquency and its threat to home-front stability were predominantly caused by African American and Mexican American communities. Indeed, most governmental efforts to address juvenile delinquency, even those like the grand jury's that ultimately reflected sympathy with the disadvantaged and limited life chances of nonwhite youth, proposed to ease the crisis by limiting the criminal behavior of Mexican Americans and African Americans. It was assumed, in other words, that nonwhite youth were guilty of something, whether or not they had committed any crime.

As if in concert with local authorities, the mainstream press in Los Angeles ruthlessly campaigned to focus attention on the alleged criminal and delinquent behavior of Mexican American youth and their African American counterparts. Throughout the last several months of 1942 and the first half of 1943, the Los Angeles *Times, Daily News,* and *Evening Herald and Express* and nearly every other local daily and weekly routinely published headlines reporting muggings, violence, drug use, and robberies by Mexican American and African American gangsters. As city authorities employed mass roundups and arrests of nonwhite young people in ghettos and barrios, the mainstream press described them as "roving gangs of blood-thirsty, marihuana-crazed young men, committing arson, rape, and robbery" and condemned them as a morally bankrupt drain on the war effort. Nonwhite youth were linked to rumors of an extensive drug culture and presented to a court of public opinion that equated the smoking of marijuana with the wasting of time, effort, and money that might otherwise be funneled into war production.[39]

As the crisis of juvenile delinquency spun out of control—more in newsrooms than in the streets of Los Angeles—the zoot style of African American and Mexican American youth came to symbolize their criminal and immoral disruption of the home front. Particularly after the Sleepy Lagoon incident and during the trial, it was common for nonwhite youth to be described as "gangsters" or "hoodlums" in newspapers. Much of the press coverage of Sleepy Lagoon was a witch hunt for African American and Mexican American teens. The Los Angeles papers sensationalized nonwhite youth crime waves with condemning headlines such as "Mexican Goon Squads," "Zoot Suit Gangs," "Pachuco Killers," and "Juvenile Gang War Laid to Youths' Desire to Thrill."[40] Exposés on the illegal activities of zoot suiters were published regularly under titles that explicitly linked Mexican American and African American youth to violence and crime. Articles like "Six Arrested in

Figure 3. Mexican American girl-gang roundup, Los Angeles, 1942. *Los Angeles Daily News* Negatives Collection, Department of Special Collections, Charles E. Young Research Library, UCLA.

Gang Death," "New Zoot Gangster Attacks Result in Arrest of 100," "Idle Time Seen as Crux of Youth Problem," and "City and County Take Action to End Boy Gangs" helped fuel the hysteria over juvenile delinquency.[41] Although local officials initiated much of the focus on African American and Mexican American youth, the mainstream press fanned the flames of the racialization of juvenile delinquency and helped make the zoot suit an emblem of the problem.

While the mainstream press portrayed Mexican American and African American youth in a largely negative light, the ethnic and leftist press chimed in with its own coverage. Some newspapers, most notably the *California Eagle,* run by African American Charlotta Bass, and the *Eastside Journal,* edited by Al Waxman, criticized the racialization of juvenile delinquency. Others, however, such as the more conservative Spanish-language paper *La Opinion* sought to solidify their own position as an integral part of wartime LA by condemning the behavior of nonwhite youth and accepting their alleged criminal nature with little

Figure 4. Mexican American boy-gang roundup, Los Angeles, 1942. *Los Angeles Daily News* Negatives Collection, Department of Special Collections, Charles E. Young Research Library, UCLA.

argument. In fact, *La Opinion* published among the most seething attacks on the immoral and violent threats allegedly posed by Mexican American youth at the same time that it lauded the efforts of city police to stem the tide of youth crime. One editorial, for example, even claimed that the Mexican American women who participated in zoot suit gangs were sex fiends who demeaned their cultural identity as Mexicans.[42]

The Los Angeles press began to link the activity of local zoot suiters with others around the country in what was viewed as a nationwide decaying of youth culture. In October 1942, for example, the *Los Angeles Times* headlined a story "Death Penalty to be Asked for Jitterbug Killers of Teacher," which reported the case of two high school students in New York. A sixteen-year-old and a nineteen-year-old were arrested on homicide charges for the killing of a math teacher in Brooklyn. While the two waited in prison without bail, it was reported that they entertained their jailers and fellow prisoners with the intricacies of the zoot suits they were wearing. The two boys, claimed the wire report, both wore their haircuts in the fashion admired by young girls and showed no remorse and little sympathy for the widow and two children of the victim.[43] The conflation of African American and Mexican American youth with zoot suits and crime quickly became a national pattern as nonwhite youth were increasingly portrayed as a drain on the war effort.

THE RACIALIZATION OF JUVENILE DELINQUENCY IN WARTIME NEW YORK CITY

Led by the liberal mayor Fiorello La Guardia, New York City authorities were less explicit in characterizing nonwhite youth as subverting home-front unity. Perhaps because there was no single event or court case that garnered as much publicity as the Sleepy Lagoon incident in Los Angeles, the debate over juvenile delinquency in New York was more subdued and not nearly as volatile in the months after the United States entered the war. Still, a perceived crisis in juvenile delinquency plagued the city. As the war progressed, those who discussed it did not take long in adopting predominantly racial terms. Whereas Mexican American youth took the brunt of attention in Los Angeles, in New York City it was African American youth who in early 1943 found themselves accused as domestic enemy number one for the alleged threats they posed to a cohesive patriotism. While many city leaders tried to separate the politics of youth from those of race, they dealt constantly with colleagues and a city at large that did, in fact, conflate black youth with danger, crime, and violence. Ultimately, despite the efforts of Mayor La Guardia and others to define juvenile delinquency as not simply an African American issue, the wartime discourse concerning juvenile delinquency in New York became racialized.

The problem of juvenile delinquency was not, of course, natural to any particular ethnic or racial group. The increase in leisure time for youth and decreasing supervision by parents and other authorities as the war unfolded—considered by many a prime cause of juvenile delinquency—combined with young people's usefulness in the defense of and production for the United States to affect white as much as African American youth. In fact, the wartime delinquency of white youth had concerned black New Yorkers since at least early 1942. In March of that year, the *People's Voice* reported on a series of incidents in which white "hoodlums" stalked and terrorized African American residents in the Washington Heights neighborhood because they did not approve of blacks living in the area. Two black families in the area had milk bottles and iron pipes thrown through the windows of their home and garbage left in the yard and were the victims of the apparently age-old teen prank of doorbell ditching. After several months of such activity and little police response, African American residents in the area feared for the their safety.

The debate over juvenile delinquency grew more heated in late 1942 and early 1943, as evidenced in extended coverage in the black press. In May 1943, another New York–based African American newspaper, the *Amsterdam News*, challenged the assumption that youth crime was essentially a black problem. Relying on the commentary of Charles Kellar, president of the New York State Youth Conference and a Kings County probation officer, the newspaper adamantly denied that juvenile delinquency, or illegal activity by adults for that matter, was limited to any race of people. Recent statistics, Kellar maintained, showed that crime rates among African American youth had actually fallen in the early war years and were not substantially higher than those for white youth. Kellar went on to suggest that for those African American youth who did break the law, it was important to consider whether economic factors, such as coming from low-income families and being the last hired and first fired in war industry jobs, affected their motivation.[44]

Despite efforts to characterize juvenile delinquency as a problem not defined solely by race or ethnic makeup, the politics of youth in New York were soon couched in racial terms. As was the case in Los Angeles, New York City authorities went to great lengths to investigate the problem of youth crime. Mayor La Guardia created a committee on juvenile delinquency and engaged in an ongoing debate with the citizens of New York over race and the politics of youth. The 1943 Kings County Grand Jury launched an inquiry into juvenile delinquency, and the New York Police Department viewed adolescent mischief as a serious citywide concern.[45] Although La Guardia and other city leaders denied the racial nature of youth crime, the bureaucratic process they initiated to address the problem ended up framing the issue as race based and ultimately helped racialize juvenile delinquency.

The intensity and importance of the debate over juvenile delinquency in New York in early 1943 was reflected in hundreds of letters between Mayor La Guardia and city residents. These exchanges reveal the deep-seated discrimination in the city, as well as the ways La Guardia sought to distance himself from such thinking. Perhaps most important, however, the letters illustrate how the politics of youth in wartime New

York came to center on a debate about who and which communities were worthy of full membership in the city and its war effort.

In one letter sent to the mayor in February 1943, Jeanne Seeley Schwartz denounced what she viewed as La Guardia's failed policy in response to juvenile delinquency. Schwartz admonished the mayor for downplaying juvenile delinquency during a recent radio address and suggested it was "time someone took you in hand and instructed you in the facts of life." Describing herself as an "ordinary housewife with two children," Schwartz wrote that all she wanted was a decent city for her children to live in. Citing what she believed to be a threat to that way of life, Schwartz asked the mayor, "Do you realize that Manhattan is full of gangs of boys between the ages of eight and 16 who go around preying on children, often with knives?" Claiming that her own son had been held up for spare change more than five times and that police had said they could do nothing about it, Schwartz got to the main point of her letter: "In this neighborhood the gangs are made up mostly of Negroes and Puerto Ricans and occasionally of white boys." She closed by demanding the mayor not ignore the situation for fear of losing votes from black and Latino communities.[46]

La Guardia responded to Schwartz's letter and others like them by following up on citizens' allegations with local NYPD precincts. For example, in direct response to Jeanne Schwartz's letter, officers from the 23rd Detective Squad interviewed her at her home and prepared a report later shared with the mayor's office. The investigation concluded that Schwartz had exaggerated the number of assaults on her son, overestimated the damage inflicted by gangs in her neighborhood, and displayed a paranoiac belief about gangs committing rape and destroying public parks that was derived largely from newspaper accounts.[47]

In another letter to La Guardia, Ethel Olsen of the Bronx levied her own attack on the city's African American youth. Olsen complained that her daily subway commute was routinely made unsafe by black youth. "Every morning on a train leaving the Bronx Park Station," she wrote, "a crowd of young colored boys and girls get on at Prospect Avenue . . . with hoots and yells, pushing and jostling, annoying all the other passengers." In what she deemed a particularly disturbing incident, a white man protested the behavior of the African American youth, only to soon find himself in a flurry of "arms and fists flying in the air." An innocent white girl was hit in the eye in the scuffle, she added. Olsen voiced her desire to move from New York, demanded better police protection, and threatened never to vote for La Guardia again if he did not do something about the situation.[48] In response to Olsen, La Guardia wrote that the young African American youth were probably going to school, could just as easily have been a group of white boys, and concluded, "I don't see what race has to do with it because I have seen the same thing happen with white boys and girls." La Guardia ended by saying he could not have a policeman on every subway in the city and that "boys will be boys and girls will be girls, regardless of race, color and creed; always have been and always will be, and there are certain things that grown ups have to put up with."[49]

In yet another, more detailed correspondence with the mayor, Leonie Gray similarly blamed black youth for juvenile delinquency in New York City. Gray bitterly complained in her letter about African American boys in her West Manhattan neighborhood who, she wrote, often attacked white children and prowled around, causing riots. Gray detailed the behavior of the youth she accused:

> These colored children are working with a clever system to throw the blame on white children, which has happened in a couple of instances I have known of since this riot started. . . . They post a small child to start an argument with a white boy (or girl) much larger than themselves; and if they can't succeed in arguing with the child, they start kicking or hitting them to make the white child fight back, and as soon as they do there are a group of colored, to jump in and attack the white child, with the alibi that they were protecting the little child.

Gray alleged that in another trick used by black youth, a girl would go up to a white boy on the street and slash his arm with a penknife. When the boy defended himself, a group of African American boys would jump him for fighting a girl. Afterward, the white boy was blamed and "by then the girl had no knife and was a perfect lady." Although Gray claimed not to be prejudiced against any race or color, she did clarify that "it is true that I don't choose to live with the colored people," because

> these are not a race of people that you can say please to and expect the same respect which you get from the white people; I don't say that there are not refined and cultured colored people, far from it; but not the trash that we have to contend with here, they haven't gotten the cannibal out of their systems yet, and revert to it on the slightest pretext. To handle these people, you can take a lesson from our President and use and allow our police to use 'soft words with a big stick', and you would soon find that you would have peace and calm; or are you afraid of the votes you would lose!!!!!!!![50]

As La Guardia faced an onslaught of criticism for his inability to control the allegedly wild and illegal behavior of black youth in the city, he was forced to respond to those who viewed young African Americans as violent and dangerous. In perhaps his most direct move to counter such criticism, in February 1943 he formed a citywide committee to study juvenile delinquency. Made up primarily of city council members, the committee was expected to "discuss the facts and present recommendations relating to a particular aspect of the broad problem of juvenile delinquency." The committee studied court cases involving juveniles, observed court proceedings, and conducted surveys on topics such as the probation system, truancy, recreation facilities, venereal disease among young people, and youth participation in the war effort. Its first report included statistics on juvenile delinquents, criminal prosecutions, and truancy in the city, but made no direct mention of race as linked to youth crime. The committee did, however, strongly imply that juvenile delinquency was a problem centered in specific areas of the city, especially Harlem.[51]

In 1943, the year La Guardia formed his committee on juvenile delinquency and the year after the Los Angeles County Grand Jury explored the problems of youth crime, the Grand Jury of Kings County, New York, made a similar investigation focusing on the predominantly African American neighborhood of Bedford-Stuyvesant in Brooklyn. Although much of the grand jury's final report and the testimony of numerous civic leaders, police officers, clergy, businessmen, and other notable citizens did not specifically identify juvenile delinquency as a race problem, the grand jury proceedings nonetheless directly linked youth crime with the city's African American community. Despite its claim that juvenile delinquency was "in no sense a race problem" and was "purely a social and law enforcement problem which calls for prompt action and immediate attention," in drawing its conclusions, the grand jury invariably focused on areas where African Americans and Puerto Ricans constituted the majority of residents.[52] Authorities conflated crime, juvenile delinquency, and violence with black and Latino neighborhoods by describing these areas as sustaining a deplorable state of lawlessness and immorality. The youth in these neighborhoods were painted in broad strokes as violent criminals who ran unsupervised around the streets wreaking havoc. "Groups of young boys, armed with penknives of all sizes and other weapons," the grand jury reported, "roam the streets at will and threaten and assault passersby and commit muggings and holdups with increasing frequency. Gangs of hoodlums armed with such knives and weapons commit holdups, stabbing, homicides, and other serious crimes."[53] One incident cited by the report entailed the attack of a sailor by a fourteen-year-old boy and four of his friends. The sailor was allegedly stabbed at least six times before he died. While youth violence was certainly cause for concern, the debate over juvenile delinquency was often generalized as a race problem.

In addition to violent assaults, the grand jury cited prostitution, venereal disease, and petty theft as common in African American neighborhoods. Its final report also emphasized the "unhealthy moral condition" stemming from prostitution carried on in dozens of apartments in Bedford-Stuyvesant, making it one of the worst areas for the crime in all of New York State. Prostitution, argued the grand jury, facilitated the spread of venereal disease and threatened the safety of the wider public. On top of the dangerous sexual conduct of area residents was a plethora of petty crime, including window smashing, shoplifting, pocketbook snatching, mugging, and holdups. The grand jury claimed that "most crimes are committed by young children below 21 years of age."[54] The characterization of nonwhite youth by local authorities as out of control, poised at any moment to commit a felony, and constantly threatening the safety of law-abiding New Yorkers helped define the role of black and Latino youth in the city. For those residents who needed no convincing that nonwhite youth were the source of nothing but trouble, the grand jury surely only solidified their beliefs.

The grand jury further blamed nonwhite communities for giving New York a black eye in its fight to be known as the greatest city in the United States. Citing the prostitution, gambling, and carousing at bars in Bedford-Stuyvesant, the grand jury's final report placed unhealthiness, in terms of both disease and moral degeneration, squarely in African American areas. It also blamed parents who were unable to control or discipline their children appropriately. "Parents, where are your children tonight?" the grand jury asked. "Where are your children right now? What company are they keeping?" The report urged a citywide curfew to aid parents in keeping their kids off the streets.

The grand jury's assessment of city officials' handling of the situation was mixed. It reserved its most seething critique for Mayor La Guardia. It demanded a greatly improved approach from his administration if the problems of nonwhite youth were to be remedied, concluding that "the fault lies with the responsible public officials, and particularly, with the Mayor of this city in failing to invoke the power at his command and take all the steps necessary to prevent the lawlessness we have referred to."[55] At the same time, the grand jury's report noted ironically that the NYPD was doing a fantastic job of containing juvenile delinquency.

Among the NYPD actions the grand jury commended was the department's April response to complaints of disorderly groups of boys in Washington Heights. Police had patrolled poolrooms, dancehalls, clubs, and playgrounds in the area—a sweep that rounded up eighteen African American gangs and six white gangs.[56] The grand jury argued for more such action and additional police staffing in predominantly black areas of the city. The grand jury's recommendation for a more militarized policing of African American neighborhoods also included calls to change the law to prohibit the gathering of crowds and harsher court rulings against youth criminals.

Although La Guardia vociferously and carefully crafted an anti-discrimination posture—an attitude that dated back to at least his response to the 1935 race riots in Harlem, when he strengthened his reputation as a sympathetic and serious advocate for the city's black community—he also characterized juvenile delinquency as a nonwhite issue. He assumed that criminal activity by youth was more a problem for the black community than for any other. La Guardia's committee on juvenile delinquency claimed that East and central Harlem accounted for more than half of the delinquent juveniles in Manhattan in 1941 and 1942.[57] Though the mayor's office pinpointed city areas rather than specific nonwhite communities, and thus tried to avoid racializing juvenile delinquency, its tactics were often quite transparent. In a moment of frustration while explaining how city authorities were handling problems with youth, for example, La Guardia himself said, "Let's be more frank about it—this is the Negro question we are talking about. I know the Police Department is making a sincere and honest effort to control it. Well, it is pretty tough; when a neighborhood changes its complexion that way there is bound to be trouble. . . . Some of these younger criminals are pretty bad."[58]

Other city officials were not as subtle as La Guardia. In a letter to the mayor in February 1943, for example, city assemblyman S. Robert Molinari conflated African American behavior with crime and immorality. Lamenting the craps and dice games, vandalism, loafing, and mushrooming of gangs in Harlem, Molinari directly correlated such activities with petty theft, mugging, and robbery of innocent citizens after dark. Whether "innocent" citizens was code for "white" citizens we cannot be sure, but that Harlem and its many black youth were considered a threat to the rest of the city was clear. Neither did Molinari exclude young women from his analysis. Although he denounced an increasing number of incidents of insults and violence against women, Molinari blamed the young women themselves for the trend, which was, in his view, largely a result of their "becoming very careless and daring through the lure of the uniform." Sympathizing with the efforts of middle- and upper-class homeowners to keep taxes down and protect their neighborhoods from the encroaching threat of maladjusted youth, the assemblyman suggested only the alternative of increasing police protection.[59]

Although no single incident in New York City spurred the frantic racialization of juvenile delinquency as the Sleepy Lagoon case did in Los Angeles, the local courts played an important role in conflating black youth and crime. In July 1943, for example, a case against a purported gang of young African American boys did not generate the national interest that Sleepy Lagoon did but shared some eerily similar traits and captured the public attention of New York City. Following an investigation in which over 250 New York youth were caught in dragnets and questioned about the killing of fifteen-year-old William Manuel in Harlem, twelve boys between ages fourteen and sixteen were arrested for murder. In what was said to be a battle over a toy pistol, Manuel had been stabbed twenty-three times by the group of boys who police claimed were part of the Bachelor Cubs gang.[60] The black press reported on the case of the Bachelor Cubs gang daily, energizing the city's African American population to respond to the growing outcries over juvenile delinquency.

Building from city leaders' condemnation of black juvenile delinquents, the mainstream press in New York City launched its own frontal assault on black youth. The coverage of juvenile delinquency by such New York newspapers as the *Times, Post,* and *Daily News* gave great attention to crime waves in Harlem and other black areas said to be a major cause of the city's deterioration. During the last months of 1942 and first six months of 1943, reports on the alleged crime wave added fuel to the fire. In one week alone, between October 28 and November 5, 1942, articles with titles like "Delinquency Rise among Girls Told," "Midnight Curfew for Girls under 16 Urged Here to Curb Delinquency," "Closing of City Parks to Children Urged as a Curb on Delinquency," "City Park Curfew for Children Urged by Judge to Curb Rising Delinquency," and "Teachers Predict Delinquency Rise" appeared in the *New York Times, New York Post,* and *Bronx News.*[61] The depth and volume of the reporting on juvenile delinquency surely cultivated fear of nonwhite youth in many New Yorkers, identified nonwhite youth as dangerous and immoral, and contributed to the growing crisis, regardless of whether the reality of youth crime was as bad as newspapers

made it out to be. The very real possibility remained that the crisis of
juvenile delinquency was as much a product of wartime hysteria as it
was a response to the youth's actual behavior.

As the article titles noted above indicate, the alleged role of young
women in juvenile delinquency was not overlooked. Many young women,
both African American and white, were viewed as prostitutes carrying
venereal disease that they passed on to unsuspecting servicemen. Discussing the growing problem of youth prostitution, one article argued, "It is
not the fault of the servicemen who pick up the girls. It is rather the fault
of mothers who clothe their children as they themselves are clothed; permit them to rouge, lipstick, mascara, and wear heels three or four inches
high. These little girls can easily be mistaken for girls 18 years old when
they are dressed up like their mothers."[62] Young women were thus to
blame for immoral sexual activity and the spread of venereal disease
because they appealed to soldiers and sailors.

The gendered and racialized nature of mainstream press coverage of
the juvenile delinquency crisis further identified young black males as
sexual predators and a threat to white women and girls. One editorial in
a Long Island publication reported that "six flashily-dressed Negroes
have been arrested in Hempstead and are reported by the police to have
confessed guilt in a series of 'mugging' attacks and petty robberies in
that village. While these boys apparently are not charged with rape, if
permitted to pursue their career of crime it is only a question of time
until this outrage would be added to their other offenses. The citizens of
Nassau County are not safe with these men at large."[63] In addition to
urging harsher methods of punishment and control by city police, the
press emphasized the threat young black men posed to white women
who worked in the defense industry or were the wives or sweethearts of
men in the armed forces. As in Los Angeles, the clothing style of nonwhite youth was used to identify them as delinquent and their masculinity as deviant. The exaggerated style of baggy drape pants, long coats,
and thick-soled shoes so much a part of zoot style was interpreted as an
affront to the way youth should dress and carry themselves. Young
African American males in New York, moreover, were seen to pose the
threat of sexual and social mixing of diverse racial and ethnic groups.
Responding to the exaggerated fear of miscegenation, New York papers
cited increases in juvenile delinquency, called for curfews for the city's
youth, and blamed prostitution on young nonwhite women and violence
on their male counterparts.[64]

The city's black press responded by protesting the negative portrayals of African American youth. Both the leading African American newspaper in Harlem, the *Amsterdam News,* and the *People's Voice* routinely criticized the mainstream New York press for inventing crime waves. The papers consistently noted the smear campaign against black neighborhoods; acknowledged that such propaganda led the armed forces to bar servicemen from entering areas for fear of exposing them to gambling, drinking, and prostitution; and asserted that these journalistic trends negatively influenced the city's view of Harlem and other predominantly black areas. Throughout late 1942 and into the spring of 1943, the black press called for an end to the lies in mainstream newspapers about Harlem and the city's African Americans.[65]

URBAN SOCIAL REFORM AND THE POLITICS OF YOUTH

Urban social reformers organized to limit the violence exerted by city officials against nonwhite youth and challenge the press's characterizations of them as criminal and hypersexual. One of the most important consequences of government and press attention to juvenile delinquency was the political mobilization of diverse coalitions to combat the racialization of juvenile delinquency. Despite their noble intentions and successes on behalf of nonwhite youth, however, Mexican American, African American, and white social reformers viewed the politics of youth as a vehicle to push a broader agenda that prioritized wartime assimilation. Social reformers contributed, albeit inadvertently, to the racialization of juvenile delinquency by failing to adequately challenge the assumption that nonwhite youth, crime, and violence were inherently linked. Rather than push for a deeper understanding of the economic and social factors that contributed to the difficult conditions faced by nonwhite youth who lived in the wartime United States, most reformers viewed the debate over juvenile delinquency as a forum in which to push for full national belonging. At the same time many of these groups worked tirelessly to secure nonwhite youth more wartime economic opportunities and social services, they often assumed that wearing a zoot suit and dancing the jitterbug was un-American, facilitated the growth of juvenile delinquency, and were contrary to the normative identities nonwhites should be crafting.

In Los Angeles, area activists responded to the Sleepy Lagoon case and the subsequent crisis in youth crime swiftly and forcefully. Most African American and Mexican American activists stressed that the problem could best be solved by incorporating troubled youth more fully into the war effort. With the war dominating public consciousness, many believed the perceived problem in youth crime and the dehumanizing discourse about Mexican American and African American youth could be eased by further assimilating those young people into U.S. society.

Much of the political work addressing the crisis of juvenile delinquency grew out of the uproar over the Sleepy Lagoon case. Most notably, the Sleepy Lagoon Defense Committee (SLDC), which developed from the efforts of the Citizens Committee for the Defense of Mexican American Youth, won national recognition for its fight for the release of the convicted defendants.[66] Chaired by Carey McWilliams, but spearheaded by its primary administrator, Alice McGrath, and organizers such as Luisa Moreno, the SLDC drew support from such celebrities as actors Rita Hayworth and Orson Welles. It inspired hundreds of advocates, including Jews, Mexican Americans, African Americans, communist party supporters, and labor organizers. The long hours of hard work that went into the committee's efforts demonstrated that not all social reformers subscribed to the views of nonwhite youth articulated by city, state, and federal authorities. McGrath, who coordinated much of the committee's day-to-day operations, even challenged the predominant view of the zoot suit as a style, praising its impressive look and admitting that even she wore drape pants on occasion.[67]

After several years of seemingly thankless work fund-raising and organizing, by 1945 the SLDC had helped win the release on appeal of all the Sleepy Lagoon defendants. The SLDC's multiracial makeup was among its greatest strengths, as involvement in the committee came from virtually every community in Los Angeles. Charlotta Bass, owner and editor of the African American newspaper the *California Eagle*, for example, was an active member of the SLDC. The *California Eagle*, even more than the Spanish language newspaper *La Opinion*, consistently supported the SLDC's efforts from the beginning. Bass, who was also the first African American woman on the Los Angeles County Grand Jury and who served on the 1942 grand jury that investigated juvenile delinquency, championed the SLDC in her newspaper, abraded city leaders for their handling of the crisis in juvenile delinquency, connected the struggles of Mexican American and African American Angelinos against discrimination, and even drew links between the treatment of nonwhite youth in Los Angeles, New York City, and other urban areas. In late 1942 the *California Eagle* published pieces entitled "Our Mexican Neighbors," "Mexicans Face Police Terror Round Ups," and "Vile Press Slurs: Link L.A. Anti-Mexican Drive with So-Called Harlem Crime Wave."[68]

While the SLDC was focused primarily on winning the release of the Sleepy Lagoon defendants from prison on appeal, it necessarily engaged the broader discourse of juvenile delinquency. Shortly after the arrest of the defendants in August 1942, Carey McWilliams argued that the Mexican American youth gang problems in Los Angeles were due to lack of proper recreational and educational facilities and opportunities.[69] Others echoed McWilliams by recommending that nonwhite youth enroll in Boy Scouts, that police departments initiate athletic leagues for troubled youth, and that the city increase budgetary expenditures for playgrounds.[70] Even the Los Angeles Board of Education supported these sorts of policies by keeping playgrounds open after school, utilizing school buildings around the clock, and sponsoring "character building" activities under proper supervision.[71]

Besides the SLDC, perhaps the most active organization in the debate over wartime juvenile delinquency in Los Angeles was the Citizens Committee for Latin American Youth (CCLAY), formed under the auspices of the mayor and local officials but made up of prominent Mexican American lawyers such as Eduardo Quevedo and Manuel Ruiz as well as other professionals. Whereas the SLDC focused its energies solely on the appeal of the Sleepy Lagoon defendants' convictions, the CCLAY addressed the broader implications of the conflation of juvenile delinquency and race. The CCLAY led the charge against the maltreatment of nonwhite youth, especially Mexican Americans, by city authorities and against the negative press reporting so common during the era.

On the heels of the Los Angeles *Times, Herald Express,* and *Daily News'* routine characterization of Mexican American and African American youth as responsible for crime waves, the CCLAY argued that such blatant misrepresentation slanted public opinion against these youth and frustrated their efforts to contribute to the war effort. In a letter to Norman Chandler, owner of the *Los Angeles Times,* for example, the CCLAY insisted that the newspaper's vendetta against nonwhite youth resulted in too many articles that disrupted home-front unity, a practice explicitly condemned by the U.S. Department of War Information and California governor Earl Warren. How could Mexican American and African American youth find jobs in defense industries or be inspired to join the service, asked the CCLAY, when they were constantly depicted as threats to national security? Ironically, it was often charges of a lack of patriotism that pushed many young Mexican

Americans and African Americans to commit more seriously to the war effort. Indeed, according to the CCLAY, "the accusation that so called gang members hate servicemen, when practically all of them have brothers and sisters in the armed forces of the United States, many of whom are heroes and have died heroes' deaths in defense of the Stars and Stripes, makes the indictment contrary to common sense."[72]

Among the CCLAY's primary goals were to challenge the assumption that Mexican American youth were a threat to the war effort and to coordinate programs within the Latino community to ease the delinquency problem. The organization argued that indulging in a program of Americanization would be no more effective in achieving its goals than one of "Mexicanization" or "Cubanization," and that the American way of living was no more a solution to juvenile delinquency than a Mexican way of living. In one public statement, the CCLAY asserted that it was not willing "to admit that gangsters are a by-product of the American way of living any more than it is willing to admit that juvenile hoodlums are a product of some national philosophy of life."[73] Despite such intentions, however, the CCLAY's actions, policies, and programs emphasized incorporation into U.S. society as the basis for any solution to juvenile delinquency. To such ends, the CCLAY spearheaded several programs that proposed to help prevent juvenile delinquency; raise the moral, social, educational, and economic standards of Spanish-speaking youth; and coordinate activities between Latino groups and law enforcement and social agencies.[74] Irrespective of race, ethnicity, or language, argued the CCLAY, juvenile delinquency was a societal problem that could be solved only by assimilating Mexican American communities into wartime society on a full and equal basis.

In areas where Mexican American and African American residents predominated, the CCLAY took measures to increase job opportunities for nonwhite youth and persuade the press and public officials to end negative characterizations of them. One such effort was the Alpine Street Project, aimed at curbing the juvenile delinquent activities of the Mexican American Alpine Street gang. Linked to citywide attempts to limit the growth of gangs in Los Angeles, the Alpine Street Project intended to provide group therapy, individual case work, recreational activities, and leadership development for area youth.[75] Despite the intentions of such initiatives, however, they largely failed to address the structural causes of poverty and inequality so pervasive in the city.

Most other Mexican American political organizations in Los Angeles similarly underscored assimilation and the performance of normative

U.S. identities as the primary strategies for improving wartime living conditions. The Federation of Spanish American Voters, Inc., attended a meeting of the Adult Education and Citizenship group in Los Angeles in 1942 where the hosts promised to renew efforts at helping Mexican Americans to better understand American ways of living. One participant captured the excitement surrounding the meeting: "We feel that by our sincere desire to present to these people our standard of living, our many solutions to their problems of health and sanitation by interpreting for them the rules and regulations which govern our country, we may be assisting them to become better members of our community."[76]

In fact, the assimilation-based political strategy was not unique to the many Mexican American groups that espoused it, but was shared by many other nonwhite activists. The Nisei-led Japanese American Citizens League, for example, combated internment and demonization as the enemy within the United States and displayed patriotism and nationalism to make its case for equality and national belonging. As Mexican American activists mobilized against the racialization of juvenile delinquency, their objectives and strategies were often interchangeable with Americanization programs advocated by governmental and public sentiment. Consequently, the bulk of organizing by the CCLAY and other similar organizations focused on promoting the participation of nonwhite youth in the war effort.[77]

The response of social reform groups in New York City to the racialization of juvenile delinquency mirrored that of activists in Los Angeles. Political organizations ranging from the local branch of the NAACP to the City-Wide Citizens Committee on Harlem (CCCH) and the West Harlem Council of Social Agencies (WHCSA) battled the mainstream press's negative coverage of the crisis. They also stressed the need for more organized and supervised activity for African American youth as a primary means to incorporate them into the city's war effort.

A number of New York community organizations sought to combat the rumormongering by the New York *Times, Post, Daily News,* and *Herald-Tribune.* The CCCH called for mass protests against major city newspapers for the inordinate attention they gave to Harlem crime news. The committee claimed to be attempting "to awaken both the city authorities and the public to the dangers of prejudice, segregation, and discrimination against our Negro citizens" and declared that "the association of the terms 'mugging,' 'Negro,' and 'Harlem' with crime and delinquency are out of all proportion to the facts and contribute to the prejudice that is the basis of the trouble."[78] The CCCH claimed that white juvenile delinquency had risen more and marveled that African American delinquency wasn't higher considering low incomes, inadequate social services provided by the city, and lack of employment opportunities. For the CCCH, the conditions in Harlem "all mean frustration and bitterness and desperation."[79] While many African American community leaders advocated increased city funds dedicated to more police, prisons, and social control, many joined the CCCH in arguing that better standards of living could result only from eliminating discrimination in employment and improving social and health facilities.

Other political groups similarly focused on incorporating black youth into the war effort as the number-one strategy to address juvenile delinquency. Like the CCCH, many of these organizations focused on Harlem. Having centered its efforts on the area since the late 1930s, the WHCSA intensified its work when the crisis in juvenile delinquency reached its apex following U.S. entry into the war. Made up of reverends, YMCA and YWCA administrators, public school teachers, Colored Orphan Asylum workers, and representatives from the Department of Welfare, the New York Urban League, and the Brotherhood of Sleeping Car Porters, the WHCSA viewed the crisis in juvenile delinquency and the need to incorporate African Americans more effectively into the war effort as two sides of the same coin. As WHCSA executive secretary Helena Coates argued as early as August 1941, concerns over juvenile delinquency and prostitution were directly linked to the need for more vocational and emergency defense training programs.[80]

Other social reform groups focused on the crisis of nonwhite juvenile delinquency. Neighborhood groups intent on curtailing youth crime formed in the Bronx, Brooklyn, and other sections of the city. Organizations such as the New York State Young Communist League and the Committee of Juvenile Aid of the Boy's Brotherhood Republic also made juvenile delinquency an important issue on their agendas.[81] Reacting in part to state and federal anti-discrimination legislation, these political groups planned to curb delinquency through "orderly channels," mainly by making nonwhite youth effective war industry laborers or members of the armed forces.[82] The Youth Council of the National Negro Congress, for example, argued that the most effective strategy to secure jobs, civil rights, and educational and recreational opportunities and to achieve security and peace was for African American youth to serve the war effort.[83]

Many activists identified improvements in social activities for nonwhite youth as the most feasible solution to delinquency problems. Some argued that any programs addressing juvenile delinquency should include restoring educational and recreational budgets, boosting appropriations for playgrounds, hiring more teachers, and extending facilities into Harlem, Jamaica, and Bedford-Stuyvesant, which suffered from overcrowding and discrimination.[84] A citizens group from Brooklyn, for example, complained to the mayor in 1943 that playgrounds with unsuitable facilities for baseball and handball led older boys to resort to all kinds of gambling, noisy and vulgar arguments, and meeting with girls in the area for "immoral purposes which requires no further detail."[85] The answer to such problems for concerned Brooklyn residents was to limit "rowdyism" by instituting more control over the area's youth through adult supervision and improved facilities.

New York City authorities, as well, supported improved leisure activities for African American youth. The NYPD made direct links between the purported rise in juvenile delinquency in areas like Harlem and Bedford-Stuyvesant and the lack of proper recreational facilities. The police helped organize and sponsor athletic leagues and playground and park programs for city youth in order to combat what they viewed as a rise in gang activity. Moreover, the NYPD argued that if more attention and resources were given to its police athletic leagues, they would have a better chance of recruiting youth from "potential crime classes" into the war effort.[86] Similarly, the same 1943 Kings County Grand Jury report that claimed juvenile delinquency had nothing to do with race asserted that the problem would be greatly eased if the number of playgrounds and recreational facilities in Bedford-Stuyvesant were increased and put to greater use. The report cited "too little parental supervision of the children" and a great need "to keep the children occupied in sports and other games in which they can use their excess energy in a proper and healthy environment, instead of in cellar clubs, bars, grills and other places where they should definitely not be."[87]

The tactics that most activists and city leaders in Los Angeles and New York adopted for dealing with juvenile delinquency contained at least two fundamental flaws. First, they largely failed to address structural conditions of poverty, discrimination, and poor life chances that most nonwhite youth faced. The limits of such reformist organizing, in other words, were evident in its objectives. Most reformers argued that the most effective solution to juvenile delinquency consisted of more recreation centers, leisure projects, and adult supervision for nonwhite youth. Their programmatic functions were dominated by plans for filling youth's idle time, especially that of young men, with constructive

Figure 5. Lineup of African American boys alleged to be
delinquent (one at far right wearing zoot suit), receiving
instruction from unseen police officers for participation in
police athletic leagues in Harlem, 1944. Herbert Gehr/Time
and Life Pictures/Getty Images.

activities. This position assumed that if nonwhite youth spent their spare
time playing football or basketball, boxing for golden gloves tourna-
ments, or camping in the woods with the Boy Scouts while under adult
supervision, juvenile delinquency would decrease dramatically.

Second, despite the critical role played by city, state, and federal governments in criminalizing nonwhite youth, community organizations
focused largely on the press as instigators of the conflict over juvenile
delinquency. Although government negligence was condemned in isolated instances, most Mexican American and African American leaders

lauded the efforts of the police department and city officials to control what they agreed were disgraceful outbreaks of youth violence during the war. While these civil rights groups may well have feared the growth of crime in their own communities, by choosing to focus on the mainstream press as the major culprit in the defamation of nonwhite youth, they excused police departments, mayors' offices, and state legislatures for their active role in the process.

Both of these flaws, the failure to address structural conditions and to move beyond a critique of the mainstream press, reflected an implicit acceptance of the need to "improve" and Americanize the social behavior of Mexican American and African American youth. While the CCLAY, SLDC, CCCH, and WHCSA challenged government and police characterizations of nonwhite youth as criminal, they also strongly implied that these youth needed to act more American. In the larger world of ethnic politicization, working-class juvenile delinquents potentially subverted the Americanization and assimilation efforts of middle-class Mexican Americans and African Americans. Many middle-class Mexican American and African American activists thus unwittingly denied the dignity of working-class youth by viewing their class and race identities as a threat to the stability of the U.S. home front. Through what legal race scholar Ian Haney Lopez might identify as their shared common sense of class, city officials and the nonwhite middle class publicly performed their class identity at the expense of young Mexican Americans and African Americans. If class identities in the early 1940s intersected with race, were produced in a range of social and institutional settings, and were practiced in relation to disparate readings of local politics, ways must be found to account for the perspectives and experiences of racialized working-class youth in the urban United States during World War II. In part II of this book, chapters 3 and 4 explore in more detail how African American and Mexican American youth responded to the denial of their dignity by reclaiming their physical bodies and urban public spaces, challenging the dehumanization thrust upon them, and charting novel social relationships on the home front.

PART TWO

The Struggle for Dignity

Zoot Style during World War II

CHAPTER 3

Zoot Style
and Body Politics

On March 20, 1944, more than two years after tens of thousands of American citizens of Japanese descent were forcibly incarcerated for suspected disloyalty to the United States, *Life* magazine published the first feature article on the Japanese American internment to appear in a major U.S. periodical. Accompanying the article was a photo depicting five male Japanese American internees with a caption that read in part, "These five Japs are among 155 trouble makers imprisoned in the stockade within the Tule Lake Segregation Center." Known as the most notorious of the "relocation centers" because it housed the most fervent resisters to Executive Order 9066, Tule Lake was home to hundreds of so-called "No No Boys," those predominantly young Japanese American men who responded negatively to items 27 and 28 on the loyalty questionnaire, which asked whether the internee would serve in the U.S. armed forces and swear allegiance to the United States. Although an older man clutching a pipe is part of the group in the photo, the others appear to be in their teens or early twenties. All appear to be encircling and looking down on the photographer, as if their racialized and masculine bodies might strike fear in and threaten those that cross their path.

This may seem an odd way to continue exploring the experiences of African American and Mexican American youth, but the *Life* magazine photo provides a useful starting point for thinking about how youth cultural politics during World War II influenced, were shaped by, and intertwined with the lives of young people from different race and ethnic

communities. Indeed, in her book *An Absent Presence,* cultural critic
Caroline Chung Simpson notes that all five men in the photo wear rum-
pled and slightly ill fitting clothes, with the dominant figure having the
posture and garb of a "greaser." He "wears a leather bomber jacket and
his hands are stuffed in his pockets as he acknowledges the camera's
presence with the barest hint of amusement."[1] Along with his long hair,
moustache, goatee, and beard, the youth's style and apparently defiant
attitude suggest cross-racial identification with Filipino, Mexican, and
African American youth of the time, many of whom were similarly
deemed threats to home-front stability for their flashy zoot suits and for
the public perception of them as being hypersexual and criminal and
refusing to participate in the war effort. While the *Life* magazine feature
was probably intended to convey the dangerous character of the "No
No Boys" to the reading public, it also reveals the more complex position occupied by Japanese American and other nonwhite youth in the
wartime United States. The men in the picture appear to be knowingly
posturing their bodies for the camera, displaying a stout togetherness,
and enjoying the experience of being gawked at during a time when
many Americans would rather have kept them out of the public eye.
They seem to have mobilized their own bodies to claim a sense of dignity
amidst the dehumanizing and humiliating experience of incarceration in
the internment camps.

    Rather than assume that nonwhite youth were powerless in the face
of wartime social, political, and economic forces, this chapter explores
the dissonance between the negative characterizations about them and
their everyday lives. It uncovers how nonwhite youth employed their
own bodies and each other as resources to create a multiracial cultural
space, generate dialogue with the rest of society, and challenge their own
subordination. Despite racial, regional, and gender differences among
zoot suiters, their struggles for dignity linked them as a class, where class
functioned not just as a predefined group of people identified by similar
relations of subordination or exploitation to capital but also as a group
based on members' *insubordination* to domination. The class nature of
zoot culture was, in part, a relationship of struggle shared by youth who
experienced antagonism between their own social practices or creativity
(work in the broadest sense) and dehumanization at the hands of local
authorities, through home-front rhetoric, or in the wartime political
economy. Zoot struggles for dignity may best be understood as the convergence of different *dignities* that simultaneously recognized and transcended ethnic or race-based identity. Rather than erase the differences

Figure 6. Japanese American "No No Boys," Tule Lake Relocation Center, 1944. Carl Mydans/Time and Life Pictures/Getty Images.

among them or ignore their engagement with the home front more generally, zoot suiters regenerated style, fashion, and wartime popular culture to make their lives more livable, meaningful, and dignified in the face of poverty, patriarchy, and violence, as well as discrimination in war industries. Just as historians have learned from the past struggles of aggrieved populations to win better wages, working conditions, or political representation, we too can learn from their struggles for dignity.[2]

The physical bodies of nonwhite youth were sites of opposition against the popular discourse that labeled them as juvenile delinquents and immoral threats to the home front. Zoot suiters *mobilized* their bodies to confront the dehumanizing social and economic conditions imposed by the wartime political economy and created by local officials, the mainstream press, and leaders of their own African American and Mexican American communities. As cultural critic Randy Martin suggests in his study of the performative aspects of dance, the concept of "mobilization" does not limit subordinated groups to defensive movements intended to block the offensive movements of more powerful forces. Mobilization, according to Martin, can be proactive in its potential to avoid co-optation and preserve spaces for new social and political relationships to germinate and in its "refusal to unsee what difference difference makes in the world."[3] By mobilizing their own bodies and occupying public space, zoot suiters challenged the indignities forced upon them at the same time that they created their own cultural identities and social relations. In this instance, power, resistance, and domination existed not as essential or elementary traits but as relationships negotiated, struggled over, and challenged by working-class African American and Mexican American youth as much as by high-ranking politicians.[4] If nonwhite youth were denied their dignity through discrimination, violence, and negative discourse, zoot suiters reclaimed it by asserting control over their own bodies and performing unique race and gender identities.

While some in the African American and Mexican American communities mobilized by buying war bonds, pushing for Americanization, demanding civil rights, or claiming whiteness, zoot suiters mobilized through a body politics of dignity. Through what Stuart Hall and other cultural critics refer to as a process of "stylization," nonwhite youth associated the material elements of zoot culture—the drape pants, the fingertip-length coats, and other accessories—with certain social practices, such as jitterbug or Lindy Hop dancing, "hanging out," and valuing leisure, to produce a cultural world and a set of social relationships that helped them make sense of wartime society.[5] The bodies of African American and Mexican American youth were also much more than texts to be read. They were also home to lived, sufferable experiences, making them the terrain for joy, pain, fear, and desire.[6] The "body politics of dignity," albeit often unorganized, unselfconscious, and unarticulated, was one way for zoot suiters to challenge normative behavior and social mores.[7]

Zoot culture also encompassed social practices that reinforced the marginalized status of nonwhite youth by reifying racial and gender hierarchies. Their patterns of popular cultural consumption, for example, often depended on interacting with the same political economy that denied them full access to wartime opportunities. Zoot suiters also often privileged one gender or race identity over another and in the process denied the dignity of others as they claimed their own. Part I showed

Figure 7. African American teens dressed in zoot suits at soda fountain, 1943. Copyright Bettmann/Corbis.

how the bodies of nonwhite youth and the public spaces they inhabited were sites of oppression; this chapter highlights how the bodies of zoot suiters functioned as a location for the contradictions of resistance and cultural politics. While some zoot suiters formed identities that disrupted popular notions of wartime race and gender as fundamentally white, others strengthened race or gender inequalities.

The mobilization and stylization of their bodies was part of zoot suiters' experimentation with what amounted to a politics of the possible in which zoot suiters explored the possibilities and limits of wartime race and gender identities. When young African American and Mexican

Figure 8. Mexican American youth in zoot suit, 1943. Copyright
Bettman/Corbis.

American men interpreted experiences of race and class denigration as
attacks on their gender identity, for example, masculinity emerged as the
terrain upon which they struggled to reclaim dignity. Young nonwhite
women also responded to attacks on their race and working-class identities by articulating new femininities and masculinities. Zoot suiters produced a variety of gender identities, some of which starkly diverged
from the heroic masculinity of servicemen, factory workers, and women
heads of household during World War II. They often challenged normative binaries of gender, making evident in their cultural practices that
masculinity was not the sole property of men and femininity did not

belong only to women. As much as they disrupted popular notions of the ways young women and men should behave, however, the gender identities of zoot suiters were often misinterpreted by the rest of U.S. society.[8] The behavior of many zoot suiters also diverged from the politics of middle-class nonwhites who believed deeply in strategies of Americanization or in claiming whiteness to secure equal citizenship. Zoot suiters practiced their own cultural politics, based at least in part on creating, sharing, and exchanging styles among a variety of youth. At the same time, many zoot suiters developed normative identities by joining the service or working in defense industries. Their cultural politics cannot be fully explained by assuming them to have been either products of alienation from the mainstream or part of the popular strategy to assimilate into wartime society. Their cultural politics, in other words, exposed a range of gender and race identities that were marginalized yet simultaneously were a critical component of the war effort. There was, to put it another way, no one way to be a zoot suiter in the wartime United States.

ZOOT STYLE AND THE POLITICS OF PLACE IN THE URBAN UNITED STATES

There are nearly as many theories about where zoot suits originated as there were possible combinations of colors, patterns, and accessories that made up the style. The *New York Times* reported in the summer of 1943 that Clyde Duncan, an African American busboy from Gainesville, Georgia, invented the first zoot suit when, several years before, he had had one of his suits altered in an exaggerated and baggy style.[9] In fact, the zoot was a popular youth style long before U.S. entry into World War II. Some believe that Clark Gable helped initiate it when he wore long coattails as the popular Rhett Butler character in the 1939 film *Gone with the Wind*.[10] Others suggest that youth were inspired by Frank Sinatra, who often sang and danced while wearing loose-fitting suits.[11] A number of Chicana/o historians argue that the zoot style of Los Angeles was influenced by westward-moving migrants who brought elements of the pachuco culture from El Paso, Texas.[12] Some argue that Mexican film sensation Tin Tan, who wore zoot suits in several motion pictures during the 1930s and 1940s, helped popularize the style among Mexican American youth. Others trace the influence of the Mexican film industry on the zoot back to the 1920s, when images of the smartly dressed and gender-bending young men known as the Fifi were quite common on the big screen.[13] In her excellent work on the taxi dance halls in Central California during the Great Depression, cultural critic Linda España-Maram shows how the McIntosh suit craze among male Filipino immigrants foreshadowed the zoot suit style.[14] The popularity of the zoot among such black jazz artists as Cab Calloway in the 1930s and early 1940s also helped circulate the style in big cities across the United States. These many narratives of the zoot's emergence and growth not only underscore its popularity but also highlight its mass appeal among a diverse group of youth in a variety of locations.

Although often considered to have been largely a Mexican American phenomenon in Los Angeles or an African American one in New York, the zoot crossed racial, ethnic, and regional boundaries. These two youth groups and urban centers were loci of zoot activity and, for that reason, are the focus of this chapter, but the zoot was also popular among Filipino, Japanese, and Euro-American young men and women all over the country. In his article on the Nisei underclass, for example, historian Paul Spickard demonstrates that Japanese American youth from Los Angeles, San Francisco, other California cities, and as far away as Chicago fashioned zoot style before and after the war. In typical fashion, one Japanese American youth named Tadashi Najima, ironically nicknamed "Blackie," was described "every inch the zoot suiter. His hair was long and slicked back. His zoot suit, or 'drapes,' included a wide-brimmed felt hat; suit jacket with huge padded shoulders tapering to narrow waist; trousers pleated wide at the hips and then cutting sharply down to narrow cuffs; long shoes with pointed toes; a chain looped from the belt almost to the ground; and a stiletto in the pocket."[15] Another Japanese American young man from the Los Angeles area, Bill Katayama, was described by a friend as "a typical Nisei 'zoot suiter.' In appearance he looks Filipino. He wears a 'pachuco' haircut style and he has several 'zoot suits.'"[16]

Moreover, as historian Valerie Matsumoto shows in her study of Japanese Americans since World War II, many youth in internment camps in places like Amache, Colorado, and Jerome, Arkansas, drew on pre-internment urban sensibilities by wearing zoots and cultivating a Nisei pachuco style as a substitute for lost pride and sense of belonging. One observer recalls that these Japanese American zoot suiters were "easily spotted . . . by their 'uniforms' and long haircuts and zoot suits[; they] crash social affairs [and] settle all personal grudges with physical assault."[17] Along the Pacific Coast, Filipino American youth also crafted zoot style. In fact, as España-Maram argues, Filipino youth had long used suits and clothing style "in their search for places that afforded them some sense of dignity and relative freedom of expression."[18] As these snippets from the lives of Japanese and Filipino American youth suggest, the world of wartime youth culture included a matrix of Afro-Latino-Asian connections and influences. Thus, the more recent long-running theatrical production *A Jive Bomber's Christmas* featured Jackson Omata, a hip Nisei zoot suiter nicknamed the Jive Bomber who cons, trades, and barters everything from toilet paper to Frank Sinatra records to improve his lot in the internment camp at Heart Mountain, Wyoming, in 1943. The Jive Bomber is not just a creation of the playwright's imagination but also an integral part of the history of the zoot and wartime youth culture.[19]

Though not a focus of this book, Asian American zoot suiters further underscore the multiracial milieu at work in wartime youth culture. The outlandish style and bold behavior of many Nisei zoot suiters, in particular, including their drinking, partying, gangster lifestyles and active sex lives, are critical elements in the story of wartime youth culture because they clashed so visibly with the political strategies of other Japanese Americans. Nisei zoot suiters departed from programs of assimilation and accommodation sponsored by the Japanese American Citizens League (JACL), which assigned to them the role of "model minority" and acquiescent subjects.[20] Like Mexican American and African American zoot suiters who clashed ideologically with the Mexican American and African American middle classes, Japanese American zoot suiters articulated a cultural politics that rejected their inferiority and were skeptical of the desire to be like the rest of U.S. society.

Although a diverse group of nonwhite youth shared zoot style, its many incarnations resulted in different meanings depending on who wore it and where they lived. As cultural critic Dick Hebdige explains in his classic account of the punk subculture, the cultural meaning of style is often derived from the young people's selective relocation of signs, activities, or commodities in different contexts to produce fresh meanings, social relations, and ways of life. This process, called bricolage by Hebdige and others, also existed in zoot suit culture and depended on the specific convergence of people, time, and place.[21] The zoot suit, in other words, was not inherently political but acquired meaning from its historical context.

In an era defined largely by calls for political consensus and economic conservatism, the zoot's excessive use of fabric, flashy colors, and exaggerated style functioned as countercultural statements. Japanese American youth who wore a zoot suit in an internment camp may thereby have refused to accept quietly the indignity of incarceration. For African American youth in Harlem the zoot may have been part of a much longer history of black fashion and cultural production that rejected their marginalization and segregation in the city. The zoot experience of Mexican American women in Los Angeles may have emerged from their struggle with the oppressive forces of familial patriarchy or the Catholic Church that expected them to be socially submissive. Whether worn by African American hepcats in New York, Mexican American pachucas/os or Filipino youth in Los Angeles, or young Japanese Americans in internment camps, zoot suits were integral to local experiences.

Beginning with the suit of clothes itself, zoot style was practiced differently in Los Angeles and New York. As evident in Malcolm X's memories of his youthful days, the zoot suits popular among African Americans in the Northeast were unique for their bright red, blue, and yellow colors, thin-soled and knob-toed dancing shoes, and outrageous measurements. Many black youth, in fact, were known to brag about the number of inches their trouser hems ballooned just above the knee compared to how closely they were tapered at the ankle. On the West Coast, particularly in Los Angeles, Mexican American, African American, Filipino, and Japanese American young men preferred white or dark-brown or black materials for their zoots, slightly more conservative measurements than their eastern counterparts, and double- or triple-soled Stacy Adams shoes. Antonio Alvarez, a Mexican American who spent several years as a zoot suiter in Los Angeles, recalled the typical West Coast zoot: "Yeah, everything was brown. And the coat came down to here [pointing to the knees], right down to here. And the silver chain from the pocket, and the wide, like a pancake, hat, with a real wide brim. If you were short, you would look like a thumbtack! And we used to dress up like that to go to the dances. All of us. All wear the same thing. With the big chain, we'd twirl the chain."[22] The geographic differences in zoot style resulted from a combination of factors including race and ethnic background, unique cultural traditions, and the availability of specific materials and accessories.

No matter where the zoot was worn or who was wearing it, the bodies of the youth who fashioned the style were intended to look and feel good in the face of wartime conditions that portrayed them negatively and often excluded them from the national polity. Ramón Galindo, who

High Rise
Pant

Figures 9 and 10. Sketches of zoot suits by tailor Ramón Galindo.
From author's personal collection.

worked as a tailor specializing in zoot suits for African Americans and
Mexican Americans in central Texas in 1942 and 1943, remembers well
the bold statement made by zoot suiters and how the contours of their
bodies fueled their style.

> They [zoot suits] did look very good. Especially on a young man that was
> tall and thin and they could wear those suits and they'd look very good.
> You take a thin guy, say six foot two or three, and their shoulder wasn't
> broad. But they pad 'em with a lot of shoulder padding to make it broad
> and make the coat look good. Once they took the coat off you see that
> skinny guy wearing that big 'ol coat. Look like a football player with all
> those shoulder pads. But that was the style.[23]

Interestingly, Ramón suggests that zoot suiters could also alter their
body's appearance to achieve a particular effect. In this case, the heavy
shoulder pads made for a more imposing and impressive look. One resident of the Central Avenue district in Los Angeles recalls that "wearing

a zoot suit gave you an identity, and it gave you pride; not wearing work clothes probably boosted your ego."[24] By looking good and taking great care of their appearance, many youth challenged through their daily activity the idea that they were undisciplined, wild, and out of control or that they should always be working on behalf of the war effort.

Despite long-standing family- and society-imposed limits on their behavior, many nonwhite young women experienced more unsupervised time and encountered the growing world of wartime popular culture as both producers and consumers.[25] As elaborated later in this and the following chapter, many young women in fact cultivated their own zoot style and worked in tandem with their male counterparts to make up the zoot's intricately gendered cultural world. For young Mexican American women, in particular, style was just as much a part of their everyday lives as it was for their male counterparts.[26] One Southern Californian observed that "the girls, too, the 'pachucas' had their version of drapes. This included very short dresses; very long bobby socks, and an elaborate hairdo with a high pompadour."[27] In her somewhat patronizing outsider's look into the world of young pachucos and pachucas in Los Angeles during the war, author Beatrice Griffith commented similarly about young Mexican American women: "The girls wore their own style of dress, consisting of a long finger-tip length coat or letterman's sweater, draped slacks or a short, full skirt above or just to their brown knees, high bobby socks, and huaraches or 'Zombie' slippers. They usually made up heavily with mascara and lipstick, and the favorite hair style was a high pompadour with flowers and earrings. As important as the costume itself was the manner in which it was worn. A bravado and swagger accentuated the dark beauty of these girls."[28] With their skirts or draped slacks, black fishnet stockings or bobby socks, the same coats worn by male zoot suiters, oxford shoes, and heavy mascara and lipstick, pachucas—or "slick chicks," as they were often labeled—combined elements of men's and women's fashion to craft their own style. One former pachuca, aged fifteen at the time, remembers that she and her friends in Los Angeles would "wear zoot suits too, with the skirts short and the jackets long. We'd wear socks up to here [pointing to the knees]. We'd buy them at the men's department. Men's socks. I even had a friend who used to put glue on her leg so her socks wouldn't fall down!"[29] The pachuca style, common among young women from working-class barrios, emphasized their own independence and beauty. The use of men's clothing illustrates, moreover, that these young women challenged normative gender binaries by choosing for themselves what

Figure 11. Mexican American female gang, Los Angeles, 1942. *Los Angeles Daily News* Negatives Collection, Department of Special Collections, Charles E. Young Research Library, UCLA.

they wore, what they considered attractive, and as shown below, how they behaved. As much as male zoot suiters did, young women mobilized their bodies to highlight how they differed from the rest of society rather than how they conformed.[30]

Zoot suit style was distinguished by much more than clothing, as many youth complemented their flamboyant apparel with distinctive hairdos and tattoos. Each of the various elements of zoot style helped nonwhite youth regain control over their own bodies, craft a public presence that demanded attention, and cultivate social practices often hard for outsiders to decipher. Zoot suiters challenged their dehumanization by taking great pride and care in their individual appearance and public personas. Like young pachucas with their pompadours, male Mexican American zoot suiters in Los Angeles had their own haircut of choice, according to one contemporary—"the hair style known as 'duck bill'—generous in length and combed toward the center in the back."[31] It was also not uncommon for Mexican American youth to employ "tattooing and the wearing of chin hairs" to further distinguish their bodies.[32]

Like their Mexican American counterparts, many young African American men added to their zoot appearance with special haircuts. Rather than the ducktail, however, many black youth were fond of the conk. According to Malcolm X, the conk was intended to straighten coarse hair and involved combing through the hair a "jelly-like, starchy looking glop" made of thinly sliced potatoes, lye, and eggs mixed together. Because of the lye, the conking process created a burning sensation on the scalp until the concoction was rinsed out with water. Enduring a few minutes of painful heat, however, was worth the end result: a head of straightened hair more easily combed and styled to fit the zoot suiter, or hepcat, image. Recalling his first conk, Malcolm X claimed, "My first view in the mirror blotted out the hurting. I'd seen some pretty conks, but when it's the first time, on your *own* head, the transformation, after the lifetime of kinks, is staggering. . . . And on top of my head was this thick, smooth sheen of shining red hair—real red—as straight as any white man's."[33] Though in later life, Malcolm X remarked that the conking of hair was a "stupid" and "ridiculous" attempt to look white and a big step toward his self-degradation, at the time he did it, the results were desired, extravagant, and in a word, "cool."[34]

These "politics of cool" crafted and exhibited by zoot suiters also included distinct speech patterns inflected by region and ethnicity. The informal language spoken often by West Coast pachucos was a hybrid of English and Spanish that journalist Beatrice Griffith identified as a "melange, composed of 'calo,' Hispanicized English, anglicized Spanish, and words of pure invention. Its vitality comes from its flexibility and the constant flux and flow of new words. It is essentially a language of convenience, utilizing lingual inventions with remarkable exactness of meaning. Humor and circumstance play an important role."[35] Griffith speculated that caló evolved from the speech patterns of Mexican immigrants who crossed the border into El Paso and traveled to Los Angeles in the 1920s and 1930s. The pachuco vocabulary, she wrote, included words and phrases like *gacho* (lousy), *chavala* (girl), *tanda* (hat), *rolando un frajo* (rolling a cigarette), *ese* (homeboy *or* that guy), *horale, bato* (hi, fellow), and *ai te watcho* (I'll be seeing you—good-bye). Griffith noted that "another characteristic of Pachucano slang is its quick, nervous rhythm" and that "there is often a tendency to eliminate the last vowel of a word, and the effect is definitely sing-song, marked broken rhythm." She also observed that "the Pachucos' facility for creating new words tends to build a wall between their speech world and that of their parents," as "the Pachuco argot is usually not understood by parents."[36]

The Coordinating Council of Latin American Youth in Los Angeles, made up of prominent Mexican American professionals, similarly complained that "many of these youths speak very little Spanish or English, relying on their own lingo which is a slant conglomeration of the two languages."[37] What many of these observers failed to realize was that caló functioned as a hybrid linguistic form that helped distinguish the social world of those who spoke it from the activities of most white youth and often rendered that world unintelligible to outsiders.[38] Caló was so distinct, according to historian Edward Escobar, that it "not only made their talk incomprehensible to their Spanish-speaking elders and white English-speaking authority figures, it also intensified pachucos' sense of uniqueness and generational solidarity."[39]

Interestingly, and not surprisingly, "it was inevitable," Griffith observed, "that jive talk should cut its way into the language of the devotees of jitterbug dancing, whether the rug-cutters were Mexican-American, Negro-American, Japanese-American, or any other minority." A number of words, phrases, and linguistic patterns from black jive became staples of Mexican American and Asian American speech, including "slick chick," "fine chick," and "sharp."[40] Black zooters and hepcats had long invented their own mode of communication, a hipster's lingo that emerged from jazz. Soon after his arrival in Boston as a young man in the early 1940s, Malcolm X encountered an array of slang terms for the first time. He remembers that "children threw around swear words I'd never heard before, even, and slang expressions that were just as new to me, such as 'stud' and 'cat' and 'chick' and 'cool' and 'hip.' Every night as I lay in bed I turned these new words over in my mind."[41] As historian Bruce M. Tyler explains, "Hip jive language was an urban dialect that separated the country hick from the city slicker." Tyler elaborates:

"Harlemites" spoke "Harlemese" this way: "Struttin' on the Avenoo" in my "glad rags doin' the streets up brown." They were "in there" with the "foldin' stuff, that is the root of all evil" (money). "I capped an underground rattler to the land of nod" (I took the subway to Broadway.) "Groovy." "Here, one can see Zoot suits and drip drapes with reat pleats, that really come on in a big way." "Homeboy—a suit-suiter." "Cats, gaitors" (alligators, a cool animal and reptile, and alligator shoes and purses, etc. were admired as expensive and classy) reject war waste theory. . . . "Dig This Gate With The Solid Kicks and Drape; He's Solid Tuitty." (Look at this man (alligator) with the good looking and expensive shoes and jitterbug (wide pants with tight fitting angles [ankle?] hems called "pegged") on; he's real boss (tuitty is the Italian word for boss).[42]

As caló did for West Coast pachucos, for many black zoot suiters, Tyler concludes, "jive language, Zoot Suits and fancy 'kicks' (shoes) bound hipsters into a world apart and style that often completely befuddled the uninitiated."[43]

Zoot suiters of all ethnicities in areas across the United States incorporated jive into their daily speech patterns. Ramón Galindo recalls that in central Texas both Mexican American and African American youth "had their own language," which emphasized style, appearance, and being cool. The same observer suggested that a typical exchange between a young woman and man during the early-forties zoot days might resemble the following:

> Young woman: You going to the dance tonight?
> Young man: Yes, I'm going to the dance.
> Young woman: Are you gonna look cool?
> Young man: Yes, I'm gonna look cool? You know it too! Well, don't you know that![44]

Such an exchange suggests that in addition to incorporating multiple cultural influences, both caló and jive were deeply gendered. Being in the know and able to converse in slang empowered the gender identities many youth sought to embody. Speech patterns helped make masculinity, in particular, a central feature in the politics of cool. A large part of young men's gender identity, for example, included talking about women and to women in ways that made the women necessary participants in zoot culture and frequently objectified them as objects of sexual desire. For young women, on the other hand, their use of slang not only afforded them access to and participation in zoot culture but also made their speech and related behavior appear more masculine at times for their complicity in what was often deemed a male social world.

Big band jazz great Cab Calloway, known for wearing his trademark white zoot suit during on-stage performances, highlighted the centrality of African American slang in songs whose titles sprang from everyday expressions: "Boogit," "Jumpin' Jive," and "Zaz Zu Zaz." In another tune, Calloway asked his listeners, "Are you hep to the jive?" Recognizing the popularity of black slang in the late 1930s and early 1940s, Calloway published seven annual volumes of *The Cab Calloway Hepster's Dictionary*. Unless one was a part of jazz and zoot culture or read the *Hepster's Dictionary*, one would not likely know the meaning of such terms as *jitterbug* ("swing fan"), *got your boots on* ("you know what it is all about, you are a hepcat, you are wise"), *hard* ("fine" or "good"), *joint is jumping* ("the place is lively, the club is leaping with fun"), *kopasetic* ("absolutely okay, the tops"), *slide your jib* ("to talk freely"), or *togged to the bricks* ("dressed to kill, from head to toe").[45] Because jive was part of everyday discourse for many nonwhite youth; was used regularly in movies, on stage, and in songs; and spread to people from all walks of life and even to places as remote as Italy, North Africa, and Germany (wherever the U.S. armed forces served), Calloway understood his dictionary to document the contribution of African American hepcat and zoot culture to the evolution of the English language. His assumptions were validated by multiple printings of the dictionary and by its inclusion as the "official jive language reference book of the New York Public Library."[46] Calloway even published his booklet *Professor Cab Calloway's Swingformation Bureau* to accompany the *Hepster's Dictionary* and instruct readers how to apply the words and phrases learned in the dictionary. Introducing people to the hepster's etiquette, the "killer-diller" songs performed by popular musical artists of the day, and nicknames of the country's best-known musicians, the *Swingformation Bureau* provided a glimpse of jazz culture and its links with zoot suit style for people who did not live it every day. So when Cab Calloway defined a hepcat as "a guy who knows all the answers, understands jive," or zoot as "overexaggerated as applied to clothes," he was not just speaking to other zoot suiters, hepcats, or jazz artists but was also helping to articulate a cultural identity practiced by countless youth to a broad cross-section of the U.S., and even international, community.

Still, the zoot suit itself was the most visible symbol of the perceived criminal, hypersexual, and dangerous character that pachucos and hepcats were said to be. In one incident in the summer of 1943, the actions of lifeguards in Santa Monica illustrated the power of this symbol. The lifeguards were warned that a "zoot suit gang" was headed for the beach and might cause trouble. After searching up and down the beach amidst hundreds of bathers, the lifeguards could find no zoot suiters. The search leader, lifeguard captain George Watkins, later remarked that "some of them had long hair, which curled up at the back like a drake's tail, but their bathing togs weren't any different from those of the others. So, we were unable to tell just how many, if any, were gang members." Journalists covering the incident concluded that it was indeed a challenge "to tell a zoot suiter, when he isn't wearing his zoot suit."[47]

Along with the other elements of zoot culture, nonwhite youth used the suit of clothes to carve out a style with which to evade authority figures, create spaces of cultural and social autonomy, and make life more enjoyable. Though zoot culture varied from place to place, one common feature was the style's potential as a "third space," where, as historian David Gutiérrez theorizes, the youth "attempted to mediate the profound sense of displacement and other stresses raised by their daily existence as members of a racialized and marginalized minority."[48] Rather than dealing with their displacement in more overt, organized ways, these youth put on a zoot suit.

ZOOT CONSUMPTION AND THE POLITICS OF COOL

Many nonwhite youth dealt with displacement and dehumanization by creating and practicing a style that identified them as "cool." While much of the wartime United States viewed the zoot as an icon for juvenile delinquency, thousands of young African Americans and Mexican Americans wore the zoot because it helped convert their social alienation, economic exploitation, and political marginalization into a sense of security and "coolness" that enabled them to navigate the highly segregated and discriminatory society in which they lived.[49] These "politics of cool" shaped the patterns of cultural production and consumption of nonwhite youth at the same time that those patterns were conditioned by the wartime economy. Zoot suiters' desire to be cool privileged leisure and abundance at a time when society demanded that they buy war bonds and conserve materials vital to the war effort.

Acquiring a zoot was often a rite of passage into "coolness." Shortly after walking out of the store dressed in his first zoot suit, Malcolm X felt transformed into a genuine hepcat, expressing a newfound confidence previously lacking in this recent rural emigrant. One of the first things he did in his new clothes was to model them for his sister Ella and visit a photographer. "I took three of those twenty-five cent sepia-toned, while-you-wait pictures of myself, posed the way 'hipsters' wearing their zoots would 'cool it'—hat dangled, knees drawn close together, feet wide apart, both index fingers jabbed toward the floor. The long coat and swinging chain and the Punjab pants were much more dramatic if you stood that way."[50]

Two young African American men arrested in New York during the summer of 1943 similarly understood their zoot style as a badge of strength and pride. While being interrogated, they bragged to one another and their police captors about the number of inches their pants ballooned at the knee. One youth proclaimed proudly that his pants

Figure 12. African American students at Bethune-Cookman College in Florida wear pants and shoes of the zoot style, 1943. Copyright Gordon Parks/Corbis.

were pegged at fourteen and twenty-eight inches, while the other was said to have shamefully confessed that his were pegged at only fifteen and twenty-seven inches.[51] Growing up in Harlem during the war, Perry remembers how young black men "used to talk about them [their pants]. Twenty-two! Fifteen! They had all these numbers! I mean, the way these guys used to talk about pants!"[52] These young men used their physical bodies to exhibit confidence, security, and dignity—attributes markedly different from popular images of zoot suiters as morally and culturally bankrupt. The carefully manicured style and purposeful demeanor of those who valued their zoot style countered allegations that they were savage and dirty, animal-like carriers of disease. In fact, their attention to style and looks put forth an identity that was the opposite—sharp, clean, and extremely well maintained. If anything, zoot suiters prioritized impeccable grooming and expensive dress and paid attention to every last detail of their appearance.

Most zoot suiters were entangled in the circuits of U.S. capitalism through their consumption of clothing, entertainment, and leisure. Zoot style would not have been possible had the growing wartime markets not provided young Mexican Americans and African Americans opportunities to purchase suits and needed accessories, spend time at concerts and dances, or just shoot pool at a local bar, catch a movie at a nearby theater, or sip sodas at the corner malt shop. Recognizing zoot consumption, however, does not relegate their style to the nonpolitical. Zoot suiters' preference for items and pastimes that many considered extravagant and leisurely flouted popular constraints on consumption in favor of contributing to the war effort. Many believed that rationing wartime goods would help win the war and ensure that increased consumption would be among the postwar spoils. Zoot suiters' consumer gaze reflected not only their desire for commodities but also their power to objectify goods and uniquely engage the wartime economy—cultural practices most often executed by white males. Zoot suiters' consumerism was not entirely controllable by their parents, business owners, or local government officials.[53] What they did with the clothes, watch chains, and hats they bought, and how they used those commodities to stylize their bodies, both expressed their own aesthetic autonomy and revealed their unique perspective on wartime consumption.[54] Moreover, zoot consumption quite possibly revealed nonwhite youth's willingness to be a part of wartime society, as long as their identity and dignity were respected.

One of the primary contradictions of the zoot was that its aesthetic autonomy depended on participation in the same wartime economy that consistently denied nonwhite youth access to the most lucrative jobs, and on use of a public discourse that pitted them against the patriotic contributions of servicemen and factory workers. Despite extensive and systematic racial discrimination against African American and Mexican American laborers in Los Angeles and New York, zoot suiters pursued a wide range of economic strategies to facilitate their style. Some secured entry-level jobs in shipbuilding and aircraft construction yards as the war progressed. In part because these positions afforded little upward mobility, many zoot suiters found other ways to earn money. As a young man growing up in the Echo Park neighborhood of Los Angeles, for example, Bob participated in numerous money-making endeavors, including delivering newspapers and, in his teens, prizefighting. He spent much of his earnings on draped pants, porkpie hats, and outings to the Central Avenue district to catch the live performances of touring jazz bands.[55] As a teen in Harlem during the height of the zoot craze in the early war years, Perry recalls, he earned his spending money from a newspaper route and, later, working in the New York Public Library.[56]

In the early days of zoot style during the Great Depression, it was perhaps even more difficult for nonwhite youth to maintain reputable employment and steady sources of spending money. Antonio Alvarez was a young Mexican American in the late 1930s when he left his mother's home in the small town of Lemon Grove, southeast of San Diego, and joined the Civilian Conservation Corps (CCC) as part of the New Deal. He spent most of his weekdays helping carve fire trails in the Glendora Hills on the outskirts of Los Angeles or working in the camp galley as a cook. On those weekends he did not return to San Diego, Antonio accompanied friends to their homes in East Los Angeles, where he was introduced to the world of the zoot suit. The twenty-five dollars a week the CCC paid him helped him buy his one and only brown zoot suit and pay for his evenings of dancing, drinking, and shooting pool with fellow members of the 21 Club, a group of Mexican American youth who hung out and socialized together. In Antonio's case, the New Deal was not only the means to the end of facilitating his zoot style but also the reason he got involved with the zoot to begin with.[57]

Some youth who found themselves on the outside looking in on the surge in wartime economic prosperity did participate in underground networks that formed illicit economies in big cities like Los Angeles and New York, sometimes turning to petty theft and misdemeanor criminal behavior. During one of his weekend stints in East Los Angeles, for example, Antonio and a group of his fellow zoot suiters plotted to rob a furniture store. Although he "chickened out" at the last moment and did not participate, Antonio was picked up by police and held overnight for questioning. Loyalty to his friends kept him silent as to the details of the robbery, and in light of his innocence, he was released the next morning.[58]

Malcolm X, after spending much of his youth shining shoes, selling sandwiches on railcars, and doing any number of other odd jobs, searched for more "easy money" by running numbers, committing burglaries, pimping, and "hustling" in other ways. As his involvement in the illicit wartime economy of Harlem grew, one of Malcolm X's most lucrative enterprises was selling marijuana. He recalls, "I sold reefers like a wild man. I scarcely slept; I was wherever musicians congregated. A roll of money was in my pocket. Every day, I cleared at least fifty or sixty dollars. In those days (or for that matter these days), this was a fortune to a seventeen-year-old Negro. I felt, for the first time in my life, that great feeling of *free!* Suddenly, now, I was the peer of the other young hustlers I had admired" (his emphasis).[59] For many Americans, the illegal activity of Malcolm X and other nonwhite youth confirmed stereotypes that characterized zoot suiters as the antithesis of wartime patriotism—criminals wasting time and money that could otherwise be funneled into the war effort. Through his illegal activity, however, Malcolm X found not only a steady income but also feelings of freedom and dignity that were unavailable through more conventional means. The lure of financial success in the narcotics business and, perhaps, the thrill of being a big-time hustler soon led Malcolm X to begin traveling by train along the East Coast, peddling reefers to touring jazz performers.[60] This sense of freedom derived from participation in the illicit economy supports historian Robin D. G. Kelley's claim that zoot suiters' hustling was in part a refusal to allow wage labor to be the primary signifier of their working-class identity.[61] By creatively finding ways to ease their own poverty, zoot suiters formed a class in as much as they shared the struggle against the pressures of the wartime economy and understood their money-making efforts as a means for sustaining their style.

Having found ways to put a little money in their pockets, nonwhite youth became consumers in an emerging market that catered to young people. According to Harlem native Perry, the economic surge from U.S. involvement in the war was critical to the development of zoot culture because "the war took away the scarcity of material and other things" that people suffered through during the Great Depression.[62] If zoot suit culture was one reflection of wartime abundance and the renewed consumer power of many Americans, there were many ways to acquire a zoot suit. One might purchase one at any of the hundreds of local tailor shops that dotted city streets and specialized in handmade suits, or at a larger retail department store that sold them off the rack, or via mail order catalogues or the newspaper. Or one could use a sewing machine, often with the help of mothers, aunts, or sisters, to stitch homemade clothes or alter pre-owned nonzoot clothing to fit the latest trend.

The highest-quality zoot suits were those made by a tailor. The sure-fire method for looking good involved walking into the tailor's shop, choosing the fabric and colors, getting a suit cut to exact measurements, and topping it all off with a matching belt, hat with feather, and pocket watch with chain. In the words of one former zoot suiter from Los Angeles, if he and his friends could afford it, "we had them tailor made. You wanted to look sharp."[63] The same was true for black youth growing up in Harlem. As a teenager in the early 1940s Perry observed that "all of these [zoot] clothes were custom made, tailor made. So they would go in [to the store] and pick the colors and it was a real deal! Get the hat to match and, you know, get the feather to go in it. Ahh man!"[64] Of course, tailor-made zoot suits were not always cheap. Perry remembers that in Harlem, "guys would save up all year and borrow money to buy these threads!"[65] Despite the cost, Bob said, in Los Angeles, if "you wanted to look flashy, you had them made."[66] According to Ramón Galindo, the Mexican American tailor from central Texas who worked as an apprentice before opening his own shop catering to both African American and Mexican American youth, if a pancake hat, coat, and shoes were included with the pants, the price often exceeded one hundred dollars, a rather hefty sum for anyone during the 1940s.[67]

Youth who could not afford tailor-made zoots could resort to popular clothing stores that sold drapes and coats off the rack. In Los Angeles, outlets like Murray's on Broadway sold zoot suits that, according to Bob, looked almost "the same way" as tailor-made suits. "You could buy a set of drapes for five or six dollars, you know," Bob said. "You want to get expensive, you pay twelve dollars for some good material [and then have them made]. That was my level, twelve bucks."[68] Clothing stores that sold drape pants for as little as $5 in Los Angeles, or two pair for about $18 in Chicago, or as low as $3.95 in Harlem provided non-white youth more affordable options.[69] When Malcolm X bought his first ready-made zoot suit as a teenager in Boston, he remembers,

> the young salesman picked off a rack a zoot suit that was just wild: sky-blue pants thirty inches in the knee and angled-narrowed down to twelve inches at the bottom, and a long coat that pinched my waist and flared out below my knees. As a gift, the salesman said, the store would give me a narrow leather belt with my initial "L" on it. Then he said I ought to also buy a hat, and I did—blue with a feather in the four-inch brim. Then the store gave me another present: a long, thick-linked, gold-plated chain that swung down lower than my coat hem.[70]

After just a few minutes of shopping, one could leave dressed to the hilt in a brand-new zoot suit with all the appropriate accessories.

Those youth for whom even off-the-rack zoot suits were too expensive turned elsewhere. One alternative lay in scouring African American newspapers such as the *Pittsburgh Courier* for mail-order advertisements for drapes selling for as little as $5.95. One national clothing store that sold full suits, coats, and pants for men, boys, and women specialized in drape and jitterbug styles with wide knees and tapered ankles. By sending a one-dollar deposit and measurements, one would receive the order COD within twenty-four hours.[71] A similar ad for a New York–based clothier claimed to bring "New York Shoe Styles Directly to You," emphasizing to potential buyers that shoes were crucial to proper style since drape pants drew attention to the feet and one should avoid getting caught in "ugly shoes."[72]

While consumption enabled zoot suiters to craft their style and claim dignity, such patterns in many ways offered an illusory and short-lived form of empowerment, as they were complicit with the dominant wartime ideology that alienated many nonwhite youth to begin with. The consumerist nature of zoot culture led many youth to purchase suits on credit, for instance. Malcolm X was "forever sold on credit" after his companion Shorty helped him secure his first zoot suit though he lacked the cash to pay for it. Before too long, Malcolm X bought another one, the salesman noting that he had missed only one weekly payment on his first zoot and so qualified for "A-1" credit.

> I studied carefully everything on the racks. And finally I picked out my second zoot. It was shark-skin gray, with a big long coat, and pants ballooning out at the knees and then tapering to cuffs so narrow I had to take off my shoes to get them on and off. With the salesman urging me on, I got another shirt, and a hat and new shoes—the kind that were just coming out into hipster style; dark orange colored, with paper-thin soles and knob style toes. It all added up to seventy or eighty dollars.[73]

The accumulation of debt through credit functioned as a double-edged sword. Nonwhite youth employed middle-class purchasing strategies to maintain their zoot style. At the same time, purchasing on credit reinforced their working-class status by sinking them into debt and, presumably, setting them on a never ending cycle to obtain additional clothes and other goods.

While some zoot suiters found the appeal of buying on credit too tempting to refuse, others, particularly young women, made their own clothing. The production of skirts, blouses, sweaters, and jackets among pachucas in Los Angeles included a communal network of home-based production and sharing of fabric. Maria, a Mexican American pachuca who grew up in Los Angeles, remembers that during the height of the zoot era, she, her sisters, and her friends often sewed their own clothes, only to take them apart and remake them in a style suitable for wearing to a Friday or Saturday night dance.[74] Altering a skirt or blouse for an evening out illustrated the creativity of women zooters and merged their consumption of the zoot with its production. Although they had to purchase the material with which to make clothes, or the skirt or blouse that they then rearranged into something new, these young women staked a claim to the production of zoot commodities and thereby demonstrated one generative principle of zoot style: the ability to use commodities in ways that diverged from their intended use and, in their remade form, give them new meaning.[75]

Despite the myriad options available to keep up with current style, many youth could afford only part of the zoot uniform. Wearing only the draped pants, for example, was not uncommon when a porkpie hat, coat, and watch chain were financially out of reach. Bob reports that those youth in LA who did not have the money to buy newly made drapes, or even the fabric to make their own, still managed to exhibit a semblance of cool. "[If you] had regular pants, [you] could somehow afford to get somebody to have [them] draped out, to have the narrow cuffs, and then they high-waisted the pants. The Filipinos down there [in Little Manila] were good at that. I think that's where they got the idea from or where it came from."[76] Wearing only a portion of the zoot style was common throughout the United States. As the son of a mail carrier and parents who both graduated from Tuskegee Institute, Perry remembers a strict childhood in Harlem, where he was often on the outside looking in on the latest fashion trends. Still, Perry negotiated with his parents the right to craft his own part-time version of zoot style. He recalls, "They [his parents] wouldn't let me peg my pants. . . . I can remember I had a pair of pants that were like this [regular pants] and managed to convince my mother to let me peg my pants. . . . The concession was I could have those pants pinched to maybe a couple of inches at the bottom, but that was it."[77] Perry's insistence on pegging his pants even just a little shows the powerful draw of the zoot for youth in urban areas. Even though he "was out of that group" of youth who wore the full zoot suit style, Perry attests, "Oh God, did I want to!"[78] For Perry and countless others, it was enough to participate on the fringes of zoot style.

Perry's negotiation with his parents over the extent of his style reveals the deep generational conflict implicit in zoot culture. Many older members of Mexican American and African American communities viewed the zoot suit as a sign of disrespect because of its often confrontational nature and popular association with wartime delinquency, violence, and drug use. One African American youth recalls that purchasing a pair of drape pants was all he could think about during a train ride from his home in Tennessee to visit his grandmother in Chicago. His hopes were quickly dashed upon arrival in the Windy City, however, when his grandmother told him if he wanted a pair of those kind of pants, he better get back on the train to Memphis because she wasn't going to buy them for him.[79] Similarly, Vernon Malvoueox, a black youth from Louisiana, was reprimanded by his father after obtaining two pairs of pegged pants by mail order from a clothing outlet in Chicago. His father confiscated the pants, admonishing Vernon, "Those are not church going pants."[80] Part of the zoot's appeal for many youth surely had to do with its departure from the straight-and-narrow approach to life they viewed in their parents.

Not all nonwhite youth, of course, aspired to wear a zoot suit. Nor was it only older generations that considered zoot suiters to be trouble-makers. While many zoot suiters may have looked on fellow young people who did not wear zoot suits as "squares," those who chose not to participate in the zoot scene had their own opinions of zoot suiters. Mary Luna, who was nineteen years old when she began working for the Douglas Aircraft Corporation in Long Beach, California, in 1942, recalls when she met her cousin's zoot suiter boyfriend. "When I first saw him he had these little—remember those pleated pants—Pachuco pants and the hat and everything. My cousin told him, 'You wear those pants and that hat, I'm not going out with you. I don't want to be seen with you like that.' So, he kind of eased up a little and got away from all that stuff."[81] Rose Echeverria Mulligan, who graduated from Garfield High School in East Los Angeles in 1944, similarly distanced herself from the activities of zoot suiters. "I was certainly not a part it," she insists, referring to zoot culture.

> There were the zoot suiters and they were pathetic in their clown suits. We used to call them their 'clown suits.' They were tailor made and the material in them was [tremendous,] great big baggy suits, little tiny cuffs, long jackets. They were conned into those suits by the tailors, I always thought, so they could charge them all this money for a tailor-made suit. They were so dumb and they fell for it and then, of course, it became a sort of trademark.[82]

Despite her conception of the zoot suit and those who wore it, Echeverria Mulligan admitted that her husband "wore those clothes," but only because "this was all you could buy at the stores." She addressed the prevailing negative propaganda about zoot suiters by stressing that "there were a lot of young men who couldn't buy any other types of clothing in the stores and their pants were all tapered and a little bit on the zoot suit side." For Echeverria Mulligan, wearing the zoot style did not amount to being a zoot suiter. Those like her future husband, she recalled, were not the same as "the really bad zoot suiters" who "overdid everything."[83]

When recalling her own youthful days in Los Angeles, Margarita Salazar said of the zoot style,

> we didn't approve of it and we didn't dress that way, so we must have kept away from those people. I've got pictures galore of my brothers and none of them have anything like that. . . . The pants we wore were relaxed, but not exaggerated. The same with our friends. . . . So, I just think we kept away from them and just didn't become involved. That was an entirely different bunch of people probably than what we were. . . . We figured it's [zoot culture] a little thing that's going to come up now and it's going to go away, an exaggerated style of dress that's going to come and go away, never expecting them to take over as much as they did eventually, you know. You saw them all over, but I think we figured, leave them alone, don't mix with them.[84]

Beatrice Morales Clifton, who was in her late twenties when she worked as a riveter and assembler for Lockheed Aircraft during the war, claimed of the zoot suit style, "Well, we didn't like it. Us, of course. I don't know about the other people, but our family didn't think much about it, because we didn't think they [zoot suiters] should be doing [it]."[85] Even Bill Katayama, described by close friends as a "Nisei zoot suiter," did not claim the title for himself. In fact, Katayama described a friend's zoot style somewhat disparagingly. His friend, Hiroshi, he suggested, "turned out to be a very extreme 'yogore' [gangster] and zoot suiter and he went around in a gang just like himself. I did not even class myself with his group. Hiroshi hung around with a lot of young punks who thought they were tough and his gang was always looking around for a fight. . . . They were at their best a gang and they fought dirty and some of them even carried knives."[86] Not all nonwhite youth romanticized the zoot or sought to embody its politics of cool. Yet whether they thought the style unbecoming or believed the press and political propaganda that demonized the zoot, many non–zoot suit youth still helped define the zoot's politics of cool because they marked it as different, dangerous, sometimes hypermasculine, and exotic.

From Los Angeles to New York, zoot fashion and style generated debate about the place of nonwhite youth in the wartime United States. Zoot suiters were not just participating in a passing trend but also engaging the wartime economy as new and increasingly powerful consumers, voicing political differences with others in Mexican American and African American communities, and crafting a cultural style unique to their generation. Their politics of cool, from the double- or triple-soled shoes to the colorful feather often adorning a pancake-brimmed hat, became a key feature in home-front political debates about the war effort and domestic stability and, ultimately, about whether the United States would win the war.

CONSTRUCTING GENDER, CHALLENGING WHITENESS

Although there was nothing inherently political about the zoot suit, wartime society imbued it with different meanings depending on who wore it, where it was worn, and who else they encountered when they wore it. If the bodies of zoot suiters were the vehicles for their politics of cool, gender was often the terrain on which they claimed dignity and practiced such politics. Some zoot suiters—like the hundreds in Southern California who had complaints filed against them by area servicemen for insulting them as "yellow Navy bastards" or for assaulting them without provocation—mobilized their bodies to craft a masculinity critical of wartime patriotism.[87] Others constructed a different masculine challenge by joining the service and stressing their own duty to the nation alongside white servicemen. Neither did these divergent experiences necessarily exclude each another. Historian Kevin Starr, for instance, has noted that some Mexican American youth viewed their zoot suiting days as a kind of last fling before joining the army or navy.[88]

Whether zoot suiters expressed their masculinity by criticizing the armed forces or entering the service, their style—with the loose-fitting pants, excessive use of fabric, bright colors, feathered hats, and ducktail, conk, or pompadour hairstyle—contrasted sharply with images of the dominant wartime masculinity of white U.S. servicemen. In their tight-fitting, all-white starched uniforms, white American sailors defined their own masculinity against that of zoot suiters and proposed a dramatically different vision of manhood that emphasized patriotism, nationalism, and dedication to war production. The white color of the naval uniform, in fact, served as a metaphor for the whiteness of sailor's masculinity, a gender identity that excluded even the many African American and Mexican American youth who served in the military. The masculine performance of nonwhite zoot suiters, when compared to that of servicemen, was a stark reminder of how gender could reflect the ethnic and racial fissures on the home front.

As Lorena Oropeza argues in her study of the Chicano movement and the Vietnam War, access to national belonging in U.S. history has often been based on claims to whiteness, manhood, and military service.[89] The World War II era was no different. Zoot suiters often contested the assumption that being a man depended on fighting for U.S. democracy overseas. Being a man for many male zoot suiters also entailed fighting in cultural terms for oneself or one's race on the home front. The zoot's exaggerated pants, hat brim, coattails, and sometimes flashy colors, not to mention its generous use of fabric, were all deemed excessive in an era of wartime shortages and detrimental to popular campaigns to conserve resources. The ducktails and conks worn by young Mexican American and African American zoot suiters and their "Spanglish" and jive dialects further marked them as acting outside the boundaries of proper male behavior. Some observers also considered male zoot suiters as overly feminine for their constant attention to dress, hairstyle, and appearance, further marking them as a gendered other.[90] One reporter, for example, noted that "the tails of the [zoot] coat [worn by nonwhite young men] swirl like the girls' skirts during a pirouette."[91] Characterized as pleasure seekers obsessed with leisure, zoot suiters were a foil to hardworking, responsible, and devoted sailors and soldiers. By proffering an alternative U.S. manhood—nonwhite, rebellious, and extravagant—zoot suiters undermined popular home-front values.

The outlandish cultural practices and attire of African American and Mexican American youth also contested popular views about gender and race within nonwhite communities. In the case of Mexican Americans, as historian Neil Foley has shown, many community leaders believed the most effective way to secure civil rights and equal citizenship during and after the war was to establish that Mexican Americans were in fact part of the white race.[92] Although most members of African American and Mexican American communities during World War II favored what historian Oropeza calls a politics of supplication when engaging the rest of U.S. society, the masculinity of zoot suiters suggests that segments of those populations believed national belonging was not contingent upon performing whiteness and normative manhood.[93]

Just as nonwhite youth employed the zoot to challenge popular ideas of gender and race, some white youth used it to perform blackness or brownness. Malcolm X, for one, remembers white youth involved in the zoot life in Harlem during the war years. "A few of the white men around Harlem, young ones whom we called 'hippies,' acted more Negro than Negroes," he wrote. "This particular one talked more 'hip' talk than we did. He would have fought anyone who suggested he felt any race difference. . . . Every time I saw him, it was 'Daddy! Come on, let's get our heads tight!' . . . He even wore a wild zoot suit, used a heavy grease in his hair to make it look like a conk, and he wore the knob-toed shoes, the long swinging chain—everything."[94] In Los Angeles, as well, young white men such as saxophonist Art Pepper were attracted to jazz, zoots, and the cultures that accompanied them.[95] Observing zoot suiters in Southern California, author Beatrice Griffith noted that "it is natural that boys and girls of other ancestry than Mexican are occasionally absorbed into Pachuco gangs. You find youths of Scotch-Irish, Protestant, Jewish or Italian, Russian or Negro backgrounds who have learned to speak Spanish with Pachuco emphasis, wear the traditional Pachuco clothes and haircuts, and otherwise become lost in the group."[96] Griffith recalled a "blue-eyed Irish boy living in a Mexican community who has so completely adopted the Pachuco culture pattern that he sings and creates corridos, the old Mexican folk ballads that the Pachucos make up for purposes of song and gang gossip." She noted further that "Negroes are similarly accepted" and that, "though this integration is not on a countywide basis, Pachucos as a rule feel closely allied with Negro youth, and their attitudes are friendly except where outside leadership has consciously tried to change it."[97]

On the backs of young white men, the zoot took on different meanings. Many white youth may have been attracted to the zoot for its flamboyant, seemingly exotic character, the dangerous and hypersexual portrayal it received in the press, or the means it offered to rebel against their own white working-class parents and community. As cultural critic Steve Chibnall argues, "The young white jitterbugs of the war years, although less committed to the style than their black counterparts, employed it in a similar way to establish an identity and define their relationship to their parent culture. The zoot added the vital element of stylistic rebellion to the other emergent focal concerns of the nascent teenage culture—hedonism, narcissism, faddism, star idolatry and conformity to subcultural codes—but it also highlighted the dependence of that culture on black innovation."[98] The zoot's popularity among white youth highlights the malleable nature of racial, ethnic, and cultural identities among young people during the war. Whiteness, blackness, and brownness were social creations performed by a diverse group of young people who engaged in cultural borrowing, exchange, and relationships despite the rules of segregation that governed much of U.S. society.

The extent of the challenge posed by zoot suiters to the heroic masculinity and whiteness of servicemen was contingent upon the beliefs of individual youth. Zoot suiters were not as a whole opposed to the war and articulated a broad range of opinions about home-front politics.

Some zoot suiters, like Malcolm X or his close friend Shorty, did oppose the war. Malcolm X recalls the strategies he and Shorty considered to avoid the draft: Shorty "was worried sick himself about the draft call that he knew was soon to come. Like hundreds of the black ghetto's young men, he was taking some stuff that, it was said, would make your heart sound defective to the draft board's doctors. Shorty felt about the war the same way I and most ghetto Negroes did: 'Whitey owns everything. He wants us to go and bleed for him? Let him fight.' "[99] The assumption that the zoot suit and the military uniform were diametrically opposed was underscored by the mainstream press. Even the black press, however, occasionally piled on the negative reporting of the zoot suiter. According to historian Bruce Tyler, in the *Pittsburgh Courier*,

> [a] drawing with the caption "Quartermaster" revealed a Black Zoot Suiter in full garb trying on a military hat while looking in the mirror. His wide-brimmed Zooter hat with a long feather in it rested on the counter. The military hat was too big. The Black Zooter told the Black Quartermaster, who had an angry scowl on his face, "Nope, Sarge, It Ain't Quite Me!" The message was that the Zoot Suit was a uniform that Zooters were passionately attached to, and the military uniform and code of conduct had no attraction for Zoot Suiters who were perceived by many Whites and some Blacks as "slackers" or draft dodgers.[100]

As Tyler and other scholars have demonstrated, however, at the same time that some zoot suiters went to elaborate measures to avoid the service and make known their opposition to the war, countless others willingly entered the army, navy, and marines. The forceful call of local Mexican American and African American leaders to support the Double V campaign inspired thousands of young men to shed their zoot suits for military uniforms. After serving in the New Deal's CCC during the late 1930s and spending his weekends zoot suiting around Los Angeles, Antonio joined the navy, spending most of his time as a cook. He recalls, "You did a little bit of everything. You cooked a little bit, you peeled potatoes, you peeled carrots, you did everything. I did it. . . . Then I made first cook running the galley, then I made chief cook running the fucking thing. Everybody. Forty-eight people. It was a good job. They gave me a war certificate for working there. Signed by the admiral and everything else."[101] Similarly, Bob was drafted into the army in 1943, after several years as a teenage zoot suiter and pachuco in Los Angeles, served in the European theater, and was wounded in combat.[102]

Whether they served in the armed forces or not, the masculinity of young male zoot suiters was often performed at the expense of nonwhite young women. If masculinity was the terrain on which male zoot suiters claimed dignity, they did so in ways that denied the dignity of their female counterparts. It is likely, for example, that zoot suiters in Los Angeles were suspicious of servicemen who visited the historically black Central Avenue area or the Mexican East Los Angeles area seeking the companionship of African American or Mexican American women. Rumor had it that men in uniform were attracted to such areas of the city in search of young nonwhite women who were easily seduced.[103] Such rumors undoubtedly aggravated tension between nonwhite civilian youth and servicemen, leading to fights over the companionship of young women. While zoot suiters performed their own manhood in ways that threatened the training and masculinity of white servicemen, for both zoot suiters and servicemen, women were often merely objects of their desire, another way to fuel their masculine style.

Of course, young women were more than sexual objects in the gaze of young white, black, or Mexican American men. Combining men's and women's clothing—such as skirts or draped slacks, oxford shoes, and the same coats worn by their male counterparts—and heavy makeup, many female zoot suiters transgressed the popular boundaries of femininity and masculinity.[104] Pachucas used their own bodies to simultaneously extend the limits of womanhood and craft an alternative female version of wartime masculinity that emphasized their independence and cultural difference.[105] Pachuca style diverged from the anticipated performance of wartime female masculinity that exalted the image of "Rosie the Riveter"—the dedicated factory worker dressed in heavy-duty work clothes, helping to produce war materials—or that of women who became heads of household when men left to go fight overseas. Streetwise women zoot suiters further challenged long-standing familial and communal patriarchies that contained their masculinity even when it was expressed in the acceptable forms of U.S. nationalism. By challenging notions of feminine beauty, sexuality, and race that prescribed how they should behave, they discarded the submissive roles that parents, middle-class activists, and even their zoot boyfriends expected them to play. In a letter to the editor responding to a *Los Angeles Times* article that had depicted pachucas as prostitutes, for example, several young women declared that they were dedicated war workers and would even volunteer to be examined to prove their virginity.[106]

The collective effort of these young women to restore their dignity shows that the mobilization of nonwhite youth was not always an individual practice. As primary vehicles for the struggle to carve social and cultural space for themselves, zoot bodies were not isolated from one another. Just as zoot suiters were often deemed a threat to the morality and security of the United States because they sometimes socialized in groups, zoot suiters seemed to recognize that they had more power to fight their dehumanization when they did it together, even if their association was often viewed by the rest of society as gang warfare. If the discourse of gangs among Mexican American and African American youth was used to paint them as criminal, gang life—or participation in social clubs, as it was often characterized by the youth themselves—took on a different meaning for those directly involved.[107]

On his weekends off from working in the Civilian Conservation Corps, Antonio often visited friends in East Los Angeles and soon joined a Mexican American gang. He spent most weekends hanging out with one friend in particular, Joe, who lived near First and Mott streets, close to the Belvedere neighborhood. Joe soon introduced him to a group of guys who made up one of the many gangs in the area. "And when I went to L.A.," Antonio recalls, "and got going with my friend Joe and started going with him to this club, they called it the 21 Club. I started going with him and the other guys . . . they looked you over and see how you are and see what kind of a guy you are. They weren't really bad bad guys. . . . It was kind of a deal. They had different gangs. They had the Belvederes, the 21 Club, the 1st Avenue Club, and stuff like that. Different gangs." He also remembers the tight-knit nature of the group and what it meant to be part of it. "There was something about them liking me, the whole gang, the whole club. They were really like a brother, they were all like brothers. Yeah. Strange, but that's the way I felt."[108] Occasionally, as "Blackie" Najima attested, youth who lived in racially mixed neighborhoods in Los Angeles even formed multiracial gangs. Najima, for example, recalls that when he was young, he joined a gang of "three or four Nisei kids, three Mexicans, and one kurombo (African American)."[109]

Young women, particularly pachucas in Los Angeles, formed similar clubs that politicized their same-sex relationships. As the following chapter reveals in more detail, the activities of many female zoot suiters, such as going to movies, concerts, or dances, took on different meanings because they were done by groups of young women. While the homo-erotics of female-female relationships may have enhanced perceptions that pachucas were disrupting domestic norms, pachucas formed neighborhood groups that, though labeled as gangs, functioned as support and social networks. Maria, the former pachuca who came of age in wartime LA, remembers that "the best-looking ones that dressed nice

were the girls from [the] Maravilla [barrio in East Los Angeles]. The
Black Widows! They all dyed their hair black. Some of them had natural
little streaks. They were pretty. I used to look at them at the dances, we
all used to go to the dances, and they used to come in their little groups
from different areas from all over."[110]

If the body was the vehicle for zoot suiters to display a sense of self
and affiliation with one another, their articulation of masculine and
feminine identities shifted depending on the social situation. Zoot suiters
performed their gender differently when dancing in a night club or trying to impress prospective sexual partners than when seeking to intimi-
date zoot suiters from another neighborhood or confronting city police.
From his youthful zoot days in Los Angeles, Bob vividly remembers
what it meant to put on a zoot for a big night on the town. "The time
you really see the pachuco's attitude is on the weekends. You gonna go
somewhere, you dress up with your drapes and collarless shirt, you
know. And your black hat. My brother was a good one for that. He had
black shoes, black pants, and . . . a big zipper on [the side of] his pants.
He had to unzip them to get out of them. I looked at him and I says,
'Man.'"[111] Compared to the confrontational behavior some zoot suiters
employed to mark themselves as undesirable in the eyes of the U.S. army,
the display of this zoot suiter's zipper and black attire was meant to convey an impressive and desirable masculinity.

In addition to challenging normative gender roles in the wartime
United States, the overt sexuality of many zoot suiters often marked
them as a threat to other American conventions. Of Mexican American
pachucas in Los Angeles, for example, white social critic Beatrice Griffith
wrote that "many of these Pachuquitas were 'little tornadoes of sexual
stimuli, swishing and flouncing down the streets.'"[112] Of course, young
men were also very much concerned with sex and their relationships
with young women. As a young Mexican American zoot suiter in Los
Angeles, Bob recalls,

> where I was hanging around it was a tough neighborhood. Now, I'm not
> talking about down by the schoolyard or the malt shop or candy store. . . .
> So everything was down here. The pool halls, restaurants, Filipino,
> Mexican, and the rest, you know. And that was when it really, well that
> was the corner for prostitutes and pimps, and as long as you mind your own
> business, they don't bother you or you don't bother them. But, if you want
> to hang out in the neighborhood, you had to know what the hell you're
> doing while you're there. Everybody's wheeling and dealing, the broads are
> wheeling and dealing and dealing guys, you know. And I was always afraid
> I'd get sick and get some kind of disease.[113]

In his autobiography, Malcolm X recounts sexual encounters and the social capital that came from being with Sophia, a white woman he went with during his early zoot days in Boston. He writes that "to have a white woman who wasn't a known, common whore was—for the average black man, at least—a status symbol of the first order."[114] The theme of interracial sex is also documented by Nisei zoot suiter "Blackie" Najima, who remembers having regular sex with many different women, including Japanese Americans but also white, black, and Mexican American women.[115] The phenomenon of interracial sex among hepcats and pachucos, particularly when white women were involved, surely intensified the threat that zoot culture posed to dominant sexual mores and added to fears of miscegenation. When the perceived hypersexuality of male zoot suiters targeted white women in particular, it underscored their masculinity and sexuality as threats to the moral and social stability of the home front.

For young women, parents, authorities, and the public rarely saw their being sexually active as positive, and such views marked them as deviant by reputation alone. If young men were considered macho and more of a man for their sexual activity, young women were probably considered "easy" and of low morals for theirs. Rose Hayashi, when she worked as a beer hall waitress, often hung around with fellow Nisei youth who gambled and drank in the worlds of the zoot. "I guess I was quite wild," she reflects. "I had always planned to go someplace where nobody knew me at all. . . . There was so much talk going around about me and I got pretty tired of it. They thought I was a prostitute and I was spreading syphilis among the Nisei. That wasn't true at all."[116] Similarly, Maria recalls the rumors that circled in the Los Angeles newspapers about pachucas like her because of their dress and style. "That was comical, actually, to hear about things like that," she says. "Every girl was going from one guy to another, you know, for sexual favors. The papers made us out to be real tramps. They said [Mexican] girls met a boy and that was it. They were like married already! That's a lie! And I know it not just for me, but my girlfriends."[117]

Juxtaposed to the heroic masculinity of white servicemen and Rosie the Riveter, the gender identities of many zoot suiters formed a stark contrast. At the same time, however, many of these zoot suiters demonstrated through their military service that their unique performance of manhood or womanhood was not outside the bounds of their identity as U.S. citizens. Through their body politics, zoot suiters used alternative gender identities to claim dignity, challenge the dehumanization and violence forced upon them, and ultimately, reveal the complicated and often contradictory nature of what it meant to be a nonwhite youth growing up in the United States during World War II. The identities and cultural style of many nonwhite youth also diverged from the dominant politics of the many other African Americans and Mexican Americans who demanded assimilation and accommodation. The style of zoot suiters was a challenge, even if unconscious, to the conformity of homogeneous wartime discourse that privileged whiteness, maleness, and consensus. One of the ironies of the zoot was that the more it provided a means for youth to define their own identity and claim dignity, the more it became a target of dehumanizing rhetoric and violence from authority figures and society at large. The following chapter offers a fuller discussion of the ways African American and Mexican American youth practiced their style in the streets, dance halls, and other urban public spaces in order to challenge conventional ways of thinking about race and gender.

CHAPTER 4

Zoots, Jazz, and Public Space

At the beginning of Spike Lee's film *Malcolm X*, a young Malcolm Little, played by Denzel Washington, and Shorty, Malcolm's homeboy played by Lee, strut down a busy street near Boston's Dudley Street Station in the early 1940s. With Malcolm sporting a sky-blue zoot suit and a pork-pie hat complete with red feather, and Shorty decked out in a red and black checkered zoot with red hat and dark sunglasses, the pair walk shoulder to shoulder, seeming to take up the entire street, not to mention our viewing screen. As they cut diagonally across a busy intersection, Malcolm and Shorty pass directly in front of a group of sailors in uniform, stop to wave exaggeratedly at several young women, and elicit gawks of both disgust and admiration from others on the street. The brief scene ends with Malcolm walking straight into the camera, as if to hammer home the point that, if nothing else, the public performance of the two young African American zoot suiters is a spectacle to be seen, whether by those who despised them or those who loved them.[1]

In the opening scene of Luis Valdez's *Zoot Suit*, the film's narrator, El Pachuco, played by Edward James Olmos and dressed in a deep-blue zoot with red shirt, broad-rimmed hat, and gold watch chain, parades slowly across a theatrical stage made to look like a dance hall in wartime Los Angeles. In front of a theater full of spectators, El Pachuco snaps his fingers, and the other characters on stage jump into action. To the rhythm of a fast-paced big band tune, the dance hall's clientele, including several Mexican American male zoot suiters, an African American male zoot suiter, a white sailor, a number of Mexican American pachucas, an African American young woman, and an Asian American young woman, dance the night away. As they turn, twist, and rub their bodies against one another, the dancers also form loosely affiliated ethnic cliques, exposing the racial tensions of wartime Southern California. When the scene ends and the dancers fade from view, El Pachuco bursts onto the stage by tearing through a massive front page of the June 5, 1943, evening edition of the *Los Angeles Daily Express,* ripping a hole in headlines about the city's Zoot Suit Riots, World War II, and the Sleepy Lagoon murder. From the stage to the dance hall to the most public of discursive spaces, the big-city newspaper, Valdez, like Spike Lee, suggests that the zoot was a most public exhibition of style.[2]

Malcolm X and *Zoot Suit* both illustrate the central role public space played in attributing meaning to zoot style during World War II. Just as individual bodies were sites of struggle for dignity by many African American and Mexican American youth, so too were the many public locations they frequented. Both of the scenes described above demonstrate that zoot suiters carved social space for themselves and that, even at a time when their opinions were often excluded from more formal channels of public discourse, they articulated their own ethnic, gender, sexual, and class identities. With their wide-brimmed hats, flowing coats, and draped pants, they literally and figuratively claimed space by flaunting and celebrating the cultural difference and privileging of leisure that prevailing social norms so often condemned. As zoot suiters across the country claimed street corners, dance halls, and local watering holes as their own, their occupation of public space elicited concern and distaste from many Americans, who continued to view them as immoral, dangerous, and threatening to the war effort. The "congested terrain" of public space, which included movie theaters, restaurants, and nightclubs, emerged in the early 1940s as perhaps the single most contested arena where zoot suiters reclaimed dignity and challenged their own alienation.[3]

Zoot suiters' occupation of public space was politicized by wartime conditions, which included what historian Arnold Hirsch describes as the making of "the second ghetto." According to Hirsch's study of Chicago in the years following World War II, the increasing number of nonwhite residents in urban areas threatened to disrupt patterns of segregation. In response, white power brokers employed restrictive housing covenants, federally mandated housing projects, and police presence on and surveillance of city streets in order to prevent changes to long-standing

Figure 13. Pair of African American zoot suiters in Detroit, Michigan, June 1943. Gordon Coster/Time and Life Pictures/Getty Images.

residential segregation.[4] As discussed in chapters 1 and 2, race discrimination and police violence in Los Angeles and New York during the early 1940s infringed on the freedom and dignity of nonwhites. Against this backdrop, zoot suiters made themselves seen when urban authorities attempted to keep them off the streets and urged them to meld into home-front society.[5] When they walked down the street, frequented local hangouts, or used public transportation, zoot suiters claimed dignity by asserting their public presence while much of wartime society denigrated them as a negative influence. Whether one admired or loathed zoot suiters, their public persona made them a part of the home front that could not be ignored.

Although virtually every U.S. metropolis harbored centers of zoot culture, including Detroit, Philadelphia, Baltimore, Chicago, and Houston, this chapter continues the book's focus on the vivid cases of Los Angeles and New York City. As two of the most celebrated and active areas of zoot suit style during World War II, the Central Avenue district in Los Angeles and the Harlem neighborhood in New York City deserve special attention for several reasons. First, Central Avenue and Harlem were the heart of the West Coast and East Coast jazz scenes, respectively, and provide rich portraits of the deep connections between the music and zoot suit culture. Second, highlighting what Robin D. G. Kelley calls "the beauty and complexity of lived experience" for those African American, Mexican American, and other youth who frequented Central Avenue and Harlem reveals the regional breadth of the zoot suit and jazz lifestyles.[6] Finally, the West Coast–East Coast frame underscores the ways that local geography, demography, and politics shaped how zoot suiters claimed public space and challenged popular wartime notions about proper nonwhite youth behavior.

In this chapter I argue that the public spaces occupied by zoot suiters and other nonwhite youth in Los Angeles and New York functioned as subaltern counterpublics. The concert venues the youth attended and sidewalks they traversed facilitated the formulation of oppositional ethnic, gender, and class identities that valued difference rather than hiding it, prioritized dignity instead of dehumanization, and practiced sexual transgression. As elaborated by social theorist Michael Warner, subaltern counterpublics are evident when subordinate groups create spaces that facilitate the circulation of social discourse and behavior counter to the dominant culture.[7] The public spaces in which jazz and zoot cultures converged along Central Avenue and Harlem functioned as subaltern counterpublics, precisely because the social practices of nonwhite youth challenged mainstream U.S. conceptions of race, sexuality, and labor.

Public space functioned as a zone of race, gender, and sexual experimentation for many zoot suiters. By creating and participating in a social world that included Mexican Americans, African Americans, Asian Americans, and whites on a relatively equal footing, many youth directly confronted segregation, sexual norms, and expectations of work. The oppositional nature of zoot suiters' public performance lay partially in the lifestyle they shared across racial boundaries. If only for a transitory moment, the mixing of black, brown, yellow, and white bodies on the dance floor of the Savoy Ballroom in Harlem or the Avedon Ballroom in Los Angeles blurred racial and ethnic boundaries. What is more, young men and women dancing the close and often sex-laced moves of the jitterbug or Lindy Hop—particularly when white youth joined zoot and jazz social circles—further confronted the demonization of miscegenation. The sexualized social practices of zoot suiters were deemed immoral by parents, the press, and local officials on the grounds that the young women involved acted unladylike and disregarded patriarchal authority.

Public attention to zoot suiters' sexuality was partly due to the shifting nature of sex during the war, when the sexual exploits of servicemen and the era's economic boom may have been related to a more general loosening of sexual mores. But zoot sexuality also drew condemnation because nonwhite youth, especially young women, were blamed for the deterioration of proper values and accused of leading white servicemen astray. Besides challenging the racial and sexual mores of wartime U.S. society, the very public behavior of many zoot suiters flaunted their privileging of leisure over work, another practice that many believed undermined the war effort. The public behavior of nonwhite youth thus reminded the rest of society that race, gender, and sexuality were not fixed sets of practices, but made up of multiple and shifting social relationships.

Zoot suiters' public performance was riddled also with contradictions. Just as they disrupted the myth of U.S. race, sexuality, gender, and nation as fundamentally white, so too did they reaffirm racial, sexual, gender, and class hierarchies. Struggles for ownership of zoot style or turf wars between different groups of zoot suiters, sexual violence by male zoot suiters against their female counterparts, and the incapacity of a lifestyle centered on leisure and recreation to promote upward social mobility all contributed to the regeneration of subordination that many zoot suiters un-self-consciously challenged in the first place. As a result, public performances of zoot suiters were often simultaneously oppositional and accommodationist.

THE ZOOT, JAZZ, AND PUBLIC SPACE IN WARTIME HARLEM

Upon his arrival in New York City in 1929, Cab Calloway, the great jazzman who would later help popularize the zoot by wearing his famous white drapes in the 1943 film *Stormy Weather,* could not contain his excitement over his first extended trip to Harlem, the internationally known center of black American cultural activity. Calloway recalls,

> I will never forget coming into New York City. I had never been there before, nor had Betty [his wife to be], though a few of the musicians [in his band] had. On the road we had all listened to their stories about how hip New York was and how big and jazzed up the nightclubs were. By the time we got to New Jersey I was a bundle of nerves. . . . We could see big, bad old New York across the river. Of course there wasn't as many skyscrapers as there are now, but we could see the enormity of the city. I was scared to death and excited as hell. We all stood there, five or six carloads of people,

waiting for the ferry, with that wide beautiful Hudson River all that separated us from New York. Finally the ferry came, and we got on and made
that long, slow trip across the river to 125th Street. We drove around
Harlem for a while, awestruck by the whole scene. I had never seen so
many Negroes in one place before in my life. . . . It was beautiful. Just
beautiful. People out in the streets, and nightclubs all over, nightclubs
whose names were legendary to me.[8]

While most of the thousands of African Americans who migrated to
northern, midwestern, and western cities between the late 1920s and
early 1940s came in search of employment, Calloway was drawn to the
vibrant cultural world that emerged in New York and other urban areas
as a result of that migration.

Prior to Calloway's arrival, Harlem had enjoyed an international
reputation as a locus of black intellectual activity, music, literature, and
art. The Harlem Renaissance of the 1920s had placed the busy blocks of
uptown Manhattan squarely at the center of the world's cultural map.
Writers, intellectuals, and artists such as Langston Hughes, Zora Neale
Hurston, Claude McKay, Countee Cullen, James Weldon Johnson,
Aaron Douglas, Jesse Fauset, Alain Locke, and Marcus Garvey, among
many others, produced an impressive body of work in the form of
poetry, essays, novels, and dramas that explored U.S. race relations,
black race consciousness, black experiences of alienation and marginalization, and African Americans' relationship to Africa and Africans. In
addition to its literature, the music of the Harlem Renaissance established race and the black experience as key features of U.S. society. In
particular, the widespread use of the spiritual and blues traditions and
the rapidly growing genre of jazz had made Harlem a capital of African
American music by the time Calloway and his companions set foot on
125th Street in 1929.[9]

When Malcolm X arrived in Harlem around the time the United
States entered World War II, he recalled, "up and down along and
between Lenox and Seventh and Eighth Avenues," it was like a "techni-
color bazaar."[10] The social scene in Harlem also included soapbox politicians who, according to one native resident, were always sparking
conversations from their perches on street corners. Sometimes such commentary included seething critiques of wartime race relations. Perry
recalls, for instance, that "when Pearl Harbor was bombed, this guy [a
soapbox orator] said in many speeches, 'Thank God for the Japanese.'"
Although this particular individual was arrested for sedition, his sympathy for the Japanese nonetheless reflected the complicated relationship

between race and nationalism in Harlem and in the United States more broadly. Harlem, home to a large African American population, also contained pockets of West Indian, Afro-Latino (including Puerto Rican), and Italian settlement and was something of a hotbed of interracial relations. What is more, from the 1930s into the 1940s, Harlem's entertainment and night life grew in popularity among residents elsewhere in the city. Following in the footsteps of the city's white population during the Harlem Renaissance twenty years earlier, residents of all colors frequented the area's clubs, bars, and eateries, eager to socialize with, emulate, or simply gawk at the young people who were the impetus behind Harlem's cultural production.

Among the biggest draws in Harlem were the live jazz performances. When asked about spending his teens in Harlem during the war and the musicians he saw perform live, Perry replied, "Name somebody! I can't think of anybody who I haven't [seen]. Every jazz great that you can think of: Miles Davis, the Bird, Dizzy Gillespie, Louie Armstrong, Duke Ellington, Count Basie . . . I mean there was literally nobody who didn't play."[11] These and other artists, such as Thelonious Monk and Max Roach, popularized Harlem jazz at such clubs as Jimmy's Chicken Shack, the Nest Club, the Savoy Ballroom, Small's Paradise, the Lenox Club, and the Apollo Theater. Perry remembers that the Apollo had the "toughest audience in the world," meaning it was hard to please.[12] Along with jazz, the zoot became a central an element in the public behavior, recreation, and style of many Harlem youth. Calloway—"in his white zoot suit to end all zoots, and his wide-brimmed white hat and string tie, setting Harlem afire" with songs like "Tiger Rag" and "Minnie the Moocher"—was among the biggest stars who wedded jazz and the zoot.[13] Harlem was a center of social and cultural innovation in the city—in Perry's words, "*the* cultural Mecca. No question about it."[14]

The number of white patrons who regularly attended nightly jam sessions, dances, and beauty contests led Malcolm X to remark, "Blacktown crawled with white people."[15] Perry also recalls whites coming to Harlem to attend all the shows and that at nearly every event he went to, there were "always a few whites."[16] The influx of white New Yorkers into Harlem, particularly in the context of the city's long history of racial strife and violence, increased interracial tension as whites continued "slumming." Jazz pianist Mary Lou Williams, who regularly attended Minton's nightclub during the early 1940s when Thelonious Monk and others routinely participated in jam sessions, recalls the skepticism many black artists had toward white patronage of the club.

It finally got downtown about this new music that was going on at
Minton's. And these sessions were really terrific. The cats would come in
around nine-thirty or ten o'clock at night, and even later, and they'd jam all
night . . . and the place was jammed. And in no time, the commercial world
from downtown was coming in on it, and they tried to learn it. I heard some
of the guys speak about not wanting to play downtown or play in the open
so everybody could take it from them. Because you know the black creators
of the music have never gotten recognition for creating anything.[17]

Although Harlem's social scene sometimes brought black and white
city residents together, it also reinforced the discrimination and segregation of the larger society. Jazz did not by itself blunt the reality of
wartime race relations; rather, it was embedded in them. When Cab
Calloway was hired to play the Cotton Club with his band, for example,
he was of course excited to be performing at the world-famous hot spot.
But, he recalls, the "ordinary folks in Harlem never did get to see the
inside of the Cotton Club," known as "the Aristocrat of Harlem,"
because of club policy barring black and racially mixed parties. Although
some African American celebrities were occasionally admitted, "brutes"
always stood at the door to enforce segregation.[18] For the many world-
renowned black musicians who played the Cotton Club, its racial segregation was a not-so-subtle reminder of the times in which they lived.
The Cotton Club even sought to replicate the ambiance of a slave plan-
tation; the layout of the club, Calloway remembers, was similar to a
southern mansion:

> With huge white columns and a backdrop painted with weeping willows
> and slave quarters. The band played on the veranda of the mansion, and in
> front of the veranda, down a few steps, was the dance floor, which was also
> used for the shows. The waiters were dressed in red tuxedos, like butlers
> in a southern mansion, and the tables were covered with red-and-white-
> checked gingham tablecloths. There were huge cut-crystal chandeliers, and
> the whole set was like the sleepy-time-down-South during slavery. Even the
> name, Cotton Club, was supposed to convey the southern feeling. I suppose
> the idea was to make whites who came to the club feel like they were being
> catered to and entertained by black slaves.[19]

In contrast to the Cotton Club's efforts to maintain a division between
the races through apartheid measures, spots such as the famous Savoy
Ballroom facilitated a multiracial social scene. The Savoy was famous
for its cutting-edge performances by musicians like Dizzy Gillespie,
Dinah Washington, Lionel Hampton, Duke Ellington, Billie Holiday,
and Ella Fitzgerald, and the energy of nights at the Savoy were legend-

ary. Malcolm X recalls his first visit to the Savoy on a night when Lionel Hampton was on stage:

> The ballroom made the Roseland in Boston look small and shabby by comparison. And the Lindy-hopping there matched the size and elegance of the place. Hampton's hard-driving outfit kept a red-hot pace with his greats such as Arnett Cobb, Illinois Jacquet, Dexter Gordon, Alvin Hayes, Joe Newman, and George Jenkins. I went a couple of rounds on the floor with girls from the sidelines. Probably a third of the sideline booths were filled with white people, mostly just watching the Negroes dance; but some of them danced together, and, as in Boston, a few white women were with Negroes.[20]

Race mixing occurred at the Savoy regularly, to such an extent that historians Shane and Graham White estimate that upwards of 30 percent of the Savoy's patrons were white during the early war years.[21]

The Savoy was perhaps the most famous of all the Harlem clubs, well known in the city and around the world as home of the Lindy Hop and jitterbug. The club was such an icon that when the 1939 World's Fair was held in New York City, a display replica of its famous ballroom was created for the fairgrounds in Flushing Meadows. Dizzy Gillespie recalled, "That was some weird shit. They built a Savoy Ballroom, a pavilion, out in the World's Fair for a 'Lindy Hopper Show.' They used Teddy Hill's band; no dancing was allowed, just a show."[22] The Savoy exhibit at the World's Fair helped bring jazz and zoot style to the world's attention. Like the zoot renditions put forward by Spike Lee and Luis Valdez decades later, the World's Fair exhibition identified nonwhite youth culture as a public performance, one that deserved attention from the rest of society.

The interracial socializing fomented by jazz was not limited to Harlem. Gillespie remembers playing gigs in such other areas of the city as Brooklyn, the Bronx, and lower Manhattan, where white and black communist organizers made up a majority of audiences. Amid attempts at recruiting him for membership in the communist party, he recalls,

> All kinds of stuff was happening. Most of the guys, most of the musicians, almost everybody up there was [racially] mixed. White-black relationships were very close among the communists. I think they were trying to prove how equalitarian they were by throwing together the white or the black counterparts of the opposite sex. A lot of white girls were there, oh yes. I thought it was pretty funny myself, being from the South. I found it strange that every couple, almost, was a mixed couple one way or the other. That was the age of unity.[23]

Figure 14. Young African American men in zoot suits at the
Savoy Ballroom in Harlem during the 1930s. Copyright Bettman/
Corbis.

One musician claimed that jazz and zoot cultures were "strictly interracial," leading at least one scholarly team to argue that "this new youth
culture—vibrant, autonomous, and not segregated—was of concern to
authorities."[24] Many New Yorkers criticized the casual mixing of races
that included many white soldiers and civilians. In particular, many
whites condemned the attention some white women gave to black male
musicians. When leaving clubs after their performances, a number of
black musicians, including Gillespie and Billy Taylor, faced verbal abuse
and physical violence from white male audience members because of the
adoration they received from white women.[25]

Part of Harlem's appeal to New York City residents at large, and one of the reasons it drew the attention of urban reformers and moralists, was that New Yorkers often viewed it as an "exotic" cultural location where visitors could participate discretely in immoral or illegal activity. White servicemen were routinely barred by their superiors from visiting Harlem for fear of their involvement in prostitution, drug use, robberies, or street violence. In fact, city police were known to discourage white civilians from going uptown, though it was virtually impossible to stop them. Harlem's reputation as a place where sex could be had easily and where interracial sex was not always frowned upon helped make prostitution among the most frightening elements of the neighborhood for white New Yorkers committed to segregation. Recalling Harlem's sexual discourse and behavior, Malcolm X wrote, "Every man without a woman on his arm was being 'worked' by the prostitutes. 'Baby, wanna have some fun?' The pimps would sidle up close, stage-whispering, 'All kinds of women, Jack—want a white woman?'"[26]

City authorities denounced the race mixing and sexual independence associated with the public character of jazz and the zoot. By May 1943, for example, the Savoy's reputation as Harlem's finest nightclub attracted the attention of local authorities who caused great controversy when they shut the club down. The NYPD and the city's Licensing Commission cited as reasons for the closure the Savoy's role in facilitating the spread of venereal disease among servicemen who frequented the club and the establishment's failure to prevent prostitution—arguments that stoked public fears of the predatory and dangerous sexual nature of Harlem and its residents. The conflation of black bodies and Harlem's public space with disease, however, was viewed by the Savoy's management, the city's African American population, and much of its multiracial clientele as trumped-up charges used to mask the real reason for closing the club: to end race mixing.

Shortly after the closing, the *Amsterdam News* ran the headline "Mixed Dancing Closed Savoy Ballroom," and the *People's Voice* asked whether the closing reflected police efforts to bar New York's white population from socializing in Harlem. In a telegram to Mayor La Guardia, Walter White and other leaders of the NAACP charged that the police department unfairly outlawed the world-famous "home of happy feet" because management had consistently refused to stop mixed-race dancing. Those close to the Savoy management insisted that authorities had long looked with disfavor on the practice of blacks and whites dancing and socializing together. Despite the pleas by the city's black leadership, La Guardia claimed his hands were tied and he could do nothing to reopen the Savoy, all the while denying that race or politics or dancing had anything to do with the closing. Rumor and fact regarding the closing of the Savoy, however, quickly became entangled in debates over what appeared to be the city's unstated policy of endorsing segregation.[27]

La Guardia's failure to respond affirmatively to the calls for assistance in clearing the Savoy's record undermined his reputation as a friend of the city's African American community. The *People's Voice* insisted that the mayor "was not powerless to act, if he wished to take some action as the chief magistrate of the city."[28] Criticism of the mayor and the NYPD for singling out the Savoy for serving a multiracial clientele were not unfounded. Following the Savoy's closure, numerous reports surfaced that it did not have nearly the problem with drugs and prostitution as dance halls in downtown Manhattan. One investigative reporter for the *People's Voice* claimed that after having "thoroughly covered eight of New York's better known taxi-dance halls with two witnesses" during the first week of May, he had found that "depravity and degradation run rampant." Among the charges of the report were that hostesses made after-hours dates with the men who spent the most money in the club, that obsessive drinking occurred, and that illegal drugs were available. The investigative team also cited prostitution, "sex-perversion," and sex for money and described the goings-on on dance floors and in corners as "an orgy of semi-fornication." Witnesses also stated that police stationed outside the venues did not interfere with such behavior, particularly when it involved white servicemen, who made up to 75 percent of the clientele involved in sex-for-money operations. The report claimed that "many men who frequent these 'meat-centers' do so with the objective of getting a woman to go to bed with them. If they have enough money they will succeed." The *People's Voice* concluded that the Savoy was, by comparison, a "Christian youth center."[29]

The response to the Savoy closing was rife with class conflict and competing political strategies. On the one hand, in depicting the shutdown as unfairly singling out the Savoy, black New Yorkers demanded equal protection of the law and fair treatment in the press. The *Amsterdam News* even noted that the allegedly vile nature of the Savoy and other dance joints "would seem rather embarrassing" to many prominent white citizens who frequented such places, including, according to Savoy manager Charles Buchanan, James Cagney, Orson Welles, members of the Rockefeller family, and Gene Tunney, among others.[30] On the other hand, in their arrogant condemnation of other city nightclubs similar to the Savoy, the black press and community leaders emphasized conformity to the conservative morality that city authorities espoused during the war. Moreover, both the city's black leadership and the mayor's office failed to recognize, or at least admit publicly, that charges of sexual misconduct and race mixing were related, in the sense that popular fears of miscegenation and the sexuality of nonwhites were probably behind both sets of concerns. Neither black leaders nor the black press ever openly argued that nonwhites seemed to be getting blamed for the broader societal shifts in sexual activity.

Despite a failure to acknowledge the dual nature of the threat posed by the Savoy to wartime conceptions of sex and race, many in the African American community were outspokenly critical of the Savoy's closing. They argued that the reasons for the shutdown were clear to all. A. Phillip Randolph, head of the Brotherhood of Sleeping Car Porters and leader of the March on Washington, denounced the Savoy closing as an "insult to the Negro people of New York City in particular and the country in general." One city musician accustomed to playing in the city's nightclubs declared in utter frustration, "It's most unfair that police restrictions seem to apply to Harlem only. Regulations are applied to Negroes which are in force in no other part of town." An employee for the Brooklyn YWCA identified the closing as another attempt to stigmatize Harlem as a vice-ridden area and to segregate New York's citizenry.[31] Shortly after the Savoy was closed, an unknown author published a poem in the *People's Voice* that captured much of the frustration African Americans felt:

> Guilty of national unity
> Of practicing real Democracy
> By allowing the races, openly
> To dance and mingle in harmony[32]

The closing of the Savoy made transparent what many zoot suiters and jazz enthusiasts had long known: many Americans considered nonwhite communities a threat to the economic, political, and social stability of the home front.

While the Savoy's closure was understood by black New Yorkers as a slap in the face to the Double V campaign, particularly in light of the war bond sales, anti-fascist rallies, and other patriotic activities the Savoy had hosted, it was not the only venue to encounter such repression. By the beginning of 1943, federal and local authorities began closing other nightclubs and harassing black musicians for corrupting and exploiting soldiers and civilians by playing jazz and selling booze, drugs, and sex that weakened their health and morals and, ultimately, undermined their ability to win the war. Nightclubs and black music, it was believed, kept people out late, facilitated tardiness and absenteeism in the war industry workplace, and eroded the fitness of soldiers and sailors, impairing the ability of the United States to hone and strengthen its war effort. All along New York's famous 52nd Street jazz scene, local officials raided jazz- and zoot-affiliated businesses in hopes of shutting them down.[33]

THE ZOOT, JAZZ, AND PUBLIC SPACE IN WARTIME LOS ANGELES

In his autobiography, the great jazz saxophonist Art Pepper recalls the social scene on Central Avenue in Los Angeles during the early 1940s, which, not unlike Harlem, was the center of black cultural activity in the city. An intriguing character who battled drug addiction and prison time, Pepper was a white musician in a jazz world dominated by African Americans. He described the sights and sounds of a weekend evening on the avenue.

> The [black] women dressed up in frills and feathers and long earrings and hats with things hanging off them, fancy dresses with slits in the skirts, and they wore black silk stockings that were rolled, and wedgie shoes. Most of the men wore big, wide-brimmed hats and zoot suits with wide collars, small cuffs, and large knees, and their coats were real long with padded shoulders. They wore flashy ties with diamond stickpins; they wore lots of jewelry and you could smell powder and perfume everywhere. And as you walked down the street you heard music coming out of every place. And everybody was happy. Everybody just loved everybody else, or if they didn't, I didn't know about it.[34]

While Pepper's recollections might be a bit romanticized, they nonetheless depict the vibrant social scene that was Central Avenue.

The Central Avenue district had long been the city's black center and a locus of leisure and entertainment. Beginning with the steady growth of Los Angeles at the turn of the century and continuing during the Great Migration, the city's African American population increased apace with the region's growing economy. As early as the 1920s, according to historian Lawrence de Graaf, "most blacks were living in one physical ghetto stretching approximately thirty blocks down Central Avenue and several blocks east to the railroad tracks, or in a few detached islands, especially on West Jefferson, Temple Street, and just south of the city of Watts."[35]

The Central Avenue social scene grew during the early years of the war. Historian Josh Sides calls Central during the 1940s an urban anomaly—a ghetto benefiting from temporary wartime prosperity whose residents, though often living in squalor, spent much of their money on leisure.[36] As the hub of the LA black community, Central Avenue was home to a variety of clubs, shops, and restaurants. Although many establishments in the area were white owned, Central Avenue was the location of several black-owned businesses. John Somerville, for example, the first black graduate of the University of Southern California and a prominent area dentist, built and owned the Somerville Hotel in the 1920s to accommodate black visitors to the city, who were denied service at most of the downtown hotels. One of the finer hotels for blacks in the country, the Somerville offered fine dining, as well as a flower shop, barber and beauty shops, and a pharmacy. Soon after the Great Depression the hotel changed ownership and was renamed the Dunbar, but it continued to be a city landmark and an example of African American entrepreneurship. The Dunbar was a popular spot among the many black entertainers who visited LA. Housing the Breakfast Club, an after-hours night spot, and the barber shop, which also served as a local hangout, the Dunbar was an institution in black Los Angeles.[37]

Nearby was the Alabam, one of the city's most popular nightclubs, where jazzmen Charles Mingus, Dexter Gordon, and Art Pepper played in the house band. In addition to Pepper, other white musicians such as Johnny Martisza and Jimmy Hanson also made their mark jamming on Central. But it was the volume of quality performances that made the Central jazz scene so spectacular. The Dunbar and Alabam were two of a large collection of entertainment venues in the district, including places like the Downbeat and the Chicken Shack, which, along with a popular Mexican restaurant, were close to the Dunbar. Within just a few blocks were the Ritz Club on Central and Vernon, Jack's Basket, Hi-De-Ho, and the Crystal Tea Room. The amazing array of establishments regularly attracted people from all over the city, including black celebrities such as Jackie Robinson and Jack Johnson.[38]

The rich social scene along Central even led one observer to characterize it as "an elongated Harlem set down by the Pacific."[39] While jazz was a crucial component, it was only one aspect of Central Avenue culture. Jazz historian Ted Gioia notes that as much activity occurred on the streets as inside the clubs. "Sometimes," he writes, "much of the show took place in the street: Mercedes and Bentleys, Cadillacs and Lincolns, movie stars and athletes, singers and dancers. The avenue contained a round-the-clock cacophony of comings and goings."[40] Many Angelino youth flocked to the area to shop for the latest in fashion, style, and accessories for their zoot attire. Bob, a Mexican American zoot suiter who used to purchase his wide-brimmed hats on Central Avenue, remembers, "Even after the war I used to go down there and listen to the jazz sessions." He recalls many moments "down at 4th and Central. And the young guys be standing out there, see who comes in and how they're dressed."[41] As one longtime resident described it, "You didn't want to hit the Avenue with dirty shoes."[42]

The jazz and zoot scene blossomed in other areas of the city as well, including farther south near San Pedro where clubs like the Avalon, Zanzabar, Twin Bells, and Last Word were happening joints, or in Little Tokyo, where many African Americans settled following the Japanese Americans internment. Visitors to Little Tokyo saw such jazz greats as Gerald Wilson and Coleman Hawkins perform nightly at Schepp's Playhouse and Club Finale. As along Central, the nightlife and social scene in Little Tokyo involved not just blacks but also well-to-do whites, Hollywood celebrities, war workers, servicemen, and youth from around the city. Young people also frequented downtown LA, where a number of theaters and ballrooms hosted dances with touring jazz and big band performers. The Orpheum Theater on 9th and Broadway, the Million Dollar Theater just six blocks away on 3rd and Broadway, and the All Nations Club on 1st and Main held concerts by the likes of Glen Miller and Cab Calloway. Recalling her arrival in Los Angeles from Hempstead, Texas, during the war years, Fanny Hill, an African American woman then in her early twenties, describes the social scene that she along with many other blacks and Angelinos were part of:

> There were a ton of good little night clubs. I mean, they kept you entertained fairly well. . . . We used to go down to a theater called the Orpheum and that's where all the Negro entertainers as well as whites went down there. And we used to go there all the time and see the big name bands and what have you. . . . And the funniest thing about it, though, it would always be in our night clubs. A white woman would come in there with a Negro man, eventually. She would. She always has broke the barrier, when it says coming out in the open. But the white man would very seldom come out in the open with a black woman."[43]

The Avedon was another popular establishment. Located on Spring Street near the Orpheum Theater, the Avedon was remembered by the

African American trumpeter Gerald Wilson, who played with Count Basie, Duke Ellington, Cab Calloway, and Ella Fitzgerald, among others, as a "fine ballroom" where "all the bands played."[44]

Whether along Central Avenue, in Little Tokyo, or elsewhere in the city, jazz-oriented nightclubs, big band concert halls, and the surrounding streets, restaurants, and businesses served as a public stage on which young people performed their zoot style. As the politics of youth gained importance on the local and national home front, public space became a battleground where the general public, city authorities, and nonwhite youth clashed. Vicente Morales, a young Mexican American zoot suiter, recalls the reaction of many white Angelinos whom zoot suiters encountered on city streets. "They didn't like us," he says, "and I remember when I used to go downtown to the stores and the restaurants usually I'd get dirty looks like I was going to rob something from them, and they didn't like the way I dressed or the way I looked. But the way I saw it, I'm not going anywhere I'm not wanted, and I don't want them to bother me and I won't bother them, that's the way I felt."[45] Similarly, Antonio Alvarez claims that when he wore his zoot suit in downtown Los Angeles, "a lot of people would remark. Say some kind of remark. 'Look at that asshole' or say something like that."[46] Lupe, a self-identified pachuca and zoot suiter, recalls that when African American and Mexican American youth used the city's public transportation they created a moving theater of social conflict. When she and her fellow pachuca friends would "take streetcars downtown . . . people talked about us, the way we were dressed, our hair. I remember it and it didn't hurt me or embarrass me. I liked the way I was. I liked the way we dressed. . . . We weren't looking for trouble."[47]

The youth cultural worlds of wartime Los Angeles allowed young Mexican American and African American women, in particular, to find new freedoms outside the confines of home and parental control. Regardless of whether young women viewed themselves as pachucas or zoot suiters, going out to dances, movies, and parties defied their confinement to the private sphere and challenged long-standing familial patterns of policing the sexuality of young women, which were often shrouded in promises of security and safety. Many young women found their parents working more or that they themselves were asked to work more outside the home, allowing for more independent activity. As discussed in chapter 3, young nonwhite women who found work in war industries often expressed disdain for zoot suiters and pachucas, perhaps because such figures were deemed counterproductive to the war effort.

Many of these same women, however, actively participated in the jazz and zoot social scenes despite consciously disidentifying themselves from zoot suiters and pachucas. Mary Luna, for example, observes, "I think that working really helped me to make a lot of friends, to get out and see what the world was like." She elaborates: "We really didn't get into going downtown, like to dances where you met others, until [we were] about twenty, twenty-one [in 1942–1943]. Before that, I didn't. It wasn't until I went to work at Douglas that I met some girls. They'd tell you they're having dances here. That's how I got to start going out. That's where I met him [her husband] at a dance, because he's from LA [and] I'd never met him otherwise."[48] Lupe Rivas recalls heading out on the town to attend evening dances with friends. "They had [the dances] downtown, down in L.A. They had a place called the Avedon. They had some good bands. . . . They had well known bands. . . . It was a nice place. They had built it brand new. Then, there were some other places that weren't brand new. They were like dance halls and night clubs. . . . All my girlfriends invited me to go and I'd go with them. I got to get around [laughs]."[49]

Although the war expanded social freedoms previously unavailable to some Mexican American women, familial patriarchy still informed the lives of many others. Although the tradition of chaperoning young girls on the town declined during the war, many young women were still expected to be accompanied by a brother or uncle.[50] In fact, Mary Luna remembers one dance she was allowed to attend only after her brother agreed to accompany her. Dressed in his naval uniform, her brother quickly met several young women and left the dance, leaving Mary alone. She enjoyed herself, however, and was taken home on a streetcar by her future husband. Even so, prior to meeting her husband, Mary remembers that she had few dates during the war years. "I used to go out with the girls," she recalls, "because I was kind of leery of all the servicemen. . . . Mostly I just used to like to go to the dances and come home with a girlfriend. I don't know. Like I tell you, I wasn't very secure [laughs]."[51] Another friend of Luna's was twenty-six years old and not permitted by her parents to leave the house unless with her brother. It's likely, however, that on many occasions young women and their chaperones made arrangements so that each could spend the evening with his or her own date or group of friends before they all headed home for the night. Lupe, for instance, recalls that she and her sisters fooled their mother into allowing them to go out at night. "We would tell her we were going to the [movie] show. I remember the *movidas* we made behind her back!"[52] More than pulling a fast one on their parents, however, many of these young women used their time out in public to meet young men, including servicemen on leave, and establish connections that could lead to dances together, home visits on the front porch, or even longer-term romantic relationships.

Regardless of whether they were chaperoned or not, young women found ways to have fun. Recalling one of many enjoyable excursions, Luna says: "I remember meeting these two sisters. We would go to a dance and they would say, 'stay overnight at our house.' Like when we went downtown. I would tell my father I'm going to stay with my girlfriends down there, so I wouldn't have to come home by myself alone. I stayed at their house and got to meet their families, and get to be a part of their life. I didn't have that many women, except for my cousins next door—to see other women and how they were. That was nice."[53]

Rose Echeverria Mulligan, who avoided direct affiliation with zoot suiters and pachucas, similarly recalls venturing out with her girlfriends in wartime LA. They often gathered at one another's homes to visit for hours at a time, making sure the young fellows they were interested in meeting knew where they were. "And sometimes they'd end up at my house, and really, we just take pictures [laughs] of each other. If they got together, you see, it would be four or five or six in one car, in a brother's car or some car. And they couldn't afford to take us anywhere because they didn't have any money."[54]

Even before the war, dances were hosted by local clubs at private homes, recalls Margarita Salazar, who grew up in LA's Boyle Heights neighborhood in the 1930s. Open or private, parties, dances, and balls attracted large groups of young people. Other times, she and her friends would leave the city to go swimming or horseback riding in the low mountains surrounding the city. Informal social clubs afforded a mechanism for young Mexican American women and others to create social space and freedom in their lives.[55] Adele Hernandez Milligan, who moved to LA in 1936 at age six and entered teenhood as the war unfolded, met a group who called themselves the Gardeña Girls and ended up becoming friends with them. Together they attended pier and beach dances during the war where "we always went with a bunch of girls, and met all the guys there and had a lot of fun and just danced away. Then we just got in a great big old car, all the girls and just come home." Hernandez also remembers dating a number of Jewish guys and picking up servicemen at many of the dances. "We'd go to all those dances and we'd meet these sailors and soldiers that had no one here.

We'd bring them home to my mother's and feed them and they'd stay overnight. But there was never any hanky panky, you didn't think of those things for some reason. Heck, I was old enough then, but you really didn't." For Hernandez and her friends, many of the servicemen they met and dated were white.[56]

The meaning of young nonwhite women's social behavior depended on who they associated with. Going to the movies with parents was different from going with a boyfriend or a group of girlfriends. Mixed-gender dates pushed the boundaries of acceptable behavior by enabling pachucas to interact with the opposite sex as consumers and participants in a wide range of social networks often unavailable at home. For those who identified as pachucas, style was also politicized by same-sex social relations, since for them, going to a concert or dance together was not uncommon. Cultural critic Rosa Linda Fregoso, in discussing the representation of pachucas in feature-length films, observes that pachucas "refused to be contained by domesticity or limited by the prevailing orthodoxy of appropriate female behavior." By "refusing to stay in the place assigned them by Chicano society," Fregoso argues, "pachucas are trespassers in public spaces, violating the boundaries of femininity." They are "often viewed by adults as transgressive girls who disturbed private and public patriarchy, la familia, and the Catholic Church" by speaking and acting in the public sphere about sex and thus threatening traditional family gender structure.[57] Although Fregoso is addressing more recent representations of the pachuca, 1940s-era pachucas also rejected parental norms by refusing to stay inside the home, using provocative language and clothing in public, and pushing the limits of *familia* and patriarchal order.[58] By crossing into the public sphere from the home, pachucas disrupted the notion that public and private spheres were unchanging. Because men deemed housekeeping, family care, child rearing, and other work women performed at home as unimportant, public space and discourse were often privileged as male and masculine. Pachucas, however, boldly asserted that public space could be inhabited by women. Further, pachucas likely transformed the private sphere, viewing it as an important site where public discourse and life were learned, engaged in, and shaped through visits with friends and boyfriends, house parties, and informal gossip.

For both young men and women, public space was critical to their social experimentation. Young African Americans and Mexican Americans had little access to recreational facilities, as public swimming pools, theaters, and other establishments were often closed or restricted on the basis of race. Consequently, many youth turned to concert halls, hotels, and nightclubs that hosted dances, or playgrounds, pool halls, and street corners as places to congregate and, depending on the place, participate in organized social events.[59]

Many youth also turned to the comforts of their own homes or those of friends and family to find space for their extracurricular activities. House parties, birthday gatherings, family get-togethers, and send-off parties for young men entering the armed forces were routine throughout the war years, providing additional opportunities to dance, exchange fashion tips, and just hang out. Lupe recalls, "It was during the war, every weekend there was a party or a dance or farewell. Every pachuco I know went in the service, all of them from my neighborhood, from his [her ex-husband's] neighborhood, his two brothers, himself, my cousin, and friends. Some were in the navy, but most were in the army. They were all drafted, all of them."[60] Youth often heard about such parties through word of mouth and showed up for the gathering whether or not they had been invited or even knew the hosts.

The occupation of public space by nonwhite youth and their penchant for turning private residences into the sites of more public, openly attended social gatherings helped make their social world multiracial. While parties in private homes were probably less cosmopolitan than events in public establishments, and while even the most open of nightclubs were riddled with racial and ethnic tension, Los Angeles was home to a uniquely diverse youth culture. Many of the youth involved crossed paths daily and thereby produced a multicultural milieu that was not lost on their wartime contemporaries. Central Avenue, in particular, was like a magnet for all of the city's youth, especially zoot suiters. Bob, the former Mexican American zoot suiter, recalls the attraction of Central Avenue's African American culture. "Yeah. I used to go down there to listen to the jam sessions. Louie Armstrong and Duke Ellington and all those guys. All those world-known musicians used to go there near 4th and Central. They called it the Chicken Basket. That was the name of a nightclub where they had all them jam sessions . . . and the movie stars used to go down there. At nighttime they would come out. They would just sit at the bar and listen to the jam sessions."[61] Lupe and her friends rarely missed a top show down on Central. "There were a lot of African Americans coming to LA at that time [early 1940s], and the dances we used to go to, I'm not kidding you, we had all the big bands, Duke Ellington, Count Basie. . . . They would have it at the places on Central Avenue. And we would hear about it and we would be there."[62]

At the Diana or Avedon ballrooms downtown, as well, zoot suiting youth congregated to hear the sounds of touring big-time jazz performers. After taking LA streetcars to downtown dance halls, one of the most memorable characteristics of these dances for Lupe was the multiracial makeup of the crowds. "Everybody from all over LA would come to the big dances at the Diana Ballroom or other places near Central to hear the big bands. Mexicans, blacks, Filipinos, and even the white kids. I remember, the black guys always looked so sharp and were the best dancers. We used to love to dance with them."[63] Japanese American youth Bill Katayama, who grew up in Boyle Heights, lived the typical life of a young zoot suiter, spending "most of his free time hanging around night clubs, getting drunk, trying to pick up girls, and jitterbugging." Katayama was sexually active from the age of fourteen or fifteen with Nisei, Mexican American, and African American girls, as well as white prostitutes.[64] Many zoot suiters broke public taboos against integration and race mixing by socializing together and participating in public events that encouraged the sharing of space by youth from different racial and ethnic backgrounds.

Thinking back to his piano-playing days in the 1930s and early 1940s, Coney Woodman, the oldest brother in the Woodman Brothers Biggest Little Band in the World, which played regularly along Central Avenue, said he performed for a number of different youth groups.

> People began to know about us. We played at the Elks and the Masonic temple, where the colored people had their big formals. The Elks was where all the young kids came and had their formals. We played at the Follies. My dad (who managed the group) got us up there. We played any kind of music. For Mexicans, we played Mexican. We played for movie stars. We played for all the communists. [laughter] A lot of movie stars were communists. They wanted us to join the Communist Party. We never got around to it. It's a good thing I didn't; I probably couldn't have worked at Rockwell [the war industry plant]. [laughter] We didn't give politics a thought. We played for this black guy that wanted to take everybody back to Africa—Marcus Garvey. We played for anything, man. We didn't care what it was. [laughter] But we weren't thinking about being active. Everybody wanted us to be active, but we didn't take it seriously. Because we were too young. We weren't even twenty-one, man.[65]

Though Woodman doesn't claim to have participated in any organized movements opposing the war or mistreatment of nonwhites, or even to have been thinking about anything other than having a good time, the music he played and the relationships that grew from it had a politics all their own. Woodman, other jazz artists, and zoot suiters displayed a rejection of the conservative social, sexual, and racial conditions of the day. Their everyday cultural activity and way of life formed an alternative method of navigating the wartime United States, one different from those of the middle-class activists and professionals who stressed assimilation, and from that of local authorities who regarded nonwhite youth as perpetrators of crime and immoral behavior.

The diversity of youth culture in areas like Central Avenue grew in part from the multiracial lives that many young people experienced in school and in their own neighborhoods. When some area high schools were integrated in the late 1930s and early 1940s, African American, Mexican American, Japanese American, Chinese American, and white ethnic students shared classrooms. The interaction among youth in school was related to relationships they shared after school hours. Several black jazz musicians, including trombonist Britt Woodman, remember attending integrated high schools such as Jordan High. Woodman notes,

> People got along, and everybody was beautiful. Now, the Mexicans were beautiful. Mexicans were like us in a sense—minority. They couldn't go into certain sections over there because that was the white neighborhood. Now, the whites went to our school, but we couldn't mingle over there. One day when we were rehearsing in our home, some of the white fellows asked if they could come and listen. We said sure. So one of them made a statement—I never forgot it—"Britt and Coney," he said, "I sure wish you could meet my mother and father, but the neighbors, they'd resent it, you coming over there." The white neighborhood was on about 96th to 101st Street right off of Wilmington Avenue. Just like the Japanese. The Japanese lived off of Compton Avenue. And the Chinamen, they had a little community where they lived. It was all divided. You know, the Japanese had the grocery stores in the neighborhood where the blacks would go. But they all were going to our school.[66]

Bassist David Bryant, a mainstay of the late-1940s LA jazz scene has similar recollections of his youth and early education in the Watts area. "There were mostly black and Mexican families in our area. And through grammar school, I think there might have been a couple of white kids. Then it was junior high and senior together at Jordan High School. That was before they built Markham Junior High. At Jordan it was multiracial: white, Mexican, black, Asian."[67] Closer to downtown, Jefferson High School also served a diverse student body. From at least the late 1930s and well into the mid-1940s Jefferson was quite integrated. William Douglass, later a well-known jazz drummer, recalls that the students at Jefferson "were, I guess, predominantly black, but we had Caucasian, Japanese, Chinese, Hispanic. I mean, they all attended the same schools."[68] For Art Farmer, a young trumpeter who arrived in Los Angeles at age sixteen from Phoenix, attending Jefferson High was like "a whole new world, this big school with all kinds of white people, black people, Chinese, Mexican. Everybody was in this school."[69]

During her school days at Garfield High in East Los Angeles, Rose Echeverria Mulligan had regular contact with many Russians, Jews, and others. She recalls,

> I really lived in Boyle Heights, I lived right on the boundary. Over here [indicating direction] was Roosevelt and this is where it was all predomi-nantly Jewish. Roosevelt High School—I mean, Jewish students—and very proud of their scholastic standing and college bound. [laughs] Garfield, too. But the majority of kids were cosmopolitan, really, and when we went there, there were Japanese and there were just about everything, every imaginable nationality and we were proud of that. We were a proud bunch. I sometimes think that that's how come we won the war.[70]

Another former Mexican American zoot suiter recalls his neighbor-hood near Temple Street starting to become more multiethnic during the years just preceding the war:

> My mom was going with this guy, a record guy, who made records. Then a Jewish guy comes in the neighborhood and there's a lot of Jews around. Well after a while they started moving down closer. We was one of the first Mexican families to move in that area, that neighborhood. And I didn't think it was long, maybe six months and you had a *tortillería* there, and they made sweetbread, and chicken stores, and matza balls and a Jewish bakery. Then you move down two blocks toward Figueroa and there's some Filipino restaurants down there and Chinese. Grocery store was run by a Japanese guy.[71]

The constant interaction among different race and ethnic groups in close quarters also produced its share of conflict and tension among young people in Los Angeles. Whether because of competition over romantic partners, competing claims to neighborhood turf, or prejudices inherited from the older generations of ethnic communities, there were limits to the degree nonwhite youth crossed social boundaries. Many youth, in fact, did not maintain a consistent or high degree of social interaction with their counterparts from other communities, though it is difficult to imagine young people in Los Angeles not having any contact with youth from ethnic communities other than their own. While youth of all colors often encountered one another in dance halls, for example, they were less apt to establish interracial dating relations. Lupe recalls that "black guys were good-looking, but we were just friends. They used to go to the dances too and we'd dance with them if they asked us to."[72] Because of pressure from parents who disapproved of interracial relationships or larger society's disapproval of racial mixing, youth seldom cultivated long-lasting romances with members of other racial and ethnic communities. Bob, who remembers Central Avenue as a common ground for all Los Angeles youth, also recalls predominantly Mexican dances where he saw few African Americans or Asian Americans.[73]

Violence, in addition to sex and romance, also helped define the public persona of zoot suiters, as it was not unusual for physical confrontations to erupt among nonwhite youth, especially males who disapproved of others socializing with young women from outside their own ethnic and racial circles or neighborhoods. The Avedon Ballroom, which was known for attracting a mixed clientele, was described by Bob as "open territory. Because of the girls, a lot of guys went there."[74] Although intra-ethnic neighborhood conflicts were sometimes put on hold while youth jitterbugged and listened to the newest sounds, conflicts did arise. Bob, a self-proclaimed tough guy, recalls one incident when he began talking to a young woman friend from the Flats neighborhood, far from his own home in Echo Park. The widely known Alpine Street gang eyeballed him the entire evening and finally confronted him. Bob tells the story:

> At the Avedon, I put down six guys there from Alpine. I knew 'em all, they knew me. They wanted to pick a fight with me 'cause I was dancing with a chick from Flats. She was my friend. Those guys got a lot of nerve, "Get away, get away," you know. They came up to me. The guy's looking like he's gonna hit me, so I knocked the guy down. Knocked him out cold. Here comes another one, they're all standing on the sidewalk. So here comes this one, I says "Oh man." So they're comin' for me and I'm hitting them, laying them out. Six of them on the floor. The [security] cop [at the Avedon], he sticks his head out the door and says, "Hey buddy, keep it outside." So I start walking down the street, you know. So I'm leaving. I didn't have a car at that time and I'm looking behind me. I'm looking behind me as I'm going down 29th Street. Here they come, all six of them, coming at me. So I turned around and I'm gonna pound these guys if they come near me, you know. I had a stick to use like a sword. I got lucky. A car was coming down the street with six guys in it, young guys. As a matter of fact, two of them turned out to be my friends and they drove by and said, "Oh shit." So they got out of the car and they stood behind me and I says, "Hey now. Just make sure that somebody don't crawl on my back when I'm gonna do this." I go after the first guy, bang he's down. Boom, boom, all the way down. The other guy's screaming, "No, no, don't hit me, no, no." He was cursing. I just go like that [feigning a punch] and didn't even hit him again. He goes, "Oh no." I turned around and said, "Let's get out of here."[75]

Antonio recalls similar confrontations from his zoot suit days in Los Angeles when macho bravado and fisticuffs were key components of zoot suiters' masculinity. "Well," he says, "you know, once or twice we got into it. Real bad one time. Real bad. I mean there must have been forty guys fighting. Bad. Fighting and kicking and everything else."[76]

While most of the intraracial violence was carried out by male zooters, young women were also involved. Rose Echeverria Mulligan remembers that when she was in the eleventh grade at Garfield High, "there was a big gang fight and darned if it didn't turn out to be a fight between [girls]. I don't know what they were. How can I describe it to you? Non-Mexican and Mexican. They were tough. They'd try to act tough."[77] Zoot suiters' habit of crashing private parties also led to misunderstandings and clashes between rival neighborhood groups. More often than not, the violence was spurred by competition for the companionship of young men or women. When Lupe was dating a zoot suiter who was supposed to have been going steady with one of the Black Widows, the pachuca gang from the Maravilla barrio, the Black Widows crashed her friend's party. "They came in and they jumped me. They were beating me up. They didn't do any damage, they scratched my face a little." The boys soon jumped in, and the "next thing you know, it was a free-for-all."[78] That women zoot suiters participated in fist fights and "free-for-alls" demonstrates yet another way by which they flouted expectations that girls behave in a "ladylike" and submissive manner.

Zoot suiters' violent acts in public formed an important part of their place in home-front society in at least two ways. On the one hand, zoot violence may have justified society's aggressive and negative stance toward nonwhite youth. On the other, through violence, zoot suiters also exerted their own identity, often in the form of very local attachments to place via neighborhood or even street affiliations. In either case, however, violence usually worked to mark them as a threat to the peace and stability of the home front, especially because such activity often occurred in public view.

ZOOT MUSIC, DANCING, AND THE HORIZONS OF PUBLIC SPACE

According to historian Douglas Henry Daniels, the claiming of public space by zoot suiters and jazz enthusiasts in New York City and Los Angeles functioned as a declaration of independence on the streets of the urban United States.[79] From coast to coast, the intertwining of jazz and zoot cultures produced a social milieu that valued difference and the mixing of diverse youth rather than the homogeneity of popular wartime discourse that exalted masculine whiteness and segregation of the racialized other. Whether labeling themselves "Terrific as the Pacific" or "Frantic as the Atlantic," or accentuating that "certain swing that they walked with,"[80] zoot suiters put dignity at the center of their cultural performance and functioned as a community that, as anthropologist Steven Gregory suggests, is best understood "not as a static, place-based social collective but a power-laden field of social relations whose meanings, structures, and frontiers are continually produced, contested, and reworked in relation to a complex range of sociopolitical attachments and antagonisms."[81] In spite of their own geographic separation, zoot suiters formed an imagined community in which "spaces are *localized*—located in a specific place—but unlimited, i.e., without defined limits."[82]

Zoot suiters' ethnic, gender, and class identities were made up, at least in part, of the networks and relationships that grew from borrowing, exchanging, and sharing cultural practices and styles with one another. Although not explicitly concerned with social change or political reform, zoot and jazz cultures functioned, to employ scholar-activist Gustavo Esteva's conception, as a social horizon encompassing "a myriad of personal and communitarian initiatives, shifting and moving away, as do rainbows, with their growing interactions among and between them."[83] The open, uneven, and unorganized character of jazz and the zoot suggests that no one specific political objective or experience connected pachucos and hepcats, but that they were linked through their sharing of the everyday cultural practices and social relationships that stemmed from their race, class, and gender positions in U.S. society. Zoot suiters were able to craft distinct race, gender, and class identities, yet simultaneously transcend such categories of identity by living in the many cultural, social, and economic conjunctures of their diverse communities.

Jazz music helped drive the popularity of the zoot across the country during the early 1940s. The early seeds of what would become the bebop revolution were evident in the dynamic sounds of East Coast swing, black southern blues, and Kansas City big band tunes. While Harlem was the metaphorical home of jazz, the sound and style, including the zoot, were circulated to cities far and wide. Still, it was in Los Angeles and New York that the color line was most often crossed in the music world. In Los Angeles and the rest of California, especially, the popularity of such white musicians as saxophonist Art Pepper and trumpeter Henry James with many Mexican American, African American, and Filipino zoot suiters points to the far-reaching appeal of music. A young Cesar Chavez, for example, experimented with the zoot and jazz long before becoming an icon in the Chicano movement for his work with the United Farm Workers. That he and his fellow Mexican American friends used to travel from Delano to Fresno in Central California to hear the likes of Duke Ellington and Billy Eckstein illustrates the cross-racial appeal of the music.[84]

While a diverse group of youth closely followed the performances of black musicians who played regularly at night spots along Central Avenue and cruised Central to hang out and see the latest fashion styles, the music makers themselves also constituted an ethnic and cultural mix of black, Latino, and white musicians and singers. As historian Anthony Macias demonstrates in his work on 1940s Los Angeles, the city boasted a music scene that was something of a "multi-cultural crucible" growing from the creation and sustenance of "social spaces of urban civility" where diverse youth intermingled.[85] Drawing on influences ranging from black American jazz, Afro-Cuban orchestras, other Afro-Caribbean sounds, and Latin American musical traditions such as Mexican trios, musicians such as Eduardo 'Lalo' Guerrero and Don Tosti and his orchestra manufactured early forms of Latin Jazz, or what Macias calls "society rumba" or "Hollywood Latin."[86] As historian Daniel Widener reminds us, Japanese American drummer Hideo Kawano also gigged at the Club Alabam, that night spot in the heart of LA's African American neighborhood on Central Avenue that was so popular among Mexican American, Filipino, and Japanese American youth. Kawano also played with Mexican American groups and, in later years, sat in on sets with musician and producer Johnny Otis, who, though the son of Greek immigrants, considered himself "black by persuasion."[87]

Well after the end of World War II, in fact, musicians helped spread zoot and pachuco style, illuminating the intersections between the cultural worlds of African American and Mexican American youth.[88] Songs like "Pachuco Boogie" and "La Pachuquilla" could be heard on juke boxes from LA to Tucson and beyond. Originally from El Paso, but having attended Roosevelt High School in Boyle Heights, Edmundo Tostado, or Don Tosti, had a huge hit with "Pachuco Boogie."[89] The song became an anthem among Mexican American youth during the late 1940s, as it showcased the pachuco caló language and glorified zoot style. Recorded on the spot in 1948 by a group of session players that included Raul

Díaz (drums and vocal), Bob Hernandez (saxophone and flute), and Eddie Cano (piano), the song took its cue from the black music scene along Central Avenue and the *danzones* and mambos from Cuba, Mexico, and New York City. Because union musicians were prohibited from recording due to a dispute over radio airplay, the song was recorded under the pseudonym of Cuartero Don Ramon, Sr., the name of Tosti's father. The liner notes by Chuy Varela to the 2002 rereleased version of the song note the African American influence on these young Mexican American musicians: "The music swung with a raw hard sense of improvisation. The sound of the Pachuco Boogie Boys—Raul Díaz scatting like a jazz singer, Hernandez blowing like a Chicano Lester Young, Tosti walking the bass like his hero Jimmy Blanton—demonstrates the affection they had developed for swing and jazz music."[90] The lyrics of "Pachuco Boogie" underscore the value, pride, and dignity many youth derived from the zoot suit style and document the theory that it spread from El Paso to Los Angeles.

Boogie
Que alalva el boogie
Boogie que alalva el boogie
Pachuco boogie
Pachuco boogie
Pachuco boogie

Raul Díaz: Ese, donde la lleva pues?

Don Tosti: Nel ese, pues si no voy ese, vengo del paciente ves. Un laugar que le dicen El Paso, nomas que de alla vienen los pachucos como you eh. Me vine aca al Los Ca ve, Me vine a parar gara porque aqui esta buti de aquella ese. Aqui se pone but alerta todo, ve. Oiga sabe vamos a dar un volteon ese. Vamos y nos ponemos buti tirili, y luego, ay mano pos que suave, Se Venga, porque quiero que me cante . . . quiero que le hago mucho al alva? eh. Orale ese canteme una cancionita ese, nos ponemos buti alterta ese. Canteme, suenele viejo . . . suenele.

[Boogie
get in the groove with the boogie
get in the groove with the boogie
Pachuco boogie
Pachuco boogie
Pachuco boogie

Raul Díaz: Where are you going man?

Don Tosti: No man, I'm not going but coming from El Paso. A place called
El Paso, where pachucos like me come from. I came to LA, see,
I came to show off my clothes because it's very cool. Here everything gets charged up. Come on, let's take a spin, man. Come
on and let's get real high and then, bro, we'll be cool. Come on
because I want you to sing . . . give it a lot of groove, eh? Let's
go, man, sing me a song, we'll get real charged up. Sing it, hit it
man . . . hit it.][91]

Raul Díaz's vocal style in this song was similar to the African American
method of singing described by Cab Calloway: "Scat singing, all that
hi-de-hoing, those zoot suits and wide-brimmed hats, they were all a
way of communicating joy to people. They were a way of telling people
'Listen, I know its rough out there, but drop that heavy load for a while.
Laugh and enjoy yourself. Life is too short for anything else.'"[92]

Several other pachuco songs, such as "Me Estaba Sonado un Frajo"
(I Was Getting Doped Up with a Torch) and "Estaba Rolando un Frajo"
("I Was Rolling a Cigarette"), highlighted in their lyrics the zoot style,
marijuana smoking, and a general rebelliousness. For many pachucos
and pachucas it was the style, not simply drugs and illicit behavior, that
made the zoot and *pachuquismo* worthwhile. Many of the songs demonstrated a daring and assertive masculinity that many young men found
appealing, while yet other songs spoke of love and romance. One in
particular illustrates that, like the music that combined Latin American
and U.S. cultural influences, those who danced to it often came together
across lines of nationality. In "El Bracero and la Pachuca" Dueto Taxco
con Mariachi Caporales del Norte told the story of a Mexican immigrant and a female zoot suiter who met on the dance floor, only to over-
come their cultural differences.

El bracero y la pachuca se fueron a vacilar
y en el baile del sobaco fueron a retozar.
Como eran muy diferentes comenzaron a bailar
y el bracero entusiasmado la comenzo a enamorar:

"Oh mujer del alma mia o amame porque te quiero, o quiereme porque te
    adoro,
porque tu aliento perfuma, linda princesa encantada, como si trajeras rosas
de esas rosas encarnadas que con sus lindas aromas a mi pecho
    cautivaras . . ."
Poesia del Tastarudo

La Pachuca no entendia lo que le quiso decir,
lo miraba y se reia y ella sigio su vasil:
"Ya tireme bute chancla traserito sin sabor,

ya me esta cayendo suna."
La pachuca dijo asi:
"Nel ese, ya parale con sus palabras del alta que por derecho me aguitan ese,
mejor pongase muy alalva con un pistazo de aquella,
y un frajito del fuerte pa' despues poder borrar. Ja . . ."
Poesia del Tirili

Muy prontito se engancharon y suspiraron los dos,
votaron mucho la chancla, y gozaron sin cesar,
orto dia por la manana, cansados de borlotear,
el bracero y la pachuca se tuvieron que amarrar.

[The bracero and the pachuca were out on the town,
and to the dance at "The Armpit" they went to have fun.
Since they were such opposites, they started to dance together,
and the bracero, in his enthusiasm, started to whisper in her ear:

"Oh woman of my soul, love me because I want you,
or want me because I adore you, because your breath perfumes,
beautiful enchanted princess, as if you carried roses,
some of those full-fleshed roses with whose wonderful aromas you captivate
    my heart . . ."
Poetry of Tastarudo

The pachuca didn't understand what the bracero was trying to say,
she looked at him and laughed, and she started to kid him:
"Cut it out and let's dance, you're so square that you're getting on my
    nerves."
So the pachuca said:
"Slow down, man, cut out that high-toned poetry jazz,
you're really bringing me down. You better have a drink and get with it
and then smoke a joint to mellow out. Ha!"
Poetry of the Reefer Man

So right away they got hooked on each other, and they both sighed,
they danced and danced together, and enjoyed the evening without
    stopping.
The next day in the morning, tired from all that partying,
the bracero and the pachuca went and tied the knot.][93]

The phenomenon of the pachuco songs took off in the late 1940s, spreading like wildfire, with songs such as "La Pachuquilla" selling over 60,000 copies. The trend reveals the social interaction among and overlap between diverse youth, including Mexican American musicians. As historian Douglas Henry Daniels suggests, the lyrical content of such songs was quite similar to the themes that popular black artists sang about, echoing the masculine performance of such African American icons as Stagger Lee.[94]

As African American, Cuban, Mexican, and other Latin American musical styles shaped and influenced the expressive culture of many Mexican Americans, so too did the pachuco style in turn influence others. In 1952, for example, African American tenor sax player Chuck Higgins hit it big with his recording of "Pachuko Hop." Like many LA-area black musicians, Higgins had a very strong following in many Mexican American neighborhoods and capitalized on his local stardom by playing numerous gigs in East Los Angeles.[95] The enormous popularity in Los Angeles of Higgins and other local black artists such as Big Jay McNeely and Joe Houston underscored the connection between African American and Mexican American youth who often listened to each other's music, shared their interests in car clubs, and helped create a web of ethnic overlap in Southern California.

The multivalent culture of jazz and the zoot was related directly to what would become bebop by the late 1940s and 1950s—the emerging series of sounds and cultural expressions described by cultural critic Eric Lott as ostentatious in its virtuosity, mobile like the instruments played, and suggestive of a "mocking defiance that made a virtue of isolation." Amiri Baraka has called it the "willfully harsh, anti-assimilationist sound of be-bop."[96] Like bebop, jazz and zoot styles contained a strain of social protest and political challenge that made these cultural expressions a threat to the racial norms of the wartime United States. Commenting on the improvisation required in much of the era's musical performance, Ralph Ellison observed that there were no agreed-upon rules of conduct and no social limits as there were in racial segregation.[97] This was evident, for example, in the popularity of Duke Ellington's anti-racism among a variety of youth, including African Americans, Mexican Americans, and Filipino Americans.[98] The music was also often linked in nonwhite communities with the Double V campaign, as if to suggest that pachucos, hepcats, the zoot, and jazz were part of the U.S. war effort and their practicing of democracy on the home front. At the same time, the music often criticized the war and related protests against it to battles against race discrimination on the home front. Buck Clayton and other jazzmen who met at military camps across the country after they were drafted, for example, created several anti-military songs.[99] Musician Lionel Hampton, though few considered him radical in his political views, captured the challenge put forth by such artistic expression when he said in 1946, "Wherever I see any injustice or any unfair action against my own race or any other minority groups 'Hey Ba Ba Rebop' stimulates the desire to destroy such prejudice and discrimination."[100]

In characterizing bebop as "a politics of style beyond protest" and a moment of struggle in "live and irreverent art," Eric Lott might also have been describing the dancing styles that accompanied jazz and the zoot in the 1940s.[101] While music and fashion were often the most recognized traits of wartime youth culture, the way youth moved and manipulated their bodies on the dance floor further illumined the intricacies of their cultural politics.[102] Historian Robin D. G. Kelley argues that wartime dance halls were zones of pleasure that could negate bourgeois pretensions by rejecting work and celebrating multiple working-class identities.[103]

Dance halls in urban areas like Harlem and LA's Central Avenue district, perhaps more than any other public spaces, enabled African American, Mexican American, other Latino, Asian American, and white youth to experiment with new social, racial, and sexual relationships. By claiming dance halls for themselves, many youth challenged their exclusion from the public's eye, as if to say, "Here we are, look at us; we can do as we wish." The sheer enjoyment youth derived from dancing and the often sexual nature of the act itself helps explain why it was such a popular activity. Lupe, for example, remembers that in LA "the dances were held at different place, different balls. The Sons of Herman was one of the more popular. There must have been half a dozen places that would have them. When we found out the big bands were there, we were there. They were fun."[104] Antonio and his buddies from the Club 21 used to "do a lot dancing" in LA:

> I used to like to dance a lot. So did Joe, my friend, a real good dancer. The whole club used to go, which was quite a few guys. They would all stand, they would all go into the hall. . . . Each group would be in, like on one side of the hall. We would be on that one side [motioning], another group over there, another group here, another group over here. And these guys would tell you to go over on that side and dance with a girl, even if you didn't know her. Yeah, they would say, "Go, go on over there." To see what they would do. And usually the girls would get up and dance. Yeah, I always had pretty good luck.[105]

The male bravado and the viewing of women as sexual property or potential sexual conquests were an appealing draw for many young men and important elements in gender relations at dance halls.

The jitterbug and Lindy Hop departed from more conventional dancing by requiring dance partners to move, twist, and merge their bodies in new ways. The zoot suit itself was, in fact, designed to facilitate such dancing, with the closely tapered cuffs helping to prevent tripping and

Figure 15. White zoot suiters dancing, 1942. Library of Congress, Prints and Photographs Division, FSA/OWI Collection, reproduction no. LC-USW3–010936-D.

the baggy pants and long tails creating a visual extravaganza as dancers moved about. The fluid movements, fast-paced rhythms, and closeness of bodies and the twirls, leaps, and tosses into the air effectively marked zoot dancing as a challenge to standard behavior. Like hip-hoppers and break-dancers of more recent generations, these youth made their bodies move in seemingly impossible ways. As one scholarly dance critic suggests, "Dancing can provide a release from many of the accepted social norms and customs of the 'civilised' social spaces of everyday life, such as social distance, conformity and reserve or disattention."[106] Dancing enabled zoot suiters during World War II to create a space where they controlled how they moved, interacted with one another, and engaged the world around them.

The often interracial and explicitly sexual nature of zoot dancing was not lost on observers. One contemporary noted that when young women danced the jitterbug with skilled male partners, "you could see the whole world" when the guys threw them over their heads, twisting and twirling them high in the air.[107] Malcolm X describes a night of dancing during his zoot days:

> Once I got myself warmed and loosened up, I was snatching partners from among the hundreds of unattached, freelancing girls along the sidelines— almost every one of them could really dance—and I just about went wild! Hamp's band wailing, I was whirling girls so fast their skirts were snapping. Black girls, brownskins, high yellows, even a couple of the white girls there. Boosting them over my hips, my shoulders, into the air. Though I wasn't quite sixteen then, I was tall and rawboned and looked like twenty-one; I was also pretty strong for my age. Circling, tap-dancing, I was underneath them when they landed—doing the "flapping eagle," "the kangaroo" and the "split."[108]

Recalling the zoot dancing scene in Harlem, Perry remarks, "The dancing was just fantastic! And when somebody got going really good, the crowd would just stop and look at them. And sometimes they were white kids! Some [of] those white guys were as good as any of the black guys. Because I can remember some of the white couples could dance as well as the blacks. They were usually Italian! We considered Italians black white guys!"[109]

There was pride at stake in how well one could dance. Perry remembers the competitive nature of dancing and playing music:

> They [other patrons] would crowd around and egg them on. And at that time it was not unusual for it to turn into a kind of contest. That was a neat thing about the music, there were all these contests to see who was the best. Among the pianists it was called "cutting time." And the pianist would get down and play and the other one would try to outplay him. And the crowd would more or less decide who was the best by applause. And this was common. And they would do it with the sax too. Oh man, it was the best![110]

For some, to be a zoot suiter required being able to dance really well. Demanding remarkable athleticism to keep up with the frantically paced music, not to mention endurance and stamina for those who danced several times a week for several hours at a time, dancing was not for the faint of heart.

Just as youth had their own preferences when it came to fashion, there were also different ways to dance. Some historians suggest that improvisation was not valued as much by male Mexican American zoot suiters, who preferred reduced movement to maintain a subdued "coolness" and allow their female dance partners to exhibit more creativity.[111] There were exceptions, however, as youth of all backgrounds performed a variety of dancing styles. Bob, the Mexican American zoot suiter from LA, describes his dancing in ways that evoke the kind of flashy and quick movements that Malcolm X describes. Bob recalls,

> Well, they played the usual standard-type musics and jitterbug and all that. I got acquainted with a girl that I was talking to when I got in a big fight down in Flats. The girls down there they used to go to the dances and the guys from my neighborhood would go, and they taught them how to do the jitterbug, the choo choo, and all that. That was what we did. You had to be a good dancer to step the side step and all that. Bounce back and forth. There's a reason for that, you know. You get the guy, like a snake, used to watching you when you're dancing. You gonna do this every time and all of a sudden, you know![112]

One young African American woman, J. K., who attended Jefferson High School in LA during the late 1930s and did sheet metal work for North American Aviation in 1942–43, used to sneak out to the dances at the navy base in Long Beach on the weekends, where she would dance the night away. "And I'll never forget. I was dancing with this guy Sonny. I could really dance, knew all the latest steps and everything. And this guy was one of these dancers where you pirouette around and I had to keep my foot close to his to keep my balance. We danced and everybody backed off and watched us. So, I really had a lot of fun, socially, even though I had to sneak off."[113] Beatrice Morales Clifton remembers that during the war many young Mexican American and African American women went to more dances, drank more, and attended more live music venues in downtown LA than they had previously.[114] Videll Drake, an African American woman in her late twenties during the early war years who worked for North American Aviation as an installer, recalls that dances at the Dunbar Hotel near all the Central clubs were among the most popular destinations for young nonwhites.[115]

Those who witnessed a dance room filled with young people surely saw bodies sharing rhythmic motions and involved in a sensual, if not sexual, experience. Wartime sociologist Fritz Redl even claimed that the zoot was an important "part of an expressional dance cult" in which participants "perform their dance with tribal fanaticism, with a high degree of absorption and devotion visible in their execution." Resembling an "orgiastic performance," Redl wrote, it qualified as a "grotesque form" of behavior.[116] In her investigative report on zoot culture, *Washington Post* journalist Agnes E. Meyer wrote of zoot dancing, "In some places this orgiastic tendency increased in vehemence and intensity. The original enjoyment of the dance was replaced by an interest in tough guy behavior, in alcoholic excesses, in uninhibited and ostentatious sex behavior."[117]

The sexual behavior of nonwhite youth—not to mention their nightlife, which sometimes included drinking, smoking marijuana, engaging in violence, and gambling—was part of the rebelliousness of wartime youth culture, but it also functioned as a space of social and cultural possibility. As cultural studies scholar Les Back deduces from his ethnography of reggae dance halls in England during the 1990s, dancing held a special power to promote new social relations. According to Back, it was "as if for one brief moment the divisive identities of race and nation were up for grabs. It was a carnival of identity, a place where time and social designation seemed temporarily suspended under the omnipresent groove of the drum and the bass. One could feel things opening up."[118] It is not hard to imagine that something similar unfolded at the Avedon, Orpheum, and Savoy ballrooms in New York and Los Angeles during the early 1940s. When Lupe did the jitterbug with young black males, or young white women flipped and twirled with Malcolm X while doing the Lindy Hop, the dance hall, in the words of Back, was "a place where social divisions [could] be temporarily suspended."[119] These public spaces were redesigned by zoot suiters and jazz musicians as arenas where new forms of identity and community triumphed.

Zoot dancing revealed group affiliations, social attitudes among nonwhite youth, and ways they used their bodies and claimed social space. In the confines of the dance hall, zoot dancing, at least temporarily, broke sexual taboos and eclipsed the social boundaries of Jim Crow segregation. Just as the dignity of zoot suiters was denied by the mainstream press and local officials, however, the dignity of pachucas and female zoot suiters was more than likely denied by their male counterparts who may have objectified them, expected sexual favors, or groped them on the dance floor. When zoot suiters performed deviant sexualities in the dance hall, they confronted the notion that one's sexual identity should be suppressed for the good of the war effort. Their interracial relationships also challenged popular condemnation of miscegenation, rampant concerns about the spread of venereal disease, and efforts to control the behavior of nonwhite youth. The "counter" in the zoot's counterpublic was evident in the ways different zoot suiters imagined and practiced social relations in the wartime United States.

Much of white America deemed the occupation of public space by zoot suiters a threat. According to social critic Howard Odum, who wrote extensively on race relations in the United States during the 1940s, the wearing of zoot style signaled sympathy for race mixing and the liberal social policies of First Lady Eleanor Roosevelt. Rumors abounded, especially in the South, that zoot suiters were a key component in Roosevelt's efforts to secure black and women's rights.[120] In Alabama, according to historian Bruce Tyler, it was rumored that "whenever you saw a Negro wearing a wide-brimmed hat with a feather in it, you knew he was wearing the sign of the Eleanor Club."[121] Other rumors involving race, sex, and patriotism—though perhaps strongest in the South, where some nonwhite enlistees and draftees spent periods of their service— revealed beliefs popular during the war about the mixing of the races. In South Carolina, for example, it was rumored that "when white men go to the Army, the Negro men will have all the white women." In Virginia, it was said, "a Negro made the remark that he had his white girl 'picked out' just as soon as the Negroes take over." An African American in Georgia reportedly said, "Aren't we going to have a time with these white women, when all these white men go off to war!" Another black man allegedly told a white couple, "You'd better be necking now because after the war we'll be doing the necking." An African American in South Carolina reportedly told a white man, "When you come back from the Army, I'll be your brother-in-law."[122] Such rumors indicate that jazz and the zoot in particular, and black masculinity more generally, often challenged black subordination and the subservient roles many white Americans expected African Americans to play. One prominent senator even claimed that "racial amalgamation" could be seen on the streets of New York and all over the United States and that such intermingling would drag down the Caucasian race.[123] As much as sex and race may have become more openly talked about during the war, nonwhites were still blamed for any perceived erosion of social mores.

In addition to challenging popular notions of race and gender, many youth contested the ethic of wartime labor. In his essay on the zoot days of Malcolm X, Robin D. G. Kelley suggests that many zoot suiters refused to allow work to become the primary signifier of their identity.[124] They refused, in other words, to behave like the good proletariat that many of their compatriots expected them to be. The practice of hustling, including the predatory and exploitative business of prostitution, emphasized an indifference to "real" work. Against the disciplined, controlled workplace and bodily movements of ship and aircraft builders, the fluidity of zoot suiters' social movements and their occasional refusal to work created an alternative way of life that did not always contribute to the wartime economy. Many zoot suiters and jazzmen were viewed as leeches living off of their women or, even worse, profiting from illicit and illegal behavior such as pimping. Zoot suiters, furthermore, often mocked the proper channels of moneymaking by valuing both legal and illegal "fast money"–making schemes. Though most zoot suiters were linked by their relationship, or lack thereof, to the means of wartime production, their "working-classness" did not presume their total subjugation to the U.S. economy. The working-class nature of the zoot was as much about the mobilization of available resources for cultural expression and insubordination against work as it was the triumph of wartime capital. The working-class quality of zoot and jazz culture did not hinge solely on its exploitation, but as E. P. Thompson argues, "happened" as part of the struggle of everyday life.[125]

Of course, the politics of the zoot were not as simple as refusing to work, challenging the war, and crafting a radical cultural identity. Zoot suiters had a much more complex relationship to wartime society that included service in the armed forces and working steadily for the war effort. Zoot suiters reflected the reality that many nonwhites were neither fully alienated nor fully assimilated. Zoot suiters also revealed racial identities contingent on the intermingling of and overlap between different ethnic and racial groups. As Malcolm X and countless others like him shed work clothes as a shoe shine boy, soda fountain jerk, or railroad car sandwich peddler for a racy zoot, the public places of Harlem, Los Angeles, and elsewhere became, in the words of scholar Eric Lott, a kind of "magic[al] place, a refuge that lent young musicians, triply alien—migrant, Negro, occupationally suspect—the courage to conquer."[126]

For many nonwhite youth, jazz and the zoot functioned as a subaltern counterpublic that was not fully understood by their contemporaries. Far from being silent, however, zoot suiters mobilized their own bodies and claimed public space to challenge the demeaning and negative discourse about themselves that stemmed from debates over the politics of youth. Zoot and jazz cultures offer a glimpse of a world where ideas about race, sex, and labor were not always regulated by the state, the wartime economy, or the dominant culture and where the possibility of novel social relations existed. Although some might argue that such cultural activity was too disorganized to have much political value, for many nonwhite youth it was a critical part of their lives and their power to find a voice during World War II. Their social behavior and cultural practices were rooted in struggles for dignity and in debates over race, gender, and national identity on the home front. As the war unfolded and calls to support it on the home front intensified, nonwhite youth, and zoot suiters in particular, found themselves at the center of debates about who and what were considered American. In the next chapters, I turn to how seriously the activity of zoot suiters and other nonwhites were taken by the rest of the country. It was not long before the conflict, controversy, and debate over zoot suiters took a more violent turn, erupting in race riots in urban centers across the United States.

PART THREE

Violence and National Belonging on the Home Front

CHAPTER 5

Zoot Violence in Los Angeles

On the evening of June 7, 1943, in Los Angeles, Vicente Morales carefully dressed in one of his tailor-made zoot suits for a night on the town. The young Mexican American teenager planned to dance the night away with his girlfriend to the jazzy sounds of the Lionel Hampton Band at the Orpheum Theater. Midway through the show, however, Morales was accosted by a group of white sailors who, without provocation, began shoving him and screaming obscenity-laced insults. Before long, Morales recalls, "about eight sailors got me outside of the theater and they started beating me up. It happened so fast, I passed out. I woke up with a cracked rib, a broken nose, black and blue all over. I was really beat."[1] After his girlfriend covered him with her coat because his attackers had stripped him of his own clothes, Morales was handcuffed by Los Angeles police, arrested on charges of disturbing the peace, and transported by paddy wagon to a city jail.

Although the reckless brutality and injustice of Morales's experience is appalling, his is not an unfamiliar story to many Mexican Americans and African Americans who lived in Los Angeles during World War II. As Chicana/o historians have demonstrated, hundreds, if not thousands, of young Mexican American men were violently attacked by white servicemen on the streets of LA during the first week of June 1943.[2] Although most of the violence was carried out by white navy, army, and marine personnel, supported by white civilians, the weeklong series of skirmishes came to be known as the Zoot Suit Riots. Countless youth who wore the drape pants and fingertip-length coats were stripped of their clothes, beaten in front of gathering crowds of onlookers, and subsequently arrested for disturbing the peace, vagrancy, and a number of other offenses.

Most previous accounts of the riots have highlighted Mexican American males as victims of the violence, have noted that the riots served as a flash point for the political mobilization of the Mexican American middle class in Los Angeles, and have focused mainly on the role of the mainstream city press in fanning the flames of the attacks.[3] This chapter builds on these interpretations by accounting for the experiences of young Mexican American women such as Morales's girlfriend and the African American, Asian American, and white zoot suiters who were also targets of the rioting servicemen. Although Mexican American males suffered most of the violence, virtually all zoot suiters, regardless of their ethnicity, and many nonwhite youth, regardless of whether they wore zoot suits or not, were subject to attack. This chapter, consequently, explores the Los Angeles Zoot Suit Riots as a multiracial and gendered experience. Rather than view nonwhite youth as mere victims, this chapter, in part by considering the content of rumors among both servicemen and zoot suiters, also understands the riots as part of the ongoing struggle by those youth to maintain control of their own identity and claim dignity. The role of zoot suiters in the riots, to put it another way, cannot be reduced to that of innocent victims or deserving street thugs.

Taking into account the multiracial and gendered character of the riots, along with the perspectives of the nonwhite youth involved, yields fresh interpretations. As previous studies have emphasized, the violence carried out by white servicemen and city residents stemmed in large part from the intensification of wartime xenophobia, concerns over domestic security, and attempts to blackball anyone perceived as not contributing to the war effort.[4] This nationalist rhetoric served as the ideological base for the riots, but also functioned as retaliation against the nonnormative race, gender, and sexual behavior of nonwhite youth. Chapters 3 and 4 explore how nonwhite youth mobilized their own bodies and occupied public space to claim dignity in the face of poverty, discrimination, and dehumanization. This chapter investigates the riots in Los Angeles as one effort by the white mainstream to strip that dignity away again. Nonwhite youth in Los Angeles, zoot suiters in particular, were singled out for their sexual, masculine, and sometimes racially mixed behavior, which challenged wartime social mores. If zoot culture enabled the youth involved to explore the possibilities of wartime identity, the Zoot Suit

Riots were a resounding statement of disapproval of such activity by white servicemen, urban authorities, and the general public.

The Los Angeles Zoot Suit Riots raised critical questions about what and who was considered a legitimate part or member of U.S. society during World War II. In what was a very public ground zero during the first week of June 1943, local authorities, the military, the media, and the public fought over nothing less than who was included in and excluded from the wartime polity.[5] The riots underscored the denial of nonwhite youth from full and equal belonging in the United States in that their experiences and cultural identities did not always easily fit within the dominant ethos of wartime patriotism or even within the efforts of nonwhite communities to accommodate to the war effort. While this chapter examines the violence between zoot suiters and servicemen, it also suggests that the line between the two groups was increasingly blurred. Large numbers of nonwhite youth—including many zoot suiters themselves—entered the service. Joining the army or navy not only provided a way for them to prove they were as American as anyone else but also threatened the equation white servicemen and other Americans maintained between their white racial identity and masculinity on one hand and patriotism on the other. In their angry response to zoot culture, white servicemen and civilians could draw more exclusive boundaries around U.S. identity. The Zoot Suit Riots illustrate that nonwhite youth and their cultural practices were at the center of debates over national identity.

A LONGER HISTORY OF ZOOT SUITER— SERVICEMEN CONFLICT

The tension between zoot suiters and servicemen in the Los Angeles area began well before the Zoot Suit Riots. As early as the mid-1930s, when zoot style was just catching on as popular fashion among nonwhites, fist fights and verbal confrontations on city streets between African American and Mexican American civilian youth and white servicemen were not uncommon. Antonio Alvarez, the former Mexican American zoot suiter, recalls that in the years leading up to the riots, sailors "had it against the zoot suiters real bad in those days. They had it against them real real bad. If they caught you by yourself wearing a zoot suit, they'd kill you, them bastards."[6] Although murder was quite rare, Bob, another Mexican American zoot suiter, recalls the regularity of violent battles in the late 1930s and early 1940s: "At that time I was fourteen, fifteen years old. Oh man, I got in a lot of fights with soldiers and sailors and marines."[7] These recollections underscore the steady and escalating conflict between zoot suiters and servicemen during the early war years, but indicate little about their competing notions of race and masculinity.

Historian Mauricio Mazón suggests that the increasing U.S. involvement in the war and Southern California's role as a civilian and military center on the Pacific Coast contributed to the escalating conflict between servicemen and zoot suiters. Following the bombing of Pearl Harbor, rumors multiplied throughout 1942 and into early 1943 of Japanese attacks targeting the city. Many Angelinos used such threats to rally for home-front unity and worked feverishly to expose the danger posed by Japanese Americans and other fifth-column saboteurs. According to Mazón, it was as if Angelinos were almost proud of the fact that their city was among the most likely to be attacked by the Japanese.[8] One result of the increasing war hysteria was open hostility against those considered subversive of the war effort. Just north of LA, the district attorney of Ventura County made clear who was included in such accusations when he claimed that "zoot suits are an open indication of subversive character."[9] The zoot thus emerged as a symbol of anti-Americanness on the home front.

The confrontation between servicemen and zoot suiters was also fueled by their routine contact around the city. The two groups often encountered one another in such popular areas as downtown and Hollywood and even in East Los Angeles, where sailors and soldiers often sought the companionship of young Mexican American women.[10] In fact, much of the city's military infrastructure, including barracks where enlisted men resided, was located near Mexican American or African American sections of town, including the naval compounds at Chavez Ravine, the naval operations base at San Pedro, army facilities at Fort MacArthur, military installations at Terminal Island, and the coast guard base at Long Beach.[11] When the navy established a massive training school and armory just north of downtown in Chavez Ravine (displacing hundreds of working-class Mexican families who had long lived there), the area between downtown and Chavez Ravine became among the most traveled by servicemen entering the city while on leave. Figueroa Boulevard and Main and Grand streets stretched from Chavez Ravine through the Alpine and Temple neighborhoods and south into downtown, linking the new navy headquarters with one of the main arteries of Mexican settlement in Los Angeles, as well as significant numbers of Italian and central European immigrants who shared the area.[12] With upwards of 50,000 servicemen on leave pouring into Los Angeles nearly every weekend, the Mexican and black neighborhoods that skirted the downtown area served as a meeting ground for civilian youth and servicemen.

During the early war years the military police recorded hundreds of complaints against zoot suiters by servicemen that reveal the contested nature of race and manhood in wartime LA. During the Zoot Suit Riots the commandant's office of the Eleventh Naval District in Southern California compiled complaints from the months and weeks prior to the riots that highlight at least four major themes: the protection of white women, sexuality, military service, and masculinity.

Among the complaints were a number of charges by white sailors that zoot suiters insulted them and their white female companions. In May, for example, two white sailors reported that a close friend of theirs, Miss Shubin, was accosted by several zoot suiters after she hosted the servicemen for dinner one night. After she walked the two sailors to the corner near her house so they might find a ride back to their base, several zoot suiters allegedly grabbed her and started tearing at her blouse. One zoot suiter said to her, "Don't scream or Ill knife you." Miss Shubin did scream, however, which prompted her sister to run to the window of their home, which scared the zoot suiters away. Also in early May, another sailor complained to his superiors that his wife had been accosted by two zoot suiters cruising by in a car as she walked along Chavez Ravine after visiting the sailor at the nearby military base. According to the sailor, the zooters pulled up alongside her, asked her to get in the car, and propositioned her by cursing, "How about a fuck?" The same woman was allegedly cursed at again by a different group of zoot suiters just two days later.[13]

In another complaint, dated May 26, a sailor claimed that a group of zoot suiters drove by his girlfriend and tried to pick her up as she walked along Chavez Ravine on her way to visit him. When she refused, they cursed her and asked if she thought she was too good for them. Just the next day, on May 27, yet another sailor reported that his wife, who worked at Lockheed, was about to board a streetcar on the corner of Whittier and Euclid when a group of zoot suiters insulted her and tried to entice her to join them. The very next night, the same group waited for her as she passed by the same corner on her way home from work. Upon seeing them, she ran screaming until a neighbor came out of his home; he remained with her until her streetcar arrived. According to the sailor, it became necessary for him to have his wife escorted each night, as it was not safe for her to walk the streets or wait for her streetcar alone. Just a few days later, on May 29, another white sailor filed a similar complaint. He and his cousin, along with two girlfriends, were walking down Main Street when the men decided to enter a drugstore to purchase cigarettes. When they exited the store, they found two zoot suiters molesting the women. When a fight ensued, the zoot suiters ran and hid in a nearby pool hall.[14]

The reports filed by sailors accusing zoot suiters of accosting, propositioning, and harassing white women reveal important clues about the interconnectedness of race and gender identities during wartime in Los Angeles. For many servicemen, their whiteness and masculinity were inseparable. Their manhood depended on its whiteness just as their whiteness relied on being manly. Being white and masculine stemmed in large part from protecting the presumed virtuosity of their white mothers, wives, girlfriends, and sisters from the vulgar, hypersexual, and violent threats posed by nonwhite youth. Such white male bravado was intertwined with their patriotism and defined in contrast to the nonwhite, unmanly, and unpatriotic behavior of young African American and Mexican American zoot suiters and the hyperfemininity, sexual purity, and helplessness of white women.

For both the sailors who made such reports to their superiors and the zoot suiters they accused, charges of homosexuality were a common way to question the other's masculinity. In early March, for instance, a sailor reported that he was between 2nd and 3rd streets on Broadway, walking home from the Hollywood Canteen, when a group of men dressed in zoot suits stood on the sidewalk and cursed him as a "fucking Navy bastard" and a "cock-sucker of the first water." In mid-April, two sailors at the Arcade Bowling Alley on Broadway were reportedly accused by a zoot suiter of tripping a lady. While the sailors denied the accusation, the zoot suiter insulted them as "God-damned swab-jockeys" and cursed them in "Mexican," as several other zoot suiters gathered to gang up on the sailors. In another incident, on a Monday night around 11:30 in early May, a sailor was walking in the vicinity of Figueroa and First streets when rocks started landing around him. He soon discovered two zoot suiters standing in a vacant lot throwing stones at him and cursing him as a "cock-sucker and a yellow bastard." On the evening of Friday, May 14, a white sailor encountered a group of six zoot suiters as he left a barbershop at the corner of Figueroa and Sunset. The sailor claimed the group taunted him and ridiculed his uniform by sarcastically saying, "You look pretty good," before cursing him and following him down the street. While another sailor was in the restroom of the Palladium ballroom, three Mexicans in zoot suits approached him, he claimed, and asked him if he joined the navy to stay out of the army. They said they would not join the service until they were drafted and then there would be one "hell of a time" trying to find them. Later in the lobby, the same Mexicans called the sailor all kinds of profane names including "patriotic bastard" and "Uncle Sam's pet cock-sucker."[15]

Insults to their patriotism and decision to serve in the military was another theme in the allegations sailors made against zoot suiters. In the middle of May, for example, a sentry on duty at the Naval Training School encountered a "gang" of zoot suiters passing by his post. From the street, the zooters cursed him, called him all manner of "vile names," including "boy scout," "bastard," and "son of a bitch." A similar incident was reported by a group of sailors on May 17 who claimed six zoot suiters approached them and shouted, "Look at those chicken shit sailors. Fuck those guys." On May 22 another report by sailors contended that several zoot suiters approached a sailor who was in the lobby of the Paramount Theater in Ocean Park smoking a cigarette. When the zoot suiters asked for a light, the sailor lit a match, only to have one of the zooters blow it out and state that he would not light a cigarette from his match. The zoot suiters then condemned him for joining the navy and cursed him until ushers from the theater broke up the confrontation. A week later, on May 29, a white sailor walking through Pershing Square at 10:30 P.M. noticed two zoot suiters start to follow him. Before too long, the sailor reported, they began telling him how rotten the navy was and that navy men were "a bunch of dirty looking sons of bitches." The zooters told him that he was a sucker for being in the navy when there were so "damn many ways to keep out of it." Later the same evening, five zooters standing on a street corner reportedly encountered a sailor in uniform and said, "There is another one of those sons of bitches" and spat at the uniform. Also on May 29, another sailor reported that a group of ten to fifteen Mexican American zoot suiters ran after a group of sailors, throwing rocks at them and cursing them without provocation. The same group of sailors recounted that on May 31, while sitting in the Alpine Café, a man in a zoot suit saw the sailors as he passed by on the street. Shortly thereafter, zoot suiters began arriving in twos and threes until about ten were inside the café and another forty outside. Insulting remarks were made about the sailors and their uniforms, though the servicemen were allowed to leave without being physically molested. Yet another confrontation was detailed by two servicemen who asserted that while they were at the Lincoln Park skating rink, four Mexican Americans in zoot suits came up to them and said, "You had better stay out of this district if you don't want to get your ass cut out of that nice navy uniform and that beautiful pair of bastard pants."[16] Since zoot suiters' versions of these events are not readily available, we cannot be certain of the accuracy of such reports. Still, because insults to military duty was a flash point in the sailor complaints, it is likely that some zoot suiters were voicing an antiwar politics, lashing out at authority figures, or loosely criticizing a home-front society that expected them to serve in the armed forces yet did not afford them first-class citizenship.

Another common theme in the charges made by sailors against zoot suiters was that the latter did not fight fair, often outnumbering servicemen or initiating violence in sneaky ways. Not only did servicemen consider the zoot suiters' allegedly violent behavior, especially their reported penchant for sucker punches and ganging up, as unmanly, but also their views mirrored the stereotype in wartime Los Angeles of the Japanese and other "enemies" of the United States as being fond of sneak attacks. One sailor, for example, reported in early April 1943 that at 10:30 on a Tuesday night, he was threatened with gang violence by zoot suiters at the Tip Toe Inn on Whittier Boulevard. Allegedly, a zoot suiter confronted him, told him it was not healthy for servicemen to eat in the establishment, and said, "If you don't leave now you will be in one fucking mess when you get in town, if you are able to get there after we are through with you." In the same month, another group of sailors was returning to the armory from downtown around midnight when three men dressed in zoot suits approached from the opposite direction and blocked the sidewalk. When the sailors stepped off the sidewalk in order to pass, one of the zoot suiters hit a sailor in the jaw before all three zooters took off running and calling the sailors "suckers." The next month, on May 22, another sailor reported that he was walking along Pershing Square when two zoot suiters walked by and hit him in the eye before yelling "Oh, the Navy!" and running away. Two days later, a group of sailors were walking along Figueroa near Sunset when four men in zoot suits crossed from the opposite side of the street, broke bottles on a garbage can, and approached the sailors menacingly. No attack was made. On May 25, yet another sailor claimed that while he was walking down the street, minding his own business, a group of fifteen zoot suiters ran after him. A few days later on May 30, a sailor reported that while he was drinking a Coca-Cola at the Casino Ball

Room in Ocean Park several men dressed in zoot suits came in and attacked two sailors and a civilian. On May 31, as tensions between the two groups continued to increase, several servicemen were on Main Street headed downtown about 8:30 P.M. when, without any warning, zoot suiters attacked them from all directions, throwing rocks and bottles. A general fight ensued. Some of the zoot suiters launched their rocks and bottles from the tops of buildings, leading one sailor to suffer a broken jaw. All of the sailors eventually fought their way free of the violence and left the scene. Just the next night, as if to further foreshadow the violent events of the weeklong riots to come, a sailor drove in front of a group of zoot suiters near Wilshire and Figueroa and was cursed at. "You God-damned sailors think you own the streets," the zooters allegedly said.[17]

The hundreds of complaints against zoot suiters by sailors and other servicemen during the spring of 1943 stemmed in part, historian Mauricio Mazón theorizes, from the pent-up frustrations of military men who were trained for war and pumped up to fight the enemy yet were stationed or on leave in a city where zoot suiters were identified as subversives. As Los Angeles resident and prominent community organizer Alice McGrath later remarked, "It was [as] though the frustration of not being able to go over and kill Japs, or whatever it was that they [the navy] were building them [sailors] up to, they could go beat up on kids with zoot suits."[18] Both zoot suiters and sailors valued their own race and gender identities at the expense of the other's. For the white sailors, their whiteness, manhood, and sexuality depended on their ability to protect white women from nonwhite men, their military service and patriotism, and their willingness to fight like men. Juxtaposed with the alleged cowardly, vulgar, and weak zoot suiter, their masculinity and whiteness was the epitome of the wartime hero.

Although these reports were made by sailors to naval authorities without any input from zoot suiters and often not recorded until weeks after the alleged incident, they do reveal something about the nonwhite civilian youth involved. Zoot suiters were not simply victims of servicemen, but sometimes initiated conflict, refused to quietly be characterized as second-class citizens, and performed their own race and masculine identities. While white sailors viewed their protection of white women as critical to their manhood, zoot suiters may have seen their potential social interactions with white women as a way of infiltrating, and potentially claiming, the whiteness so central to the wartime identities of many U.S. residents. If imagining and pursuing social relations with white women was one way for nonwhite young men to claim a sense of dignity in a society that outlawed such behavior, they may of course have done so at the expense of white women's dignity. Similarly, if zoot suiters could bolster their own manhood by questioning the sexuality of white servicemen, they simultaneously denigrated the dignity of young Mexican American and African American women, gays, and lesbians. It is also likely that many zoot suiters in Los Angeles were suspicious of servicemen who visited the historically black Central Avenue area or Mexican East Los Angeles seeking the companionship of African American or Mexican American women.[19]

The early months of 1943 also saw an increase in violence carried out by the LAPD, which contributed to racial tension in the city. Since the Sleepy Lagoon case in August of the previous year, the LAPD's reputation in African American and Mexican American communities had steadily declined. During the weeks leading up to the riots, a number of high-profile cases of police aggression occurred involving Mexican Americans and African Americans. In early March, for example, a thirteen-year-old African American boy named Ronald Hudson was shot and killed by police officers when he was caught riding in a stolen car. Hudson's family and much of the black community in LA considered the police action reckless. Reports showed that the bullet that killed Hudson was fired through his eye, despite police claims that they fired at the car as it was being driven away from them. Rumors spread among black Angelinos that Hudson was shot while facing the police and that, despite his record of several minor offenses, he had never shown himself to be a violent threat to the officers.[20] In another incident at the end of March, two young men, one a twenty-three-year-old African American and the other a seventeen-year-old Mexican American, were shot by police after they were allegedly involved in a fight with a third man.[21] In early May, the LAPD was involved in the shooting of a young Mexican American male. After Manuel Rueda, a Mexican American private in the army, reported that he was attacked by four zoot suiters while on leave near San Pedro, the police arrived on the scene and fired shots that injured Alfred Rubio, a twenty-year-old Mexican American who claimed he was not part of the zoot suit quartet.[22] Rueda's initial allegations confirm that the conflict between servicemen and zoot suiters was not always simply racial in nature. The wounding of Rubio further inflamed the Mexican American community's resentment of the LAPD.

At the end of May, the LAPD made headlines yet again when an officer shot and killed thirty-six-year-old African American defense worker

Lenza Smith. The tragedy unfolded after a vehicle driven by Smith struck a parked police car at 2:30 in the afternoon. According to the officer at the scene, Smith claimed he was on his way to kill a man who had stolen twenty dollars from him. When Smith ran toward a house, the officer followed him. After trailing Smith into the house, the officer claimed, Smith threatened his life and, though Smith had no weapon, the officer fired twice at point-blank range. When Smith tried to grab the gun away from the officer, he was shot two more times and stumbled bleeding from the house. He was then transported by ambulance to a local hospital, where he died. Soon after the shooting, a crowd of African American residents from the area gathered around the police car, shouting in protest that a man who had committed no crime should not be shot. As the crowd began to get rowdy, one man snatched the antenna from the police car. When backup LAPD officers arrived on the scene, three African Americans were arrested for inciting riot, a maneuver that quelled the tension, at least for the moment. One of the three arrested was E. Harrison, a deacon at Calvary Baptist Church and a nineteen-year employee of the city's garbage disposal unit. At the police substation where he was held, Harrison claimed, he was beaten and cursed. An officer allegedly told him: "You are one of those smart Eastern niggers. You and the niggers down on Central Avenue are listening to a bunch of Russian communists who are trying to convince you that American white people aren't treating you right. The white man would be treating the Negro right if he would kill all you smart niggers." Following the Smith shooting, the local branch of the NAACP held an emergency meeting to discuss the unstable race relations and violence in the city.[23]

The incident that perhaps most foreshadowed the Zoot Suit Riots occurred in Venice in May, just a week before the rioting began. The Lick Pier and nearby beachfront had become a locus of potential trouble because it was a favorite hangout for both sailors and zoot suiters. During the second weekend in May, a group of Mexican American zoot suiters were dancing at the nearby Aragon Ballroom when a rumor spread that a white sailor had been stabbed. Before too long, despite the efforts of local LAPD officers to quell the unrest, an unruly mob of sailors, white high school students, and other civilians gathered outside the Aragon and attacked the Mexican American youth as they left the dance hall. A group of some five hundred sailors and civilians chased zoot suiters down the boardwalk shouting, among other threats and insults, "Let's get the chili-eating bastards!" The rioters proceeded to beat the Mexican American youth they encountered, and according to one eyewitness cited by historian Edward Escobar, "They didn't care whether the Mexican kids wore zoot suits or not . . . they just wanted Mexicans." Other reports of the incident established that the zoot suiters did not submit weakly to the onslaught but fought back, even attacking police officers. The violence in Venice soon spilled over into Santa Monica and lasted until nearly 2:00 A.M. Even though white servicemen and civilians had been the instigators, police later blamed the Mexican American youth involved. One officer explained the LAPD's reaction: "The sailors and high-school kids got hold of rumors," he stated. "Everybody was upset with jittery emotions wanting to let off steam. So you had a riot, and the zoot suiters were the safety valve. You'll have to admit the only thing we could do to break it up was arrest the Mexican kids."[24]

The trial of eleven of the Mexican American boys arrested during the Venice riot sparked more controversy when the presiding judge in the case, Arthur Guerin, lectured the boys, urging them to join the army as an outlet for their aggression and to serve their country patriotically. Alfred Barela, one of those so admonished by Guerin, and whose experience helps begin this book's introduction, responded to the judge's charges in a letter. Far from meekly accepting the judge's stern disciplining or the LA public's denigration of zoot suiters and Mexican American youth in general, Barela eloquently articulated his struggle with wartime society, questioning why the police who unfairly arrested him did not earn the judge's wrath:

> Why don't you bawl those cops out? How come he [the police officer] said there were twenty-five hundred people in that mob and only a few Mexican kids, but all the arrests were of the Mexican kids and none of the others arrested? Why do cops hate the Mexican kids and push them around? You should see the way the cops searched us for knives and guns as though we were gangsters. They didn't let us call our folks and my ma was plenty worried about what happened to me. You say we've got rights like everybody else. Then how can they do this to us?[25]

There is little doubt that zoot suiters' account of the violence and tension sweeping Los Angeles differed from those of servicemen, police, and the general public—a version of the truth that did not single out nonwhite youth as the source of the problem. In fact, in the weeks leading up to the Zoot Suit Riots, servicemen in the Los Angeles area were reportedly involved in at least eighteen incidents of unlawful violence that did not involve zoot suiters, including events that led to the deaths of seven Angelino civilians in which servicemen were the prime suspects.[26] What is more, the penchant for violence by servicemen was not limited to Los Angeles. In April, for example, white marines and sailors stationed near San Francisco invaded Mexican American and African American neighborhoods in Oakland and assaulted civilians, beating and stripping several zoot suiters.[27]

Racial conflict had also been simmering among California servicemen since a December 1942 riot between black and white sailors in Vallejo. In this case, more than two hundred sailors clashed after a fight broke out between a white and a black sailor and rumors spread that a white marine had stabbed a black sailor. In a move that sparked the rioting, the navy ordered more than one hundred black sailors not to leave a nightclub in order to question them. When the group refused to obey the order, a shore patrolman fired into the crowd, wounding two sailors—Leo Shaw, age eighteen, and George Carpenter, age twenty-six, both black cooks in the navy. After the shooting, fights broke out and grew into a riot that spread through the club and out into the streets. Naval authorities claimed that African American sailors had been planning the outburst for months, alleging that they were angry over favoritism toward whites in their units. Within weeks of the incident the NACCP urged the secretary of the navy to punish all those involved, noting that black sailors were injured by fellow servicemen when the troops charged with keeping the peace turned their guns on the crowd.[28] Although the black sailors wore navy uniforms, not zoot suits, the violence against them in Vallejo underscores again the point that white servicemen's race identity was intertwined with their masculinity and patriotism. For many of them, being white depended on being "manly" and an American, just as being an American or "manly" was contingent on being white. The growing numbers of black and other nonwhite persons in the armed forces, many of whom may have been zoot suiters, encroached upon what many white servicemen may have viewed as a stronghold of white masculine patriotism.

By late May 1943, racial tensions in Southern California had reached an all-time high. Signs multiplied that Los Angeles, in particular, was a racial tinderbox. On Sunday, May 30, a group of zoot suiters fought with eleven sailors in the Mexican American barrio of Alpine. The next night, a group of soldiers and sailors clashed with zoot suiters near Chinatown. When one of the sailors had his jaw broken, a melee ensued with rocks and broken bottles used as weapons. A few days later, just before the riots began, conflict arose again between servicemen and zoot suiters, according to several reports. One sailor reported that he was on liberty with a fellow serviceman crossing Figueroa when they saw four boys and two girls, all Mexicans, with the boys dressed in zoot suits. When they passed the group, the sailors claimed, they were called all manner of vile names, and the zoot suiters raised their hands in the Nazi salute and screamed "Heil Hitler!" Another sailor reported that as he made his way back to the armory with a busload of fellow servicemen, two zoot suiters standing on the corner of Alpine and Figueroa called the sailors "sons of bitches and bastards" without any provocation from the sailors.[29]

The growth of racial tension and the rising number of skirmishes between zoot suiters and servicemen propelled Los Angeles's African American newspaper, the *California Eagle,* to charge in late May that "powerful interests in Los Angeles are desperately attempting to provoke a mass race clash in the city through piling grievance after grievance upon the Negro and Mexican community, on the one hand, and through smearing Mexicans and Negroes as 'zoot suit killers' on the other." In response to such concern, the local chapter of the NAACP sponsored a community meeting to discuss strategies to curb racial conflict and prevent further violence. Held the week before the riots, the meeting drew more than fifteen hundred citizens but was unable to prevent what was to come.[30]

THE ZOOT SUIT RIOTS

Fears of mass violence in Los Angeles were realized on the night of Thursday, June 3. Eleven white sailors walking along Main Street in East Los Angeles were, they later claimed, jumped and beaten by a gang of at least thirty-five zoot suiters. In this predominantly Mexican American neighborhood, Main Street was lined with "ramshackle" houses, a large brewery on one side, and a series of bars, small factories, and boarded-up storefronts on the other. The group of white servicemen suffered only a few minor injuries. LAPD officers responding to the call, many of them off duty at the time, dubbed themselves the Vengeance Squad and arrived at the scene to arrest Mexican American zoot suiters.[31] The next day, more than two hundred sailors hired a caravan of at least twenty taxicabs and set out for East Los Angeles. When sailors in the lead car spotted a young Mexican American in a zoot suit, a signal was sent to the rest of the procession, and the boy was beaten within minutes.[32] Violence against Mexican Americans and African Americans, many wearing zoot suits and others not, continued for the next four days and nights, leading *Time* magazine to declare a few weeks later,

"California's zoot-suit war was a shameful example of what happens to wartime emotions without wartime discipline."[33]

For most of the first day of the violence, many of the city's nonwhite youth were unaware that a riot was under way. Ironically, the same night the violence began, a group of at least thirty-five Mexican American boys from the Alpine neighborhood met with police at the Central Police Station on First Street to discuss strategies to reduce juvenile delinquency and keep Mexican American youth off the streets. During the meeting a report was received from a Mexican American sailor that a group of white sailors was roaming the neighborhood hunting for zoot suiters and seeking revenge for alleged attacks on servicemen. The meeting was prolonged in hopes of preventing an incident, but when the boys left the meeting to go home, many of them were attacked and beaten by the sailors. Residents reported that the group of sailors roamed the streets and theaters, including the Carmen Theater at the corner of Alpine and Figueroa, where they beat and stripped a Mexican American youth in the audience.[34]

In one of the few written testimonies of a zoot suiter, Rudy Sanchez, a young Mexican American who attended the anti-gang meeting with LAPD officers in Alpine, related in a letter the incidents leading up to the beginning of the riots. Several weeks after the riots Sanchez wrote:

> I am writing this letter, in behalf of the so called "zoot suiters." We all got together (the so-called zoot suiters) a few weeks ago. Boys from each neighborhood were present, Lee Chapman a detective, and a few business men around the neighborhood are all helping us to keep out of trouble, by trying to make a club for us (zoot suiters) to keep us out of the street, and we were all for it. We went to four straight meeting's [sic], trying to make some progress, to keep us out of trouble. Everything was going along very nicely in fact there hasn't been a fight between a gang of "zoot suiters" for quite some time. In spite the fact rumors have it that the so-called "zoot suiters" always start everything, meaning all these gang fights that have taken place lately, but its not true, they only fight back to defend there selfs, and that's only natural. Last Thursday we had a meeting at the Central jail on first street between Broadway and Hill, to see what could be done about getting us that club. After the meeting a former "zoot suiter" (now a sailor) came to the meeting to warn us, that about fifty sailors were walking and riding around our neighborhood with sticks, boards, clubs, rocks, and even guns looking for any "zoot suiters" they could find to use their weapons on. When we got back to our neighborhood, (Alpine and Figueroa) we saw a crowd of people in front of our neighborhood theatre (Carmen) we stopped to see what had happened. The girls, boys, ladys, men and manager of the theatre informed us that forty or fifty sailors broke in the show and beat up "zoot suiters," grown up men and even boys as young as twelve and thir-

teen years old. Men and "zoot suiters" getting beat up is pretty bad, in fact
its bad enough like it was before "zoot suiters" fighting each other, but
when the sailors of the United States of America beat up twelve and thirteen
year old kids of the same country just because their Mexicans, you can
imagine how brave they must be. Some of the sailors victims twelve and
thirteen year old kids were taken to hospitals for injuries they suffered at
the hands of the pitiless sailors.[35]

Naval officials had a different understanding of how the riots began.
Lieutenant Charles Bacon wrote in his official report that the trouble on
June 4 all started when an unspecified number of zoot suiters gathered
on Figueroa Street between Alpine and Sunset. When shore patrol officers were dispatched to investigate the situation, they learned that there
had been some conflict between servicemen and zoot suiters in the area
earlier in the evening, and quickly took control of the scene. Enlisted
men returning from leave that same night reported to superiors that they
had heard rumors of fights with zoot suiters and even witnessed a few
confrontations, but no one claimed any firsthand knowledge of the conflicts, though at least one navy man returned to the base with lacera-
tions. It was also reported that when liberty for servicemen expired at
11:00 P.M. that night, an unusually high number were not yet back in
their barracks. Further investigation revealed that large numbers of servicemen and civilians were gathered on Main Street near Second Street
in search of zoot suiters. According to most of the servicemen interrogated, they were responding to rumors that a group of zoot suit men had
jumped some sailors and still held them captive. Although Bacon believed
that "there was very little actual fighting," the recollections of nonmili-
tary residents in Los Angeles dispute this.[36]

The violence soon escalated when white soldiers and marines joined
sailors to cordon off sections of city blocks, raid places of business, and
form posses in an attempt to purge LA's streets of zoot suiters. Former
Mexican American zoot suiter Bob, who lived through and participated
in the riots, recalls the early skirmishes with sailors and soldiers:

One night they [sailors and soldiers] came down [to the neighborhood
around Alpine] and we wondered what the hell was going on. We never
seen [that many] sailors or soldiers down there. So there was three or four
of us that were hanging together, you know, at one of those restaurants
down by the corner with the nightclubs. The bar, that's where all the prostitution happened. . . . It was bad enough that we seen a bunch of white
cats, and we said what the hell's going on? So they go to this restaurant and
somebody comes out and says, "Hey, you guys are Mexicans, you guys better go." "Why?" "They come looking for Mexicans." I says, "Oh, yeah?

Figure 16. Servicemen armed with bats and clubs during Zoot Suit Riots, June 1943. Copyright Bettmann/Corbis.

Well let 'em come. Come on." So as [the sailors and soldiers] are coming out, boom bang boom, you know. There was only about seven or eight of them. There was four of us, but we kicked some good ass, you know. And they left. All that started. That was on a Monday or Tuesday evening. Come Friday, man, five hundred guys coming through there.[37]

For four days, zoot suiters were beaten, stripped of their clothes, and left humiliated in front of gathering crowds of onlookers. Although much of the initial violence occurred in the northern part of downtown between the city's center and the naval training base, Belvedere, Boyle Heights, El Monte, Baldwin Park, Montebello, San Gabriel, and virtually any other neighborhood where Mexican Americans lived were targets for the rioting servicemen. Carey McWilliams later recalled, "They'd [sailors] barge into the downtown theaters, and drag them [zoot suiters] out of the theaters, and work them over, and all that sort of thing. And the zoot suit costume was an incitation to these mobs that were roaming the city. They went on for about a week before it quieted down."[38]

Beatrice Griffith, the Los Angeles writer and social worker, recounted that "it was like the whole of Los Angeles had busted out with riots— Central, Watts, Dogtown, Flats, Happy Valley, Clanton, Hazard, Mariana, Pecam—all different territories had fights at once. Those sailors and soldiers sure got around the Mexican streets."[39] Servicemen made the rounds of the city's dance halls and public meeting places in search of zooters. Soldiers used army jeeps to transport themselves from one scene of rioting to another, while sailors used naval oars to block off streets in hopes of containing zoot suiters. Streetcars were stopped and motormen forced to open the doors as rioters searched for victims. Rioters targeted theaters, where they forced theater managers to turn on the lights, took youth in zoot suits from the audience, and beat them on the streets outside. In its feature article on the riots, *Time* magazine noted that beatings occurred across the city in or in front of the Arcade, Roxy, Cameo, Broadway, Central, and New Million Dollar theaters.[40] In several cases, young men were taken from beside their wives, girlfriends, parents, and even children.[41] Bob remembers that "when we were fighting with the sailors and soldiers in downtown, they were running in the theaters and grabbing any Chicano. But first they used to check you over to see if you had drapes on, and it got to the point where they couldn't find too many of those guys anymore. They were hanging around the neighborhoods, in case we came their way. So, anybody that's Mexican they dragged their ass out there and take your pants off in the middle of Broadway."[42]

Recalling the brutality of the riots many years later during an interview, longtime Los Angeles resident Rose Echeverria Mulligan, who did not consider herself a zoot suiter or pachuca, asked, still in disbelief,

> Did you hear about the riots? That wasn't right . . . because everybody got lumped in (with the zoot suiters). I didn't live there [in the part of town where the rioting occurred], I just heard about it. See, we had a different neighborhood and I heard where the Navy or servicemen came in and attacked. They went into homes and beat up the women. Is that right? I mean, that isn't right. . . . And then that area over there was off limits to them after that. But they were just poor people, I guess, and there was a lot of anger, a lot of anger. My brother told me about that. He was in the service and he had to hear all of that. It's hard.[43]

Another Mexican American youth present at the time simply remembers that "sailors were beating up Chicanos and stripping them of their suits, and the Chicanos were doing the same to the sailors."[44]

Lupe, the former pachuca and zoot suiter, recalled that white service-

Figure 17. Servicemen cruising streets of Los Angeles during Zoot Suit Riots, displaying shreds of clothing from beaten zoot suiters, June 1943. Copyright Bettmann/Corbis.

men "beat up on any Mexican, whether they were young kids or older kids. . . . I remember it because I saw it. To the degree that younger people [Mexican Americans and African Americans] in the streets were hiding behind houses" so as not to be seen by sailors.[45] Lupe says she felt "sorry for those poor guys [zoot suiters]. I think now, if I would have had sons and grandsons at that time and they beat up my kids like that, I'd have been right in there with them. But they'd have to beat me up with them. I wouldn't be fighting with sticks and candles either; I'd be out there with shovels and rakes and whatever I could get my hands on."[46] Maria, a teenager during the riots, remembers how the sailors "picked on the weak" by singling out zoot suiters who were walking on their own and were badly outnumbered, sometimes by as many as fifteen to one.[47]

By June 5, the second night of the riots, Carey McWilliams reported, squads of sailors joined by soldiers and marines paraded through downtown, four abreast, arms linked, stopping anyone whose clothes they did not like and ordering him to change by the following night or else suffer a fate similar to those beaten the night before.[48] In his own eyewitness account, Al Waxman, editor of the *Eastside Journal* and long a sympathizer with the plight of Mexican Americans in Los Angeles, wrote:

> At Twelfth and Central I came upon a scene that will long live in my memory. Police were swinging clubs and servicemen were fighting with civilians. Wholesale arrests were being made by the officers.
>
> Four boys came out of a pool hall. They were wearing the zoot-suits that have become the symbol of a fighting flag. Police ordered them into arrest cars. One refused. He asked: "Why am I being arrested?" The police officer answered with three swift blows of the night-stick across the boy's head and he went down. As he sprawled, he was kicked in the face. Police had difficulty loading his body into the vehicle because he was one legged and wore a wooden limb. Maybe the officer didn't know he was attacking a cripple.
>
> At the next corner a Mexican mother cried out, "Don't take my boy, he did nothing. He's only fifteen years old. Don't take him." She was struck across the jaw with a night-stick and almost dropped the two and a half year old baby that was clinging in her arms. . . .
>
> Rushing back to the east side to make sure that things were quiet here, I came upon a band of servicemen making a systematic tour of East First Street. They had just come out of a cocktail bar where four men were nursing bruises. Three autos loaded with Los Angeles policemen were on the scene but the soldiers were not molested. Farther down the street the men stopped a streetcar, forcing the motorman to open the door, and proceeded to inspect the clothing of the male passengers. "We're looking for zoot-suits to burn," they shouted. Again the police did not interfere. . . . Half a block away . . . I pleaded with the men of the local police substation to put a stop to these activities. "It is a matter for the military police," they said.[49]

In her own fictional account of the riots, Beatrice Griffith imagines what being caught on the streets of LA when the violence started might have been like for two Mexican American zoot suiters:

> It was like the sailors and marines were taking over the whole city. Only now there were soldiers too, yelling with all the gabachos [white people] helping them. They had bottles and belts, clubs and iron pipes in their hands. They were waving them over their heads. We got pushed against the building by the crowd who was looking up the street where there was a lot of shouting and where somebody was getting beaten. The people were filling the streets, packing them from building to building, yelling like they were drunk or crazy. They didn't see us yet cause we had on leather coats and they couldn't see our pants in the mob. The air was full of excitement.[50]

Griffith's protagonists continue to roam the streets of Los Angeles during the riots, hearing sailors call out, "Come on you Pachucos, you yellow bastards, we'll get you . . . all of you," or "Gangway, here comes the Navy. We're hunting for zoot suits to burn!"[51]

Manuel Ruiz, the Mexican American lawyer and LA activist who had long championed the assimilation of Mexican American youth, claimed that his clientele increased dramatically during the riots. "On one occasion," Ruiz recalls, "I got a telephone call . . . from three mothers. Their youngsters were in jail. The police were enforcing a curfew for young Mexican-Americans. I think it was 10:00pm and it concerned the Diana Ballroom on Pico Street in Los Angeles. The Police just drove up with about 15 paddy wagons and paraded everybody out of the ballroom and threw them all in jail. I had, all of a sudden, 150 clients. The charges were for resisting an officer, some for breaching the curfew law, others for unlawful assembly."[52] Ruiz details the beating of one of his zoot suiter clients:

> The story of the Mexican minority in Los Angeles is the story of Pedro Garcia. Pedro Garcia is a senior in Roosevelt High School, the son of Mexican parents, who was born in Los Angeles and thinks of himself as an American. On the 7th of June, 1943, Pedro went to the movies at the RKO on Hill Street. Halfway through the picture, groups of servicemen burst into the theater, yelling for Mexicans. Pedro, who was sitting in an aisle seat, was seized and dragged out onto the street corner. There the sailors who had captured him ripped off his clothes, kicked him, and beat him into unconsciousness. A group of bystanders grinned in excitement as they watched. Several policemen in the crowd looked on, but didn't make a move to interfere. When it was all over, they formed a circle around Pedro until an ambulance arrived to take him to the hospital.[53]

Also on June 7, a mob of soldiers and marines entered the Meralta Theater at the corner of East 1st and St. Louis streets and forced the manager to turn on the house lights. The Hollenbeck Heights Division of the LAPD was less than three hundred feet from the theater, yet, despite the pleas of concerned citizens, the officer in charge refused to dispatch patrolmen to stem the violence.[54]

Mexican Americans in zoot suits were the prime targets of violence by white servicemen, civilians, and police, but others were also attacked, including African Americans, Filipinos, and even some white youth.[55] After the first days of rioting, the NAACP's branch office reported that several African American youth wearing zoot suits had been attacked in the downtown area, with at least four suffering serious injuries.[56] In another instance, Milford Brewer, a twenty-one-year-old African American, and several of his friends were the targets. After celebrating his induction into the army at a farewell beach party, Brewer and several companions, including three women, at least one of whom was white, were stopped by police while on their way to the bus depot to check the

Figure 18. An injured African American man with police in ambulance during
Zoot Suit Riots, June 1943. Copyright Corbis.

schedule for departures to Des Moines, Iowa, where Brewer was to
report for duty. The group was ordered out of their car, searched, and
told to "wait there." Within moments, a group of white soldiers arrived
and stripped the boys of their trousers. The *Amsterdam News* reported
that the violence was "prompted by the presence of a young white
woman" with Brewer.[57]

The *California Eagle* reported that black Angelinos were subject to
violence whether they wore zoots or not. On June 10, just as the riots
subsided, headlines in the *Eagle* included "Zoot Riot Jolts Watts," Watts
being a large African American neighborhood near Central Avenue. The
article included a picture of John Zion, a young black man who was the
son of a Baptist minister and who had been pounced on, beaten, kicked,
and cursed at 2:00 on Sunday morning by white servicemen. His lip had
required stitches. The caption of the accompanying photo of Zion simply read "Dragged from show." Reporting that the rioting had skirted
African American communities for several days, the *Eagle* noted that

"telephone reports from Watts last night picture a seething riot scene as Negroes, Mexicans, and servicemen engaged in bloody fisticuffs through streets." The *Eagle* further noted that the corner of Central Avenue and 12th Street was a particular hot spot for battles between groups of non-white youth, bands of roving servicemen, and city police.[58]

In what is considered the most serious injury of the riots, Lewis Jackson, a twenty-three-year-old black defense worker, was attacked by a mob of sailors and soldiers on Monday during the riots. Jackson was stabbed and gouged in the eye with a knife after he was engulfed in the street by a mob of up to two hundred rioters. A recent migrant from Louisiana, Jackson was employed in the shipyards and was not even wearing a zoot suit at the time of his attack.[59] While initial reports conjectured that servicemen rioters stopped at the edge of the black district for fear of possible retaliation before heading back to the Mexican East Side, reports from the *Eagle* suggest that the African American population in Los Angeles was also under attack.[60]

As the beating of Lewis Jackson makes clear, riot targets included those not dressed in full zoot garb. At the time, Carey McWilliams estimated that only half of the victims wore zoot suits.[61] Maria, who was eighteen years old in 1943, recalls that after the second or third day of violence, any Mexican American youth became fair game, regardless of the degree of his zoot style. "They [sailors] got the boys in our neighborhood," she remembers, "and they weren't even the real heavy-duty pachucos. They were moderate and they got beat up!"[62]

Neither was everyone attacked a Mexican American or African American. Reports also indicate that several white zoot suiters came under assault from servicemen.[63] The young white men who lived in black or Mexican areas, had Mexican American or African American friends, and were culturally part of such groups were also attacked. *Time* magazine reported in its June 21 edition, for example, the beating of a seventeen-year-old Russian boy, Pete Nogikoss, by sailors who saw him talking with two Mexican American zoot suiters on a street corner. The Los Angeles branch of the NAACP also reported that on June 10 a group of sailors beat up a white boy wearing a zoot suit in front of the Paramount Theater at the corner of 43rd Street and Broadway.[64]

That sailors and soldiers included black and white zoot suiters in their attacks, as well as non–zoot suiters, is of no small significance. White servicemen rioters may have been defending their own whiteness, masculinity, and patriotism against public performances of nonwhiteness by zoot suiters. Their tirades against black and white youth, how-

ever, suggest that they associated more than a single race or ethnic identity with the zoot's subversive qualities. It is quite possible that the riots
may, at least in part, represent a response to the multiracial ways that
zoot suiters mobilized their bodies and occupied public space. Attacks
on white zoot suiters further suggest that the rioting servicemen did not
see race in monolithic black, brown, and white terms, but rather in varying degrees of each. The white zoot suiters attacked were not quite white
enough, or perhaps too black or too brown, to be spared. The servicemen may have seen them as race traitors or foreign to U.S. whiteness, as
many of them hailed from Eastern European immigrant communities,
some of which shared residential districts with Mexican American and
African American Angelinos.

Of course, the racial identities exhibited by servicemen and zoot suiters were related in complex ways to their ideas of gender, sexuality, and
patriotism. While the gendered and sexual nature of the riots was evident in the myriad male-to-male interactions that occurred, the role of
young women is also worth noting. Young Mexican American women,
in particular, actively participated in the riots. Although they were not
targeted to the degree that their male counterparts were, young women
did endure physical harassment. One Mexican American girl who was
thirteen at the time, remembers, "My best friend was attacked by some
white sailors. They asked her if she had been in Tijuana the week before
with them. Four of them grabbed her. I was the only one she told."[65] In
her fictionalized version of the riots based loosely on her personal observations, author Beatrice Griffith notes that young Mexican American
women did not escape the attention of the crowds that gathered to watch
the beatings of male zooters. When the clothes of a male zooter were
passed through a mob after he had been beaten, Griffith writes, "a
blonde girl near us jumped and caught the tan coat that went sailing by.
She grabbed it, then she squirmed until she got it on. She danced around
in a circle yelling, 'I'm a Pachuca, I'm a Pachuca.' She was laughing and
kissing the sailor next to her like she was nuts."[66] Griffith also describes
a meeting between several young men and women at the home of a
Mexican family during the initial stages of the riots:

> Pretty soon you heard the sound of breaking bottles and a lot of yells down
> the street. Ernestina looked out the window and yelled, "Here they come.
> They're coming in here!" And in that minute in rushes a whole gang of
> sailors and marines with bottles and belts and sticks.
>   One little guy, drunk and yelling names, busted into the door, called
> out, "Any zoot suiters live here?" When he saw us guys and the girls in

the room he stopped a minute, then he yelled, "Here's a mess of 'em. Come on guys, come and get 'em." The fight was on. From the door in the kitchen my mother call [*sic*] them in English, "You disgrace your uniform . . . verguenza . . . verguenza . . . shame . . . these boys have done you nothing."

But one of the sailors yelled her back, "Ah dummy up. If you weren't a lady we'd do the same to you. These guys raped our wives!"[67]

A number of observers blamed the violence on competition for young women between male zooters and sailors. Pachucas, it was rumored, appealed to servicemen and thus were jealously guarded by many Mexican American boys, much as white servicemen thought zoot suiters threatened white women.[68] In this scenario, Mexican American women were viewed less as active participants in zoot suit culture and wartime society than as sexual property. This sexual tension was observed by African American writer Chester Himes, who recounted in an article for the *Crisis* a conversation he overheard on a Central Avenue streetcar. When three drunken white sailors bragged about their prowess as fighting men, he heard them say, "Ah'm tellin' yuh, Ah fought lak a white man!" When a young Mexican woman boarded the car at the next stop, the sailor leered at her and bellowed, "Boy, did those native gals go fuh us." The sailor continued bragging that "uh white man can get any gal he wants" and asked those around him "Can't he, boy, can't he git 'em if he wants 'em?" Himes, noting other instances when white servicemen attempted to pick up Mexican American girls, observed, "We hate to think of what might have happened to a darker-skinned Mexican in a white bar in a white district, trying to pick up a white girl."[69]

Unlike Himes, however, others blamed the Mexican American girls themselves. In a nationally syndicated article in *Newsweek,* for instance, it was noted that "a sailor with a pocketful of money has always been fair game for loose women and the girls of the Los Angeles Mexican quarter were no exception."[70] LA County supervisor John Anson Ford also faulted the presence of young Mexican American women for the outbreak of the riots. Servicemen looked upon their stay in LA as a sort of last fling before being shipped overseas, he claimed, and so "they went up and down the streets of the downtown area . . . and painted the town red." Because "some of the boys in uniform were very much taken with some of the Mexican girls, because of their pretty ways and faces, this resulted in conflicts with some of the Mexican American boys. The result was that some fierce fistfights occurred. Then the thing snowballed into really what eventually became know as the Zoot Suit Riots."[71]

Others also saw the conflict over young Mexican American women as critical to the onset of the violence. Los Angeles mayor Fletcher Bowron suggested that "the so-called 'zoot suit' riots resulted from sporadic street fighting, which in turn resulted from individual fights between sailors and young Mexicans over girls."[72] Alice McGrath, one of the main organizers of the Sleepy Lagoon Defense Committee, argued that white sailors regularly went looking for Mexican and black girls because they thought they were "easy" and that this led to fights with zoot suiters.[73] Even one former pachuca, Lupe, remembers that although she met many servicemen downtown who were respectful of her and her friends, the reputation of Mexican girls among many sailors and soldiers was that they were "loose" and "wild." They were considered "fair game" by military men, who often harassed and insulted them on the streets, in clubs, and in restaurants.[74]

Rumors of rape also circulated among zoot suiters and servicemen, helping to fuel the hysteria and the violence of one group against the other. According to Bob, the rumor of a zoot suiter having raped a white woman helped spark the violence. "Well, from what I understand," he says, "there was a rape case. There was some guy who was really a real nasty type guy, you know. Real rough, tattoos, and drapes and all that. The kind [of drapes] you had to use the zipper to get out, you had to unzip your pants to get them off. That's what I heard."[75] Such rumors support historian Kevin Starr's contention that sexual tension led to the Zoot Suit Riots, and historian Marilynn Johnson's argument (discussed in chapter 6) that gendered and sexual rumors often circulated during the initial stages of urban race riots across much of the United States during the summer of 1943.[76]

Rumors of another enemy attack on U.S. territory after Pearl Harbor, particularly in Los Angeles and along the Pacific Coast, also fueled the backlash against zoot suiters because they were considered subversive to the war effort. The animosity against zoot suiters grew from rumors spread by the press and general public that zoot suiters were active members in a network of fifth-column *sinarchistas* working on behalf of Hitler's master plan to disrupt the unity of the U.S. home front.[77] Although no evidence supports such claims, the rumors nonetheless indicate that zoot suiters and nonwhite youth in general were labeled enemies of the U.S. state. While the notion that zoot suiters were fascist agents helps explain the servicemen's violence against them, the theory also serves as an apology for their unruly, undisciplined, racist, and violent behavior.

The wartime hysteria in Los Angeles makes more sense as an impetus toward the riots when it is considered in relation to other causes, including the structural conditions in the city. Several local officials cited the economic position occupied by nonwhite youth as a prime factor in their discontent and alleged hatred of servicemen. County Supervisor Ford wrote in a June 9 letter to Nelson Rockefeller: "The cause or causes of these outbreaks are somewhat difficult to define. Basically there is the long smoldering restlessness due to racial friction and economic inferiority on the part of many Mexican youth."[78] Similarly, in an editorial published the week after the riots ended, the *California Eagle* asserted that although African American and Mexican American youth might be criticized for their role in the violence, it should be recognized that "slums manufacture delinquency" and that poor housing conditions and lack of recreational facilities resulted in problems regardless of race, ethnicity, or the kind of clothes one wore.[79] A report by a civilian group charged with investigating the riots noted emphatically the lack of adequate housing and recreational facilities for the city's black population, as well as two other "irritants" for African Americans in Los Angeles: an increasing recognition that the armed forces relegated blacks to low-level positions and refused to protect them from civilian violence, and that city officials were pushing to stop black migration into the city, an apparent violation of constitutional rights.[80] Class friction, though its recognition often led to the mistaken assumption that nonwhite youth, not white servicemen, were the primary perpetrators of violence, was nonetheless a key factor in the long-standing conflict between zoot suiters and servicemen.

The economic and social causes of the riots were exacerbated by the role of the mainstream Los Angeles press. Many of the city's progressive political activists, including Carey McWilliams and Alice McGrath, argued that the press, especially the Hearst-owned *Examiner,* had helped conjure up an imaginary threat of zoot suit youth disrupting home-front stability. Even LAPD chief C. B. Horrall blamed the press for instigating the riots and publicizing zoot gangs. Horrall's criticism was also a thinly veiled attack on zoot suiters themselves, who, he claimed, rioted only to get their pictures in the paper.[81] While mainstream press coverage certainly fanned the flames of the zoot suiters–servicemen conflict and enhanced public anxiety once the riots began, it was only one factor that caused the violence.

Ultimately, the Zoot Suit Riots were the result of a myriad of political, economic, and social factors that underscored the racial, gender, and sexual conflicts between zoot suiters and servicemen and consistently marked zoot suiters as a threat to the safety of the general public. The angry and violent behavior toward zoot suiters, however, was not just a matter of conditions and attitudes external to nonwhite youth. The riots were also a direct response by white servicemen, local authorities, the mainstream press, and the general public to the challenges posed by zoot suiters' unorthodox social mores. The multiracial nature of zoot culture, its valuation of different masculine identities, and the propensity of some zoot suiters to value leisure over much-needed wartime labor all helped provoke the violence. Moreover, because so many young nonwhites, including many zoot suiters, did join the military, white servicemen rioters may have felt they were defending the armed forces as a kind of last bastion of whiteness, masculinity, and patriotism. In the end, the conflict between zoot suiters and servicemen was largely about drawing the boundaries of the national polity during wartime. On the one hand, zoot suiters made a case, whether conscious or not, that national belonging and cultural citizenship should be broader, more flexible, and more inclusive. White servicemen, on the other hand, proposed narrower, more rigid, and more exclusive criteria for considering who was an equal member of wartime society.

LOS ANGELES RESPONDS TO THE RIOTS

The LAPD generally supported the rioting servicemen's actions. In a letter to Martin Popper of the National Lawyer's Guild dated June 9, 1943, Carey McWilliams claimed that "the evidence clearly indicates that the police stood by laughing and kidding while the mob beat, insulted, and humiliated every Mexican boy they could lay their hands on (including also Negro youngsters)."[82] Chester Himes observed that police often waited until after zoot suiters were beaten and stripped to intervene, only to arrest the zoot suiters for disturbing the peace or for vagrancy.[83] The hands-off policy of the LAPD may have also stemmed in part from sympathies many officers had with servicemen because many of them were veterans of World War I.[84] Seeing police officers in cars and on motorcycles accompany taxis full of servicemen looking for zoot suiters through the streets of East Los Angeles, McWilliams remarked sarcastically, "It's strange that in L.A. with one of the most efficiently equipped police systems, for tracing such disasters as stolen cars, the police were apparently unable to keep track of a caravan of twenty automobiles loaded with over two hundred uniformed men." Despite the arrest of

Figure 19. Mexican American zoot suiters chained together, waiting to board sheriff's bus after Zoot Suit Riots, June 1943. Copyright Corbis.

hundreds of zoot suiters during the riots, the LAPD took only a few sailors into custody before turning them over to the shore patrol.[85]

Maria remembers that "instead of arresting the sailors, they [LAPD officers] helped kick them [Mexican American and African American zoot suiters] around! The cops were even leading them [sailors] to the areas they could find them [zoot suiters]."[86] Another Mexican American teenager at the time, Lupe, states simply that the police "allowed them [sailors] to do it."[87] Such protocol left many Mexican Americans and African Americans in a no-win situation. As Maria recounts,

> Who could you complain to? When the police themselves were beating you up and kicking you around! Who are you going to complain to? They'd deny it. I seen kids taken out of a theater for throwing popcorn in the show, which every kid does at sometime or another. They took 'em out of the

show and took them to the police station and then later on that night they
dropped them off all bloody. This was in East LA at one theater. They
dropped the kid off all beat up. You think the parents are gonna complain?
There are ways of thinking that the police are always right, that they were
just there for our good. The kids knew they weren't. They were there for
their own good.[88]

Mexican American lawyer Manuel Ruiz recalls that rumors abounded
of police brutality during the riots. "Through the grapevines," he recalls
hearing that "there were some of them [zoot suiters] that allegedly committed suicide in jail and things like that. Of course at that time we
didn't have the monitoring systems that exist at the present time."[89] The
number of zoot suiters who committed suicide or were killed or beaten
in police custody during the riots is impossible to ascertain. What is
clear, however, is that the LAPD was not interested in protecting Mexican American or African American youth from the violent onslaught of
servicemen and civilians.

Military authorities also did little to prevent servicemen from continuing their foray through the streets of LA. As in his analysis of the
LAPD, Carey McWilliams noted that the shore patrol was unable to
locate hundreds of sailors rioting throughout the city and only symbolically arrested a few of them once they returned to base camp at Chavez
Ravine.[90] Initially, in fact, the shore patrol and military police hesitated
to restrict any movement of servicemen through the city. Public calls for
more decisive military action came from Carey McWilliams and such
other Angelino activists as Josefina Fierro de Bright, who was one of
the primary organizers of El Congreso del Puebla de Habla Española
(Spanish-Speaking Congress) and traveled to Washington, D.C., during
the riots to urge the Roosevelt administration to help quell them. But
these requests had no effect.[91] After four full days of rioting, naval officials finally announced the city as a restricted area for enlisted men. The
army quickly followed suit. In its official statement announcing the ban,
the navy described its sailors as defending themselves against the city's
"rowdy element."[92] Despite the restrictions, however, mob violence in
the city, involving many servicemen on leave, continued for another two
days and nights. The navy showed little desire to stem the violence
against nonwhite youth and refused to seriously punish sailors for their
behavior. Perhaps for fear of exposing an inability to control its enlisted
men or because superiors shared the condemnation of zoot suiters, the
navy suggested, rather than ordered, measures that would bring a
quicker end to the violence. LA County supervisor Ford claimed that the

military's refusal to close downtown to military personnel may have been prompted by city entrepreneurs who depended heavily on the dollars spent by servicemen on leave and did not want them outlawed from shopping and entertainment districts. Regardless, in what amounted to what historian Rudolfo Acuña calls a low-profile cover-up, the navy's internal memos show that top officials did not view violence against zoot suiters as a serious charge against uniformed men.[93]

It is no surprise that most city and county officials supported the actions of area servicemen and the LAPD. Mayor Fletcher Bowron publicly legitimized the police and military, discounted race discrimination as a factor in the uprising, and blamed the disturbances on the activities of local gangs. Despite the role that LAPD officers had played in permitting and even promoting violence, Bowron commended Police Chief Horrall for his unit's emphasis on "acts and conduct, not citizenship, color, or location in city or parentage of persons" when making arrests.[94] The mayor adamantly denied that race had played any role in the riots. In fact, he argued, there was "no substantial anti-Mexican feeling and . . . all those involved have been treated alike, regardless of race, color, or creed."[95] To avoid having his city pegged as a caldron of racial strife, Bowron insisted that "there is no question of racial discrimination involved" in the riots or their aftermath.[96]

Despite this contention, Bowron blamed the outbreak of rioting on youthful gangs of Mexicans who displayed a "lack of restraint and discipline" and on Mexican American girls who promoted fights between sailor and zoot suiters.[97] In an ironic public statement the week of the riots, Bowron argued that "there are too many citizens in this community, some of them good intentioned and a few whose intentions I question, who raise a hue and cry of racial discrimination or prejudice against a minority group every time the Los Angeles Police make arrests of members of gangs or groups working in unison." He concluded, "They all look alike to us, regardless of the color and length of their coats."[98] Bowron further claimed that the riots were "a bad situation as the result of the formation and activities of youthful gangs, the members of which, probably to the extent of 98 percent or more, were born right here in Los Angeles."[99] According to the mayor, it was the gang members, not the servicemen, who were to blame for "some very disgraceful and regrettable scenes on the public streets and in cafes and theaters in L.A."[100]

Such thinking concluded that zoot suiters were to blame for the riots and supported city and military authorities whose job it was to protect the city's law-abiding citizens from such dastardly threats. Bowron defended the sailors in the aftermath of the riots. "We are going to see that members of the armed forces are not attacked," he said. "If young men of Mexican parentage or if colored boys are involved it is regrettable, but no one has immunity and whoever are the disturbers are going to be sternly dealt with, regardless of the protests of the sentimentalists and those who seemingly want to throw so much protection around the disturbing element in the community that good citizens cannot receive proper protection."[101] Bowron's condemnation of servicemen's involvement in the riots had a significantly lighter tone. He maintained that military police, not city police, should bear responsibility for disciplining any uniformed men who might have acted out of line. Bowron claimed in essence that the city expected "cooperation from officers of the Army and Navy to the extent that soldiers and sailors do not pile into Los Angeles for the purpose of excitement and adventure and what they might consider a little fun by beating up young men whose appearance they do not like."[102]

Although he publicly blamed zoot suiters and supported the military police and shore patrol's efforts to curb the violence, however, Bowron privately blamed military officials for not doing enough to control their men. This may have been a ploy to divert attention from the well-publicized charges that city police refused to arrest sailors and soldiers during the riots and aided their efforts. Nonetheless, in a letter to police chief Horrall, Bowron wrote that "criticism of the Navy Shore Patrol might be conveyed . . . by showing that it has been the practice and understanding that the MP will take care of soldiers and the Shore Patrol will look after sailors." He further believed that "while we cannot disclaim all responsibility for acts of violence in which sailors were involved, necessarily police officers could not be on the scene wherever a fight occurred, and it was very difficult, if not impossible, to identify sailors, and therefore few, if any arrests of sailors were made by police officers."[103]

Whether Bowron intended to pass the buck to military authorities or not, he was acutely aware that his response to the riots would influence local, regional, national, and even international politics. Downplaying race as a factor in the riots was certainly meant to appease federal authorities who were concerned that the riots threatened the nation's Good Neighbor policy with Latin America, particularly Mexico.[104] Unity among the Americas was considered critical to the Allied victory over Hitler, Mussolini, and the Japanese. In the aftermath of the riots,

Bowron clashed with Alan Cranston, appointed by the Office of War Information (OWI) to investigate the riots. Cranston, who had also investigated the Sleepy Lagoon case the previous year, allied himself with several Mexican American activists who claimed that an anti-Mexican sentiment permeated both the riots and the city's response. In reaction, Bowron dispatched a letter to Elmer Davis of the OWI. The mayor wrote that it would have been easy for Cranston to secure accurate information from official city resources, but he mistakenly joined a group "composed of a few good citizens, some wholly impractical social workers, some young attorneys who like to get publicity to further their professional careers, and a few others who do not enjoy a good reputation in this community."[105] Bowron's underlying charge was that to declare that the riots had targeted persons of Mexican descent harmed U.S. foreign policy. Bowron warned that such inaccurate reports would result in "irreparable damages to the city of Los Angeles" and "probably some misunderstanding created on the part of the Mexican officials."[106] Bowron confided to LAPD chief Horrall that he wanted to tell the State Department that

> no Mexican citizen was arrested by the police department, that, so far as the police department can determine, no Mexican citizen was set upon by sailors, soldiers, or civilians, . . . that not only in connection with the recent outbreaks, but in connections with the handling of the entire zoot suit matter and youthful gangs, instructions had been given to all police officers that racial discrimination would not be tolerated and that any action the police officer in any arrest should be without reference to race, color or creed, that the Police Department has been careful to fully protect the rights of Mexican citizens, that it is unfortunate that many local young men of Mexican blood have been arrested but it is at the same time regrettable that young men of Mexican blood have violated the law. The Police Department has merely attempted to enforce the law and keep the peace and this requires vigorous action because of the nature of the activities of the young hoodlums involved.[107]

Ironically, Bowron's insistence on claiming no Mexican citizens' rights had been violated during the riots implicitly recognized those zoot suiters who had been attacked as full-fledged U.S. citizens, deserving equal membership in U.S. society. In late June, Bowron publicly conveyed as much when, in a speech at the downtown Biltmore Hotel welcoming the secretary of the navy to the city, he asserted that in Los Angeles "we have some good people and true to make up our population, exclusive of zoot suiters, we now have close to 1.75 million."[108] Despite their political posturing to the contrary, city officials viewed zoot suiters as outsiders, not part of the local Los Angeles, or broader national, community.

While Bowron tried to smooth over the explosive racial nature of the riots, not everyone was so subtle. Just as the riots began, G. M. Montgomery, the principal of Dorsey High School in Los Angeles, stated in a schoolwide assembly, "I don't want any of that low zoot suit stuff from the Eastside on this campus."[109] The Los Angeles City Council followed suit when it considered a proposal making it a jailable offense to wear "zoot suits with reat pleats" within city limits. Supporters of the proposal argued that police had lost control of the riot situation, that zoot suit "hoodlums" now had the cops "buffaloed," and that it was up to the city government to limit any further disturbances.[110] Though the proposal was not officially passed, it helped set the stage for further anti-zoot action. In the first measure of its kind, for instance, the U.S. Department of Justice outlawed the manufacture and sale of zoot suits on the grounds that the material used was unlawfully cut and in violation of orders to conserve fabric by the War Production Board.[111]

The immediate response of county officials following the riots also downplayed the racial tension and seriousness of the violence. In his assessment of the riots, Los Angeles County supervisor John Anson Ford stated that "some of this lawlessness was little more than college hazing carried on on a large scale, yet some of it inevitably produced retaliation and did serious bodily harm."[112] Like Bowron, Ford wanted to avoid negative publicity that might reflect poorly on Los Angeles, undermine U.S. foreign relations, or imperil local government's relationship with state and federal leaders. On June 8 Ford stated: "While deeply deploring these outbreaks, the board of supervisors wishes to record its conviction that a generally cordial relation exists between residents of Anglo and Latin ancestry, many of whom have lived side by side for years, as have their parents before them. We do not believe that recent lawless outbreaks in any way indicates any change in that basic cordial and friendly relationship." Responding to observations by the progressive press and even First Lady Eleanor Roosevelt that race had, in fact, played a role in the riots, Ford said that "while racial aspects of the current disturbance have been emphasized, we believe that this situation is primarily arising from restlessness of youth in war time." Ultimately, Ford hoped the county would not only "restore order in a just manner, but . . . aid in reassuring our neighboring Latin American countries of our sincere esteem and deep desire to treat them as Allies and neighbors."[113] Further evidence of Ford's concern with the Good Neighbor policy lies in correspondence with his nephew, James B. Ford, a lieutenant and assistant naval attaché stationed at the American embassy in Guatemala City, Guatemala. In August 1943 Supervisor Ford, as he often did, quoted his nephew from a letter James had sent: "The Los Angeles zoot suit riots and the Detroit affair [which had occurred earlier that summer] made a very strong and unfortunate impression down here [in Latin America] and they are both to be very much regretted."[114] The supervisor further argued that the "deplorable" zoot suit situation brought to the fore the important activities of many private citizens and public officials who were trying to ameliorate interracial tension with Latin America.[115]

Given time to reflect on the riots, however, Ford altered his analysis. Not quite a year later, in March 1944, Ford explicitly identified race as a factor in the uprising. The riots, he now argued, were "prompted in part by typical racial antipathies and in part by special circumstances," including the "youthful desire of boys on newly acquiring uniforms to assert their military status. Likewise, the young lads of both Negro and Mexican ancestry, wearing zoot suits, undoubtedly felt the urge aggressively to emphasize they belong to racial minorities" to compensate for an inferiority complex. "Among them too," Ford added, "have been many whose very inadequate training in childhood has made them lawless and others very vicious."[116] Ultimately, the county supervisor highlighted competing notions of masculinity, race, and national identity as prime reasons that the violence occurred.

The response of California state authorities was a bit different from those of local officials. In a letter to U.S. attorney general Francis Biddle several months after the riots, Governor Earl Warren blamed the LA-area press for overdramatizing the threat of zoot suit gangs and implicated the LAPD for being "derelict in their duty in failing to stop the rioting promptly."[117] The governor's citizen committee, appointed to investigate the riots and chaired by the auxiliary bishop of Los Angeles, Joseph T. McGucken, demanded "that crimes of violence be brought to justice, and the guilty must be punished regardless of what clothes they wear—whether they be zoot suits, police, army or Navy uniforms. The streets of Los Angeles must be made safe for servicemen as well as civilians, regardless of national origin."[118] McGucken's committee asserted, "The wearers of zoot suits are not necessarily persons of Mexican descent, criminals, or juveniles. Many young people today wear zoot suits. It is a mistake in fact and an aggravating practice to link the phrase 'zoot suit' with the report of a crime. Repeated reports of this character tend to inflame public opinion on false premises and excite further outbreaks."[119] The committee further condemned the LAPD, arguing that "mass arrests, drag-net raids and other wholesale classifications of groups of people are based on false premises and tend to aggravate the situation."[120] Concluding its report in direct opposition to the statements of local officials, the committee emphasized that "it is significant that most of the persons mistreated during the recent incidents in Los Angeles were either persons of Mexican descent or Negroes. In undertaking to deal with the cause of these outbreaks, the existence of race prejudice cannot be ignored."[121]

The analysis of the governor's committee, however, was overshadowed by coverage of the riots in the popular press. Throughout the week of rioting, the mainstream press condoned physical violence, supported the actions of city police and servicemen, and spewed culturally violent propaganda against nonwhite youth.[122] Building on months of sensational criminalization of Mexican American and African American youth as zoot suiting punks, the press supported the actions of white servicemen rioters and vilified zoot suiters as deserving of every punch, kick, and injury they received. After the first night of violence, for example, the *Herald Express* ran the headline "Sailor Task Force Hits LA Zooters" and justified the riots as a defense of the morality, patriotism, and safety of wartime Los Angeles.[123] Championing the efforts of the servicemen, the *Times* reported on June 7 that "those gamin dandies, the zoot suiters, having learned a great moral lesson from servicemen, mostly sailors, who took over their instruction three days ago, are staying home nights."[124] Much of the press coverage emphasized the few servicemen injured in the violence, ignored the hundreds of zoot suiters wounded, and juxtaposed photos of zooters brandishing knives next to innocent-looking and bandaged servicemen.[125] Major newspapers across the country similarly characterized zoot suiters as gangsters who threatened the stability of Los Angeles, one of the country's most important war production sites. During the week of the riots, headlines in Washington, D.C., Chicago, Atlanta, and elsewhere blared, "Zoot-Suiters Again on Prowl as Navy Holds Back Sailors," "Los Angeles' Zoot War Called 'Near Anarchy,'" and "Army, Navy Promise to Halt Zoot Riots."[126]

The Los Angeles press did not spare young Mexican American women, either. The *Times* took a particular interest in reporting alleged attacks by Mexican American girls on white women. Headlines during the week of the riots included "Brass Knuckles Found on Woman Zoot Suiter" and "Zoot Girls Use Knife in Attack as War Eases." In the first case, twenty-two-year-old Amelia Venegas, who claimed to have a husband serving in the navy, was arrested for disturbing the peace and carrying a concealed weapon after questioning the way police were treating a group of zoot suiters outside her home in East LA.[127] In the second case, a white woman claimed she was attacked by three "slick chicks" when the girls jumped her at the entrance to the 3rd Street tunnel, sat on her chest, kicked her, and slashed her face with a razor.[128] As with their male counterparts, women zooters were pictured in the *Times* and other publications as ruthless hooligans on the prowl for white women.[129] Similar stories marking zoot women as un-American ran in most LA-area newspapers. Former pachuca Maria remembers how the press described the popular hairdos of young women zooters: "They made it out like we had knives in our hair and all that. . . . We laughed when we talked about it. Hey, did you do what they said you did? Heck no, you know. Girls talked just like anyone else. They made up lies. Us carrying knives and things in our hair. You just can't believe the stories they put out."[130]

In contrast to the mainstream press, the black-owned *California Eagle* was among the most ardent voices in defense of the African American and Mexican American youth involved in the riots.[131] On June 10, as the violence was beginning to subside, the *Eagle* announced "Zoot Riot Jolts Watts." Citing numerous telephone reports from black residents who lived in the Watts neighborhood, located near the Central Avenue district, the *Eagle* portrayed a "seething riot scene" where African American and Mexican American youth engaged in bloody fisticuffs with servicemen. Noting that many black youth wearing zoot suits and some nonzoot African Americans were the targets of mob violence, the newspaper stressed that whites were responsible for most of the violence, noting that although "negroes have been attacked throughout the downtown area by servicemen[,] no mass rioting by negroes . . . has been reported."[132] The *Eagle* also faulted "bands of roving servicemen, soldiers, and sailors," city police, and the press for ignoring or participating in the violence.[133] In an open letter to the mayor, for example, the *Eagle* charged that "a white heat of lynch fury" was whipped up by the mainstream press and, as a cause of the riot, was second only to the performance of police, who aided sailors and soldiers against Mexicans, looked the other way in attacks against Mexicans, arrested scores of innocent Mexican youth, and sowed a whirlwind of disunity.[134] Numerous editorials in the *Eagle* echoed these sentiments and noted commonalities in the police violence, discrimination, poor housing, and poverty suffered by African American and Mexican American communities. A few of the editorial headlines capture the paper's position: "The Papers Are Responsible," "Press, Police Caused Riot," and "Daily Press Made Zoot War!"[135]

While the *California Eagle* and national black newspapers such as the *Chicago Defender* and *Pittsburgh Courier* defended the nonwhite youth attacked in the riots and condemned the role of the armed forces, police, and city government as an extension of Jim Crow policies,[136] *La Opinión*, the major Spanish-language newspaper in Los Angeles was slower to react to the riots. Perhaps because Mexican Americans in the city were able to more effectively claim whiteness as a way of proving their national belonging, *La Opinión* was less critical of the military, police, and white civilian involvement in the riots. Editor Ignacio Lozano was known for his more conservative political bent. As the violence captured the attention of the city, *La Opinión* routinely published and supported claims by LAPD officials that nonwhite youth were the key culprits in the rise in wartime juvenile delinquency and deserved blame for the instability of the home front and, consequently, the riots themselves.[137]

A number of leftist and communist-leaning publications, such as the *Eastside Journal*, *PM*, and the *Daily Worker*, were much more critical of the role of city authorities and servicemen. Several well-known public figures, Carey McWilliams among them, contributed to such forums and highlighted the role of the mainstream press in exhorting violence. McWilliams argued in an article for *PM*, for example, that the Hearst press incited campaigns against Mexicans, promoted police raids, and generally sought to ignite clashes between racial groups.[138] In another *PM* article, Peter Furst suggested that the Good Neighbor policy was in jeopardy because Mexican officials blamed the LA-area press for instigating the riots by claiming that zoot suits were the badge of gangsters and that zoot suiters were bent on hurting innocent bystanders. Furst further claimed that on Central Avenue, "the Los Angeles Harlem," a young African American male encountered by journalists said to them, "You gonna take pictures of us so you can put them in them damn Hearst papers and call us gangsters again? You won't take no pictures here and make us look like murderers to white people—too much damn prejudice, that's what!"[139]

Many leftist critics believed fascism was at the heart of the riots. Some in leftist and communist circles, in fact, argued that the U.S. servicemen rioters and the mainstream journalists egging them on were working on Hitler's behalf to disrupt home-front stability and democracy.[140] Al

Waxman, for example, claimed that the riots were a "sinister" force aimed at undermining home-front unity.[141] In a mid-June article in the *Daily Worker,* George Morris blamed the fifth-column leanings of the Hearst press for creating divisiveness and linked the Zoot Suit Riots to other violent outbreaks around the country. Morris wrote that "within less than two weeks we have the zoot suit events in L.A. County spreading to Philadelphia, Baltimore, the KKK [Ku Klux Klan] striking against the upgrading of Negroes at the Packard Car Co., the strike at Mobile, Alabama shipyards growing out of anti-Negro race incitement and only two days ago, the virus spread to a Brooklyn plant where an unauthorized walkout occurred against Negroes."[142]

Among the most important consequences of the riots was the mass political mobilization of nonwhites in Los Angeles. Following months of campaigning against the racialization of juvenile delinquency, the NAACP, CCLAY, and SLDC urged authorities to take immediate and firm action against those responsible for the rioting. Arguing that violence against nonwhite youth was a disgrace to the United States' democratic ideals, disrupted home-front unity, and gave a black eye to efforts for hemispheric cooperation, these organizations called for collective meetings, rallies, and protests. Just as zoot suit culture itself crossed ethnic and racial lines, many Mexican American, African American, and Jewish activists together challenged popular discourse about the riots.[143] According to SLDC secretary Alice McGrath, this diverse mix of activists was at least partially motivated by concerns that "stirring up race hatred and prejudice is not confined to action against any one group. Today it can be Mexicans and Negroes. Tomorrow it can be Jews (for them today in Axis countries). As a Jew I feel that I am protecting my future by fighting discrimination in any form."[144] Many of these activists further identified fundamental social problems—including unemployment, inadequate housing, segregation, and lack of recreational facilities—that required attention if nonwhite youth in Los Angeles were to be provided fair life chances. Union organizers, including the Los Angeles council of the Congress of Industrial Organizations (CIO), also blamed the riots on the mainstream press and the failure of police to maintain order. For the CIO, the riots divided people in vital war production areas, created new and unjustified prejudices against Mexican Americans and African Americans, and strained relations with Mexico. As initiatives to be addressed in post-riot debates, the organization thus called for the end of discrimination in war industries, equality in housing, and equal protection for nonwhite communities under the law.[145]

While the activism in response to the Zoot Suit Riots politically mobilized the nonwhite middle class and, as historian Edward Escobar argues, helped make Mexican American a political identity to be reckoned with in Los Angeles, such activism often had more to do with Mexican Americans and African Americans demonstrating their patriotism and national belonging than with nonwhite youth's experiences and struggles for dignity. The NAACP, for example, issued a public statement the same day the riots began that read: "There will be no riot in this community to divide and disrupt the war effort which must carry weapons to the black and white soldiers who offer blood sacrifices on every continent of the world."[146] The struggles for civil rights and inclusion by predominantly middle-class activists, in other words, were often different from the struggles for dignity by working-class youth, and these activists rarely considered the perspective of the youth themselves. Ironically, one might even argue that the intensity of the riots was as much a response by white Angelinos and servicemen to the increased efforts of Mexican American and African American activists to discredit the racial nature of juvenile delinquency as it was a response to zoot suiters themselves.

One of the shortcomings of a narrative of the Zoot Suit Riots constructed from newspaper reports, military records, and the archives of middle-class activists is that the voice of zoot suiters is lost. Although much of the historical record on the riots is devoid of nonwhite youth's perspectives, and although understanding how others viewed the riots is important, it is still possible to illuminate how zoot suiters themselves responded to the events of June 1943 in Los Angeles. Like local leaders, the press, and activists in their own communities, Mexican American and African American youth had their own version of how the riots unfolded. Listening to their stories makes clear that zoot suiters were not hapless victims but had their own critiques of how city authorities and local military personnel behaved.

Although white servicemen initiated and carried out most of the violence, zoot suiters did not submit meekly to the beatings, but actively defended themselves and retaliated with physical and verbal assaults of their own. During the week of the riots, some zooters even organized trips in pickup trucks to Southern California military bases as far away as San Diego in hopes of rumbling with servicemen. Bob remembers:

> The guys from Alpine [Street Gang]. They would get in their trucks and drive them through the neighborhoods, in their trucks, you know. And go down to San Diego to kick some ass over there. I says, "What are you guys

crazy? We got the bases there and got about a thousand guys. You guys gonna go to war and start your own war?" And they went. I never asked them what happened or what, but I heard a lot of them got their asses kicked. Driving down the freeways in those trucks. You guys are crazy.[147]

Rudy Leyvas, the brother of Sleepy Lagoon defendant Hank Leyvas, also recalls that he and other zoot suiters squared off against the mobs of servicemen. Leyvas remembers a night early on in the riots:

There was an alley behind this theater and a lot right next to it. And it was just jammed. So we was waiting, it was already getting dark. So then about 20 or 30 guys come out in the street sort of so when the sailors come they could see them. And as soon as they went out there here comes the truck loads, truck loads of sailors and civilians. And they let out a cry, there they are, there they are. And they came in. As they came in, once they got all the way in, we all came out. . . . I had myself, had a bat and I used it. And there was people hurt on both sides.[148]

LAPD officer C. D. Medley was one target of zoot suiters who fought back. In an incident during the week of the riots, Medley alleged, he stopped his patrol car to investigate a zoot suit–clad youth lying in the street. As he approached the boy, Medley claimed, "the decoy broke away and ran across the street." A nearby car with several other youth in it "came straight at me. I tried to dodge but the car swerved after me, knocking me down."[149]

Even in their efforts to fight back against the LAPD and servicemen rioters, Mexican American and African American youth sometimes pooled resources and formed alliances with one another. For example, after radio broadcasts on June 7 alerted listeners that rioting servicemen planned to invade the black district near the intersection of 12th Street and Central Avenue, the *Amsterdam News* reported that "scores" of black residents blocked the mobs of white sailors when they arrived and greeted them with the message that the Mexicans "are all right with us."[150] In what historian R. J. Smith calls the "battle of 12th Street," upwards of five hundred Mexican American youth, including boy and girl members of the 38th Street, Jug Town, Adams, Clanton, Watts, and Jardine gangs, joined with black youth armed with sticks and brickbats.[151] The racially mixed group of youth, reported the *Amsterdam News,* was soon "on the march seeking out any white servicemen they could find. Negro servicemen were not molested."[152] In another instance, an African American man lent Rudy Leyvas his car in an effort to help battle the sailors. Leyvas recalls: "There's this man, I never knew, I never seen him before. And he says, are you guys coming to fight sailors? And I says, yeah. And he said, I have a car here, it's full of gas. And at that time the gas was rationed. He says, it's full of gas, take it, use it, when you get through just leave the keys in it, put it any place on Central Avenue and I will pick it up. And he says, all I want you to do is get one of them white guys for me."[153] Journalist and NAACP activist John Kinloch, a regular contributor to the *California Eagle* and the nephew of *Eagle* publisher Charlotta Bass, underscored the commonalities between area Mexican Americans and African Americans during the riots when he noted: "Well, we've had a lot of experience along the same lines. We've felt the whiplash of oppression and we know how and where it stings. Besides, it would be us if the Mexicans weren't more convenient."[154]

In striking back, zoot suiters were responding to the violence against them, but they may also have been taking a jab at the hypocrisy of being attacked because of their race and culture at a time when the U.S. war effort sought to defeat fascism overseas. The riots "lasted only for the summertime," Bob says,

> and after that it was all over. But those guys [sailors] made a lot of people unhappy with their driving the Mexicans out. Even a lot of the white people were saying, "I thought the war was over there with the Japanese and you got Americans as prisoners over here, you know. Who's next?" "If they got all the Mexicans in jail, are we next?" the white people are saying. "Who's going to fight the war?" So they started getting all the soldiers and the servicemen to cut out that bullshit, you know. Then, after that all happened, I got drafted.[155]

Although zoot suiters were usually construed as antiwar, unpatriotic, and even pro-Axis, they were regularly being drafted or were voluntarily joining the navy and army and were serving their country with great vigor. These youth not only demonstrated zoot suiters' wide range of political perspectives and experiences, but also blurred the distinction between zoot suiters and servicemen as they were one and the same. Later, after they returned from duty in the European and Pacific theaters of war, many of them used their service in the military to bolster the movement for civil rights in the United States.

Other zoot suiters questioned the behavior of servicemen involved in the riots more analytically. In a letter to Mexican American activist and attorney Eduardo Quevedo, for example, Rudy Sanchez, writing on behalf of the "so-called" zooters, wrote, "If these sailors are setting example for the rest of the armed forces we will lose the war. They are dividing us here at home and they call us the hoodlums. We want to help win the war too, and many of us fight in the war. Whose side is the Navy on anyway, Uncle Sam or Hitler?"[156]

Manuel Reyes, one of the Sleepy Lagoon defendants, wrote from San Quentin prison to Alice McGrath that he had heard of the Zoot Suit Riots. Reyes wrote:

> I been reading and hearing over the radio about the trouble in L.A. It looks bad for us, doesn't it? I been getting the "People's World" and I pass it around to the rest of the boys. I read in it, how the police beat up two of my friends. I seen their pictures in the paper, the one with a wooden leg and the other, I know them both. It sure is terrible what's going on in L.A. I never dream that things like that would happen in the U.S.A., a land of freedom. I thought it only happens in Germany and Japan.[157]

Young nonwhite women also resented their treatment throughout the riots. A group of eighteen young Mexican American women, for example, submitted a letter to the editor that condemned mainstream Los Angeles newspapers for negative characterizations of pachuca style during the riots, but the letter was rejected by the big-city dailies. Al Waxman's *Eastside Journal* eventually published it on June 16, when the group argued publicly for their own virtuosity and patriotism: "The girls in this meeting room consist of young girls who graduated from high school as honor students, of girls who are now working in defense plants because we want to help win the war, and of girls who have brothers, cousins, relatives, and sweethearts in all branches of the American armed forces. We have not been able to have our side of the story told."[158]

As agents of violence themselves, zoot suiters marked the riots as a struggle over the edges of U.S. identity. If the servicemen rioters tried to excise the racial, gender, and sexual performances of zoot suiters from popular notions of what made one American, then zoot suiters fought back, perhaps for inclusion or perhaps to be heard and seen by those who wished to silence them. Whether fighting back with violence of their own or sticking up for themselves in the press, both men and women zoot suiters found ways to voice their own displeasure with their treatment. Zoot suiters made known that as much as the riots may have resulted from macro political and social patterns in wartime LA, they were also very much tied to the micro politics of nonwhite youth's struggle for dignity.

A FINAL NOTE ON INTERPRETING THE ZOOT SUIT RIOTS

Previous interpretations have generally viewed the riots as a mono-ethnic (Mexican American) and largely male phenomenon. The exclusive focus on Mexican Americans and males has led to prevailing arguments that servicemen symbolically annihilated the masculinity of Mexican American zoot suiters and that the Zoot Suit Riots were a watershed moment in the politicization of the city's Mexican American middle class. By focusing almost exclusively on the role of servicemen or social reformers, such analyses narrate the riots largely from the perspective of the U.S. state or the nonwhite middle class, obscuring the perspective and experience of zoot suiters and making it difficult to view them as anything other than victims. Although these arguments hold great merit because they account for the devastating effects of physical violence and the important gains made by middle-class activists, they often fail to consider the racial and gender complexity of the riots.

Although young Mexican American civilian males and white servicemen undoubtedly made up the majority of actors in the riots, young women, African Americans, and civilian whites also actively participated. Broadening the narrative framework of the riots to acknowledge their involvement does more than make the story more inclusive. It also shifts our understanding of the riots' causes and meanings. While many previous accounts have rightly suggested that wartime xenophobia was an important impetus to the riots, those who were involved in the riots were not simply pawns in the geopolitics of World War II. Servicemen, zoot suiters, other civilians, and local authorities each had their own conceptions of Los Angeles and U.S. identity that fueled their behavior. As much as the riots were part and parcel of a more general wave of xenophobia sweeping the nation, as evidenced in the Japanese American internment, they also stemmed from the particular conflict between zoot suiters and servicemen over the nature of race, masculinity, and sex during the war and the ways that entry of nonwhites into the armed forces challenged many military men's interrelated racial, gender, and national identities.

Although the riots in Los Angeles were rooted in the city's unique history of social and political struggle, the events of June 1943 in LA did not form an isolated incident. On the heels of violence against zoot suiters in Los Angeles, seemingly sporadic acts of violence targeting African Americans and Mexican Americans—many of them youth wearing zoot suits—spread to almost every metropolis in the United States. The perpetrators of violence did not discriminate against their victims based on race, gender, or region. Nor did they distinguish between those zoot suiters who were critical of the war and others who voluntarily joined the service. The next chapter turns to the spread of racial violence in the weeks and months that followed the Zoot Suit Riots. While not all of the riots that marred the summer of 1943 focused as exclusively on the zoot as the violence in LA did, the bloody confrontations in New York, Detroit, and along the Gulf Coast reflected the ongoing struggle for dignity by nonwhites in the wartime United States.

CHAPTER 6

Race Riots across the United States

On June 26, 1943, a short three weeks after the Zoot Suit Riots ended in Los Angeles, the headlines of the national edition of the *Pittsburgh Courier* read "Race Riots Sweep Nation: 16 Dead, Over 300 Hurt in Michigan, Texas, Mississippi." Writing from Detroit, where violence between African Americans and whites engulfed the city for several days, *Courier* staff correspondent John R. Williams wrote, "As I type these lines, I am sitting atop a racial volcano which has been ignited by the flames of racial hatred!"[1] On the same day, the *Amsterdam News* ran a feature story with the headline "National Race War Feared: Racial Strife Confounds Nation Fighting to Keep Democracy on Top."[2] Just a few days later, on June 29, the NAACP argued that urban violence on the home front was a microcosm of the war against Hitler in which "race was pitted against race," "bloodshed and destruction ruled," and "hatred held sway."[3] Black journalists and leaders responded to the increasing number of race riots across the United States, including skirmishes between black and white defense workers in the shipyards of Mobile, Alabama, and Beaumont, Texas; violence between African American soldiers and white military police near military bases in Tennessee, Georgia, and Mississippi; and the bloodshed caused by white and black civilians in Detroit. Before the summer was over, violence fueled by racial conflict would also strike New York City.

Rather than viewing these violent uprisings as isolated incidents, this chapter considers them as part of the larger struggle for dignity and national belonging during World War II. Although the riots sprang from local economic, social, and political conditions, each was also part of a growing trend among whites toward mob and vigilante violence as a response to the increased cultural, economic, or political self-activity of nonwhites. While the agents of violence varied, from white servicemen and Mexican American youth in LA to white laborers in the South and black residents of Harlem, and while the behavior of the rioters ranged from the symbolic stripping of victims to looting and murder, the riots were all fueled by wartime shifts in patterns of employment, demography, and xenophobia. Increased competition for jobs, housing, and public services was often reflected in racial terms, particularly when many whites panicked over diminution of what might be called their economic, political, and social overrepresentation as more nonwhites gained access to home-front resources. The riots also revealed how wartime race relations were gendered, as nearly every incident was preceded and deeply shaped by rumors of Mexican American or African American men having committed sexual violence against white women.

As historian Paul A. Gilje suggests, studying riots can help show how different class, racial, and ethnic groups engage one another; riots serve as important mechanisms for change by reflecting social discontent. Moreover, they sometimes shift economic arrangements, affect political policy, and, perhaps most important for the purposes of this chapter, illuminate instances when ordinary people articulate critiques of society.[4] Despite differences in the participants, immediate causes, and events, each riot during the summer of 1943 can be viewed as either an effort to claim dignity and national belonging in the face of the dehumanization and alienation of wartime or an effort to deny the dignity and national belonging of those considered unworthy.[5] The race riots were a national phenomenon, not limited to the West, South, East, or Midwest, and were a critical moment in the wartime debate over who and what was considered American.

While this chapter is not as explicitly concerned with zoot suiters and the cultural practices of nonwhite youth as previous chapters, it places the Zoot Suit Riots in a larger framework of urban riots during the summer of 1943. In doing so, I suggest that the violence in LA helped set the stage for the racial conflict that emerged around the country, and that the cultural politics of zoot suiters were not so different from the labor and social struggles of other nonwhites to claim dignity and equality on the home front. In fact, while the Zoot Suit Riots occurred in Los Angeles, violence against zoot suiters during the early weeks of June

1943 spread to nearly every major U.S. city where zoot culture flourished, including Detroit, Philadelphia, and New York. Following the
spread of zoot violence, racial tension around the country increased, and
local authorities began bracing for the possibility of full-fledged riots in
their own cities. The Zoot Suit Riots thus functioned as a kind of miner's
canary by foreshadowing the experiences of nonwhite laborers, soldiers,
and civilians in the racial violence to come.

THE SPREAD OF ZOOT VIOLENCE
AND THE FEAR OF RACE WAR

In her feature in the *Washington Post* on June 12, 1943, journalist Agnes
E. Meyer described zoot suit culture as a "new youth movement" with
"orgiastic," "aggressive," and "obvious gang characteristics." Despite
her clear disapproval—and unsubtle moralizing—of zoot suiters, Meyer
blamed the Zoot Suit Riots not only on nonwhite youth but also on the
navy and U.S. society as a whole for encouraging renegade violence.
One of the real dangers of such behavior in LA, according to Meyer, was
that it might spark more violence against zoot suiters in other cities.
"Obviously letting the Navy beat them [zoot suiters] up," she warned,
"is only going to increase the solidarity of this spontaneous if perverted
youth movement. On the West Coast the rioting between the sailors and
the zoot-suiters is spreading from city to city." Meyer painted zoot suiters as cartoonlike figures and forecast the danger spreading "to other
war centers where the costumed jitterbugs are numerous."[6]
    Although the violence directed at nonwhite youth in Los Angeles
stemmed in part from local conflicts, including the sharing of public
space by servicemen and zoot suiters and the economic constraints of
wartime Southern California, Meyer's prognostication was soon realized. Within days of the clashes in Los Angeles, violence against zoot
suiters spread to other urban areas in the United States. In fact, beatings,
police action, and riot activity against zoot suiters occurred in virtually
every major urban location where zoot culture flourished.
    On June 9 in San Diego, as the Zoot Suit Riots in Los Angeles were
winding down, at least two separate mobs of nearly three hundred white
servicemen scoured the streets for zoot suit–clad youth. Though zooters
escaped the wrath of the mobs without serious injury, the San Diego
chief of police warned that any persons seen in zoot suit apparel, including zoot suiters from Los Angeles seeking a safe haven, would be questioned and given "shake downs" to determine if they were concealing

weapons or if they were vagrants.[7] Within days of the end of the LA riots, violence against zoot suiters spread to the Bay Area, in Northern California. Officials in San Jose cracked down on zoot suiters in hopes of preventing an outbreak of violence similar to that in LA; rumors circulated that sailors stationed in the area sought to start another "zoot suit war"; a group of Mexican Americans were chased from a beachfront in Santa Cruz; and police roundups of groups of zoot suiters became routine.[8]

The same day that zoot suiters were chased through San Diego streets, city police in Baltimore placed extra squads on duty to watch for African American zoot suit gangs. The heightened alert came one day after at least three black zoot suiters, all allegedly members of the "brimstone gang" from northeastern Baltimore, were arrested, fined, and jailed for charges ranging from disorderly conduct to carrying concealed weapons. Police claimed that the arrested youth were part of a larger group of more than a hundred young African Americans who carried knives and pistols, attacked other black youth, and caused general havoc, especially smashing milk bottles.[9]

Just a few days later, on June 11, sporadic fights broke out between white youth and more than sixty-five black zoot suiters in northwestern Detroit. Squad cars from three police precincts were dispatched to quell the confrontation, as officers dispersed several groups from each side of the conflict after brawls left at least one seriously injured—a white youth said to have been knifed in the arm. The Associated Press reported that the zoot suiters involved were "armed with clubs, knives, and auto irons" and described the white participants as "high school students." The AP's report did note, however, that, in a scene reminiscent of the stripping of zoot suiters in LA the previous week, "a zoot suit was ripped off one youth by high school students who smashed a window of an automobile in which he had locked himself."[10]

Only the next day, four young African American men wearing zoot suits were attacked and badly beaten on a Philadelphia street corner by at least twenty-five white boys during a face-off in which several gunshots were exchanged. While the assailants escaped the scene, the zooters were treated at a nearby hospital for head and face injuries before being arrested by police "for their own protection" on charges of disturbing the peace. Also in Philadelphia on June 10, two white members of Gene Krupa's jazz band, saxophonist Boniface de Franco and pianist Michael Marmarosa, were beaten by two white sailors in uniform who said they mistook the two musicians for zoot suiters. Following a performance at a nearby dance hall, de Franco and Marmarosa were wearing their band uniforms and waiting for a train on the south-bound platform of the City Hall Station when the sailors approached them. "We didn't think anything of it at first," de Franco later said. "But the first thing we knew both sailors mumbled something about zoot suits. One punched me while the other hit Michael."[11]

Though violence against zoot suiters by white servicemen and civilians grew from local conditions, it was also likely fueled, at least in part, by the extensive coverage of the Los Angeles Zoot Suit Riots in local newspapers across the country. The attacks in LA and elsewhere led several African American newspapers, including the *Amsterdam News* and the *People's Voice* in New York City, to forecast additional racial violence in U.S. cities. The *People's Voice,* for example, argued that the mainstream press in LA and other big cities were to blame for the Zoot Suit Riots spreading and potentially growing into a massive "race war."[12] As the summer unfolded, such prognostications proved only too true.

RACE, LABOR, RUMORS OF RAPE, AND RIOTS ON THE GULF COAST

While zoot suiters and servicemen were embroiled in conflict, violence between black and white defense workers erupted across the country. A rash of wildcat strikes occurred, mounted by African American workers seeking equal pay and upward mobility. Meanwhile white workers who resented the encroachment of black workers into previously segregated jobs and workplaces waged hate strikes. Increases in the numbers of African American employees hired to work in southern shipyards, midwestern auto factories, and other defense industries were often viewed by white workers as a blow to job security and a key cause in the degradation of workplace conditions. Racial conflict between workers in such industrial centers as Detroit, St. Louis, Cincinnati, Toledo, and Philadelphia stemmed from the massive mobilization for war that brought black and white, along with men and women laborers, into contact with one another on the shop floor for the first time. As historian and cultural critic George Lipsitz argues, racial strife and labor unrest during the war escalated to the point that "workers placed democracy, equality, and the right to dignity squarely in the middle of the American agenda."[13]

Along the Gulf Coast, the desegregation of the shipyards in Mobile,

Alabama, and Beaumont, Texas, led to ugly incidents of white-on-black violence. In each case, rumors of black men sexually assaulting white women, shifts in wartime employment, and changing settlement patterns in the South fueled the violence. The populations in both Mobile and Beaumont grew by nearly 80,000 people between 1940 and 1943, resulting in housing and food shortages that heightened tensions between black and white residents. And, as Lipsitz suggests, the political mobilization of African Americans in support of the Double V campaign led many whites to deeply resent black political activity and newfound economic success.[14]

Early signs of the racial violence that was to grip much of the United States during the summer of 1943 were evident even prior to the Zoot Suit Riots in Los Angeles. As would be the case in Beaumont several weeks later, the trouble in Mobile began in late May when the Alabama Dry-dock and Shipbuilding Company (ADDSCO) hired African Americans in compliance with Roosevelt's Executive Order 8802, which outlawed discrimination in defense industries. When a number of black laborers were upgraded to better positions, white workers turned violent.[15] Although their actions were spurred by fears of competition over jobs and resentment at having to share their workplace environment with blacks, white workers' motivations for violence were also laced with rumors of rape and sexual interaction between white women and black men. As with the rumors of Mexican American men sexually violating white women that preceded the Zoot Suit Riots in LA, the *People's Voice* reported from Mobile that "the presence of white women on jobs with Negro men [gave] rise to inflammatory sex rumors, social equality bugaboo, etc."[16] Among the charges by white workers before the riots were that "Negroes are going to take our jobs . . . Going to speed-up the job . . . Going to work with our white women."[17] More specifically, a black shipyard worker was rumored to have raped a white woman.[18] To make matters worse, tensions were at an all-time high among Mobile residents, for, as a post-riot investigation by James Jackson of the Southern Negro Youth Congress (SNYC) found, the area's population had doubled within two years, and the city was plagued by "inadequate housing facilities, lack of adequate day nurseries, near absence of recreational outlets, [an] unrelieved transportation bottle-neck, shortage of foods and exorbitant restaurant prices." Alongside the "anti-labor practices and stupid and inefficient management and personnel policies of the company" and the weakness of the shipyard workers union, Jackson placed blame for the riot on ADDSCO, its white workers (many of whom were rural migrants inexperienced in and prejudiced against working with both blacks and women), and Mobile leaders for failing to effectively deal with the growing racial tension.[19]

The climax of racial conflict in Mobile came on the morning of Tuesday, May 25. Following the promotion of a group of black welders who had completed their first shift alongside white welders the previous day, hundreds of white laborers decided they had had enough. Armed with steel bars, lead pipes, and pieces of scrap iron, as many as five hundred white workers, including many white women, attacked more than two thousand black workers who were finishing up their day shift. The violence began when white welders began yelling insults and threats at black workers. Within minutes, the small gang of welders swelled into a mob.[20] As one observer recalled, the mob,

> having charged itself with the lynch spirit with the sight of their first victims['] blood and the animal yells of their leaders, they moved down the line from one ship's way to the next, swarming down upon the bewildered and unresisting Negroes, cursing them, beating them, clawing at them and rushing them from the yard. Negro men and women poured themselves over the sides of uncompleted vessels, raced across the narrow gangways—like seamen leaving a torpedoed ship. Once on land they made one mad dash toward the relative safety of the ferry landing. Through a barrage of steel bolts, wrenches and other missiles past the gauntlet of hooting, spitting, shouting throngs of young boys and women and old men, they raced on. The strong men stopping to pick up their wounded.[21]

One bloodcurdling incident involved eighteen-year-old African American Virginia Richardson, mother of a five-month-old baby and wife of a soldier. When the riot broke out, Richardson, who worked as a ship's sweeper, was ordered to stay on the job by her foreman, who assured her that the mob was only targeting welders. A few minutes later, however, a gang of white men and women demanded that Virginia "get the hell offa this ship." An unknown black worker then picked Virginia up and carried her off the ship and ran to safety. When her rescuer's arms went limp, Virginia saw his shirt stained with blood and knew he had been injured by something thrown by the pursuing mob. As she screamed for God to help her, the mob caught her. As one man struck her in the side with a lead pipe, another yelled, "Ain't got time for no God now, nigger." After falling to the ground, she was again helped to her feet by the man who led her from the ship and the two hurried for safety.[22]

By 11:00 A.M., nearly all blacks had been driven from the shipyards.

Scores of black workers, both men and women, had broken bones or bloody cuts. Although over six hundred troops were called in from a nearby military base to restore order in the shipyards, black workers throughout Mobile were not assured of their safety, and for the rest of the week, hundreds fled the city for fear of more white violence.[23] In the aftermath of the riots, some people, including Charles Hanson, the regional director of the International Union of Marine Shipbuilding Workers of America, observed that the whole chain of events was "Hitler-inspired."[24] Others suggested that the riot was "a carefully planned and cleverly led action designed to disorganize production and incite anti-Negro programs and racial clashes" throughout the South. There were even reports of several white workers who refused to join in the mob action for patriotic reasons and fled the scene with black workers to protect the latter from injury. In another demonstration of support, one white woman welder went to the superintendent's office the next day and demanded to be released from her job. After the clerk asked for a reason why, the woman responded, "That I can't stand working here any longer. I never thought I would live to see the day when members of the white race would stoop to such cruelties!" As she left the office and passed a group of black men at the door, she turned and said to them, "I hope you boys will succeed. I am sorry for what they did to you people."[25]

In its report on the incident, the SNYC discussed the importance of the ADDSCO riot for black workers. "The labor movement must see in the recent events in Mobile," the SNYC asserted, "a supreme challenge to its future existence in the South, the success of the war production effort, and thereby the future welfare of the whole people." Further, it claimed, "this reactionary strike marks the highest point yet attained in the realm of practical activity by the white supremacy wing of the defeatists in their open campaign to drive the Negro people from all war activity and citizenship life. . . . Indeed, Mobile is a challenge and a sober warning to the win the war forces in this country."[26] Whether the SNYC was referring to the war abroad, the war at home, or both cannot be ascertained. Regardless, it would soon be clear that Mobile was a precursor of more dramatic racial strife in the South and elsewhere.

By the middle of June, following the violence in Mobile and the Zoot Suit Riots in Los Angeles, attention again shifted eastward and southward to Beaumont, Texas. As in Mobile, the trouble in Beaumont, located about eighty miles east of Houston near the Louisiana border, stemmed from a combination of local pressures in employment, housing, and services; at least two different rumors that black men had raped white women; and the intensifying racial strife that stemmed from intense coverage in local newspapers of the growing number of conflicts in the United States. As in other war production centers, Beaumont's population increased dramatically during the early 1940s. By 1943, according to the *Amsterdam News,* there were over 150,000 people living in or near the city, including some 40,000 African Americans.[27] Beaumont's shipbuilding and petroleum industries helped make it one of the premiere World War II boomtowns on the Gulf Coast, attracting black and white migrants looking for work from around Texas and the rest of the South. As in other cities across the country, such growth strained race relations in housing, public transportation, and employment. When black workers began working more skilled and better-paying positions in the shipyards in the spring of 1943, racial tensions intensified as white laborers assailed such developments and even created a series of mysterious "accidents" in which, for example, rivets were dropped on unsuspecting black workers.[28]

As spring turned to summer, the situation in Beaumont worsened as a number of racially driven rumors planted a further wedge between the city's black and white residents. Among the rumors circulating in white parts of town during the early weeks of June was that the city's black population was planning a rebellion to coincide with the annual Juneteenth celebration on June 19, the day on which African Americans in Texas traditionally celebrated emancipation. Around the same time, reports surfaced that a young white woman, an eighteen-year-old telephone operator, had been beaten, raped, and stabbed by a black man in the downtown area while she was walking home from work after dark on June 5. The suspect, twenty-four-year-old Curtis Thomas, was an ex-convict and a defense worker. While being arrested, Thomas was shot by police. He later allegedly confessed in the hospital, only to die two days later while in police custody, at the same time that a mob of white residents gathered in hopes of lynching him.[29] Not more than a week later, rumors spread that a second white woman had been raped by another black man. This time, a white mother of three young children alleged that she was assaulted by a black man who had come to her front door looking for work. In her initial reports to police, the woman claimed that the man later entered her house and attacked her just after she had put her children down for their afternoon nap. However, city authorities, including the police chief and city attorney, quickly came to doubt the woman's story after she was examined by a local physician and no evidence of rape or assault was found. City police also found no fingerprints on the cup and saucer from which the woman claimed the assailant had drunk coffee just before the attack. Despite these findings, the rumor of another white woman raped by a black man soon spread through town, including the elaboration that the rapist was a draft dodger and the victim was the wife of a shipyard worker.[30] The racially and sexually charged rumors in Beaumont even spurred local authorities in nearby Houston to run a full-page ad in the *Houston Chronicle* denouncing such behavior. Bracketed by large print reading "Loose Talk Helps Hitler" and "Do Not Be a Rumor Monger," the ad began, "Baseless rumors about possible racial troubles are being circulated by loose-tongued, thoughtless people." It further admonished, "We urge you—Don't do Hitler's work. Stop circulating rumors which create tenseness and interfere with war production, and attend to your own business."[31] The power of rumormongering was later noted by one reporter who observed the intensifying racial situation in Beaumont: "In such a state of mind, fear seems to develop by a sort of spontaneous combustion, with rumor piling upon rumor and imagination getting beyond bounds, [and] the instinct of protection becomes overwrought and distorted. Quite probably, many of those who joined in the disorders at Beaumont were moved, in the beginning, at least, by an unreasoning alarm."[32]

The racialized rumors and pressures in Beaumont reached their tipping point on the evening of June 15, when more than 2,000 white workers at Pennsylvania Shipyards and Consolidated Steel Shipyards threw down their tools, walked off the job, and marched to the town jail. Once there, the mob demanded that the black man suspected of the latest rape be handed over in the name of justice. When told the man was unavailable, the mob took matters into their own hands by trying to enter the jail and extricate any black prisoners they could find. Rebuffed in such efforts, the white mob headed for Forsythe and Gladys streets, at the center of Beaumont's black district. Along the way, the rioters searched for African Americans, even stopping cars to drag out and beat passengers in the streets. Once in the heart of the black district, the mob grew to as many as 10,000 whites who embarked on a campaign of "beating, burning, and destroying!"[33]

Witnesses later attested that white rioters entered the homes of black residents, "destroyed furniture, ripped curtains from windows, tore up radios and pianos and then set fire to the houses."[34] According to one witness, "The men entered one house as if they were crazy. They tore up the furniture, hurled large pieces out of windows, and, as soon as the occupants would come out, men who composed the 'second team' would take after them and beat them."[35] Another stated that "the mob would beat the few Negroes who stuck to their homes. Many of the mob carted off valuables of the Negroes."[36] Other witnesses saw rings and jewelry worn by black women torn from their fingers and bodies. Black-owned businesses were also trashed and burned, including an ice cream parlor and two funeral homes. The Japanese American owners of a small café in the black district were not spared the wrath of the mob, as their relationship with Beaumont's blacks may only have further undercut their already precarious position as an "internal enemy" in the eyes of many white Americans. The café was demolished by white rioters wielding axes and hammers, but only after all of the whiskey on site was drunk. Rioters also targeted blacks who worked in the shipyards, as new rumors spread among African Americans that the mob intended to run all black workers out of town. In the face of such violence, some blacks in Beaumont fought back. Black residents reportedly fired several shots at the white mob; in another reported instance, a busload of fifty African American army inductees on their way to base camp injured several rioters who attacked their bus. A woman who viewed much of the violence in the black district said simply, "It was like hell."[37]

After more than fifteen hours, the violence was finally quelled when the Texas governor declared martial law. More than 2,000 state guard troops were brought in to help restore order. The city hall and jail were surrounded with barbed wire, black residents were forced to cancel all Juneteenth festivities, and Beaumont was declared off limits to enlisted army personnel. The final damage toll of what were soon labeled "Bloody Tuesday" and "Bloody Wednesday" included at least three dead (two black persons and one white), dozens seriously injured, more than twenty black-owned homes and businesses burned to the ground, and the arrest of more than one hundred white rioters. By the end of the week, local leaders blamed outside fifth-column agitators for the riot, thousands of black residents had fled Beaumont, and many city businessmen were concerned that the area's war production would continue to suffer.[38]

Various theories were offered to explain the Gulf Coast riots. Some, including many local authorities and political activists, blamed secret Hitler agents seeking to disrupt unity on the American home front.[39] Others, including the *Amsterdam News*, blamed "evil whites" and groups like the Ku Klux Klan.[40] As in the Zoot Suit Riots in Los Angeles, however, the violence in Mobile and Beaumont also stemmed from conflicting ideas about who was to be included in the national polity and who was permitted to reap the fruits of wartime economic growth.

One primary cause of the violence in Mobile and Beaumont was the unhappiness of white workers with federally mandated desegregation of war industries and the resulting refusal of many blacks to return to prewar race relations and limited economic opportunities. Beyond the personal feelings of distaste about working alongside African Americans or fear of increased competition for jobs, many white workers may have felt that the increased presence of black workers in defense industries represented a more inclusive notion of wartime U.S. identity and national belonging that was threatening to some whites' sense of privilege. For some, consequently, the logical reaction was to close, to slam shut with violence, the door of wartime opportunity for blacks. If the struggle of nonwhites during World War II included attempts to win resources and secure national belonging, the riots in Mobile and Beaumont were, if anything, efforts to deny the spoils of such efforts to thousands of African American workers along the Gulf Coast.

As much as the Gulf Coast riots stemmed from racial and labor unrest, they were also deeply layered with gender and sex. Perhaps because white residents were uncomfortable with the increasing reality that white women and black men worked with one another in the shipyards, they believed rumors that black men had raped white women. These rumors constructed black male bodies as dangerous and oversexed. Black men were viewed not only as incapable of contributing to the war effort but also as subversive to U.S. nationalism for their alleged violence to white women, who were most often caricatured as mothers of young children, wives of servicemen or defense workers, or defense workers themselves.

The power of rape rumors in the shipyards of the Gulf Coast and elsewhere were parodied by Chester Himes in *If He Hollers Let Him Go*, his novel about several days in the life of a black shipyard worker in Los Angeles. At the apex of the story line, Bob Jones, the main character, finds himself in an isolated section of a ship under construction with a fellow shipyard worker, a white woman named Madge, who makes advances toward him. When others approach, including a navy inspector who is presumably white, Madge screams, "Help! Help! My God, help me! Some white man, help me! I'm being raped." "Stop, nigger!

Don't, nigger! Nigger, don't! Oh, please don't kill me nigger." Turning to Bob, Madge—who is from Texas, not coincidentally—says, "I'm gonna get you lynched, you nigger bastard." Though falsely accused, Bob knows all too well he will never get to tell his side of the story: "Abruptly a raw wild panic exploded within me. The overwhelming fear of being caught with a white woman came out in me in a great white flame." Despite his efforts to escape the scene, Bob is severely beaten by his fellow white shipyard mates. Considering the situation he found himself in, Bob later thinks, "I could see myself trying to prove my innocence and nobody believing it. A white woman yelling, 'Rape,' and a Negro caught in a locked room. The whole structure of American thought was against me; American tradition had convicted me a hundred years before. And standing there in an American courtroom, through all the phoney formality of an American trial, having to take it, knowing that I was innocent and that I didn't have a chance." Although the veracity of Madge's story is soon questioned and he is not convicted of rape, Bob has little choice but to follow a judge's suggestion to join the army.[41]

The rape allegations and rumors in *If He Hollers Let Him Go* and during the Gulf Coast riots also highlight white womanhood as a flash point. White male workers may have rioted against blacks to protect white womanhood from the perceived dangers of black men and to demonstrate their white manhood. For the fictional Madge and the real white women in Beaumont who, according to all available evidence, falsely accused black men of rape, their behavior was one way to take protection of their white womanhood into their own hands. And, while records on the Beaumont riot do not reveal the extent to which white women rioted, numerous white women were, according to witnesses, active in the assaults on black workers at ADDSCO in Mobile. Violence and mob behavior in the Gulf Coast incidents thus included women as both agitators and victims.

The riots in Mobile and Beaumont made evident that struggles for dignity and national belonging in the wartime United States were deeply shaped by labor and class, race and ethnicity, and gender and sex. Concerns over industrial production and political unity exacerbated racial conflict, but whites and blacks also struggled to define their identity in terms of race, sex, and gender by demanding either inclusion (by blacks) or exclusion (by whites). The violent struggles for dignity during wartime were not confined to the Gulf Coast but also affected residents in the Midwest and Atlantic Northeast.

RACE, RIOT, AND WARTIME IN THE MOTOR CITY

Within days of the violence in Beaumont, the nation's attention shifted to Detroit, where race riots between the city's black and white residents erupted on June 20. For nearly four days, the city's white and black populations squared off in physical confrontations on the streets. When the rioting ended on June 23, more than thirty Detroiters were dead, more than seven hundred were injured, and more than $2 million in property damage had been done in the city. Whereas in the summer's previous incidents, nonwhites had fought back, defended themselves, and acted violently toward whites, the Detroit riot was markedly different from those in Los Angeles and along the Gulf Coast in that mob behavior originated in both black and white communities.[42]

Like other major cities during the war, Detroit experienced rapid population growth, which led to increased tension between whites and blacks in employment, housing, and public services. During the early war years, the auto industry received millions of dollars in federal contracts that helped make the city a major defense center. Nearly half a million migrant workers, including many white and black southerners, pushed Detroit's population over two million at the same time that they increased racial strife in the city. Wildcat strikes by blacks and, in turn, hate strikes by whites, along with intense debates over segregation in residential districts, schools, and public transportation, became commonplace. An incident in February 1942, more than a year before the riot, served to underscore the city's deep-seated racial divisions. Following a long battle by the city's African Americans to gain access to apartments in the Sojourner Truth housing projects—part of a larger campaign for fair housing in the city by black workers and the black church—a mob of seven hundred whites armed with rocks, sticks, and other weapons attempted to prevent blacks from moving in. The mob stopped moving vans and attacked the families numbering almost three hundred black individuals. White police officers ignored the white rioters and arrested many of the blacks who sought to defend themselves. Although fourteen black families would eventually move into the Sojourner Truth apartments under the watchful eye of nearly a thousand state guardsmen, the incident was a precursor of things to come.[43]

By the summer of 1943 Detroit was teetering on the edge of more intense racial conflict. As if the previous weeks' events in Mobile, Los Angeles, and Beaumont provided a final push, the city soon found itself embroiled in an ugly race riot of its own. The steadily increasing conflict between blacks and whites since the confrontation at the Sojourner Truth project the previous year no doubt set the stage for what would occur on June 20–23, 1943. The clash began on Sunday the 20th, a scorching day with temperatures exceeding ninety degrees, when up to 100,000 black and white Detroiters headed for the parks and beaches on Belle Isle. Throughout the day a number of minor scuffles between blacks and whites were reported, but nothing out of the ordinary. By nightfall, however, the number of reports of verbal arguments, fist fights, and other confrontations between black and white visitors to Belle Isle increased. By 10:00 P.M. the Belle Isle Bridge was packed with cars and pedestrians, and, following yet another fight between a black and white man, the two racial groups in the crowd of some two hundred soon squared off against each other. Police arriving on the scene focused their efforts on the African Americans present, searching the persons and automobiles of most blacks in the area and arresting several black youth.[44] One observer noted that in their response to the initial disturbance on Belle Isle, the police "would continue to handle racial disorders by searching, beating, and arresting Negroes while using mere persuasion on White people."[45] With their heavy-handed tactics, Detroit police quelled most of the violence on Belle Isle before midnight.

Police and city officials, however, failed to anticipate that violence between blacks and whites would quickly spread across the city. Soon after midnight, spurred on by a series of rumors, disturbances broke out in white and black neighborhoods. In a white neighborhood near the Roxy Theatre, rumors circulated that a black man had raped a white woman at Belle Isle earlier in the evening. One of several different versions of the same rumor alleged that a young black man had slit a white sailor's throat and then raped his white girlfriend. As such rumors fueled the disorder, fighting continued through the night. White mobs grew in size and number and began tracking down black residents by stopping streetcars, stoning cars, and then stabbing and assaulting the passengers.[46]

About the same time that the rioting near the Roxy began, different rumors of white atrocities committed against black women and children spread through black neighborhoods. One eyewitness to the riot in the black neighborhood of Paradise Valley, just a few miles from Belle Isle, reported: "We were besieged on every red light by Negroes telling the most exaggerated stories of the events leading to the outbreak—that two Negro women had been murdered at the local beach resort—that a white sailor (or soldier or marine) had thrown a Negro baby into the

Detroit River after striking its mother. There were many versions of these rumors which spread like wild fire thru the Negro district."[47] At one point, as the rumors gained momentum, someone at the Forest Club, a popular black nightclub in Paradise Valley, jumped onto the stage and urged the audience of some five hundred patrons to seek vengeance against whites.[48] As the crowd exited onto the streets of the surrounding neighborhood, its members began to attack whites in the area. One black witness reported that "the whites who dared to drive thru our particular 'battlefront' were stoned and late yesterday afternoon, I saw a car careen down the street, its driver unconscious at the wheel. The crazy zig-zag of that car before it crashed a few door away seemed to me to describe more graphically than words can tell the pattern of this whole sad affair."[49] That Sunday night, the battle lines had been drawn. By Monday evening, after a brief respite from the commotion, the streets were again full of "looting, fighting, and howling." On Tuesday, June 22, according to the *People's Voice,* Detroiters awoke "with the stench of hand-to-hand fighting still clinging to its nostrils after 24 hours of the worst race rioting this country has witnessed."[50] Throughout Monday, Tuesday, and into Wednesday, blacks who "crossed 'no mans land' " into white parts of town, including downtown Detroit and areas along Woodward Avenue and other major thoroughfares, were immediately beaten. In one instance, an old black man was shot by four white youths because they "wanted to have some fun."[51] Whites who found themselves in the black districts of Detroit were also the targets of violence. In one incident, a white pharmacist who worked in a black neighborhood was driven to safety by several black acquaintances. One of the black passengers recalled that "the presence of a white man in the car made us the target of abuse and threats from the mob lining the streets, and at one red light, a woman came up to the car window where I sat and demanded that the white man be let out of the car."[52]

During the riot, city police were often outnumbered by rioters and, as a general rule, responded more quickly to violence against whites than to white-against-black violence. In his report on the riot for *Crisis* entitled "The Gestapo in Detroit," Thurgood Marshall castigated the Detroit police for their inefficiency in their responding to the violence, for allowing the rioting to spread, and for using " 'persuasion' rather than firm action with white rioters, while against Negroes they used the ultimate in force: night sticks, revolvers, riot guns, sub-machine guns, and deer guns." Marshall cited one instance in which a black man was attacked by a mob on Woodward Avenue on his way to work in the bank where he had been employed for eighteen years. The mob seized him and, in the presence of at least four policemen, beat the man and stabbed him in the side.[53] The behavior of city police provoked much debate, with Marshall, the NAACP, and others claiming gross misconduct while the police themselves and other city authorities rebuffed the charges.[54] With the Detroit police unable to control the violence, and in many people's view acting to incite further violence, it was not until President Roosevelt, at the behest of Michigan governor Harry Kelly, sent federal troops into Detroit that order was fully restored. The presence of tanks, jeeps, and trucks manned by soldiers traveling up and down the main streets of the city brought an end to the violence, but the extreme racial tension continued.[55]

In Detroit, as in LA and along the Gulf Coast, such conflict was deeply gendered. The rumors of rape and sexual assault circulated by both blacks and whites in Detroit demonstrated that notions of manhood were often equated with protecting women. The contention that black women participated in the Detroit riot, corroborated by the fact that they represented as much as 6 percent of arrestees during the melee, further underscores that they were driven to protect their own womanhood, guard their families' well-being, or, like their male counterparts, lash out against wartime pressures.[56]

The riot produced divergent responses. Mayor Edward Jeffries and Police Chief John Witherspoon claimed that "white mobs" and "negro hoodlums"—"meaning those teenagers and young adults who engaged in unlawful behavior regularly"—were the instigators of most of the violence. Jeffries and Witherspoon supported one another's assertions that more whites were treated for injuries, that white riot behavior was "retaliatory," and that black youth spilled the first blood.[57] The committee appointed by Governor Kelly to investigate the riot similarly concluded that African Americans had instigated the violence. According to black critics, the committee's final report ignored the violence of whites against blacks except for one brief paragraph and failed to address the killing of black citizens by city police officers.[58] Both city and state officials, furthermore, identified black zoot suiters and "jitterbugs" and white "hillbilly" southern migrants as those who initiated the riots, did most of the looting, and were to blame for the week's most vile behavior.[59] Historians Dominic Capeci and Martha Wilkerson argue, however, that the rioters included a broad spectrum of Detroiters, including white and black zoot suiters, recent black and white migrants to the city, men and women, and people well and poorly educated, young and old.[60] Federal officials generally followed the lead of Detroit authorities. U.S. attorney general Francis Biddle suggested that African American migrants in Detroit for war production jobs caused the violence by creating overcrowded and dilapidated living conditions.[61] J. Edgar Hoover, director of the Federal Bureau of Investigation (FBI), blamed the bulk of the deaths, injuries, and property destruction on black teenage hoodlums.[62] Black leaders, in contrast, had an altogether different analysis of the riot. When Governor Kelly's fact-finding committee completed its investigation, the NAACP claimed the report "solves nothing, further embitters Negroes and destroys any lingering vestige of confidence in law enforcement authorities."[63] Other black spokespeople argued that "the report put the blame for the riot on Negroes, and completely flaunting the charges of police brutality and laxity[,] stated, 'the ordinary law enforcement and judicial agencies have thus far adequately and properly dealt with law violators.'"[64]

Citizen groups also began to view the racial violence in Los Angeles, the South, and Detroit as interconnected. National black leadership and the black press often linked the Detroit riot to other race riots in the United States by viewing them all as the product of fifth-column agents seeking to disrupt home-front unity. The National Negro Congress asserted that the riots had collectively weakened numerous war production centers. According to the NNC, "Detroiter fought Detroiter, and American fought American. . . . Detroit's vital war production program has lost one million and a quarter man hours."[65] Noting the attacks against nonwhites across the United States, the NNC further argued that "the Detroit riot was not an isolated incident. In Mobile, a shipyard center, in Beaumont, a shipyard center, in Los Angeles, an aircraft center, and in Chester, Seattle, Newark, war centers all, this same disruption of our war production effort, this same sabotage of the patriotic unity of our people has taken place. In some cases other minorities, Jewish people and Mexicans, were the victims. All of these events have occurred within the last 90 days."[66] An emergency meeting of civic groups in the first days after the riot heard reports from Harry Braverman, member of the Committee of National Unity and former chairman of the 1942 Los Angeles Grand Jury, on the rioting in Los Angeles; George Marshall of the National Federation of Labor (NFOL), who compared Detroit to the shipyard violence in Mobile and Beaumont; and Joseph Ford of the People's Committee of New York, who spoke on his city's efforts to avoid a race riot. Meeting participants urged President Roosevelt to take further measures against discrimination in employment and the armed services and to denounce the behavior of city police and courts during the recent disturbances.[67] The Detroit riot also elicited similar efforts from the NNC, the National Lawyers Guild, and several other political organizations that joined together in a national conference on race riots.[68] Lamenting the violence and destruction of the riots in Los Angeles, Beaumont, and Detroit, conference participants declared, "The recent 'insurrection' in Detroit, climaxing a nation-wide series of riots directed against the Negro and Mexican people in important war production areas, has precipitated a national crisis."[69] "If we suffered such disasters on the military front," they claimed, "the American people would insist upon new strategy and drastic action. In this total war, defeats on the home front are equally as far reaching."[70]

If the Zoot Suit Riots and Gulf Coast labor riots were dominated by violence against nonwhites, the Detroit riot was a more equal exchange of violence between whites and blacks. Following the several weeks of racial violence targeting nonwhites across the United States, events in Detroit in late June demonstrated that African Americans would not accept such treatment without a fight. Although zoot suiters fought back in LA and black workers in the South did not submit without a fight, the violence in Detroit was of a different sort. It was bloodier than the ceremonial stripping of nonwhite youth that had occurred in Los Angeles and even more forceful than the attacks on black workers and their property in the South. It was also another sign, perhaps the strongest yet in the summer of 1943, that nonwhites would not stand for what the *Pittsburgh Courier* called the "war of anti-minority terrorism" sweeping the country.[71] The Detroit riot alerted the entire country, if the Zoot Suit Riots and Gulf Coast riots before it had not, to the conditions in urban areas where massive migration led to increased population, employment, and housing pressures that intensified racial conflict. It would not be long before even stronger indications would appear that nonwhite struggles for wartime resources, dignity, and national belonging were turning violent.

RACE AND RIOT IN NEW YORK CITY

As racial tensions led to violence in urban centers across the United States, New York did all it could to avoid a similar fate. In late June, following the Detroit riot, New York mayor Fiorello La Guardia emphatically claimed that a similar incident "won't happen here!" Choosing his words carefully, La Guardia asserted, "We are in the midst of a most difficult and trying period. We require at this time more than ever before to keep calm, cool, and, above all things, to have an understanding of the other fellow's problems." Promising equal protection under the law for all city residents, the mayor continued: "We must not forget in New York City we still have the aftermath of prejudice, racial hatred, and exploitation that has existed in many parts of our country. I want to assure the people of this city that with just a bit of cooperation and understanding on the part of the people themselves, we are able to cope with any situation. I am depending upon the good people of this city to keep our record clean."[72] Other city leaders and institutions followed the mayor's lead. Throughout July rallies were planned with a "Detroit Can't Happen Here" theme.[73] Newspaper ads called on all New Yorkers to help avoid disturbances. One such ad demanded that residents clip "The New Yorkers Pledge" out of the newspaper, sign it, and send it in to the mayor's office. The pledge read in part: "In this hour of danger, when every great city is threatened by race riots, I want to join you in doing my share to keep New York from being a house divided against itself." The pledge further urged city residents to commit their "aid as a New Yorker and American" to not allowing themselves "to be provoked to disorder" and to "denounce and discredit all rumors that seek to divide and confuse the people of New York."[74]

Despite efforts to avoid racial tension in the city, race relations in New York, as in other big U.S. cities, were quite volatile by mid-1943. Several incidents in New York suggest the local flavor of the intensifying conflict between blacks and whites. In addition to city authorities' closing of the famous Savoy Ballroom in Harlem (see chapter 4), black New Yorkers were angry with the city's decisions to allow construction of a whites-only housing project and to permit the navy to use municipal buildings for recruitment in spite of its segregated policies.[75] Combined with extensive press coverage of the riots in Los Angeles, the Gulf Coast, and Detroit by the black press in New York, these controversies helped ripen the city for violent conflict of its own.

The Harlem riot of early August 1943, however, was different than those it followed. Unlike the riots in Los Angeles, Mobile, Beaumont, and Detroit, the great majority of rioters in Harlem were black. The Harlem riot was also noted more for its mass looting in black districts than for interracial violence. Despite its unique nature, however, the Harlem riot also stemmed from wartime economic, demographic, and social pressures. And, when considered as one piece in the bloody puzzle that makes up the riotous summer of 1943, the Harlem riot further underscores the point that struggles for dignity in the wartime United States were often violent and were deeply shaped by competing experiences of class, race, and gender.[76]

The trouble began in the lobby of the Braddock Hotel, at the corner of 126th Street and 8th Avenue in Harlem on the evening of Sunday, August 1. White patrolman James Collins arrested a young black woman, Marjorie Polite, for disorderly conduct after she reportedly complained boisterously to the front desk clerk about her accommodations and demanded a refund. Another black woman, Florine Roberts, intervened in the dispute and demanded that Polite be released. Roberts was in Harlem to visit her son Robert Bandy, a low-ranking military policeman in the army who was on leave from his base camp in New Jersey. Within a matter of minutes, Bandy joined his mother in protest and commented that Patrolman Collins would not hassle a white person in a similar circumstance. A scuffle between Bandy and Collins ensued in which Bandy allegedly gained control of Collins's nightstick. The confrontation ended with Collins drawing his pistol and shooting Bandy in the left shoulder. Bandy was arrested and, along with Collins, taken to Syndenham Hospital.

As the encounter between Collins and Bandy ended, rumors quickly spread through Harlem that a white cop had shot a black soldier. Different slants of the rumor included that the soldier was protecting his mother at the time of the shooting and that he had been killed in his mother's presence. As with other race riots earlier that summer, the rumors in Harlem centered on popular notions of womanhood, masculinity, and patriotism. According to the rumors, Bandy was protecting the black womanhood of Polite and his mother. Although Bandy's mother appears to have been the first one to intercede on Polite's behalf, rumors cast both women as less important than Bandy. More than protecting black womanhood, however, the rumors portrayed Bandy as asserting his own black masculinity and patriotism, as if to suggest that he, as a black man and soldier, was worthy of equal treatment. In their multiple forms the rumors reminded black New Yorkers that their dignity was routinely denied by wartime racism and that their place in the wartime United States was anything but equal to that of whites.

As the rumors spread, a crowd of angry black Harlemites gathered in front of Syndenham Hospital. After Collins was moved from the hospital to the 123rd Street police precinct, more than 3,000 Harlem residents congregated outside the station to protest his actions. Soon the mass of people began to throw bricks, smash windows, overturn cars, and fight

with police. As mobs of people began to gather on street corners throughout Harlem, the NYPD deployed hundreds of officers to disperse them.
In spite of these early efforts to quell an uprising, the streets of Harlem
did not remain quiet. By 10:30 P.M. rioters were routinely smashing
storefront windows with clubs, pipes, and chairs, and then gutting the
stores of their goods. Harlem's leading African American newspaper,
the *Amsterdam News,* reported that "hardly a window between Lenox
and Eighth Avenue escaped the wrath of the mobsters."[77]

The areas hardest hit were the several blocks on 125th Street that
made up Harlem's main artery. Pawn shops and clothing, food, and sup-
ply stores were rampaged and pillaged for anything on the shelves. The
rioters took everything, from shoes and jewelry to furniture and groceries. Most of the looting, however, targeted white-owned businesses.
Several reports indicate that many shops operated by African Americans
and favored whites were left unmolested. In its report on the riot, the
Office of War Information stated simply, "White people were not there
to fight, but their property was there to destroy."[78] The *Amsterdam
News* also noted that rioters singled out businesses run by white men.[79]
In his remarkable novel *Invisible Man,* Ralph Ellison fictionalizes the
riot, including a scene in which, in the midst of mass looting and violence
in Harlem, a store owner stands in front of his business "calling frantically, 'Colored store! Colored store!'" One passerby yells, "Then put up
a sign, motherfouler. You probably rotten as the others." "Listen at the
bastard," another says. "For one time in his life he's glad to be colored."[80]
By 3:00 A.M. Monday morning the rioting and looting had spread all
over Harlem, and people were seen carrying boxes of groceries, piles of
clothes, radios, and other items. One man struggled with a whole calf
found in a meat market. Others made off with boxes of liquor. Before
the night was over, in a scene that reminded many New Yorkers of the
Harlem Riot of 1935, much of Harlem came to resemble a war zone.
During the height of the riot on late Sunday and early Monday, August
1–2, at least five people were killed, 300 injured, 550 arrested, and more
than a quarter of a million dollars in property was damaged.[81]

During the worst of the rioting, city officials pleaded with New
Yorkers to stay away from Harlem and for those already in the area to
return to their homes. Mayor La Guardia, supported in his efforts by
Max Yergen of the National Negro Congress, Walter White of the
NAACP, and other African American labor and religious leaders, spoke
to the city via radio several times. The NYPD poured thousands of police
officers into Harlem, army vehicles were used to make mass arrests, and

more than fifteen hundred African American citizen volunteers assisted police in attempting to restore order and prevent looting.[82] By 10:00 A.M. Monday morning, these forces had effectively subdued the rioting. Mayor La Guardia then instituted a 10:30 P.M. curfew for Harlem, and city traffic was routed around the area. The curfew remained in force and the extra 5,000 police officers temporarily assigned to Harlem were kept on duty until late Wednesday.[83]

While the Harlem riot of 1943 unfolded differently than the Zoot Suit, Gulf Coast, and Detroit riots, it grew from many of the same wartime conditions that had sparked violence in other areas and was linked with the summer's previous violent episodes. If the economic and social pressures of World War II led to attacks on black and Mexican American zoot suiters in LA and on black workers in the South, and to confrontations between black and white residents in Detroit, many of those same pressures drove Harlem residents to say "Enough is enough!" Harlem was notorious for ridiculously expensive and hard-to-obtain rental units, sky-high food prices, and unaffordable commercial services. In the weeks preceding the riot, in fact, a large number of Harlem residents complained that they were unable to purchase basic foodstuffs, that storekeepers cheated customers on coupons and charged unfair prices, and that landlords routinely exploited tenants for higher-than-market rents. At one Amsterdam Avenue market, for example, patrons had to sign up a week in advance to buy chickens and were still charged 25 percent over market value.[84] A Harlem-area social worker noted that "these people get 15, 20, and 25 dollar a week jobs, but it costs 35 to 40 dollars a week to live in New York." Many felt that they were not sharing in the bounty of wartime wages, yet were still subjected to wartime prices, a situation made worse by the city's failure to enforce price ceilings in Harlem.[85] Historian Cheryl Greenberg suggests that the riot was, in part, the result of the failure of African American organizations to provide space for official protests against such conditions, leaving black New Yorkers nowhere to channel their frustrations.[86] Following the riot, the clamor over economic conditions in Harlem led Mayor La Guardia to open a local branch of the Office of Price Administration (OPA) in an effort to regulate price controls and educate consumers in the area.[87] Still, more than a year after the riot, an article in *Colliers* magazine cited the structural causes of the riot with a focus on housing. The article noted that with the "largest concentration of Negroes in the world," Harlem had "obscene living conditions" with 300,000 in housing designed for 75,000. "As a whole," the article continued, Harlem "[remains] very inflammable, dynamically race conscious, emotionally on the hair trigger, doggedly resentful of its Jim Crow estate. It doesn't ignite, it explodes."[88]

As the initial incident at the Braddock Hotel underscored, one key to the spread of the riot was the poor treatment of African American soldiers. Both black servicemen and civilians were keenly aware that the armed forces were still segregated and that whites often treated black and other nonwhite soldiers with disrespect. A number of popular catchphrases of the time illustrate that such issues were on people's mind. Among blacks in New York and elsewhere, it was not uncommon to hear "God Dam the Army," "What in the hell have I got to fight for?" or "Stay out of the dam Army as long as you can—it's a bitch."[89] Although some may have considered such sayings unpatriotic, they reflected the contradictory relationship that black Harlemites had to the war effort, including many who served valiantly in the armed forces. The service of black enlistees from Harlem, moreover, was made public by a report from the 369th Infantry, long known as "Harlem's Own" and "Harlem's Pride." The fame of the 369th came after a portion of the regiment was brought back from overseas duty in the Pacific and sent to Camp Stewart in Georgia. When members of the 369th reported constant belittling and insults from whites during their stay in the South, the troops were supported widely by African American leaders in Harlem who protested their mistreatment. Animosity directed at the armed forces was not forgotten among Harlem residents during the riot. One man interviewed after the violence claimed that "the army is run by crackers." Another rioter, the father of a soldier, remarked, "My boy told me that in the army you are told to respect the uniform, don't care who is in it. But that don't go for colored."[90]

Black New Yorkers also shared a historically troubled relationship with the NYPD, another factor that probably intensified the riot once it began. Many Harlemites interviewed after the riot did little to challenge the notion that the violence and looting was at least in part a protest against police protocol. One black businessman accused officers of being more interested in graft than in enforcing the law. Others expressed satisfaction when told about the number of police officers injured in the riot. One official investigating the violence observed an incident on the Wednesday following the riot when a group of black youth gathered in front of the 135th Street police station to watch police unload a truckful of goods seized in raids on suspected looters. One of the officers waved away one of the boys, saying, "Get out of here, you little black bastards

before I kick you in the ass." An African American bystander commented, "Listen to that bastard. If any of my family ever gets in trouble
I'm going to take a personal interest and set out to get any cop who
comes around. . . . Then there'll be two of us in trouble."[91]

Spiraling rents, high prices for basic foodstuffs, the refusal of many
whites to accept black soldiers (and, by extension, African Americans in
general) as equal citizens, and the rocky relationship between Harlem
and the NYPD all made the hopes of Mayor La Guardia and other leaders that the city would avoid a racial disturbance seem almost foolhardy.
The *Amsterdam News* put it most bluntly the week after the riot: "The
disturbance last Sunday night was inevitable to any honest and intelligent observer. The wholesale discrimination against the Negro in the
armed services of the United States, and especially the killing of soldiers
in uniform; discrimination against the Negroes in factories, and the riots
in Los Angeles, Beaumont, Texas, Newark, NJ and last but not least, the
bloody uprising and fatal clashes of whites and blacks in Detroit have
stirred the Negro soul to its deepest resentment."[92] Another observer
agreed:

> The Harlem riot was the direct result of the American system of discrimina-
> tion, segregation and police brutality against the Negro people. This, rather
> than hoodlumism, is what we must call attention to. It may be idle to spend
> precious time and the taxpayers' money searching out the technical guilt of
> this or that person. It serves no purpose to stress that a disorderly woman
> was being arrested, that a soldier tried to prevent a policeman from appre-
> hending her and was dutifully shot by this policeman. It serves less purpose
> to point out that this soldier was wounded and not killed. Much is made of
> false rumors, agitators, etc. What is not said is that what agitated the people
> was in accord with their general experience.[93]

As in other cities, the violence in Harlem prompted varied responses,
including competing explanations and strategies employed by city leaders to recover and rebuild. Much of the official response from city
authorities centered on punishing the black rioters. Some higher-ups in
the NYPD suggested that most of the looting was done by a small group
of hardened criminals—a position that allowed them to claim success in
addressing wartime concerns over juvenile delinquency in Harlem and
other poverty-stricken areas.[94] In what would turn into a weeklong esca-
pade to locate stolen goods, however, the NYPD launched a massive
campaign to identify looters and recover over $2 million in missing mer-
chandise from Harlem stores, an effort that soon showed the impact of
gender and generational factors. Although hoodlums and criminals were

blamed for much of the violence and looting, youth and women emerged as central figures in the riot. Among those arrested were more than seventy-five women accused of looting and disorderly conduct. In one case, a mother and her fourteen-year-old son were arrested on grand larceny charges for stealing a complete bedroom set. In another case, an eighteen-year-old girl was jailed for stealing thirteen dresses valued at over $100 from a Seventh Avenue clothing store. Countless others were taken into custody after police determined they were in possession of "hot goods."[95] One account described "a gray-haired elderly woman pushing a block of ice down the sidewalk before her. This was the only article she had been able to salvage out of what had become 'public property.'"[96] Marjorie Polite, the young black woman involved in the initial argument with the Braddock Hotel clerk that led to the scuffle between Bandy and Collins, was even accused of starting the riot, held on $10,000 bail, and sent to a medical institution for treatment.[97]

At the same time that black youth and black women were blamed for the rioting, a debate raged over whether the riot was racially motivated at all. High-ranking members of the NYPD postulated that the riots had nothing to do with racial conflict.[98] In public statements immediately following the riots, other city officials followed suit by downplaying or flat-out rejecting race as a central element in the disturbances. Statements made by New York justices, congressmen, and labor leaders included "no one can say this was a race riot"; "though this outburst expresses pent up anger, it in no sense expresses an interracial conflict"; "what we have to realize is that this is not a race riot, even if it is a result of resentment of what has happened all over the country"; and "this outbreak is not a race riot in the usual sense of the term."[99] Many New Yorkers argued that the prompt action by Mayor La Guardia and the NYPD to end the disturbance helped prevent a race riot by quickly gaining control of the situation.[100] The two leading black newspapers in New York, the *Amsterdam News* and the *People's Voice*; the NAACP; and the National Negro Congress joined in applauding the mayor's office and the police.[101] The *Amsterdam News* surmised, "The riot would have been much worse . . . if it had not been for the honest and courageous action of city officials and responsible Negro leaders. The action of Mayor La Guardia and the Police Department during the trouble was indeed exceptionally commendable."[102]

Opinions differed, however, as to whether race had been a factor in the riot. As historian Alan Grimshaw has demonstrated, at least two divergent views are evident in the *New York Times* coverage of the riot and the dissenting analysis of social critic Harold Orlansky. On August 3, only a day after the riot ended, the *Times* reported the following:

> Prompt and courageous action by Mayor LaGuardia and the police, plus the calm maintained by the white population and most of the Negroes of New York, kept the trouble from developing into a race riot as did the recent orders in Detroit.
>
> Both riots had similar powder-keg backgrounds in the rapid growth and overcrowding of Negro districts in recent years, charges of discrimination in the Army, Navy and war industry, demands for social and economic equality, and the rise of Negro and radical agitators preying on these conditions. Both were marked by the spread of false rumors magnifying relatively minor incidents that served as sparks for the tinderbox.
>
> There the similarity ended, however. Whereas gangs of white hoodlums organized in Detroit to hunt down individual Negroes who ventured out of the Negro district, thus emulating Negro gangs in Negro districts, nothing like this occurred in New York.
>
> Negroes from Harlem and other districts traveled to and from their work in other areas of the city yesterday, and carried on their duties without molestation.[103]

In contrast, in his 1943 report, "Harlem Riot: A Study in Mass Frustration," Orlansky wrote:

> City officials and the press were far off the truth in claiming that the riot was not racial. Although white citizens were not widely assaulted, the riot was obviously a racial manifestation. Looting was restricted almost exclusively to white property, and attacks and insults were centered on white policemen, though some Negro policemen and 1,000 Negro wardens were later on the scene; no rioter dared to spit into the face of a Negro officer. Attempts were made by the wilder elements to attack whites on the streets, buses and trolleys, but no such attempts were made against Negroes. "Hoodlumism is not racial," argued the *Times*, but at no point did the white "hoodlums" from neighboring districts engage in the looting. The precipitating incident is also indicative of this racial basis: crowds were aroused by a *white* policeman attacking a colored soldier. It can scarcely be questioned that had a *Negro* policeman shot Bandy, or had a white policeman shot a white soldier, the riot would not have occurred.[104]

In attempts to align themselves with city power brokers, social activists, African American leaders, and the black press walked a fine line between echoing local officials who downplayed race as an issue in the riots and recognizing the interconnectedness of class and race in fueling the violence. Their response to the riot was, in many ways, an effort to simultaneously bring attention to the plight of black Harlem residents, maintain active and cordial relations with white city leaders, and, perhaps most important, repair any damage the riot may have done to claims that African American New Yorkers should be important and equal participants in the war effort. For some, it was easy to pin the eruption of rioting on youthful hoodlums, particularly since they had been viewed negatively in the public eye for so long. In its recommendations to ease riot conditions, for example, the City-Wide Citizens Committee on Harlem (CCCH), made up of prominent black and white New Yorkers, proposed the immediate opening of more playgrounds, recreational facilities, and summer schools in the Harlem area to reduce juvenile delinquency.[105] Many community leaders also agreed that race was not a crucial element in the riot. Such positions were often contradictory and confusing, as in one report published by the *People's Voice*. Assuming that race was only an issue when people from different races were in violent conflict, the article claimed that "it was a riot of people goaded by their resentment of discrimination on the American scene. It was not a race riot. Negroes were not in conflict with whites. At no time was there any evidence of racial hatred."[106]

Even when the role of racial tension in Harlem was acknowledged as a key element in the riot, its explanatory value was limited to specific and individual circumstances. NAACP executive secretary Walter White suggested in one public statement following the riot that the mistreatment of African American soldiers was a "sore point" and was the sole racial factor igniting the riots. "Had it been a Negro civilian, however prominent, who was shot," claimed White, "there would have been no riot." White also stressed that it was crucial for white and black New Yorkers not to fix blame for the violence, as that would only "weaken or wreck our all out effort to win the war."[107] Many New Yorkers shared this viewpoint, stressing that reconciliation in support of the war effort was much more important than explaining the riots as a racial conflict. Even the renowned black artist and singer Paul Robeson, for example, decried the discrimination and brutal treatment experienced by many African Americans in New York by asserting, "We need more unity; we need greater production; we need all of our energies with which to defeat nazi and fascist forces—the enemy of us all."[108]

Despite their reluctance to publicly acknowledge racial tension as a fundamental cause of the riot, many community leaders did recognize that Harlem was afflicted with serious socioeconomic problems stemming from poverty and race discrimination. One labor organization declared, "The discrimination against Negroes in the armed forces, the discrimination in hiring of Negro workers, the wretched housing conditions in Harlem, the suffering of Harlem's lower income groups because of uncontrolled prices, the demoralizing effects of the failure to pass the anti–poll tax and anti-lynching bills—these are the matches that lighted Harlem's bonfire. It must be put out at once."[109] Immediately following the riot, a people's committee met at the Abyssinian Baptist Church and made several recommendations to the mayor's office for remedying Harlem's socioeconomic conditions. The committee, made up of African American church leaders and professionals, suggested enacting rent and price controls for Harlem, dismantling Jim Crow in the armed forces, and unifying African American New York.[110] Even the *People's Voice,* which steadfastly denied any racial tension in the riots, proffered a program for Harlem that included the end of Jim Crow in the military, equal job opportunities, enforcement of price controls, and the end of second-class citizenship.[111]

Despite favorable early responses to the city's handling of the riot situation, La Guardia's office gradually faced increasing resentment from some in the African American community for failure to adequately address the riot conditions. Consistently more critical of city authorities than the *People's Voice,* the *Amsterdam News* voiced displeasure with La Guardia's post-riot plan. Writing more than a month after the riot, one *Amsterdam News* journalist claimed that "Mayor La Guardia has made public no concrete steps he has taken to formulate a program which will prevent ever again such an occurrence in the community. This is looked upon as a rather deplorable situation by many citizens throughout the city, in view of the fact that this was the second disturbance of its kind in the community within eight years, the first having occurred on March 19, 1935."[112] The riot of August 1943 was indeed eerily similar to disturbances in Harlem eight years earlier, and the reoccurrence of violence did not sit well with many New Yorkers.[113] Many identified the same kind of discrimination in employment, poor housing and high rents, and inadequate educational, recreational, and health facilities in 1943 that had existed in 1935.[114] The recurrence of violence in Harlem made many skeptical of the interracial and citywide riot prevention committees established by La Guardia. One report comparing Harlem in 1935 and 1943 lamented that

> conditions in Harlem Hospital were just as bad then as they are today, housing facilities are still unfit for decent and comfortable living; the school buildings are older than they were in 1935, and not less over-crowded; the school teachers have *not grown* to tolerate their Negro pupils and they still

do all that lies in their power to train them away from academic studies; there has been no lessening in the wholesale discrimination that the Negro has always experienced in getting a job at a living wage, and the lack of health and recreational facilities are most likely to have improved on the side of deterioration.[115]

The general public in Harlem and the rest of New York also exhibited a range of perspectives on the 1943 riot. Many African Americans, as evident in letters written to and published in the *Amsterdam News*, agreed with those who blamed only a small number of black criminals for the worst of the rioting. To avoid depicting all of Harlem as inclined to violence, one citizen claimed, "It was the hoodlums, the drunken, the criminal element. Don't blame all of Harlem for the crime of the relative few."[116] Another claimed that what occurred in Harlem "was not a riot. It was a bunch of illiterates doing nothing but mass stealing from their own race."[117] In one investigative report that included several interviews of informants in the Harlem area conducted by two black and one white interviewer, there emerged key differences in the way black and white New Yorkers understood the riot. According to the initial report by the Office of War Information (OWI), in the first days after the riot, most whites thought African American rioters were directing anger at whites because of social grievances. Black New Yorkers involved in the rioting, on the other hand, saw their behavior as targeting property rather than persons. For them, the rioting and destruction targeted mostly white-owned grocery stores, chain stores, pawn shops, taverns, and liquor stores because these places housed essential and desired goods. Many whites, when asked about the makeup of the mobs, noted that they consisted primarily of young hoodlums and southern African Americans unaccustomed to northern privileges. Black interviewees generally claimed that all ages and sexes were involved in the looting and destruction. For them the riot did not involve a specific group of Harlemites, but reflected a mood to rebel shared by thousands of residents in the area. Finally, on the question of whether the riots were racially motivated, white and black interviewees starkly disagreed. Whites generally viewed the riots as unlawful looting, while blacks clearly noted the racial dimensions of poverty in Harlem.[118]

What happened in Harlem during the first days of August 1943 was deeply shaped by the ways race affected economic opportunity. In its report of the riot the OWI argued that, although black Harlemites were not battling groups of whites in hand-to-hand combat, "basically the riot was an expression of racial conflict."[119] The racial overtones of the incident at the Braddock Hotel and the selective destruction and looting of white-owned businesses supported such claims. "Sentiments expressed about the riot," the OWI report concluded, "were of a character to leave no question that this violence was an expression of antagonism directed against whites in general and practices that are nationwide."[120] Eye-witnesses added further credence to the argument that the riot was a result of the complex interrelation of the race and class positions of black Harlemites. One white shopkeeper explained that the looting did "not indicate blind furious vandalism, but the destruction of property belonging to people they wanted to injure—not necessarily as individuals, but as proximate symbols of dominance and exploitation." The same witness also remarked that the shooting at Braddock Hotel was one of countless incidents that could have set Harlem off.[121] Commenting on black leaders who broadcast over loudspeakers from moving vehicles during the riots in attempts to persuade people to stop the violence and respect the law, one African American business owner astutely identified the ways class identity was deeply intertwined with race in Harlem. Although he agreed with the idea that the rioters were hoodlums, he also claimed, "It's the hoodlums that really act like the Negroes feel. These big Negroes on these sound trucks talking so much—they ain't talking for nobody but themselves."[122]

Other white onlookers, however, refused to recognize the complexity of the situation and resorted to the criminalization and animalization of the black rioters. Another store owner commented that "lots of them just want to steal, just waiting to steal, just like to steal. They're not responsible. They're getting too much freedom. They're like an animal, still a wild animal, no matter how long you train them."[123] Still another remarked that African Americans in New York "have more opportunity up here than down south and get away with it. Down there they crack down on them. Here, they'll start looting and a laughing."[124] A white policeman assigned to help contain the violence claimed that for African Americans "looting is just natural instinct. They don't know better, they're just like savages. Don't belong in a civilized country in my estimation . . . belong back in a tree . . . only thing missing is a tail."[125]

Although the worst of the rioting in Harlem was over within about twelve hours, it was the exclamation point in a long summer of race riots. Like the riots in Los Angeles, Mobile, Beaumont, and Detroit, the Harlem riot called attention to the ongoing struggle for dignity in the wartime United States. It revealed that efforts by African Americans and other nonwhites to shed second-class citizenship for a more equitable place in the wartime United States had a long way to go. Although the violence ended relatively quickly in Harlem and other cities, the sentiment behind the riots did not easily die. Nearly a month after the Harlem riot, a sixteen-year-old black youth from Brooklyn, Charles Joseph, and a group of his friends were ordered to disperse by a white police officer or be arrested on charges of disorderly conduct for telling the officer, "What we need here is a riot like we had in Harlem."[126]

VIOLENCE AND THE STRUGGLE FOR DIGNITY IN THE WARTIME UNITED STATES

From Los Angeles to Harlem, the race riots during the summer of 1943 highlighted the inconsistency between the United States' fight for democracy overseas and a struggle for dignity and national belonging on the home front. Like the battles in Europe and the Pacific, the domestic clashes were violent, as thousands took to the streets. Some rioted to exclude from the national polity those different from themselves for fear of economic competition or racial animosity. Others rioted to voice their displeasure with being denied equal citizenship and participation in the wartime economic boom. Still others rioted to affirm and express their cultural autonomy. Some opportunistically used the riots to boost their own position in life, either by looting or by politicizing the riots to help their causes. Virtually all of those who participated in the violence or responded to the riots in their aftermath, however, sought to protect and ensure their own dignity in the face of conditions they considered threatening to their own livelihood. Many on the home front considered their dignity, like democracy overseas, worth fighting for.

Despite a variety of local causes, the riots provided a national stage on which nonwhites and whites—including zoot suiters, shipyard workers, journalists, politicians, and other citizens—sparred over who was included equally in the national polity. The battles over who was afforded national belonging and first-class citizenship reflected how Mexican American and African American civilian youth and white servicemen in Los Angeles, defense workers in the South, and black and white residents of Detroit and Harlem defined, in their own ways, the race, gender, and class dimensions of U.S. identity. Along with the continued imprisonment of Japanese Americans and the rebellion and protests by internees at the Tule Lake internment camp later in 1943, nonwhite youth culture, labor mobility, and political activity were each part of the broader story of the struggles of diverse groups of Americans to

claim a place in home-front society. For the whites who instigated urban
violence, the riots were one more weapon by which they could limit the
gains made by nonwhites and protect their own race, class, and gender
privileges.

As much as the riots stemmed from the material inequality many
nonwhites faced during the war, nonwhites' shifting role in the violence
over the course of the summer made clear that more was at stake than
the availability of housing, jobs, and wartime resources. The riots were
also the violent manifestation of the ongoing struggle of African Americans and Mexican Americans to live with dignity in a society that regularly treated them with indignity and was unable to resolve the hypocrisy of fighting for democracy overseas while it was not fully operative
on the home front. In his brilliant poem "From Beaumont to Detroit:
1943," Langston Hughes captured the essence of this critique:

> Looky here, America
> What you done done
> Let things drift
> Until the riots come
>
> Now your policemen
> Let the mobs run free.
> I reckon you don't care
> Nothing about me.
>
> You tell me that hitler
> Is a mighty bad man.
> I guess he took lessons
> From the ku klux klan.
>
> You tell me mussolini's
> Got an evil heart
> Well, it mus-a-been in Beaumont
> That he had his start
>
> Cause everything that hitler
> And mussolini do
> Negroes get the same
> Treatment from you.
>
> You jim crowed me
> Before hitler rose to power
> And you're still jim crowing me
> Right now, this very hour.
>
> Yet you say we're fighting
> For democracy.
> Then why don't democracy
> Include me?

I ask you this question
Cause I want to know
How long I got to fight
BOTH HITLER—AND JIM CROW.[127]

As Hughes suggests, it is important to see the links between the riots.
Beginning with the Mobile shipyard riots in May, exploding with the
attacks against zoot suiters in early June, and continuing into the
Beaumont, Detroit, and Harlem disturbances, racial violence was commonplace in the summer of 1943. City officials around the country
prepared for and tried to prevent the riots, though to little avail. By the
time the Harlem riot was over in August, it was clear that the different
local incidents were symptoms of a bigger, national crisis in racial, gender, sex, and cultural relations. One black leader said as much when he
remarked shortly after the Harlem riot that when Private Bandy scuf-
fled with Officer Collins in the incident that sparked the violence,
Bandy "was mad at every white policeman throughout the United
States who had consistently beaten, wounded, and often killed colored
men and women without provocation."[128] Having had enough, many
nonwhites rioted to let it be known that they too were part of the wartime United States and to demand that they be afforded the rights of
any other American.

In as much as their home-front experience was defined by struggles
for dignity that turned violent, the lives of Gulf Coast shipyard workers,
of revelers at Detroit's Belle Isle, and of Harlem residents fed up with
high prices paralleled those of African American and Mexican American
zoot suiters. The Zoot Suit Riots in Los Angeles marked the first disturbance to bring major national attention to the intensifying racial conflict
on the home front and fueled the subsequent bloody summer of '43. The
rioters—black, Mexican American, and white—wished for better lives
or sought to protect the rights and privileges they already had. They
demanded the right to live with dignity and were willing to fight violently for it.

The NAACP declared in July of 1943: "Not only do these riots
injure America in its present fight for life, but [they] threaten the very
foundation of the Republic itself. Unchecked, they may well bring
down in ruin our Constitution, our Bill of Rights, and our Declaration
of Independence along with man's best hope for a government of freedom, dignity and security of race, creed, or color."[129] For the thousands of nonwhite youth, war workers, and civilians who took to the
streets or defended themselves against rioting, and for their white

counterparts, violence was a statement about the inequality of wartime society. The race riots of 1943 showed that many in the United States, like the zoot suiters among them, refused to accept a home front that excluded them, treated them as second-class citizens, and routinely denied their dignity.

Epilogue

From Zoot Suits to Hip-Hop

On June 19, 1943, the *Amsterdam News* published an article on the Zoot Suit Riots entitled "Mexicans, Negroes Victimized." West Coast correspondent Lawrence Lamar wrote that the attacks against zoot suiters by white servicemen, police, and civilians were a way of "keeping the Mexicans and Negroes in their places." Accompanying the article was a photo reprinted from the *Los Angeles Herald-Express* of three young men in zoot suits. In the photo, a Mexican American male zoot suiter with his clothes torn looks sheepishly at the camera and stands on a bench between two male black zoot suiters, one staring ahead and the other smiling broadly while looking up at the others. The photo's caption reads, "What a Hype: Stripped and Beaten by servicemen, this Mexican youth, Paul Acevedo of Los Angeles, is shown with his pals after a skirmish with men of the armed forces."[1] Although it is impossible to tell whether Acevedo and the two nameless black zoot suiters were, in fact, friends, we do know that the *Amsterdam News* reported that they shared the experience of being attacked, beaten, and "kept in their place" by white rioters in LA.

Zoot suiters in Los Angeles, New York, and elsewhere, however, did not always accept being kept in their place. They challenged their own dehumanization and creatively found ways to claim dignity, much as defense workers, social activists, and many other Americans did. Unlike their counterparts in labor unions or more formal political groups, zoot suiters were not formally organized and did not directly alter economic

Figure 20. Mexican American youth Paul Acevedo in torn zoot suit with two African American zoot suiters during Zoot Suit Riots, June 1943. Copyright Bettmann/Corbis.

and social hierarchies of the era. They did not even share any one principle with one another, save perhaps their privileging of leisure and style. In fact, zoot suiters often intensified race and gender tensions, reinforced their own class alienations, and carried out violence of their own while voicing a variety of opinions that included everything from protesting the war to voluntarily joining the service. Zoot suiters staged their struggle on the terrain not of labor or political activism but on that of culture, employing style, fashion, and their own bodies as tools to craft complex identities and social relationships.

Rather than fetishize the suit of clothes itself, it makes more sense to prioritize the identities and social relationships that emerged from, in, and around the world of the zoot. By articulating their own racial, gender, sexual, and class identities, zoot suiters made a case for the pluralism of wartime American identity and demanded that the nation take seriously its commitment to democracy on the home front. The story of the zoot reminds us that the cultural intersections of the war's race and ethnic communities created possibilities for a world where, even if only for a transitory moment in the dance hall, wartime race, gender, and nationalism had multiple forms and was not always white. Zoot suiters' experiences also reveal that ideas of race were deeply gendered and that ideas of gender were deeply raced, as variant forms of masculinity and racial identity often intertwined to define World War II–era patriotism and national identity. In addition, zoot suiters sought not simply to assimilate (as middle-class "minority" activists often suggested) or to affirm their alienation from the rest of the nation (as local officials, servicemen rioters, and the mainstream press often noted). The perspective of zoot suiters themselves suggests they often did both at the same time. Furthermore, the seemingly disparate struggles for dignity by zoot suiters, defense workers, and rioters connects the life experiences of each in a way that suggests wartime social relations might be best understood when we consider how cultural politics are linked to labor and electoral politics and the broader political economy.

Combined with the labor and political unrest of other Americans, zoot suiters alerted the nation that not everyone was satisfied with life on the home front. If democracy—and the cultural autonomy, economic opportunity, and social freedom many believed to be its constituent parts—was important enough to fight for overseas, it was also worth fighting for at home. Zoot suiters found their weapons in fashion and music, while others used tools from shipyards or looted storefronts or attacked those they believed were infringing on their own rights. Taken together, the cultural, political, and economic activity of nonwhites during World War II helps illuminate a moment when the questions of what U.S. identity meant, who was able to claim national belonging, and who was afforded the right to live with dignity were undecided.

The pluralism of the zoot provided a glimpse of an alternative home front during World War II, but its power as a cultural icon did not end with the war. Although the popularity of the zoot suit among Mexican American and African American youth waned as the war came to a close, the style reappeared in later years with new meanings.[2] This book's

cover image, for example, depicts the increasingly international character of the zoot in the years immediately following the war. It shows three
Jamaican immigrants dressed in zoot suits upon their arrival at Tilbury,
United Kingdom, on board the *Empire Windrush* in 1948. A number of
scholars have also explored how the 1940s-era zoot suiter was heralded
during the Chicano movement of the late 1960s and early 1970s as a
symbol of resistance.[3] Others have interrogated how romanticization of
Mexican American male zoot suiters has hidden the complexity and history of female, black, and Asian American zoot suiters.[4] Still others have
shown how the zoot functioned as an important cultural symbol for
Chicana/o youth in the late 1970s, particularly as a central element in
low-rider culture.[5] More recently, the zoot has reemerged in new contexts. Since the 1990s it has made a comeback as the wardrobe of choice
among youth in the worldwide resurgence of swing music and dancing,
a trend fueled by movie stars wearing zoots suits, as Jim Carey did in
The Mask, and popular bands like Big Bad Voodoo Daddy and the
Cherry Poppin' Daddies featuring the zoot in their music, live performances, and on-screen appearances. One need only check out the number of zoot suits worn to high school proms in the early 2000s or visit
zoot suit manufacturers online, such as www.suavecito.com, to verify
that the zoot has been reincarnated as a cool and popular style. While it
always was a commodity, the challenge it once presented to wartime
cultural homogeneity and gender and race relations is not nearly as
salient. Although it still retains a flavor of youth rebellion and dissidence,
as the historical background section of sauvecito.com or the song "Zoot
Suit Riot" by the Cherry Poppin' Daddies illustrates, the zoot may be
more akin to the throwback sports jerseys so popular today among hip-
hop-oriented youth.

While a few historians have explored how the youthful zoot days of
Malcolm X in Harlem and Cesar Chavez in central California helped
shape their adult participation in the Civil Rights Movement,[6] less has
been said about how the interracial character of youth culture as a whole
was transformed in the years following World War II. Indeed, one of the
seemingly magical qualities of youth culture is that while the individuals
involved change over time, and may even grow to despise how they once
behaved, young people continue to regenerate social experimentation
and cultural expression. The interracial and gendered struggles for dignity by zoot suiters set the stage for the evolution of youth culture in the
years that followed.

As the Civil Rights Movement evolved out of the labor and cultural activism of the 1940s, nonwhite youth, some of them perhaps the children of former zoot suiters and wartime jazz aficionados, helped define the era's charged political atmosphere. In a country of social and political upheaval, young people quickly became a catalyst for social change and protest. Youth dominated the anti–Vietnam War movement; led African American, Native American, Asian American, Chicana/o, and Latina/o social movements through such organizations as the American Indian Movement (AIM), Black Panthers, Brown Berets, and Young Lords; and spearheaded the transgressive rock 'n' roll and hippie lifestyles. As evident in the striking similarities between a pair of classic sixties tunes—the exalted white folksinger Bob Dylan's classic "The Times They Are a-Changing" and the great black rhythm-and-blues artist Sam Cooke's vintage "A Change Is Gonna Come"—young people from a wide spectrum of racial and ethnic backgrounds realized they had the power to alter U.S. society.

As their predecessors did in the 1940s, many nonwhite youth in the sixties faced conditions that denied their dignity, including dismal educational opportunities, poverty, and discrimination. New obstacles, however, also surfaced with the political militancy of the times, including increased surveillance by local and federal law enforcement, renewed outbreaks of racial violence in cities such as LA and Detroit, and the ever increasing pressure of the Vietnam War draft. Like zoot suiters a generation prior, nonwhite youth in the 1960s were confronted with societal expectations to join the service and protect a country many felt failed to acknowledge their civil rights at home.

While much of the empowerment of nonwhite youth during the era stemmed from ethnic pride—an ideological position that sometimes privileged race and ethnicity over class, gender, or sexual preference—an explosion in youth cultural production also occurred, revealing an interracial and internationalist U.S. identity, one not determined completely by ethnic or cultural nationalism, but informed by relationships across ethnic, racial, and regional lines.[7] The art and style of many young nonwhites exhibited a cultural politics that reflected solidarity between anticolonial movements in the United States, Latin America, Africa, Asia, and the Caribbean. Although perhaps the best-known poem of the Chicana/o movement, for example, was Corky Gonzalez's ultranationalistic and hypermasculine "Yo Soy Joaquin," there were countless others in which the verses stressed the power of coalition building across lines of difference and feminist critique. The work of the pan-Latino literary collective Pocho-Che from the Bay Area, for example, linked the conditions of Chicanas/os with those of African Americans, Puerto Ricans, and other Latinas/os. The impact of the black beat-generation poet Bob Kaufman on members of Pocho-Che, their passion for the mixed Latina/o and African American history of improvisation and riffing in jazz music, and their engagement with artists like Carlos Santana, Tito Puente, James Brown, and writers from San Francisco's Third World Communications collective illustrate that interracial communication and community formation were alive and well.[8] The diverse and powerful body of poetry by Chicana feminists, moreover, demanded *la causa* take seriously the concerns and issues of women, gays, and lesbians, as exemplified in Marcela Christine Lucero-Trujillo's poem "Machismo Is Part of Our Culture."[9]

To take another example, cultural critic George Lipsitz shows how Chicana/o youth culture crafted an interethnic and international politics in movement-era poster art. Like the thousands of young Chicanas/os that took to the streets or walked out of schools to protest second-class citizenship, poster artists demanded they be heard by using their mobile, widely accessible, and inexpensive forum to occupy public space by plastering posters all over neighborhoods, college campuses, and local hangouts. While some posters echoed the nationalist sentiments of the time, others gave broad exposure to international issues. For example, Rupert Garcia's 1970 "Fuera de Indochina!" protests the Vietnam War, Malaquias Montoya's famous "Chicano/Vietnam/Aztlán" emphasizes the affinities between Chicanas/os and the Vietnamese, and Linda Lucero's 1978 poster "Lolita Lebron" pays tribute to the Puerto Rican struggle for independence. Others included Louie "the Foot" Gonzalez's poster in support of the Salvadorian People's Support Committee, Yreina Cervantes's celebration of Chicana/o–Central American interactions in her "El Pueblo Chicano con el Pueblo Centro Americano," and Mark Vallen's "Sandinista" and "Poetry for the Nicaraguan Resistance," expressing support for Nicaraguan forces under attack by U.S.-supported contras. All of these posters demonstrated the efforts of Chicana/o youth to forge solidarity with struggles for social justice by other aggrieved groups, no matter their national or ethnic makeup.[10]

The "Brown Eyed Soul" music movement—involving the fusion of the Motown sound, soul, rhythm and blues, rock, and jazz with local musical traditions—also resulted in a rich mixture of African American and Chicana/o cultures. Artists from East Los Angeles such as War, Brenton Wood, and El Chicano built on the tradition of multiracial bands in Southern California dating back to the 1940s and 1950s.

Tejanos from the Rio Grande Valley of South Texas, such as the heavily doo-wop- and black soul–influenced Sunny and the Sunliners, and even the many Jamaican rock steady and reggae artists who drew from black American music, further stretched the spatial dimensions of this shared soundscape. All of these musicians were part of a youth culture, whether via protest songs or love songs, that complicated and sometimes challenged the ideology of cultural nationalism by cultivating ties between diverse life experiences.

The interethnic and internationalist dimensions of youth culture did not always, or even often, reflect the dominant ideological thrust of movements for black, brown, yellow, or red power. Some argued that attention to foreign, feminist, queer, and other U.S. ethnic social movements detracted from the energy needed to grow ethnic or race-based movements, thus hardening lines of cultural, gender, and sexual difference. These contradictions, however, only further point to the multiplicity of Chicana/o, African American, and other nonwhite identities and struggles for dignity. Just as the movement era was, according to Chicana/o and African American scholars, both revolutionary and reformist, so too was it both nationalist and internationalist, both racially focused and interracial. Ultimately, like zoot suiters before them, movement poets, artists, and musicians showed that nonwhite youth did not always form their politics from their identity, but often drew their identity from their politics.[11]

Since World War II and the Civil Rights Movement, the ever deepening globalization of capital has resulted in the dizzying movement of goods, labor, culture, and ideas across national borders and has transformed further the life conditions of nonwhite youth in the urban United States. As immigration to the United States from Latin America, Asia, and the Caribbean has intensified, U.S. cities have become increasingly global in their ethnic, racial, national, and cultural makeup.[12] The continued growth of global cities like Los Angeles, New York, and Houston facilitates interracial cultural expression among youth, who often share schools and neighborhoods, yet also aggravates interracial conflict among working-class communities that compete for jobs, housing, and urban resources.

Globalization has resulted in both new forms of resistance and oppression for young people of color. Economic restructuring and deindustrialization have forced many in the urban United States to face growing rates of unemployment and dilapidated and unaffordable housing, along with decreasing local, state, and federal resources for inner-city welfare, schools, parks, and health care. Since the early 1970s, the postindustrial crisis has spurred the movement of jobs and heavy investment away from once vibrant downtown manufacturing centers and toward growing industrial areas along the U.S.-Mexico border and in places as far away as Southeast Asia where workers are paid a fraction of the wages once earned by their U.S. counterparts and where environmental regulations are looser and profits are higher. The accompanying rise in gang violence, drug use, and crime parallels the militarization of big cities and increased surveillance of urban youth as domestic terrorists.[13] In many ways, popular discourse in the United States during the 1980s and 1990s portrayed nonwhite youth as the epitome of what was wrong with urban America.

In the face of such dehumanization, youth cultural expression continues to function as a struggle for dignity in which nonwhite youth perform unique race and gender identities. Perhaps the most recognizable youth cultural phenomenon over the last thirty years is hip-hop, including rapping, dee-jaying, break-dancing, and graffiti writing. Following its emergence among African American, Afro-Caribbean, and Puerto Rican youth in the South Bronx in the 1970s—an urban area often depicted as the poster child of 1970s postindustrialism—hip-hop rapidly grew in popularity among Chicana/o, Asian American, and white youth. Latina/o rappers, in particular, have played a large role in helping hip-hop explode the traditional black-white binary in U.S. race relations, making it virtually impossible to view hip-hop as solely a white, Latina/o, Asian, or even black cultural practice.[14]

For young hip-hoppers, much as for zoot suiters in a bygone era, gender, the body, and public space have often been the terrain on which interracial relationships have formed. Many young men, in particular, have responded to the devastation of the postindustrial city, criminalization, and well-known patterns of police brutality and inflated incarceration rates by articulating and fetishizing a hypermasculinity that is evident, for instance, in rap lyrics that denigrate women, gays, and lesbians while they critique the state by mocking or cursing police tactics. Hip-hoppers have also employed style, in the form of the exaggerated fashion of baggy pants, retro sports jerseys, gold chains, and oversized jackets, and they occupy public space, in the form of graffiti on public walls or subway trains and the pounding bass of car stereos on city streets, as strategies to make themselves seen and heard in a time when the economic, political, and social mainstream encourage their invisibility and silence. Through their use of the body and technology—in the seemingly impossible movements of the spinning, twisting, and popping of break-dancing; the making of music without instruments; and the use of commodities such as speakers and albums in unintended ways—nonwhite youth have claimed for themselves at least a part of the dignity that the world in which they live has taken away from them.

As with World War II– and movement-era youth cultures, the social contradictions and political limits of contemporary youth culture are many. Hip-hop's seething critique of neoliberal economics is, for example, often undermined by many rappers' and musicians' drive for money, commodification, and merchandise sales. The frequent misogyny, homophobia, and sexism in the gangsta rap or Dirty South genres, for example, and the often patriarchal nature of the music industry sometimes make claims to dignity by heterosexual male youth synonymous with the denial of dignity to young women, gays, and lesbians. And, of course, as much as we might point in certain situations to the cooperation of politically conscious youth across racial boundaries, there are just as many, if not more, instances of relationships among African American, Chicana/o, Latina/o, and Asian American youth reflecting the conflict between their larger communities over dwindling resources in many U.S. cities.

Perhaps because of these contradictions, present-day youth culture helps us better see the multifaceted makeup of nonwhite identities and their struggles for dignity. That the efforts of nonwhite youth to navigate the difficult life conditions of globalization and postindustrialism frequently intersect with the experiences of others suggests that contemporary youth are refashioning the interethnic cultural exchange articulated in different forms by the zoot suiters and movement-era artists who preceded them. Moreover, young people's cultural politics continue to underscore that another world is possible, one that imagines, and sometimes puts into practice, social relationships that value rather than denigrate difference. As youth culture regenerates itself in the future, it will likely continue to foster cooperation and conflict across ethnic, racial, and national boundaries.

Listening carefully to zoot suiters, movement artists, and hip-hoppers may reveal that youth culture is not simply about what one wears, how one dances, or which music one listens to. It is also the place where social differences and struggles for dignity converge and from where complex and contradictory identities grow. Rather than fetishize the zoot suit, poems, or music, we might better focus on the regeneration of youth cultural spaces and the plethora of shifting social relationships among them. Part of what links zoot suiters to hip-hoppers, in other words, is not only their shared racialization and cultural commonalities, but also their efforts and desire to claim dignity and cultural autonomy in the face of powerful forces. While they may not have created viable political or economic alternatives to long-standing structures of domination or even directly challenged them in any overtly organized way, these youth did create social spaces and cultural identities that enabled them to improve, or perhaps simply enjoy more, their everyday lives. Although these efforts might seem to pale in comparison with more widely recognized movements for social change, recognizing the power of such social spaces and cultural identities just might teach us something about how people struggle to live with dignity in the face of dehumanization, poverty, and violence.

Illuminating the history of zoot suiters and other youth cultural workers forces us to recognize that race and ethnic history in the United States is not a story only of conflict or togetherness, but a complicated mix of the two. If nothing else, a deeper understanding of youth culture makes clear that capturing the full complexity of the Chicana/o or African American experience is virtually impossible without accounting for how one relates to the other. As much as these lessons learned from zoot suiters and the youth cultural workers who followed them can help us better understand the past, perhaps their greatest value is that they just might help us make better sense of our own struggles and those that lie before us.

Notes

1. Malcolm X, *The Autobiography of Malcolm X as Told to Alex Haley* (New York: Ballantine Books, 1964), 105.

2. Alfred Barelato Judge Arthur S. Guerin, May 21, 1943, Manuel Ruiz Papers, box 15, folder 16, Department of Special Collections, Stanford University.

3. Agnes E. Meyer, "Zoot-Suiters—A New Youth Movement," *Washington Post* (June 13, 1943), 4B.

4. Lupe Rivas (a pseudonym), interview with author, Los Angeles, January 13, 2000.

5. Perry Perkins (a pseudonym), interview with author, San Diego, December 20, 2001.

6. I understand the cultural politics of the zoot to be the dynamic process by which zoot suiters gave expression to their material conditions; produced social patterns, values, and ideas; and struggled in and made sense of the world. Like many others who study youth and popular culture, I have been profoundly influenced in my thinking on cultural politics by the foundational work of the Centre for Contemporary Cultural Studies (CCCS) at the University of Birmingham in Great Britain during the 1970s, particularly studies of youth subcultures by Stuart Hall and Tony Jefferson, Dick Hebdige, and Paul Willis. Employing ethnographic and literary methods, as well as Gramsci's theory of hegemony, to investigate British youth subcultures, including punks, skinheads, teddy boys, and rastas, these scholars illustrate how young people negotiated, opposed, or subverted the dominant culture in the United Kingdom by creating new identities and lifestyles that constituted a cultural struggle for control over their own lives. These studies further demonstrate that youth were often key participants in debates over national identity, class values, and the future of British society. See,

for example, Stuart Hall and Tony Jefferson, eds., *Resistance through Rituals: Youth Subcultures in Post-War Britain* (New York: Routledge, 1996); Dick Hebdige, *Subculture: The Meaning of Style* (New York: Routledge, 1994); Paul Willis, *Learning to Labour: How Working Class Kids Get Working Class Jobs* (New York: Columbia University Press, 1977). For a useful overview of scholarly approaches to subculture generally, see Keith Gelder and Sarah Thornton, eds., *The Subculture Reader* (London: Routledge, 1997). The work of these and other cultural studies scholars suggests that working-class youth often seek cultural autonomy at the same time that their lives are molded by the dominant national culture and political economy. As cultural critic and race scholar Paul Gilroy notes, it is useful in studies of culture "to preserve the tension between broadly defined political imperatives and the non-negotiable autonomy of cultural expression." Paul Gilroy, *Small Acts* (New York: Serpent's Tail, 1993), 15.

7. Antonio Alvarez, interview with author, Jamul, CA, February 25, 1994.

8. My understanding of race as a social construction that cannot be reduced to class or culture (nor vice versa), and of racialization as the process by which race draws meaning from its historical context, follows the work of sociologists Michael Omi and Howard Winant, *Racial Formation in the United States: From the 1960s to the 1990s* (New York: Routledge, 1994), and critical race and legal theorist Ian Haney Lopez, in "The Social Construction of Race: Some Observations on Illusion, Fabrication, and Choice," *Harvard Civil Rights–Civil Liberties Law Review* 29 (Winter 1994): 1–62; Paul Gilroy, *There Ain't No Black in the Union Jack: The Cultural Politics of Race and Nation* (Chicago: University of Chicago Press, 1991). For a critical discussion of race in popular culture, see Stuart Hall, "What Is This 'Black' in Black Popular Culture?" in David Morley and Kuan-Hsing Chen, eds., *Stuart Hall: Critical Dialogues in Cultural Studies* (New York: Routledge, 1996).

9. My understanding of identity as fluid over time and influenced, but not fixed, by geography, and of identity formation as political work that potentially impacts broader struggles for social change, follows the work of cultural critic and theorist Stuart Hall. See his "Old and New Identities, Old and New Ethnicities," in Anthony D. King, ed., *Culture, Globalization, and the World System* (Binghamton: Department of Art and Art History, State University of New York, 1991); as well as Stuart Hall, "Cultural Identity and Diaspora," in Patrick Williams and Laura Chrisman, eds., *Colonial Discourse and Post-Colonial Theory: A Reader* (New York: Columbia University Press, 1994).

10. I understand gender as the negotiation for and struggle over power, culture, and the meaning of history between men and women, as well as among men and among women—negotiation defined neither by biology nor by society's assumptions. This view follows the work of a number of scholars in critical gender and queer studies. See, for example, Judith Halberstam, *Female Masculinity* (Durham, NC: Duke University Press, 1998); Alejandro Lugo, "Destabilizing the Masculine, Refocusing 'Gender': Men and the Aura of Authority in Michelle Z. Rosaldo's Work," in Alejandro Lugo and Bill Maurer, eds., *Gender Matters: Rereading Michelle Z. Rosaldo* (Ann Arbor: University of Michigan Press, 2000), 54–89; Susan Lee Johnson, "A Memory to Sweet Soldiers: The Significance of Gender in the History of the American West," *Western Histori-*

cal Quarterly 24, no. 4 (November 1993): 495–518; Joan Scott, *Gender and the Politics of History* (New York: Columbia University Press, 1988).

11. On World War II–era popular culture in the United States and its potential to reveal the ethnic, class, and gender complexity of wartime identity, see, for example, Lewis A. Erenberg and Susan Hirsch, eds., *The War in American Culture: Society and Consciousness in World War II* (Chicago: University of Chicago Press, 1996); M. Paul Holsinger and Mary Anne Schofield, eds., *Visions of War: World War II in Popular Literature and Culture* (Bowling Green, OH: Bowling Green State University Popular Press, 1992).

12. Carey McWilliams, *North from Mexico: The Spanish-Speaking People of the United States* (New York: J. B. Lippincott, 1968); Beatrice Griffith, *American Me: Fierce and Tender Stories of the Mexican-Americans of the Southwest* (New York: Pennant Books, 1954); Octavio Paz, *The Labyrinth of Solitude* (New York: Grove Press, 1985).

13. Mauricio Mazón, *The Zoot-Suit Riots: The Psychology of Symbolic Annihilation* (Austin: University of Texas Press, 1988); Edward J. Escobar, *Race, Police, and the Making of a Political Identity: Mexican Americans and the Los Angeles Police Department, 1900–1945* (Berkeley: University of California Press, 1999); Eduardo Obregón Pagán, *Murder at the Sleepy Lagoon: Zoot Suits, Race, and Riot in Wartime L.A.* (Chapel Hill: University of North Carolina Press, 2003).

14. Several excellent recent dissertations and forthcoming books address zoot suiters. These include Elizabeth Escobedo, "Mexican American Home Front: The Politics of Gender, Culture, and Community in World War II Los Angeles," PhD thesis, University of Washington, 2004; Anthony Macías, *Mexican American Mojo: Popular Music, Dance, and Urban Culture in Los Angeles, 1938–1968* (Durham, NC: Duke University Press, forthcoming); Catherine Ramírez, *The Woman in the Zoot Suit: Mexican American Women, Nationalisms, and Citizenship* (Durham, NC: Duke University Press, forthcoming).

15. George Lipsitz, "Who'll Stop the Rain? Youth Culture, Rock 'n' Roll, and Social Crisis," in David Farber, ed., *The Sixties: From Memory to History* (Chapel Hill: University of North Carolina Press, 1994), 206–34. Historians Elliot West and Paula Petrik similarly argue that because of a dearth of sources highlighting the point of view of young people, "reconstructing their story is an extremely frustrating business." Elliot West and Paula Petrik, eds., *Small Worlds: Children and Adolescents in America, 1850–1950* (Lawrence: University of Kansas Press, 1992), 3. For another incisive analysis of children in the history of the United States, see Steven Mintz, *Huck's Raft: A History of American Childhood* (Cambridge, MA: Belknap Press of Harvard University Press, 2004).

16. My analysis of youth culture follows cultural critic Sunaina Maira's call for scholars to conceive of youth culture studies in a way that "revitalizes discussions about youth cultures and social movements while simultaneously theorizing the political and social uses of youth." Sunaina Maira, "Imperial Feelings: Youth Culture, Citizenship, and Globalization," in Marcelo Suárez-Orozco and Desirée Baolian Qin-Hilliard, eds., *Globalization: Culture and Education in the New Millennium* (Berkeley: University of California Press, 2004), 209–10. For surveys of youth culture in the United States and elsewhere, see, for example,

Vared Amit-Talai and Helena Wulff, eds., *Youth Cultures: A Cross-Cultural Perspective* (London: Routledge, 1995); Jonathon S. Epstein, ed., *Youth Culture: Identity in a Postmodern World* (Malden, MA: Blackwell, 1998); Johan Fornan and Goran Bolin, *Youth Culture in Late Modernity* (London: Sage, 1995).

17. In collaboration with urban education scholar Elisabeth Soep, Sunaina Maira suggests that youth culture is "a site that is not just geographic or temporal but social and political as well, a 'place' that is bound up with questions of power and materiality." Sunaina Maira and Elisabeth Soep, introduction to Maira and Soep, eds., *Youthscapes: Popular Culture, National Ideologies, Global Markets* (Philadelphia: University of Pennsylvania Press, 2004), xv. Maira and Soep view youth culture not only as a generational phenomenon or an isolated element of society but also as a phenomenon embedded in processes, experiences, and debates over globalization, citizenship and nationalism, consumption and resistance, and popular culture. Similarly, scholars Joe Austin and Michael Nevin Willard stress that the meaning of youth, like race or gender, shifts over time and with place and that institutions, policies, and processes outside the control of young people help shape the meaning of their lives and identities in relation to others. Joe Austin and Michael Nevin Willard, eds., *Generations of Youth: Youth Cultures and History in Twentieth-Century America* (New York: New York University Press, 1998), 4–5. On definitions of youth as an analytical category of analysis, see also Tracey Skelton and Gill Valentine, eds., *Cool Places: Geographies of Youth Cultures* (Routledge: New York, 1998), 2–10.

18. *Negro Digest* 1, no. 4 (Winter–Spring 1943): 301, as quoted in Robin D. G. Kelley, *Race Rebels: Culture, Politics, and the Black Working Class* (New York: Free Press, 1994), 161.

19. My understanding of dignity is deeply influenced by the Zapatistas in Chiapas, Mexico. In a communiqué shortly after their armed uprising in January of 1994, the Zapatistas located dignity at the center of their oppositional politics:

> We saw that not everything had been taken away from us, that we had the most valuable, that which made us live, that which made our step rise above plants and animals, that which made the stone be beneath our feet, and we saw, brothers and sisters, that all we had was DIGNITY, and we saw that great was the shame of having forgotten it, and we saw that DIGNITY was good for human beings to be human beings again, and dignity returned to live in our hearts, and we were new again, and the dead, our dead, saw that we were new again and they called us again, to DIGNITY, to struggle.
>
> Quoted in John Holloway and Eloina Pelaez, eds., *Zapatista! Reinventing Revolution in Mexico* (London: Pluto Press, 1998), 159.

Rather than replicate the vanguardist tradition of Marxist Leninist guerilla movements, the Zapatista's theory and practice of oppositional politics is informed by tenets of *"preguntando caminamos"* ("asking we walk") and *"mandar obedeciendo"* ("to command obeying") that center critique as a crucial component in dignity's revolt and urge that strategies of resistance be continually reimagined. Implicit in my reference to Zapatista theories of dignity and resistance is an epistemological argument about the value of alternative ways of knowing, producing knowledge, and constructing academic discourse. In short, I am reading the writings of Subcomandante Marcos and the Zapatistas as we might any other body of critical theory. For more examples of Zapatista communiqués that highlight their understanding of dignity in conjunction with struggles for hope, humanity, freedom, democracy, and justice, see "Second Declaration of the Lacandon Jungle," June 1994; "Fourth Declaration of the Lacandon Jungle," January 1996; "First Declaration of La Realidad for Humanity and against Neo-liberalism," January 1996. These and many other Zapatista communiqués are widely available on the World Wide Web and in the substantial print literature on the Zapatistas. For more on the Zapatista uprising and the growing influence of zapatismo as political and cultural praxis, see, for example, Holloway and Pelaez, *Zapatista!*; Gustavo Esteva, "The Zapatistas and People's Power," *Capital and Class* 68 (Summer 1999): 153–82; Midnight Notes Collective, *Auroras of the Zapatistas: Local and Global Struggles of the Fourth World War* (Brooklyn: Autonomedia, 2001); Manuel Callahan, "Zapatismo beyond Chiapas," in David Solnit, ed., *Globalize Liberation: How to Uproot the System and Build a Better World* (San Francisco: City Lights Books, 2004), chapter 16.

20. Stuart Cosgrove, "The Zoot-Suit and Style Warfare," *History Workshop Journal* 18 (Autumn 1984): 78.

21. Ross Chambers, *Room for Maneuver: Reading the Oppositional in Narrative* (Chicago: University of Chicago Press, 1991).

22. I conceive of the physical and discursive bodies of zoot suiters as socially constructed sites marked by the wider relations of power in which they were embedded. See, for example, Hastings Donnan and Thomas Wilson, *Borders: Frontiers of Identity, Nation, and State* (New York: Berg, 2001), 130.

23. My theory of a "body politics of dignity" follows numerous other efforts by historians and cultural critics to recognize and uncover the voice and activity of the subaltern, particularly when there is a lack of archival material that addresses such perspectives. For other such theoretical interventions in Chicana/o studies, see, for example, Emma Perez, *The Decolonial Imaginary: Writing Chicanas into History* (Bloomington: University of Indiana Press, 1999). In African American studies see, for example, Kelley, *Race Rebels*.

24. On the politics of worthiness, see Ana Y. Ramos-Zayas, "Delinquent Citizenship, National Performances: Racialization, Surveillance, and the Politics of 'Worthiness' in Puerto Rican Chicago," *Latino Studies* 2 (2004): 26–44.

25. The terms *hep cat, hipster, pachuca/o, zoot suiter,* and *zooter* were all contested during the early 1940s, and their many different meanings, including negative connotations attributed by local urban authorities and the mainstream and ethnic press, depended on who was doing the labeling. Though some hep cats and pachucos self-identified as such without wearing zoot suits, these terms, especially after the height of zoot popularity during World War II, were commonly associated with the zoot suit. Thus, while recognizing that zoot culture, *pachuquismo,* and the hep cat identity encompassed attitudes and values that prioritized leisure, style, speech, dance, and music that transcended just the suit of clothes, I use the term *zoot suiters* to refer to the many African American hep cats and Mexican American pachucos, as well as Euro-American, Japanese

American, and Filipino American youth who participated in zoot culture. For studies investigating the term and cultural practices of hep cats, see, for example, Kelley, *Race Rebels*, 161–82; Bruce Tyler, "Black Jive and White Repression," *Journal of Ethnic Studies* 16, no. 4 (Winter 1989): 31–66. For studies investigating the terms and cultural practices of pachucos and pachucas, see, for example, Arturo Madrid-Barela, "In Search of the Authentic Pachuco: An Interpretive Essay," *Aztlan* 4, no. 1 (Spring 1973): 31–60; Catherine S. Ramírez, "Crimes of Fashion: The Pachuca and Chicana Style Politics," *Meridians: Feminism, Race, Transnationalism* 2, no. 2 (2002): 1–35. For a recent comparative scholarly treatment of pachucos and hep cats, see Douglas Henry Daniels, "Los Angeles Zoot: Race 'Riot,' the Pachuco, and Black Music Culture," *Journal of African American History* 87, no. 1 (Winter 2002): 98–117.

26. For a useful overview of oral history as methodology, see, for example, Robert Perks and Alisdair Thomson, eds., *The Oral History Reader* (London: Routledge, 1997). For a discussion of the use of oral history in ethnic studies, see, for example, Matt García, *A World of Its Own: Race, Labor, and Citrus in the Making of Greater Los Angeles, 1900–1970* (Chapel Hill: University of North Carolina Press, 2001), 8–10.

1. RACE AND POLITICAL ECONOMY

1. "Mrs. Bass Philharmonic Auditorium Address, Sunday March 14, 1943," Charlotta A. Bass Collection, 1874–1968, additional box 1, folder "Speeches, 1940's," Southern California Library for Social Studies and Research. See also, Charlotta Bass, *Forty Years* (Los Angeles: Charlotta Bass, 1960).

2. This paradox can be described as part of a process of abjection in U.S. identity formation in which, as described by cultural critic Karen Shimakawa, attempts were made "to circumscribe and radically differentiate something that, although deemed repulsively *other* is, paradoxically, at some fundamental level, an undifferentiable part of the whole." Karen Shimakawa, *National Abjection: The Asian American Body Onstage* (Durham, NC: Duke University Press, 2002), 2–3.

3. For a general discussion of the increase in the numbers of women and minorities in war industry employment, see Allan M. Winkler, *Home Front U.S.A.: America during World War II* (Arlington Heights, IL: Harlan Davidson, 1986); Gerald Nash, *The American West Transformed: The Impact of the Second World War* (Bloomington: Indiana University Press, 1985); Gerald Nash, *World War II and the West: Reshaping the Economy* (Lincoln: University of Nebraska Press, 1990); D'Ann Campbell, *Women at War with America: Private Lives in a Patriotic Era* (Cambridge, MA: Harvard University Press, 1984).

4. Campbell, *Women at War with America*, 103. On the experience of women on the home front more generally, see, for example, Karen Anderson, *Wartime Women: Sex Roles, Family Relations, and the Status of Women during World War II* (Westport, CT: Greenwood Press, 1981); Susan Hartman, *The Home Front and Beyond: American Women in the 1940s* (Boston: Twayne, 1982); Maureen Honey, *Bitter Fruit: African American Women in World War II* (Columbia: University of Missouri Press, 1999); Doris Weatherford, *American Women and World War II* (New York: Facts on File, 1990).

5. Vicki Ruiz, *Cannery Women, Cannery Lives: Mexican Women, Unionization, and the California Food Processing Industry, 1930–1950* (Albuquerque: University of New Mexico Press, 1987).

6. Winkler, *Home Front U.S.A.,* 63, 67.

7. On the contribution of African American and Mexican American servicemen and communities to World War II, see, for example, Maggie Rivas-Rodriguez, ed., *Mexican Americans and World War II* (Austin: University of Texas Press, 2005); Raul Morin, *Among the Valiant: Mexican Americans in World War II and Korea* (Alhambra, CA: Borden, 1963); Christopher Moore, *Fighting for America: Black Soldiers—The Unsung Heroes of World War II* (New York: One World/Ballantine, 2004); Neil Wynn, *The Afro-American and the Second World War* (London: Elek, 1976). On race and cultural relations in the United States during World War II more generally, see, for example, Beth Bailey, *The First Strange Place: The Alchemy of Race and Sex in World War II Hawaii* (New York: Free Press, 1992); Nash, *American West Transformed*; Winkler, *Home Front USA*; John Morton Blum, *V Was for Victory: Politics and Culture during World War II* (New York: Harcourt Brace Jovanovich, 1976); John Morton Blum, *United Against: American Culture and Society during World War II* (Colorado Springs: U.S. Air Force Academy, 1983); Lewis Erenberg and Susan Hirsch, eds., *The War in American Culture: Society and Consciousness in World War II* (Chicago: University of Chicago Press, 1996); Richard Polenberg, *America at War: The Home Front, 1941–1945* (Englewood Cliffs, NJ: Prentice-Hall, 1972); Escobedo, "Mexican American Home Front."

8. John Hope Franklin and Alfred A. Moss, Jr., *From Slavery to Freedom: A History of Negro Americans* (New York: McGraw-Hill, 1988), 389–90.

9. On the African American military experience during World War II and the struggle to desegregate the armed forces, see, for example, Bernard C. Nalty, *Strength for the Fight: A History of Black Americans in the Military* (New York: Free Press, 1986); Gail Buckley, *American Patriots: The Story of Blacks in the Military from the Revolution to Desert Storm* (New York: Random House, 2001), 257–334; Richard M. Dalfiume, *Desegregation of the U.S. Armed Forces: Fighting on Two Fronts, 1939–1953* (Columbia: University of Missouri Press, 1969); Gary Gerstle, *American Crucible: Race and the Nation in the Twentieth Century* (Princeton: Princeton University Press, 2001), 203–37.

10. Winkler, *Home Front U.S.A..*

11. Gerstle, *American Crucible,* 188.

12. For examples of segregation against African Americans and Mexican Americans in Los Angeles, see, for example, Commentary on the Coordinating Council for Latin American Youth by Manuel Ruiz Jr., January 26, 1977, Manuel Ruiz Papers, box 1, folder 1; Statement of Lieutenant Edward Duran Ayres to the 1942 Grand Jury of Los Angeles County, ibid., box 15, folder 16; Carey McWilliams Papers, collection 1243, box 26, folder "Ayres, Duran Ed.," Department of Special Collections, University of California, Los Angeles; Papers of the National Association for the Advancement of Colored People (NAACP), part 15, Segregation and Discrimination, Complaints and Responses, 1940–1955, series A, Legal Dept., NAACP, Bethesda, MD; theater bulletin in Los Angeles noting "Mexican Night Every Wednesday, Colored Night Every Thurs-

day," in Alice McGrath Papers, collection 1290, box 2, folder 11, Department of Special Collections, University of California, Los Angeles.

13. On Jim Crow segregation, see, for example, George Fredrickson, *White Supremacy: A Comparative Study in American and South African History* (Oxford: Oxford University Press, 1981); C. Vann Woodward, *The Strange Career of Jim Crow* (New York: Oxford University Press, 1966); Kelley, *Race Rebels*; Neil McMillen, *Dark Journey: Black Mississippians in the Age of Jim Crow* (Urbana: University of Illinois Press, 1989).

14. David Montejano, *Anglos and Mexicans in the Making of Texas, 1836–1986* (Austin: University of Texas Press, 1987), 262.

15. On cultural citizenship, see Lisa Lowe, *Immigrant Acts: On Asian American Cultural Politics* (Durham, NC: Duke University Press, 1996); David Trend, ed., *Radical Democracy: Identity, Citizenship, and the State* (New York: Routledge, 1996); Stephen Castles and Alastair Davidson, *Citizenship and Migration: Globalization and the Politics of Belonging* (New York: Routledge, 2000); Catriona McKinnon and Lain Hampsher-Monk, eds., *The Demands of Citizenship* (New York: Continuum, 2000); David Miller, *Citizenship and National Identity* (Cambridge: Polity Press, 2000); Andrew Vandenberg, ed., *Citizenship and Democracy in a Global Era* (New York: St. Martin's Press, 2000).

16. On the histories of Los Angeles and New York, see Mike Davis, *City of Quartz: Excavating the Future of Los Angeles* (London: Verso, 1990); Robert Fogelson, *The Fragmented Metropolis: Los Angeles, 1850–1930* (Cambridge: Harvard University Press, 1967); Ricardo Romo, *East Los Angeles: History of a Barrio* (Austin: University of Texas Press, 1983); Albert Camarillo, *Chicanos in a Changing Society: From Mexican Pueblos to American Barrios in Santa Barbara and Southern California, 1848–1930* (Cambridge: Harvard University Press, 1979); Joshua B. Freeman, *Working-Class New York: Life and Labor since World War II* (New York: New Press, 2000); Gilbert Osofsky, *Harlem: The Making of a Ghetto* (New York: Harper and Row, 1971); Thomas Kessner, *Fiorello H. La Guardia and the Making of Modern New York* (New York: McGraw-Hill, 1989); Barbara Blumberg, *The New Deal and the Unemployed: The View from New York City* (Lewisberg, PA: Bucknell University Press, 1979).

17. Escobar, *Race, Police, and the Making of a Political Identity*, 156–57. For more on the growth of the western economy during World War II, see, for example, Nash, *World War II and the West*.

18. Nash, *American West Transformed*, 25.

19. Ibid., 38.

20. On the migration of African Americans to the West, see, for example, ibid, chapter 6. On Mexican immigration to the United States during the 1940s see, for example, David Gutiérrez, *Walls and Mirrors: Mexican Americans, Mexican Immigrants, and the Politics of Ethnicity* (Berkeley: University of California Press, 1995); Kitty Calavita, *Inside the State: The Bracero Program, Immigration, and the I.N.S.* (New York: Routledge, 1992).

21. Kevin Allen Leonard, "Brothers under the Skin? African Americans, Mexican Americans, and World War II in California," in Roger W. Lotchin, ed., *The Way We Really Were: The Golden State in the Second Great War* (Urbana:

University of Illinois Press, 2000), 189–90. Leonard notes that the figures for ethnic Mexicans living in Los Angeles should be considered a conservative estimate, as there is much debate about the accuracy of the 1940 census count.

22. "Report for Conference with Mr. Thomas Campbell and Mr. Walter Christian of United States Employment Service, prepared by George Gleason, December 3, 1942," including "suggestions made by Campbell and Christian," Manuel Ruiz Papers, box 2, folder 18.

23. Harry F. Henderson, Chairman of Special Committee on Mexican Relations of the Los Angeles County Grand Jury 1942, to Henry Stimson, Secretary of War, November 12, 1942, Carey McWilliams Papers, collection 1243, box 27, folder "LA County Grand Jury 1942." See also "Resolution of CCLAY," June 2, 1942, Manuel Ruiz Papers, box 3, folder 15; minutes of the CCLAY regular meeting, February 1, 1943, Manuel Ruiz Papers, box 3, folder 8.

24. Neil Foley, "Becoming Hispanic: Mexican Americans and the Faustian Pact with Whiteness," in Foley, ed., *Reflexiones 1997: New Directions in Mexican American Studies* (Austin: University of Texas Press, 1997); Foley, *The White Scourge: Mexicans, Blacks, and Poor Whites in Texas Cotton Culture* (Berkeley: University of California Press, 1999).

25. "A Summary of the Hearings of the President's Committee on Fair Employment Practice Held in Los Angeles, California, October 20 and 21, 1941, with Findings and Recommendations," Manuel Ruiz Papers, box 5, folder 4.

26. Josh Sides, *L.A. City Limits: African American Los Angeles from the Great Depression to the Present* (Berkeley: University of California Press, 2003), 57.

27. Russell R. Peterson, principal, Roosevelt Evening High School, to Eduardo Quevedo undated, box 1, folder 10; Russell R. Peterson to Eduardo Quevedo, February 10, 1942, box 1, folder 10; Russell Peterson to Eduardo Quevedo, March 26, 1942, box 1, folder 12; Elizabeth Faragoh, chairwoman of the Committee for the Care of Children in Wartime Los Angeles, to Eduardo Quevedo, September 21, 1942, box 1, folder 10, all in Eduardo Quevedo Papers, 1929–1968, collection M0349, Department of Special Collections, Stanford University; Citizens Committee for Latin American Youth to YMCA, January 30, 1942, Manuel Ruiz Papers, box 2; Civilian Defense Councils Committee on Youth Programs, Los Angeles, California, "Activities—April 1 to June 15, 1942," ibid., box 1, folder 12; "Casos y Cosas," by Eduardo Quevedo, June 4, 1942, Eduardo Quevedo Papers, 1929–1968, collection M0349, box 1, folder 10.

28. "Jim Crow in National Defense," pamphlet issued by the Los Angeles Council of the National Negro Congress, Papers of the National Negro Congress, box 21, Schomburg Center for Research in Black Culture, New York Public Library.

29. "Mrs. Bass Philharmonic Auditorium Address, Sunday March 14, 1943," Charlotta A. Bass Collection, 1874–1968, additional box 1, folder "Speeches, 1940's." See also Bass, *Forty Years.*

30. Leonard, "Brothers under the Skin?" 192.

31. Sides, *L.A. City Limits*, 62–69.

32. Chester Himes, *If He Hollers Let Him Go* (London, Falcon Press, 1947; repr., New York: Thunder's Mouth Press, 2002), 3.

33. George J. Sánchez, *Becoming Mexican American: Ethnicity, Culture and Identity in Chicano Los Angeles, 1900–1945* (Oxford: Oxford University Press, 1993), 74. On the history of East Los Angeles, also see Romo, *History of a Barrio*.

34. "Testimony of Carey McWilliams," papers read at meeting held October 8, 1942, called by Special Mexican Relations Committee of the Los Angeles County Grand Jury, Manuel Ruiz Papers, box 15, folder 16.

35. "A Tabulation of Facts on Conditions Existent in Hick's Mexican Camp," ibid.

36. Clora Bryant et al., eds., *Central Avenue Sounds: Jazz in Los Angeles* (Berkeley: University of California Press, 1998), introduction, 200–201.

37. Sides, *L.A. City Limits*, 45.

38. On the professionalization of the LAPD and wartime police brutality in Los Angeles, and for a thorough history of the relationship between the Mexican American community and the LAPD, see Escobar, *Race, Police, and the Making of a Political Identity*, 155–77.

39. Manuel Ruiz, Citizens Committee for Latin American Youth, to LAPD chief of police C. B. Horrall, November 14, 1941, Manuel Ruiz Papers, box 2, folder 12.

40. Statements of Aurora Maldinado and Peter Maldinado, undated, Manuel Ruiz Papers, box 3, folder 12.

41. Postcard to Manuel Ruiz from John Mendez of Fillmore, California, December 27, 1943, Manuel Ruiz Papers, box 2, folder 20.

42. Citizens Committee for Latin American Youth to Lieutenant Em Quibell, Hollenbeck Police Station, November 27, 1941, Manuel Ruiz Papers, box 2, folder 12.

43. On the evolution of the "Mexican problem" in California and in U.S. political discourse, and on the 1930s repatriation campaign, see Gutiérrez, *Walls and Mirrors*; Mark Reisler, *By the Sweat of Their Brow: Mexican Immigrant Labor in the United States, 1900–1940* (Westport, CT: Greenwood Press, 1976); Abraham Hoffman, *Unwanted Mexican Americans in the Great Depression: Repatriation Pressures, 1929–1939* (Tucson: University of Arizona Press, 1974).

44. Private Sal Thomas to Layle Layne, October 12, 1942," Layle Lane Papers, collection MG 54, box 1, folder "Correspondence — Soldiers, 1942–1946, Schomburg Center for Research in Black Culture, New York Public Library.

45. Cheryl Greenberg, *Or Does It Explode? Black Harlem in the Great Depression* (New York: Oxford University Press, 1991), 199–200.

46. Dominic J. Capeci Jr., *The Harlem Riot of 1943* (Philadelphia: Temple University Press, 1977), 59.

47. Greenberg, *Or Does It Explode?* 199–200.

48. "Findings and Principal Addresses, The Hampton Institution Conference on the Participation of the Negro in National Defense," Hampton, Virginia, November 25–26, 1940, remarks by Dr. Malcolm S. Maclean, president of Hampton Institute, and by Aubrey Williams, administrator of National Youth Administration, Fiorello La Guardia Papers, microfilm roll 0197, Municipal

Archives, New York City; "Youth, Defense, and the National Warfare," Recommendations of the American Youth Commission of the American Council on Education, Papers of the National Negro Congress, box 54.

49. "American Negro in National Defense Industries," memorandum, May, 7, 1941, Fiorello La Guardia Papers, microfilm roll 197.

50. Memo to "all holders of defense contracts" from Sidney Hillman, associate director general, Office of Production Management, Washington, D.C., undated, Fiorello La Guardia Papers, microfilm roll 197.

51. Flyer "Announcing the Eastern Seaboard Conference on the Problems of the War and the Negro People," sponsored by the National Negro Congress, April 10–11, 1943, Abyssinian Baptist Church, New York City, Layle Lane Papers, collection MG 54, box 1, folder 7.

52. "The Negro and the Fight for Victory," address delivered by Edward E. Strong, national secretary of the National Negro Congress, at the Eastern Seaboard Conference on the Problems of the War and the Negro People, April 10, 1943, New York City, Layle Lane Papers, collection MG 54, box 1, folder 7.

53. Ibid.

54. George F. Chapline, president of Brewster Aeronautical Corporation, to Mayor Fiorello La Guardia, February 15, 1941; D. R. Grumman, Grumman Aircraft Engineering Corporation, to Mayor Fiorello La Guardia, February 17, 1941; William L. Wilson, Director of Public Relations, Republic Aviation Corporation, to Mayor Fiorello La Guardia, February 21, 1943, Fiorello La Guardia Papers, microfilm roll 0197.

55. Charles Collier to Mayor Fiorello La Guardia, May 9, 1941, ibid.

56. "Growing Up in Harlem . . . ," pamphlet issued by Board of Directors, West Harlem Council of Social Agencies, Harlem Neighborhood Association Papers, Schomburg Center for Research in Black Culture, collection MG 364, box 1, folder 1.

57. On the wartime social and political experiences of Italian Americans, see, for example, Winkler, Home Front U.S.A., 70–71; Blum, V Was for Victory, 147–55.

58. Harrold Lindo to Mayor Fiorello La Guardia, August 30, 1941, Fiorello La Guardia Papers, microfilm roll 0197.

59. Rebecca Elliot to Mayor Fiorello La Guardia, September 26, 1941; George Sclier to Mayor Fiorello La Guardia, July 16, 1941; Pearl Cotton to Mayor Fiorello La Guardia, June 22, 1942; Anthony Piscopo to Mayor Fiorello La Guardia, June 30, 1941; Albert Nealy Jr. to Mayor Fiorello La Guardia, June 17, 1941; Henry Feldman to Mayor Fiorello La Guardia, September 1, 1941; Mrs. H. S. Wolf to Mayor Fiorello La Guardia, September 23, 1941, Fiorello La Guardia Papers, microfilm roll 0197.

60. Henry K. Craft to David Stratner, April 15, 1941, Fiorello La Guardia Papers, box 808, as quoted in Capeci, Harlem Riot of 1943, 49–50.

61. Capeci, Harlem Riot of 1943, 32. On the history of Harlem prior to the Great Depression, see, for example, Osofsky, Harlem.

62. Greenberg, Or Does It Explode?, 215.

63. Mercedes Owens to Fiorello La Guardia, June 25, 1942, Fiorello La Guardia Papers, microfilm roll 0197.

64. Florence P. Shientag, law aide to Mayor Fiorello La Guardia, to Mrs. William Owens, July 6, 1942, ibid.

65. "Growing Up in Harlem. . . . "

66. "Angry Mob Circles Hospital as Crazed Man Is Slain by Cop"; "Mounted Cop, Gun in Hand, Quelled Mob," *People's Voice,* May 16, 1942; "I Saw a Harlem Cop Slay a Helpless Man," *People's Voice,* May 23, 1942; "Harlemites Visit DA's Office in Armstrong Slaying Case," *People's Voice,* May 30, 1942.

67. "Incensed Long Island Townsfolk Clash with Cops over Brutality," *People's Voice,* May 9, 1942.

68. "Four Teenage Boys Spit Upon: Detective Had Been Warned By Judge," *People's Voice,* April 10, 1943.

69. Reverend Edward McGowan Mayor La Guardia, July 2, 1943; Isaac Siegel, Domestic Relations Court, to Honorable Lester B. Stone, Executive Assistant to the Mayor, July 16, 1943, Fiorello La Guardia Papers, microfilm roll 0197.

70. "Suspend Subway Cop Who Beat High School Girl; Trial Scheduled," *People's Voice,* April 3, 1943.

71. *New York Age,* May 8, 1943, as quoted in Nat Brandt, *Harlem at War: The Black Experience in WWII* (Syracuse, NY: Syracuse University Press, 1996), 64–65.

72. "A Summary of the Hearings of the President's Committee on Fair Employment Practice Held in Los Angeles, California, October 20 and 21, 1941, with Findings and Recommendations," Manuel Ruiz Papers, box 5, folder 4.

73. Greenberg, *Or Does It Explode?,* 202.

74. Winkler, *Home Front U.S.A.,* 62.

75. "Report for Conference with Mr. Thomas Campbell and Mr. Walter Christian of United States Employment Service, prepared by George Gleason, December 3, 1942," including "suggestions made by Campbell and Christian," Manuel Ruiz Papers, box 2, folder 18.

76. "The Negro and War Activities," by Layle Lane, August 18, 1942, Layle Lane Papers, collection MG 54, box 1, folder 7.

77. Merl E. Reed, *Seedtime for the Modern Civil Rights Movement: The President's Committee on Fair Employment Practice, 1941–1946* (Baton Rouge: Louisiana State University Press, 1991).

78. On the internment of Japanese Americans during World War II, see, for example, Roger Daniels, *Concentration Camps, U.S.A.: Japanese Americans and World War II* (New York: Holt, Rinehart, and Winston, 1970); Roger Daniels, *Prisoners without Trial: Japanese Americans in World War II* (New York: Hill and Wang, 1993); Michi Weglyn, *Years of Infamy: The Untold Story of America's Concentration Camps* (Seattle: University of Washington Press, 1996); Brian Masaru Hayashi, *Democratizing the Enemy: The Japanese American Internment* (Princeton: Princeton University Press, 2004); Greg Robinson, *By Order of the President: FDR and the Internment of Japanese Americans* (Cambridge, MA: Harvard University Press, 2003); Ronald Takaki, *Double Victory: A Multicultural History of America in World War II* (New York: Little, Brown, 2000), 137–79.

79. Eric Muller, *Free to Die for Their Country: The Story of the Japanese*

American Draft Resisters in World War II (Chicago: University of Chicago Press, 2001), 3.

80. Himes, *If He Hollers Let Him Go*, 4.

2. CLASS POLITICS AND JUVENILE DELINQUENCY

1. "Youthful Gang Secrets Exposed: Young Hoodlums Smoke 'Reefers,' Tattoo Girls, and Plot Robberies," *Los Angeles Times,* July 16, 1944.

2. Donnan and Wilson, *Borders,* 136.

3. On studies of juvenile delinquency, see "Analysis and Explanation of the Program and Budget of the Youth Correction Authority for the 95th and 96th Fiscal Years," John Anson Ford Collection, box 33, folder 11, Huntington Library, San Marino, CA; letter to Judge H. Robert Scott from the committee appointed to study so-called Mexican gang situation, December 28, 1942, ibid., box 34, folder 3. See also Escobar, *Race, Police, and the Making of a Political Identity,* particularly chapter 6, "Theories and Statistics of Mexican Criminality," and chapter 9, "Facts and Origins of the Zoot-Suit Hysteria." Making use of county supervisor, mayoral, and city police records, Escobar suggests that though crime in general decreased in the Los Angeles area during the initial years of World War II, the arrests of nonwhite youth increased.

4. See, for example, Kevin Gaines, *Uplifting the Race: Black Leadership, Politics, and Culture in the Twentieth Century* (Chapel Hill: University of North Carolina Press, 1996); Mario T. García, *Mexican Americans: Leadership, Ideology, and Identity, 1930–1960* (New Haven, CT: Yale University Press, 1989).

5. According to George Lipsitz, "Class represents both an ideological perception and historical experience." George Lipsitz, *Rainbow at Midnight: Labor and Culture in the 1940s* (Urbana: University of Illinois Press, 1994).

6. "We Have Just Begun To Fight!" Manuel Ruiz Papers, box 16, folder 5.

7. "A Statement on the Sleepy Lagoon Case," undated, Bert Corona Papers, Department of Special Collections, Stanford University, box 28, folder 25; Ben Margolis, "The Sleepy Lagoon Case," *Los Angeles Lawyer Guild* 1, no. 3 (December 1944), in Manuel Ruiz Papers, box 16, folder 5.

8. "A Statement on the Sleepy Lagoon Case."

9. Guy Endore, "The Sleepy Lagoon Case," with a foreword by Orson Welles, prepared by the Citizens' Committee for the Defense of Mexican American Youth, Los Angeles California, 1942, Bert Corona Papers, box 28, folder 25; "A Statement on the Sleepy Lagoon Case"; Margolis, "The Sleepy Lagoon Case"; "We Have Just Begun to Fight!" See also Pagán, *Murder at the Sleepy Lagoon*; Escobar, *Race, Police, and the Making of a Political Identity.*

10. "Minutes of Meeting of Citizens Committee on Youth in Wartime," November 1, 1943, Manuel Ruiz Papers, box 4, folder 1; "Summary of Recommendations and Progress to Date of the Special Committee on Older Youth Gang Activity in Los Angeles and Vicinity," ibid., box 15, folder 16; "Objectives of the Los Angeles Youth Project and the Youth It Served in 1944," ibid., box 4, folder 12; "Report of Special Committee on Problems of Mexican Youth of the 1942 Grand Jury of Los Angeles County," ibid., box 15, folder 16.

11. Numerous letters, memos, and reports addressing the 1942 grand jury in

particular and juvenile delinquency more broadly abound in both the papers of Bowron and Ford. See, for example, John Anson Ford Collection, box 75, B, IV, folders 7–8; Fletcher Bowron Collection, 1934–1970, Huntington Library, San Marino, CA, box 1, folder "Extra Copies of Letters, 1942."

12. Statement of Lieutenant Edward Duran Ayres to the 1942 Grand Jury of Los Angeles County, Manuel Ruiz Papers, box 15, folder 16; Carey McWilliams Papers, collection 1243, box 26, folder "Ayres, Duran Ed."; Papers of the National Association for the Advancement of Colored People, part 15, Segregation and Responses 1940–1955, series A.

13. Statement of Lieutenant Edward Duran Ayres to the 1942 Grand Jury of Los Angeles County; Carey McWilliams Papers, folder "Ayres, Duran Ed."

14. "Gangster Gets Six Months," unidentified news clipping, Manuel Ruiz Papers, box 16, folder 6.

15. Statement of Lieutenant Edward Duran Ayres to the 1942 Grand Jury of Los Angeles County; Carey McWilliams Papers, folder "Ayres, Duran Ed."; Papers of the National Association for the Advancement of Colored People, part 15, Segregation and Responses 1940–1955, series A.

16. Statement of Lieutenant Edward Duran Ayres to the 1942 Grand Jury of Los Angeles County; Carey McWilliams Papers, folder "Ayres, Duran Ed."

17. Victor Jew, "Getting the Measure of Tomorrow: Chinese and Chicano Americans under the Racial Gaze, 1934–1935 and 1942–1944," in Nicholas De Genova, ed., *Racial Transformations: Latinos and Asians Remaking the United States* (Durham, NC: Duke University Press, 2006).

18. Statement of Lieutenant Edward Duran Ayres to the 1942 Grand Jury of Los Angeles County; Carey McWilliams Papers, folder "Ayres, Duran Ed."

19. E. W. Biscailuz, Sheriff of Los Angeles County, to Ernest W. Oliver, Foreman, Los Angeles County Grand Jury 1942, August 20, 1942, Carey McWilliams Papers, box 29, folder "Mexicans—Juvenile Delinquency."

20. For discussion of eugenics and scientific racism, see Stephen J. Gould, *The Mismeasure of Man* (New York: Norton, 1981); Edward J. Larson, *Sex, Race, and Science: Eugenics in the Deep South* (Baltimore: Johns Hopkins University Press, 1995); Elazar Barkan, *The Retreat of Scientific Racism: Changing Concepts of Race in Britain and the United States between the World Wars* (Cambridge: Cambridge University Press, 1992).

21. C. B. Horrall, Chief of LAPD, to Ernest W. Oliver, Foreman, Los Angeles County Grand Jury 1942, August 13, 1942, Carey McWilliams Papers, box 26, folder "Ayres, Duran Ed."

22. "The Problem of Crime among the Mexican Youth of Los Angeles," by Harry Hoijer, papers read in meeting held October 8, 1942, called by special Mexican relations committee of the Los Angeles County Grand Jury, Manuel Ruiz Papers, box 15, folder 16.

23. Reference in personal notebook of Carey McWilliams (untitled entry) to letter to grand jury by LAPD captain Vernon Rassmussen, second week of August 1942, Carey McWilliams Papers, box 27, folder "McWilliams, Carey—as author." Rasmussen further stated that he did not believe the Mexican gang situation was as serious as it was assumed to be, that it did not challenge law enforcement agencies, and that the situation could be controlled without difficulty.

24. See, for example, Fletcher Bowron to Mr. Vierling Kersey, Superintendent of Los Angeles Schools, February 1, 1943; Bowron to California Governor Earl Warren, May 18, 1943, Fletcher Bowron Collection, box 1, folder "Extra Copies of Letters, 1943, Jan–June." See also "Remarks of Mayor Fletcher Bowron at the Banquet of Peace Officers' Association of the State of California, October 23, 1942," ibid., box 34, folder "Remarks at Public Events, Addresses by the Mayor, 1942."

25. "Statement by Mayor Fletcher Bowron, January 11, 1943," ibid., box 34, folder "Statements to the Press 1942–1943–1944."

26. For more on how public health officials in California, especially in Los Angeles, promulgated eugenics-infused policies affecting their Mexican constituents, see Natalia Molina, *Fit to be Citizens? Public Health and Race in Los Angeles, 1879–1939* (Berkeley: University of California Press, 2006).

27. Fletcher Bowron to Dr. Thomas Parran, Surgeon General, United States Public Health Service, Washington, D.C., October 13, 1943, Fletcher Bowron Collection, box 1.

28. Josephine Fierro de Bright, General Secretary, National Congress of the Spanish Speaking Peoples of the USA, to John Anson Ford, Los Angeles County Supervisor, September 1, 1939, John Anson Ford Collection, box 75, folder 5.

29. Nayan Shah, *Contagious Divides: Epidemics and Race in San Francisco's Chinatown* (Berkeley: University of California Press, 2001), 77–79.

30. See, for example, John Anson Ford to Dr. George B. Mangold, Chairman, County Probation Committee, March 2, 1939; John Anson Ford to Los Angeles County Youth Commission, September 14, 1939. These and several other similar letters are found in the John Anson Ford Collection, box 33, folder 6.

31. See, for example, Karl Holton to John Anson Ford, July 17, 1942; Stephen J. Keating, Secretary, Citizens Committee for Latin American Youth, to John Anson Ford, May 6, 1943; memorandum to Southern California Council of Inter-American Affairs, "Suggested Program of Committee on Racial Minorities," May 10, 1943, ibid., box 33, folder 6.

32. "Testimony of Carey McWilliams," papers read in meeting held October 8, 1942, called by Special Mexican Relations Committee of the Los Angeles County Grand Jury.

33. Escobar, *Race, Police, and the Making of a Political Identity*, 219.

34. "Testimony of Guy T. Nunn," papers read in meeting held October 8, 1942, called by Special Mexican Relations Committee of the Los Angeles County Grand Jury.

35. Ibid.

36. "Paper Presented by Consul Aguilar," papers read in meeting held October 8, 1942, called by Special Mexican Relations Committee of the Los Angeles County Grand Jury.

37. "Report of Special Committee on Problems of Mexican Youth of the 1942 Grand Jury of Los Angeles County."

38. Ibid.

39. Manuel Ruiz, "Latin American Juvenile Delinquency in LA: Bomb or Bubble?" *Crime Prevention Digest* 1, no. 13 (December 1942), in Manuel Ruiz Papers, box 1, folder 6.

40. Endore, "The Sleepy Lagoon Case."

41. "Six Arrested in Gang Death: Girl and Five Youths Held in Fatal Shooting at Wedding Shower," *Los Angeles Times,* November 23, 1942; "New Zoot Gangster Attacks Result in Arrest of 100: Complaints against 43 Issued, Accusing Them of Unlawful Assemblage in Week-end Outbreaks," *Los Angeles Times,* October 27, 1942; "Idle Time Seen as Crux of Youth Problem," *Los Angeles Daily News,* October 2, 1942; "City and County Take Action to End Boy Gangs," *Los Angeles Evening Herald and Express,* November 24, 1942.

42. "Origenes de Pachucos y 'Malinches,'" *La Opinion,* August 26, 1942. For more articles and editorials condemning juvenile delinquency, see *La Opinion,* August 1942 through July 1943.

43. "Death Penalty to Be Asked for Jitterbug Killers of Teacher," *Los Angeles Times,* October 4, 1942.

44. "Youth Conference Leader Tells of Juvenile Crimes," *Amsterdam News,* May 1, 1943.

45. "Mayor's Committee Report on Juvenile Delinquency: First Interim Report, July 8, 1943," Fiorello La Guardia Papers, microfilm roll 0112, "Juvenile Delinquency (52) to Labor-Civilian Defense Administration (25)," subject files 1934–1945; "Report on Subject Matter of Communication from Justice Herbert A. O'Brien, Domestic Relations Court, concerning Adolescence, Forwarded by the Counsel to the Governor of the State of New York," ibid., microfilm roll 0197, "Queens Borough Hall (1) to Race Discrimination (16)," subject files 1934–1945; "Presentment of the August 1943 Grand Jury of Kings County: In the Investigation of Crime and Disorderly Conditions of the Bedford-Stuyvesant Area of Brooklyn," ibid., microfilm roll 0197.

46. Jeanne Seeley Schwartz to Mayor Fiorello La Guardia, February 9, 1943, ibid., microfilm roll 0110.

47. Memo, Commanding Officer, 23rd Detective Squad, NYPD, to Commanding Officer, 18th Division, NYPD, March 31, 1943, ibid.

48. Ethel M. Olsen to Fiorello La Guardia, April 16, 1943, ibid.

49. Fiorello La Guardia to Ethel M. Olsen, April 22, 1943, ibid.

50. Mrs. Leonie Gray to Fiorello La Guardia, March 13, 1943, ibid.

51. First Interim Report of the Mayor's Committee on Juvenile Delinquency, July 8, 1943.

52. "Presentment of the August 1943 Grand Jury of Kings County."

53. Ibid.

54. Ibid.

55. Ibid.

56. Memo, Office of the Juvenile Aid Bureau to Chief Inspector, NYPD, April 14, 1943, Fiorello La Guardia Papers, microfilm roll 0110.

57. First Interim Report of the Mayor's Committee on Juvenile Delinquency.

58. "Presentment of the August 1943 Grand Jury of Kings County."

59. Assemblyman S. Robert Molinari, Richmond, to Mayor La Guardia, February 19, 1943, Fiorello La Guardia Papers.

60. "Arrest 12 Young Boys in Gang Murder Case," *Amsterdam News,* July 24, 1943; "Jail Boy Gang Leader in Murder," *Amsterdam News,* July 31, 1943.

61. "Delinquency Rise among Girls Told," *New York Times*, October 28, 1942; "Midnight Curfew for Girls under 16 Urged Here to Curb Delinquency," *New York Post*, October 31, 1942; "Closing of City Parks to Children Urged as a Curb on Delinquency," *New York Times*, November 5, 1942; "City Park Curfew for Children Urged by Judge to Curb Rising Delinquency," *Bronx News*, November 5, 1942; "Teachers Predict Delinquency Rise," *New York Times*, November 5, 1942.

62. "Closing of City Parks to Children Urged as a Curb on Delinquency," *New York Times*, November 5, 1942.

63. "Editorial Appearing in the Hempstead, Long Island *Review-Star*, Harsher Methods Needing," undated, Papers of the National Negro Congress, box 73.

64. "Delinquency Rise among Girls Told"; "Midnight Curfew for Girls Under 16 Urged Here to Curb Delinquency"; "Closing of City Parks to Children Urged as a Curb on Delinquency"; "City Park Curfew for Children Urged by Judge to Curb Rising Delinquency"; "Teachers Predict Delinquency Rise," *New York Times*, November 5, 1942; "Delinquencies Surveyed Here: Lack of Parental Care Laid to Women in War Jobs," *New York Sun*, January 11, 1943; "Mothers on Jobs Blamed for Delinquency Rise: Welfare Speakers Recommend Restrictions on Hiring," *New York Herald Tribune*, January 12, 1943; "Delinquency Laid to Penny-Pinching: Curb in Welfare Service to Children Sharply Assailed by Justice Polier," *New York Times*, April 17, 1943; "Schoolgirls Compete in Oldest Profession," *New York Daily News*, December 22, 1943. See also Fiorello La Guardia Papers, microfilm roll 0112, folder "Juvenile Delinquency—Press Clippings, November–December 1942."

65. "Daily News under Fire for Smearing," *People's Voice*, August 15, 1942; "Survey of New York Papers Reveal News' Lie Widespread," *People's Voice*, August 15, 1942; "New York Dailies Out-Garble Goebbels," *People's Voice*, March 27, 1943; "Truth behind the Harlem Smear!" *People's Voice*, April 10, 1943; "Citizens' Committee Raps Angling of Crime News," *Amsterdam News*, April 3, 1943; "Rosenwald's Daughter Raps 'Crime Wave' Reports," *Amsterdam News*, April 24, 1943.

66. On the Sleepy Lagoon Defense Committee, see Frank P. Barajas, "The Defense Committees of Sleepy Lagoon: A Convergent Struggle against Fascism, 1942–1944," *Aztlan* 31, no. 1 (Spring 2006): 33–62.

67. "The Education of Alice McGrath," Alice McGrath Oral History, interviewed by Michael Balter, tape 4, side 2, January 20, 1985, p. 157, UCLA Special Collections, collection 300/269.

68. See, for example, the editorial "Our Mexican Neighbors," *California Eagle*, October 15, 1942; "Plans Probe of Mexican 'Boy Gangs,'" *California Eagle*, October 22, 1942; "Mexicans Face Police Terror Round-ups; Vile Press Slurs: Link L.A. Anti-Mexican Drive with So-Called Harlem 'Crime Wave,'" *California Eagle*, November 5, 1942.

69. Carey McWilliams to Nelson Rockefeller, Coordinator of Inter-American Affairs, Washington, D.C., August 6, 1942, Carey McWilliams Papers, box 27, folder "McWilliams, Carey—as author."

70. CCLAY Meeting of the Board of Directors, December 1, 1941, Manuel

Ruiz Papers, box 3, folder 7; CCLAY Meeting of Board of Directors, February 9, 1942, ibid.; minutes CCLAY regular meeting, March 1, 1942, ibid., box 3, folder 8; minutes CCLAY regular meeting, March 23, 1942, ibid., box 3, folder 7; Manuel Ruiz to Judge Robert H. Scott, Superior Court, Juvenile Division, November 13, 1942, ibid., box 2, folder 13; Manuel Ruiz to Lieutenant Wallace, Hollenbeck Police Station, March 2, 1943, ibid., box 2, folder 14; Manuel Ruiz to Lieutenant Stein, Highland Police Station, March 2, 1943, ibid., box 2, folder 14; Manuel Ruiz to Captain Brewster, East Los Angeles Sheriff Sub-Station, March 2, 1943, ibid., box 2, folder 14; Alfonso Ortega, District Scout Executive of Boy Scouts of America, to Manuel Ruiz, January 22, 1942, ibid., box 2, folder 18; William T. Lindsay, Director of Organization and Extension, Boy Scouts of America, Los Angeles Area Council, to Eduardo Quevedo, September 12, 1944, Eduardo Quevedo Papers, box 1, folder 12; Myer B. Marion, Justice of the Peace, Belvedere Township, to Eduardo Quevedo, April 7, 1941, ibid., box 1, folder 9; minutes CCLAY regular meeting, April 5, 1943, Manuel Ruiz Papers, box 3, folder 8.

71. Minutes CCLAY meeting, May 3, 1943, Manuel Ruiz Papers, box 4, folder 6.

72. CCLAY to Norman Chandler, July 18, 1944, ibid., box 2, folder 15.

73. Statement by CCLAY, undated, ibid., box 2, folder 11.

74. "Articles of Incorporation of CCLAY, a Non-profit Corporation, August 31, 1943," ibid.

75. "Description of the Alpine Street Project," ibid., box 3, folder 14.

76. M. Edith Condon, Assistant Area Supervisor, Adult Education and Citizenship, Los Angeles, to Federation of Spanish American Voters, Inc., July 1, 1942, Eduardo Quevedo Papers, box 1, folder 10.

77. Untitled statement discussing Mexican American juvenile delinquency and community programs geared toward its curtailment, Manuel Ruiz Papers, box 1, folder 7.

78. "Citizens' Committee Raps Angling of Crime News"; "Rosenwald's Daughter Raps 'Crime Wave' Reports."

79. Ibid.

80. West Harlem Council of Social Agencies, Annual Report, June 1940–May 1941, Harlem Neighborhood Association Papers, collection MG364, box 1, folder 1, "West Harlem Council of Social Agencies Board of Directors, 1939–1945."

81. See, for example, statement on juvenile delinquency by the New York State Young Communist League, Chairman Carl Ross, 1943, Fiorello La Guardia Papers, microfilm roll 0110; "Report of the Committee on Juvenile Aid of the Boys' Brotherhood Republic," February 15, 1943, ibid.; "Bronx Group Will Combat Juvenile Delinquency," *Amsterdam News,* July 24, 1943; Annual Report, June 1940–May 1941, West Harlem Council of Social Agencies.

82. See, for example, "Anti-discrimination legislation recently adopted in New York and New Jersey," July 1942, Manuel Ruiz Papers, box 5, folder 4. This document cites a number of noteworthy additions to statutory law dealing with discrimination based on race, creed, or color enacted during the 1942 sessions of the New York State Legislature, the New York City Council, and the

New Jersey State Legislature. Included were bans on discrimination in defense contracts, public places of business, and advertisements for employment. See also "Bronx Group Will Combat Juvenile Delinquency."

83. "Preamble to the Constitution of the National Negro Youth Council of the National Negro Council," Papers of the National Negro Congress, box 54.

84. Statement on juvenile delinquency by New York State Young Communist League.

85. Citizens in Vicinity of P.S. 171, Brooklyn, New York, to Mayor Fiorello La Guardia, August 9, 1943, Fiorello La Guardia Papers, microfilm roll 0110.

86. President, Police Athletic League, NYPD, to Mayor Fiorello La Guardia, June 5, 1943, Fiorello La Guardia Papers, microfilm roll 0110.

87. "Presentment of the August 1943 Grand Jury of Kings County."

3. ZOOT STYLE AND BODY POLITICS

1. Caroline Chung Simpson, *An Absent Presence: Japanese Americans in Postwar American Culture, 1945–1960* (Durham, NC: Duke University Press, 2001), 24.

2. For more on dignity, see, for example, John Holloway, "Dignity's Revolt," in Holloway and Pelaez, *Zapatista!* 159–98; John Holloway, *Change the World without Taking Power: The Meaning of Revolution Today* (London: Pluto Press, 2002); John Holloway, "In the Beginning Was the Scream," in Werner Bonefeld, ed., *Revolutionary Writing: Common Sense Essays in Post-Political Politics* (Brooklyn: Autonomedia, 2003): 15–22.

3. Randy Martin, *Critical Moves: Dance Studies in Theory and Politics* (Durham, NC: Duke University Press, 1998), 13.

4. Foucault observes that the points between social bodies, whether they be man and woman, members of a family, master and pupil, or between every one who knows and every one who does not, there exist relations of power that are not simply a projection of the sovereign's power over an individual, but are the concrete and changing soil in which power is grounded, the conditions which make it possible to function. Foucault thus helps us to understand power as a multi-directional relation, operating from the bottom up as it does from the top down. See, for example, Michel Foucault, *Power/Knowledge: Selected Interviews and Other Writings, 1972–1977* (New York: Pantheon Books, 1980), 187; Hubert L. Dreyfus and Paul Rabinow, *Michel Foucault: Beyond Structuralism and Hermeneutics* (Chicago: University of Chicago Press, 1982), 185.

5. John Clarke, Stuart Hall, Tony Jefferson, and Brian Roberts, "Subcultures, Cultures, and Class," in Hall and Jefferson, *Resistance through Rituals,* 54–55.

6. Michel Foucault, *Discipline and Punish: The Birth of the Prison* (New York: Vintage, 1979), 25; Janet Price and Margrit Shildrick, eds., *Feminist Theory and the Body: A Reader* (New York: Routledge, 1999), 18; Bibi Bakare-Yusuf, "The Economy of Violence: Black Bodies and the Unspeakable Terror," in Price and Shildrick, *Feminist Theory and the Body,* 312.

7. There is an extensive literature on the politics of subculture and everyday activity. My thinking on these issues draws on, for example, Clarke, Hall, Jef-

ferson, and Roberts, "Subcultures, Cultures, and Class"; Kelley, *Race Rebels*; James Scott, *Domination and the Arts of Resistance: Hidden Transcripts* (New Haven: Yale University Press, 1992); and Hebdige, *Subculture*.

8. Judith Butler, *Gender Trouble: Feminism and the Subversion of Identity* (New York: Routledge, 1999), xxiii. Butler suggests that the unintelligibility of subaltern or subversive gender performances to producers of dominant gender discourse can render the subaltern or subversive subjects politically mute. In the case of zoot style, Butler's argument helps explain how city authorities, mainstream media, and the general public did not fully understand or seek to understand the motivations of nonwhite youth for practicing zoot style, thus leaving zoot suiters themselves without much of a political voice in the discourse about themselves in the wartime United States. On the other hand, much of this chapter and chapter 4 explore ways that nonwhite youth did in fact make known their perspective on such issues as race, class, and gender during the war through their cultural performance.

9. *New York Times*, June 11, 1943.

10. Shane White and Graham White, *Stylin': African American Expressive Culture from Its Beginnings to the Zoot Suit* (Ithaca, NY: Cornell University Press, 1998), 249–50.

11. Joe Alcoser, interview with the author, San Diego, CA, November 23, 2000.

12. See, for example, Gutiérrez, *Walls and Mirrors*, 123.

13. Laura Isabel Serna, "The Zoot Suiter and the Fifi: Transnational Origins of Chicano Resistance," paper presented at the Mexican American History Workshop, University of Houston, May 6–7, 2005.

14. Linda España-Maram, "Brown 'Hordes' in McIntosh Suits: Filipinos, Taxi Dance Halls, and Performing the Immigrant Body in Los Angeles, 1930s–1940s," in Austin and Willard, *Generations of Youth*, 118–35.

15. Paul Spickard, "Not Just the Quiet People: The Nisei Underclass," unpublished version in author's possession. For the published version, see Paul Spickard, "Not Just the Quiet People: The Nisei Underclass," *Pacific Historical Review* 68 (1999), 78–94. Subsequent citations are to the published version unless otherwise noted.

16. Spickard, "Not Just the Quiet People," 88.

17. Eddie Shimano, "Blueprint for a Slum," *Common Ground* 3 (Summer 1943): 81, cited in Valerie Matsumoto, *Farming the Home Place: A Japanese American Community in California, 1919–1982* (Ithaca, NY: Cornell University Press, 1993), 131.

18. España-Maram, "Brown 'Hordes' in McIntosh Suits."

19. Traax Production, "Jive Bomber Synopsis," www.traaxproduction.com/jive/synopsis.html.

20. Spickard, "Not Just the Quiet People," 80.

21. The notion of style as bricolage is elaborated in Hebdige, *Subculture*. See also John Clarke, "Style," in Hall and Jefferson, *Resistance through Rituals*, 175–91.

22. Antonio Alvarez interview, February 25, 1994.

23. Ramón Galindo, interview with the author, Austin, TX, June 27, 2000.

24. Richard Dunn, quoted in R. J. Smith, *The Great Black Way: L.A. in the 1940s and the Lost African American Renaissance* (New York: PublicAffairs, 2006), 32.

25. On the Depression-era and wartime popular cultural activity of Mexican American young women, its impact on expanding their social and cultural influence, and their emergence as a growing consumer market, see, for example, Vicki Ruiz, *From Out of the Shadows: Mexican Women in Twentieth-Century America* (New York: Oxford University Press, 1998).

26. Recognizing that the experiences of black women are sometimes overlooked in studies that focus on race and gender, in discussing female zoot style in this chapter, I concentrate on young Mexican American women. Although young African American women also actively participated in zoot culture, their role has been largely ignored in the archival and press records of the era.

27. "The Wearing of the 'Drape" Is No Sign of Delinquency," *Daily World,* May 21, 1945, in Alice McGrath Papers, collection 1290, box 5, folder 4.

28. Griffith, *American Me,* 6.

29. Lupe Rivas interview, January 13, 2000.

30. On zoot style among young Mexican American women, see, for example, Catherine Ramírez, "Crimes of Fashion"; Cosgrove, "The Zoot-Suit and Style Warfare"; Griffith, *American Me.*

31. "The Wearing of the Drape Is No Sign of Delinquency," *Daily World,* May 21, 1945, in Alice McGrath Papers, collection 1290, box 5, folder 4.

32. Griffith, *American Me,* 5.

33. Malcolm X, *Autobiography,* 54.

34. Kelley, *Race Rebels.* Kelley argues that many of Malcolm X's interpretations and memories of his youthful days were colored when he authored his autobiography by the lens of his position as a central figure in the Nation of Islam and Civil Rights Movement.

35. Griffith, *American Me,* 13–14.

36. Ibid., 14–18.

37. "Narrative Report and Evaluation of the Conditioning Program Undertaken by the Co-ordinating Council of Latin-American Youth with the So-Called 'Pachuco' Gangs in Los Angeles, California," Manuel Ruiz Papers, box 3, folder 14.

38. For example, David Gutiérrez describes caló as a "hybrid English-Spanish slang dialect" in Gutiérrez, *Walls and Mirrors,* 123.

39. Escobar, *Race, Police, and the Making of a Political Identity,* 178.

40. Griffith, *American Me,* 16.

41. Malcolm X, *Autobiography,* 43.

42. Tyler, "Black Jive and White Repression," 32.

43. Ibid.

44. Ramón Galindo interview, June 27, 2000.

45. *The New Cab Calloway's Hepsters' Dictionary: Language of Jive,* 1944 Edition (Cab Calloway, Inc., 1944), reprinted as appendix to Cab Calloway and Bryant Rollins, *Of Minnie the Moocher and Me* (New York: Thomas Y. Crowell, 1976).

46. Ibid.

47. "Lifeguards Can't Tell 'Zoot Suit' Bathers," *Los Angeles Times,* July 7, 1943.

48. David Gutiérrez, "Migration, Emergent Ethnicity, and the 'Third Space': The Shifting Politics of Nationalism in Greater Mexico," *Journal of American History* 86, no.2 (September 1999): 488. For more on the "third space" in cultural theory, see Akhil Gupta and James Ferguson, "Culture, Power, Place: Ethnography at the End of an Era," in Gupta and Ferguson, eds., *Culture, Power, Place: Explorations in Critical Anthropology* (Durham, NC: Duke University Press, 1997); Homi Bhabba, *The Location of Culture* (New York: Routledge, 1994).

49. Freeman, *Working Class New York*, 37. Freeman describes this process as "cultural jujitsu," suggesting that "the marginality that many working-class New Yorkers felt, which often manifested itself as timidity and social awkwardness, could be converted through a cultural jujitsu into coolness. This was a trait often associated with African Americans, but, at least to some extent, it could be found among working-class New Yorkers of all sorts."

50. Malcolm X, *Autobiography*, 52.

51. "Death Penalty to Be Asked for Jitterbug Killers of Teacher."

52. Perry Perkins interview, December 20, 2001.

53. Nan Enstad, *Ladies of Labor, Girls of Adventure: Working Women, Popular Culture, and Labor Politics at the Turn of the Century* (New York: Columbia University Press, 1999), 182. On consumption patterns more generally and the centrality of consumption in U.S. society since the Great Depression, see Lizabeth Cohen, *A Consumer's Republic: The Politics of Mass Consumption in Postwar America* (New York: Knopf, 2003).

54. I thank Sterling Stuckey for making this observation in conversations about zoot culture during the Black History Workshop at the University of Houston, March 15–16, 2002.

55. Bob Rodriguez (a pseudonym), interview with the author, Los Angeles, February 14, 2000.

56. Perry Perkins interview, December 20, 2001.

57. Antonio Alvarez interview, February 24, 1994.

58. Ibid.

59. Malcolm X, *Autobiography*, 99.

60. Ibid.

61. Kelley, *Race Rebels*, 173–74.

62. Perry Perkins interview, December 20, 2001.

63. Bob Rodriguez interview, February 14, 2000.

64. Perry Perkins interview, December 20, 2001.

65. Ibid.

66. Bob Rodriguez interview, February 14, 2000.

67. Ramón Galindo interview, June 27, 2000. Galindo worked as both a tailor's apprentice and an independent tailor before entering the service in 1944. Though he lived and worked in Austin, Texas, the prices he quotes for tailor-made zoot suits were likely close to those in other urban centers like Los Angeles and New York.

68. Bob Rodriguez interview, February 14, 2000.

69. Tyler, "Black Jive and White Repression," 33.

70. Malcolm X, *Autobiography,* 52. The *L* stands for "Little," Malcolm X's surname at the time.

71. *Pittsburgh Courier,* June 12, 1943.

72. *Pittsburgh Courier,* January 2, 1943. See also Tyler, "Black Jive and White Repression," 33; Bruce M. Tyler, "Zoot-Suit Culture and the Black Press," *Journal of American Culture* 17, no. 2 (Summer 1994), 21–34.

73. Malcolm X, *Autobiography,* 58.

74. Maria Hernandez (a pseudonym), interview with the author, Los Angeles, February 14, 2000.

75. Clarke, Hall, Jefferson, and Roberts, "Subcultures, Cultures and Class," 56.

76. Bob Rodriguez interview, February 14, 2000.

77. Perry Perkins interview, December 20, 2001.

78. Ibid.

79. Comments of Sterling Stuckey during the Black History Workshop at the University of Houston, March 15–16, 2002.

80. Tyler, "Black Jive and White Repression," 33–34.

81. Mary Luna, interview, in *Rosie the Riveter Revisited: Women and the World War II Work Experience,* vol. 20, p. 31, Department of Special Collections, California State University, Long Beach.

82. Rose Echeverria Mulligan, interview, in *Rosie the Riveter Revisited,* vol. 27, p. 55.

83. Ibid, 55–56.

84. Margarita Salazar, interview, in *Rosie the Riveter Revisited,* vol. 25, pp. 65–66.

85. Beatrice Morales Clifton, interview, *Rosie the Riveter Revisited,* vol. 8, pp. 46–47.

86. Spickard, "Not Just the Quiet People," 88.

87. For numerous examples of physical and verbal confrontations between minority zoot suiters and sailors in 1943, see Records of Shore Establishments and Naval Districts, 181, Eleventh Naval District, Records of the Commandant's Office, General Correspondence, 1924–1955, folder P8–5 (Zoot Suit Gang) 1943 [3/4], box 296, National Archives and Records Administration, Pacific Region (Laguna Niguel, CA).

88. Kevin Starr, *Embattled Dreams: California in War and Peace, 1940–1950* (Oxford: Oxford University Press, 2002), 105.

89. Lorena Oropeza, *¡Raza Si! ¡Guerra No!: Chicano Protest and Patriotism during the Viet Nam War Era* (Berkeley: University of California Press, 2005), 7.

90. Ralph S. Banay, "A Psychiatrist Looks at the Zoot Suit," *Probation* 22, no. 3 (1944): 81–85. See also Ramirez, "Crimes of Fashion," 10–11.

91. Agnes E. Meyer, "Zoot-Suiters—A New Youth Movement," *Washington Post,* June 13, 1943.

92. Foley, "Becoming Hispanic."

93. Oropeza, *¡Raza Si! ¡Guerra No!* 49.

94. Malcolm X, *Autobiography,* 94.

95. Art and Laurie Pepper, *Straight Life: The Story of Art Pepper* (New York: Da Capo Press, 1994).

96. Griffith, *American Me*, 10.

97. Ibid.

98. Steve Chibnall, "Whistle and Zoot: The Changing Meaning of a Suit of Clothes," *History Workshop Journal* 20 (Autumn 1985), 57.

99. Malcolm X, *Autobiography*, 71.

100. Tyler, "Black Jive and White Repression," 34.

101. Antonio Alvarez interview, February 25, 1994.

102. Bob Rodriguez interview, February 14, 2000.

103. "The Education of Alice McGrath," 153–54.

104. There is a growing body of research on women zoot suiters and pachucas. Stuart Cosgrove, drawing heavily from Los Angeles–area newspapers, notes the major features of pachuca style in "The Zoot-Suit and Style Warfare," 77–91. As noted earlier, Beatrice Griffith also refers to the pachuca phenomenon in her collection of short stories, *American Me*. See also Rosa Linda Fregoso, "Homegirls, Cholas, and Pachucas in Cinema: Taking Over the Public Sphere," *California History* 74, no. 3 (Fall 1995): 317–27; Ramírez, "Crimes of Fashion."

105. Halberstam, *Female Masculinity*; Lugo, "Destabilizing the Masculine, Refocusing 'Gender.'" Halberstam argues that masculinity is not the sole property of male bodies and that "heroic," or white middle-class, male masculinity is inscribed with power and privilege only when juxtaposed to alternative racialized and female masculinities. Lugo argues that questions of the masculine and feminine should be addressed not through biological or societal assumptions but through analyses of power, historical context, and gender, particularly the way men and women interact with each other and negotiate their cultural subjectivities. I would add to Lugo's analysis the way men engage other men and how women engage other women.

106. McWilliams, *North from Mexico*, 257–58.

107. On the history of Mexican American and other nonwhite gangs in Los Angeles, see, for example, Joan W. Moore, *Homeboys: Gangs, Drugs, and Prison in the Barrios of Los Angeles* (Philadelphia: Temple University Press, 1978); James Diego Vigil, *Barrio Gangs: Street Life and Identity in Southern California* (Austin: University of Texas Press, 1988); James Diego Vigil, *Rainbow of Gangs: Street Culture in the Mega-city* (Austin: University of Texas Press, 2002).

108. Antonio Alvarez interview, February 25, 1994.

109. Spickard, "Not Just the Quiet People," unpublished version, 5.

110. Maria Hernandez interview, February 14, 2000.

111. Bob Rodriguez interview, February 14, 2000.

112. Griffith, *American Me*, 6.

113. Bob Rodriguez interview, February 14, 2000.

114. Malcolm X, *Autobiography*, 67.

115. Spickard, "Not Just the Quiet People," 89.

116. Ibid., 86.

117. Maria Hernandez interview, February 14, 2000.

4. ZOOTS, JAZZ, AND PUBLIC SPACE

1. *Malcolm X*, directed by Spike Lee, 1992.
2. *Zoot Suit*, directed by Luis Valdez, 1982.
3. Kelley, *Race Rebels*, 75. The term "congested terrain" is Kelley's. On theories of space more generally, see Edward Soja, *Postmodern Geographies: The Reassertion of Space in Critical Social Theory* (London: Verso, 1989).
4. Arnold R. Hirsch, *Making the Second Ghetto: Race and Housing in Chicago, 1940–1960* (Cambridge: Cambridge University Press, 1983), xii, 10.
5. For one example of the oppositional meaning that the publicity of youth culture acquired in a historical context other than World War II, see Joe Austin, *Taking the Train: How Graffiti Became a Crisis in New York City* (New York: Columbia University Press, 2001).
6. Kelley, *Race Rebels*, 179.
7. Michael Warner, "Publics and Counterpublics," *Public Culture* 14, no. 1 (2002): 49–89. Warner extends the discussion of counterpublic spheres initiated by Nancy Fraser in "Rethinking the Public Sphere: A Contribution to the Critique of Actually Existing Democracy," in Craig Calhoun, ed., *Habermas and the Public Sphere* (Cambridge, MA: MIT Press, 1992), 109–42.
8. Calloway and Rollins, *Of Minnie the Moocher and Me*, 68.
9. On the cultural history of Harlem and the Harlem Renaissance, see, for example, Nathan Huggins, *Harlem Renaissance* (New York: Oxford University Press, 1971); Jervis Anderson, *This Was Harlem: A Cultural Portrait, 1900–1950* (New York: Farrar, Strauss and Giroux, 1982); Houston Baker Jr., *Modernism and the Harlem Renaissance* (Chicago: University of Chicago Press, 1987); Cheryl A. Wall, *Women of the Harlem Renaissance* (Bloomington: Indiana University Press, 1995); Cary D. Wintz, ed., *The Harlem Renaissance, 1920–1940* (New York: Garland, 1996).
10. Malcolm X, *Autobiography*, 74.
11. Perry Perkins interview, December 20, 2001.
12. Ibid.
13. Calloway and Rollins, *Of Minnie the Moocher and Me*.
14. Perry Perkins interview, December 20, 2001.
15. Malcolm X, *Autobiography*, 82.
16. Perry Perkins interview, December 20, 2001.
17. Dizzy Gillespie with Al Fraser, *To Be, or Not—To Bop: Memoirs* (New York: Da Capo Press, 1985), 149.
18. Calloway and Rollins, *Of Minnie Moocher and Me*, 90.
19. Ibid., 88.
20. Malcolm X, *Autobiography*, 74.
21. White and White, *Stylin'*, 132.
22. Gillespie, *To Be or Not—To Bop*, 88.
23. Ibid, 80.
24. White and White, *Stylin'*, 132.
25. Tyler, "Black Jive and White Repression," 45.
26. Malcolm X, *Autobiography*, 74–75.
27. "Mixed Dancing Closed Savoy Ballroom," *Amsterdam News*, May 1,

1943; "What's behind Savoy Closing: Is It Police Move to Bar Whites from Harlem?" *People's Voice,* May 1, 1943. For more on the closing of the Savoy, see Tyler, "Black Jive and White Repression," 57.

28. "What's Behind Savoy Closing."

29. "Downtown Dance Halls Reek with Sex Filth," *People's Voice,* May 8, 1942.

30. "Indignation Grows over Savoy Case: Check on Other Spots Shows Ballroom 'Finest' among the City's Lot," *Amsterdam News,* May 15, 1943.

31. Ibid.

32. "Guilty Savoy," *People's Voice,* May 22, 1943, as quoted in Capeci, *Harlem Riot of 1943,* 138.

33. Tyler, "Black Jive and White Repression," 48–49.

34. Pepper and Pepper, *Straight Life,* 41.

35. Lawrence de Graaf, "The City of Black Angels: Emergence of the Los Angeles Ghetto, 1890–1930," *Pacific Historical Review* 39 (1970), 335.

36. Sides, *L.A. City Limits,* 46.

37. Bryant et al., *Central Avenue Sounds,* 9–10.

38. Daniels, "Los Angeles Zoot," 99–100; Pagán, *Murder at the Sleepy Lagoon,* 52; Ted Gioia, *West Coast Jazz: Modern Jazz in California, 1945–1960* (Oxford: Oxford University Press, 1992), 4–7. For an in-depth discussion of the development of Central Avenue as the crucible of African American life in Los Angeles during the 1940s, see Smith, *Great Black Way.*

39. Gioia, *West Coast Jazz,* 4.

40. Ibid., 5.

41. Bob Rodriguez interview, February 14, 2000.

42. Bryant et al., *Central Avenue Sounds,* 198.

43. Fanny Christina "Tina" Hill, interview, in *Rosie the Riveter Revisited,* vol. 14, p. 106.

44. Bryant et al., *Central Avenue Sounds,* 336–37.

45. Vicente Morales, interview by Sandy Mercado, May 1972, transcript p. 6, Mexican American Collection, Chicano/Chicana Experience, binder 25, Department of Special Collections, California State University, Long Beach.

46. Antonio Alvarez interview, February 25, 1994.

47. Lupe Rivas interview, January 13, 2000.

48. Mary Luna interview, 32.

49. Lupe Rivas interview, January 13, 2000.

50. For a more detailed discussion of chaperonage and how it became less relevant during the war, see Ruiz, *From Out of the Shadows,* especially chapter 3, "The Flapper and the Chaperone," 51–71.

51. Mary Luna interview, 32, 39, 62, 67.

52. Ibid.

53. Ibid.

54. Rose Echeverria Mulligan interview, 48–49.

55. Margarita Salazar (McSweyn), interview, in *Rosie the Riveter Revisited,* vol. 25, pp. 46, 49, 52, 54, 59.

56. Adele Hernandez Milligan, interview, in ibid., vol. 26, pp. 27–28, 40, 43.

57. Fregoso, "Homegirls, Cholas, and Pachucas in Cinema," 320.

58. Ibid., 318.

59. See, for example, Manuel Ruiz, Citizens Committee of Latin American Youth, to J. David Orozco, Mason Theater Building, May 26, 1942, Manuel Ruiz Papers, box 2, folder 13; Citizens Committee of Latin American Youth, minutes of meeting, December 13, 1943, ibid., box 3, folder 8; flyer for dance at the Diana Ballroom, ibid., box 5, folder 12.

60. Lupe Rivas interview, January 13, 2000.

61. Bob Rodriguez interview, February 14, 2000.

62. Lupe Rivas interview, January 13, 2000.

63. Ibid.

64. Spickard, "Not Just the Quiet People," 87–88.

65. Bryant et al., Central Avenue Sounds, 97–98.

66. Ibid., 115–16.

67. Ibid., 165.

68. Ibid., 234.

69. Ibid., 264.

70. Rose Echeverria Mulligan interview, 16.

71. Bob Rodriguez interview, February 14, 2000.

72. Lupe Rivas interview, January 13, 2000.

73. Bob Rodriguez interview, February 14, 2000.

74. Ibid.

75. Ibid.

76. Antonio Alvarez interview, February 25, 1994.

77. Rose Echeverria Mulligan interview, 53.

78. Lupe Rivas interview, January 13, 2000.

79. Daniels, "Los Angeles Zoot," 106.

80. Labels accompanying sketch of zoot suit on Sleepy Lagoon Defense Committee letterhead, by M. Delgado, one of the Sleepy Lagoon defendants, Alice McGrath Collection, box 2, folder 7, Department of Special Collections, University of California, Los Angeles; Ramón Galindo interview, June 27, 2000 ("certain swing").

81. Steven Gregory, Black Corona: Race and the Politics of Place in an Urban Community (Princeton: Princeton University Press, 1998), 11. Gregory argues that communities exist as "people move into them and are excluded from them. Public authorities chart their borders and develop them. Financial institutions invest and divest in them. Politicians represent and appeal to them. And those who inhibit these bewilderingly complex fields of political and socioeconomic relations struggle to define their needs, interests, and identities by constructing and mobilizing their own often-oppositional versions of community."

82. Gustavo Esteva, "Regenerating People's Spaces," Alternatives 12 (1987): 132. On the notion of imagined communities, see also Benedict Anderson, Imagined Communities (London: Verso, 1983).

83. Gustavo Esteva and Madhu Suri Prakash, Grassroots Post-Modernism: Remaking the Soil of Cultures (London: Zed Books, 1998), 199. Cultural critic Randy Martin similarly argues that "such horizons, with their promise to enlarge the sense of what is possible, generally lost in daily experience to the enormous

scale of society, are thereby condensed and made palpable." Martin, *Critical Moves,* 14.

84. Daniels, "Los Angeles Zoot," 107.

85. Anthony Macías, "Rock con Raza, Raza con Jazz: Latinos/as and Post–World War II Popular American Music," in Frances Aparicio and Candida Jaquez, eds., *Musical Migrations,* vol. 1, *Transnationalism and Cultural Hybridity in Latin/o America* (New York: Palgrave McMillan, 2003), 183–84.

86. Ibid., 184.

87. Daniel Widener, "Perhaps the Japanese Are to Be Thanked? Asia, Asian Americans, and the Construction of Black California," *positions* 11, no. 1 (2003): 135–81; Johnny Otis, *Upside Your Head! Rhythm and Blues on Central Avenue* (Hanover, CT: Wesleyan University Press, 1993).

88. On the interracial music scene of postwar Los Angeles, see, for example, George Lipsitz, "Cruising around the Historical Bloc: Postmodernism and Popular Music in East Los Angeles," in *Time Passages: Collective Memory and American Popular Culture* (Minneapolis: University of Minnesota Press, 1990), 133–60; García, *A World of Its Own*; Macías, "Bringing Music to the People."

89. Macías, "Rock con Raza, Raza con Jazz," 186.

90. Chuy Varela, liner notes for *Pachuco Boogie featuring Don Tosti* (El Cerrito, CA: Arhoolie Productions, Inc., 2002).

91. Ibid.

92. Cab Calloway, as quoted in Tyler, "Black Jive and White Repression," 32.

93. Varela, liner notes to *Pachuco Boogie.*

94. Daniels, "Los Angeles Zoot," 107–9.

95. Bob Porter, liner notes for *Rock 'n' Rhythm and Blues* (London: Ace Records, 2002).

96. Eric Lott, "Double V, Double-Time: Bebop's Politics of Style," *Callaloo,* no. 36 (Summer 1988), 600–601.

97. Ibid, 599.

98. Daniels, "Los Angeles Zoot," 105; Pagán, *Murder at the Sleepy Lagoon,* 99; Tyler, "Black Jive and White Repression," 31.

99. Tyler, "Black Jive and White Repression," 38.

100. Horace R. Clayton, "Social Significance in Jazz Louses Good Stuff Up," *Downbeat* (December 16, 1946), 8, as quoted in Lott, "Double V, Double-Time," 603.

101. Lott, "Double V, Double-Time," 603.

102. On the cultural politics of dance, including the ways the dancing body might be construed as a vehicle for expressive politics, see, for example, Martin, *Critical Moves*; Jane C. Desmond, "Embodying Difference: Issues in Dance and Cultural Studies," in Celeste Fraser Delgado and Jose Esteban Muñoz, eds., *Everynight Life: Culture and Life in Latin/o America* (Durham, NC: Duke University Press, 1997), 33–64.

103. Kelley, *Race Rebels,* 168.

104. Lupe Rivas interview, January 13, 2000.

105. Antonio Alvarez interview, February 25, 1994.

106. Ben Malbon, "Clubbing: Consumption, Identity, and the Spatial Practices of Every-Night Life," in Skelton and Valentine, *Cool Places*, 271.

107. Ramón Galindo interview, June 27, 2000.

108. Malcolm X, *Autobiography*, 58–59.

109. Perry Perkins interview, December 20, 2001.

110. Ibid.

111. Pagán, *Murder at the Sleepy Lagoon*, 54.

112. Bob Rodriguez interview, February 14, 2000.

113. J. K., interview, in *Rosie the Riveter Revisited*, vol. 18, pp. 56–57.

114. Beatrice Morales Clifton interview, 66.

115. Videll Drake, interview, in *Rosie the Riveter Revisited*, vol. 10, pp. 47–48.

116. Daniels, "Los Angeles Zoot," 105–6.

117. Meyer, "Zoot-Suiters—A New Youth Movement."

118. Les Back, "X Amount of Sat Siri Akal! Apache Indian, Reggae Music and Intermezzo Culture," in Aleksandra Alund and Raoul Granqvist, eds., *Essays on Immigration and Culture in Present-Day Europe* (Amsterdam: Rodopi, 1995), 145.

119. Ibid., 146.

120. Howard Odum, *Race and Rumors of Race: Challenge to American Crisis* (Chapel Hill: University of North Carolina Press, 1943).

121. Tyler, "Black Jive and White Repression," 51.

122. Ibid.

123. Ibid., 56.

124. Kelley, *Race Rebels*, 174.

125. E. P. Thompson, *The Making of the English Working Class* (New York: Vintage Books, 1966), preface; John Holloway, "Dignity's Revolt," in Holloway and Pelaez, *Zapatista!* 180–85.

126. Lott, "Double V, Double-Time," 599.

5. ZOOT VIOLENCE IN LOS ANGELES

1. Vicente Morales interview, transcript pp. 9–10.

2. See, for example, Mazón, *The Zoot-Suit Riots*; Escobar, *Race, Police, and the Making of a Political Identity*; Pagán, *Murder at the Sleepy Lagoon*; Patricia Rae Adler, "The 1943 Zoot-Suit Riots: Brief Episode in a Long Conflict," in Manuel P. Servin, ed., *An Awakened Minority: The Mexican-Americans* (Beverly Hills: Glencoe Press, 1970), 142–58; McWilliams, *North from Mexico*; Solomon James Jones, *The Government Riots of Los Angeles, June 1943* (San Francisco: R and E Research Associates, 1973).

3. Ibid.

4. Ibid.

5. Following cultural critic Lisa Lowe, I rest this notion of inclusion/exclusion not on legal definitions of national citizenship but on a more flexible cultural citizenship. According to Lowe, "Although the law is perhaps the discourse that most literally governs citizenship, U.S. national culture—the collectively forged images, histories, and narratives that place, displace, and replace indi-

viduals in relation to the national polity—powerfully shapes who the citizenry is, where they dwell, what they remember, and what they forget." Lowe, *Immigrant Acts*, 2.

6. Antonio Alvarez interview, February 25, 1994.

7. Bob Rodriguez interview, February 14, 2000.

8. Mazón, *The Zoot-Suit Riots*, 15–16.

9. McWilliams, *North from Mexico*, 250.

10. On servicemen frequenting Hollywood while on leave during the spring of 1943, see, for example, Harry Meyers, Secretary of the Ways and Means Commission, to "dear friend," April 10, 1943, John Anson Ford Collection, box 76, folder 7 (1943).

11. Mazón, *The Zoot-Suit Riots*, 58.

12. Pagán, *Murder at the Sleepy Lagoon*, 146–51.

13. Records of Shore Establishments and Naval Districts, 181, Eleventh Naval District, folder p8–5 (Zoot Suit Gang), 1943 [3/4], box 296, Records of the Commandant's Office, General Correspondence, 1924–1955.

14. Ibid.

15. Ibid.

16. Ibid.

17. Ibid.

18. "The Education of Alice McGrath," 155.

19. Ibid., 153–54.

20. "Grand Jury Probe Sought," "13-Year Old Boy Killed by Cop's Bullet thru Eye," *California Eagle*, March 10, 1943.

21. "Shoot Two Who Beat Pedestrian," *California Eagle*, April 1, 1943.

22. *Citizen-News* (Hollywood), May 5, 1943, clipping in Alice McGrath Papers, collection 1290, box 5, folder 5.

23. "Near-Riot as Cop Shoots Eastside Man," *California Eagle*, May 27, 1943.

24. Escobar, *Race, Police and the Making of a Political Identity*, 230. On the riot in Venice, see also Pagán, *Murder at the Sleepy Lagoon*, 163–64.

25. Alfred Barela to Judge Arthur S. Guerin, May 21, 1943, Manuel Ruiz Papers, box 15, folder 16.

26. Mazón, *The Zoot-Suit Riots*, 59.

27. Rudolfo Acuña, *Occupied America: A History of Chicanos*, 3rd ed. (New York: Harper and Row, 1988), 256.

28. "Stories Conflict on Vallejo Riot Cause," *California Eagle*, January 1, 1943; "Navy Starts Probe of Vallejo Riots," *California Eagle*, January 8, 1943.

29. Records of Shore Establishments and Naval Districts, 181, Eleventh Naval District.

30. "Mass Meet Charges Attempt to 'Goad Riot,'" *California Eagle*, May 27, 1943.

31. On the initial sequence of events during the riots, see Carey McWilliams Personal Notebook, entry for "The Riots," Carey McWilliams Papers, collection 1243, box 27, folder "McWilliams, Carey—As Author"; "We Have Just Begun to Fight," no date, Sleepy Lagoon Defense Committee Archive, collection 107, microfilm reel 1 of 8, box 1 ("News Releases"), folder 1 ("mimeographed cop-

ies"), Department of Special Collections, University of California, Los Angeles; McWilliams, *North from Mexico*, 244–45; Escobar, *Race, Police, and the Making of a Political Identity*, 234–36.

32. Carey McWilliams, Personal Notebook, entry for "The Riots."

33. *Time* (June 21, 1943), 18.

34. Minutes, Citizens' Committee for Latin American Youth, June 7, 1943, Manuel Ruiz Papers, box 4, folder 6.

35. Rudy Sanchez (signed "a sincere so called 'zoot suiter' ") to Dear Sir, June 6, 1943, Eduardo Quevedo Collection, box 1, folder 11. References to Sanchez's letter are also found in Minutes of the Coordinating Council for Latin American Youth, June 7, 1943, Manuel Ruiz Papers, box 3, folder 8.

36. Memorandum, "Officer of the Day" to "Commanding Officer," June 4, 1943, Records of Shore Establishments and Naval Districts, 181, Eleventh Naval District.

37. Bob Rodriguez interview, February 14, 2000.

38. Carey McWilliams Oral History, "In All Things Honorable," interviewed by Joel Gardner, July 13, 1978, collection 300/195, pp. 163–164, Department of Special Collections, University of California, Los Angeles.

39. Griffith, *American Me*, 29.

40. *Time* (June 21, 1943), 18.

41. Report addressed to Robert Kenny, Attorney General of California, submitted by the interracial and multiethnic Los Angeles Committee for American Unity, June 11, 1943, Manuel Ruiz Papers, box 16, folder 5; "We Have Just Begun to Fight."

42. Bob Rodriguez interview, February 14, 2000.

43. Rose Echeverria Mulligan interview, in *Rosie the Riveter Revisited*, vol. 27, pp. 55–56.

44. Vicente Morales interview, transcript p. 8.

45. Maria Hernandez interview, February 14, 2000.

46. Ibid.

47. Lupe Rivas interview, January 13, 2000.

48. Carey McWilliams, Personal Notebook, entry for "The Riots."

49. Eyewitness account of Al Waxman, as quoted in McWilliams, *North from Mexico*, 249.

50. Griffith, *American Me*, 25–26.

51. Ibid., 26–27.

52. Manuel Ruiz, "Oral History," September 21, 1972, p. 19, Manuel Ruiz Papers, box 1, folder 9.

53. "Los Angeles' Mexican Minority," November 29, 1944, Manuel Ruiz Papers, box 1, folder 6.

54. Los Angeles Committee for American Unity, Provisional Chairman, Harry Braverman, and Provisional Executive Committee (including Carey McWilliams, Al Waxman, Carlotta Bass, Eduardo Quevedo, and Ben Margolis), to Robert Kenny, Attorney General of California, and Reverend Joseph McGucken, Chairman of the Governors Special Committee on Los Angeles Emergency, Manuel Ruiz Papers, box 16, folder 5.

55. "The Education of Alice McGrath," 161–62; "Report and Recommen-

dations of Citizens Committee," appointed by California Governor Earl Warren, June 12, 1943, Manuel Ruiz Papers, box 4, folder 1. For references to
attacks on Mexican Americans, African Americans, and Filipino Americans, see,
for example, Ruth Tuck, "Behind the Zoot Suit Riots," *Survey Graphic: Magazine of Social Interpretation* (August 1943), 313; McWilliams, *North from Mexico*, 248; Acuña, *Occupied America*, 257.

56. Thomas L. Griffith Jr. to Walter White, June 9, 1943, Papers of the
National Association for the Advancement of Colored People, part 15, Segregation and Responses, 1940–1955, series A.

57. "Loses Pants in 'Zoot War': Soldiers Relieve Draftee of His Trousers,"
Amsterdam News, June 26, 1943.

58. *California Eagle*, June 10, 1943.

59. "Mob Victim's Eye Cut Out," *California Eagle*, June 17, 1943.

60. McWilliams, *North from Mexico*, 248–49.

61. Ibid., 250.

62. Maria Hernandez interview, January 13, 2000.

63. Secretary, Los Angeles NAACP, to Elmer Davis, Office of War Information, Washington, D.C., June 11, 1943, Papers of the National Association for
the Advancement of Colored People, part 15, Segregation and Responses,
1940–1955, series A; *Time* (June 21, 1943), 18.

64. Secretary, Los Angeles NAACP, to Davis.

65. Juana Alvarez, interview with Larry R. Solomon, July 26, 1992, as
quoted in Solomon, *Roots of Justice: Stories of Organizing in Communities of
Color* (Berkeley: Chardon Press, 1998), 27.

66. Griffith, *American Me*, 26.

67. Ibid., 29.

68. Mazón, *The Zoot-Suit Riots*, 64.

69. Chester Himes, "Zoot Riots Are Race Riots," *Crisis* 50 (July 1943),
200–220, as quoted in Pagán, *Murder at the Sleepy Lagoon*, 158.

70. "Zoot Suits and Service Stripes: Race Tensions behind the Riots," *Newsweek* (June 21, 1943), 35.

71. John Anson Ford Oral History, "John Anson Ford and Los Angeles
County Government," interviewed by L. Craig Cunningham, 1967, pp.
187–188, Collection 300/50, Department of Special Collections, University of
California, Los Angeles.

72. Fletcher Bowron to Philip W. Bonsal, Chief, Division of American
Republics, State Department, Washington, D.C., August 3, 1943, Fletcher Bowron Collection, box 1, folder "Extra Copies of Letters, 1943, Jan–Jun."

73. "The Education of Alice McGrath," 153–54.

74. Lupe Rivas interview, January 13, 2000.

75. Bob Rodriguez interview, February 14, 2000. This rumor was also noted
by Lupe Rivas in her January 13, 2000, interview.

76. Starr, *Embattled Dreams*, 99–100; Marilynn S. Johnson, "Gender, Race,
and Rumours: Re-examining the 1943 Race Riots," *Gender & History* 10, no.
2 (August 1998): 252–77.

77. On rumors of zoot suiters as fifth-column agents, see, for example,
Mazón, *The Zoot-Suit Riots*, 15; Starr, *Embattled Dreams*, 103–4.

78. John Anson Ford to Nelson Rockefeller, June 9, 1943, John Anson Ford Collection, box 75, B. LA County Government, IV. Relations, 5. International (items I[cc–dd]).

79. "Slums Manufacture Delinquency," editorial, *California Eagle,* June 17, 1943.

80. Loren Miller, "Comment on draft of Guild Report on Riots," copy, Carey McWilliams Papers, box 31, folder "Race Riots, Los Angeles."

81. "Zoot-Suit Riots: 125 Hurt in Los Angeles Fights," author and magazine unidentified, Alice McGrath Papers, box 5, folder 4.

82. Carey McWilliams to Martin Popper, National Lawyer's Guild, June 9, 1943, Carey McWilliams Papers, box 31, folder "Race Riots, Los Angeles."

83. Starr, *Embattled Dreams,* 108.

84. Mazón, *The Zoot-Suit Riots,* 76.

85. McWilliams, Personal Notebook, entry for "The Riots."

86. Maria Hernandez interview, February 14, 2000.

87. Lupe Rivas interview, January 13, 2000.

88. Maria Hernandez interview, February 14, 2000.

89. Manuel Ruiz Oral History, September 21, 1972, Manuel Ruiz Papers, box 1, folder 9.

90. McWilliams, Personal Notebook, entry for "The Riots."

91. García, *Mexican Americans,* 172–73.

92. On the navy's eventual decision to restrict leave, see Records of the Shore Establishment and Naval Districts, 181, Eleventh Naval District; *Los Angeles Times,* June 9, 1943; *Los Angeles Herald Examiner,* June 9, 1943; "Los Angeles Banned to Sailors by Navy to Stem Zoot-Suit Riots," *New York Times,* June 9, 1943.

93. Acuña, *Occupied America,* 145.

94. Fletcher Bowron to C. B. Horrall, Chief of LAPD, July 19, 1943, Fletcher Bowron Collection, box 1, folder "Extra Copies of Letters, 1943, Jan–June."

95. Bowron to Bonsal, August 3, 1943.

96. Statement by Mayor Fletcher Bowron, June 9, 1943, Fletcher Bowron Collection, box 34, folder "Statements to the Press, 1942–1943–1944."

97. Bowron to Bonsal, August 3, 1943.

98. Statement by Mayor Fletcher Bowron, June 9, 1943.

99. Ibid.

100. Fletcher Bowron to Elmer Davis, June 28, 1943, Fletcher Bowron Collection, box 1, folder "Extra Copies of Letters, 1943, Jan–June."

101. Statement by Mayor Fletcher Bowron, June 9, 1943.

102. Ibid.

103. Fletcher Bowron to C. B. Horrall, Chief of LAPD, July 19, 1943, Fletcher Bowron Collection, box 1, folder, "Extra Copies of Letters, 1943, Jan–June."

104. For analysis of the response to the Zoot Suit Riots in Mexico and Latin America, see Richard Griswold del Castillo, "The Los Angeles 'Zoot Suit Riots' Revisited: Mexican and Latin American Perspectives," *Mexican Studies–Estudios Mexicanos* 16, no. 2 (Summer 2000): 367–78.

105. Bowron to Davis, June 28, 1943.

106. Ibid.

107. Bowron to Horrall, July 19, 1943.

108. Remarks of Fletcher Bowron on the occasion of the luncheon honoring Secretary Knox, June 30, 1943, Fletcher Bowron Collection, box 34, folder "Remarks, Public Events, Addresses, by Mayor."

109. "Dorsey High Principal Wants No 'Zoot Suits,'" *California Eagle*, June 3, 1943.

110. *Los Angeles Times*, June 10, 1943; "The Education of Alice McGrath," 159–60.

111. *Los Angeles Herald Examiner*, June 13, 1943; *Los Angeles Times*, June 13, 1943; *Atlanta Constitution*, June 12, 1943.

112. John Anson Ford, statement on behalf of the Los Angeles County Board of Supervisors, June 8, 1943, John Anson Ford Collection, box 51, folder 4.

113. Ibid.

114. Ford quoting his nephew in a letter to W. S. Rosecrans, August 2, 1943, John Anson Ford Collection, box 75, folder 9.

115. John Anson Ford to Jerry Voorhis, U.S. House of Representatives, June 25, 1943, John Anson Ford Collection, box 75, folder 9.

116. John Anson Ford, "What Lies behind the 'Zoot Suit' and Race Rioting and How Can These Be Prevented?" March 1, 1944, John Anson Ford Collection, box 51, folder 5.

117. Earl Warren to Francis Biddle, October 14, 1943, Robert Kenny Collection, 1823–1975, folder "General File, Zoot-Suit Riots," Southern California Library for Social Studies and Research, Los Angeles.

118. "Report and Recommendations of Citizens Committee," June 12, 1943, Manuel Ruiz Papers, box 4, folder 1.

119. Ibid.

120. Ibid.

121. Ibid.

122. I understand cultural violence to encompass ways by which the symbolic sphere of society—including ideology, religion, language, and art—can be used to legitimize physical violence, economic exploitation, or political marginalization. On cultural violence, see, for example, Johan Galtung, "Cultural Violence," in Manfred B. Steger and Nancy S. Lind, eds., *Violence and Its Alternatives: An Interdisciplinary Reader* (New York: St. Martin's Press, 1999), 39–53.

123. McWilliams, Personal Notebook, entry for "The Riots"; *Los Angeles Times*, June 5, 1943; *Los Angeles Herald Examiner*, June 5, 1943; *Los Angeles Daily News*, June 5, 1943.

124. *Los Angeles Times*, June 7, 1943.

125. See, for example, "Riot Alarm Sent Out in Zoot War," *Los Angeles Time*, June 8, 1943; "City, Navy Clam Lid on Zoot-Suit Warfare," *Los Angeles Times*, June 10, 1943; "Zoot Suit War Runs Course as Riots Subside," *Los Angeles Times*, June 12, 1943; "Punishment of All Urged to Break up Zoot Suit War," *Los Angeles Times*, June 13, 1943; "Southland Zoot Riots Reported Stamped Out," *Los Angeles Times*, June 14, 1943. See also *Los Angeles Herald Examiner*, June 8–11, 1943; *Los Angeles Daily News*, June 8–11, 1943.

126. *Washington Post,* June 10–12, 1943; *Atlanta Constitution,* June 11, 12, 1943; *Chicago Daily Tribune,* June 9, 10, 1943.

127. *Los Angeles Times,* June 10, 1943.

128. *Los Angeles Times,* June 11, 1943.

129. See, for example, ibid.; "Black Widow Girls Beat, Slash Woman; Police Tighten Controls," *Washington Post,* June 11, 1943.

130. Lupe Rivas interview, February 14, 2000.

131. Arriving in Los Angeles in 1910 from Providence, Rhode Island, Charlotta Bass and her husband, Joseph, took control of the *California Eagle* from its founder, John Neimore. After Joseph's death in 1934, Charlotta singlehandedly ran the newspaper with the clear purpose of advocating freedom and equality for African Americans. The history of African Americans in Los Angeles soon became intertwined with that of the *California Eagle,* as it served as the major media outlet for black political opinion in the region. Charlotta Bass edited the *California Eagle* for forty years before ill health forced her to retire in the 1950s. For more on Charlotta Bass and the history of the *California Eagle,* see Bass, *Forty Years,* located at the Southern California Library for Social Studies and Research, Los Angeles; "Early History of the Negro Press in California, article draft," Charlotta A. Bass Collection, 1874–1968, additional box 1, folder "Articles and Speeches, undated."

132. "Rioting Skirts Negro Community," *California Eagle,* June 10, 1943.

133. Ibid.

134. "An Open Letter to Fletcher Bowron," *California Eagle,* June 10, 1943.

135. *California Eagle,* June 10, 1943; *California Eagle,* June 17, 1943.

136. See, for example, John Robert Badger, "Inside Story of Coast Zoot Suit Riots Told by Defender Reporter," *Chicago Defender,* June 19, 1943.

137. See *La Opinion,* June 1943; Escobar, *Race, Police, and the Making of a Political Identity,* 200, 221.

138. Carey McWilliams, "Hearst Press Incited Campaign against Mexicans, Promoted Police Raids, Whipped Up Race Clashes," *PM,* June 12, 1943.

139. Peter Furst, "Press Blamed for Spread of Zoot Suit Riot," *PM* (n.d.), in Alice McGrath Papers, box 5, folder 4.

140. On the perceived threat of zoot suiters as a fifth-column, see Mazón, *The Zoot-Suit Riots,* 81–82, 107. Mazón emphasizes that after the FBI concluded an investigation in March 1945, no evidence of Mexican American activity subverting the war effort was discovered.

141. Al Waxman, "Column Left: More on Riots" (n.p.), Carey McWilliams Papers, box 31, folder "Race Riots, Los Angeles."

142. George Morris, "Pacific Firsters Incite Coast Riots," *Daily Worker,* June 12, 1943.

143. See, for example, Jon Watson, "Crossing the Colour Lines in the City of Angels: The NAACP and the Zoot-Suit Riot of 1943," *University of Sussex Journal of Contemporary History* 4 (2002); Escobar, *Race, Police, and the Making of a Political Identity.*

144. *Appeal News* 1, no. 6 (July 6, 1943), in Sleepy Lagoon Defense Committee Archive, microfilm reel 1 of 8, box 2, folder 1 ("Appeal News, v.1, n.1 to

v.2, n.6"). The newsletter *Appeal News,* written and circulated by Alice McGrath, was an important medium of communication between the Sleepy Lagoon Defense Committee and the Sleepy Lagoon defendants during their years in prison. The *Appeal News* intended to inform and update the defendants on the status of their appeal to overturn their convictions.

145. "Los Angeles CIO Council's Statement on Recent Race Riots Here" (n.d.), Sleepy Lagoon Defense Committee Archive, microfilm reel 1 of 8, box 1 ("News Releases"), folder 7 ("texts of speeches").

146. "Mass Meet Charges Attempt to 'Goad Riot.'"

147. Ibid.

148. Rudy Leyvas, interviewed in documentary film *Zoot Suit Riots,* dir. Joseph Tovares, American Experience Series (Boston: WGBH, 2001).

149. "Mexico Indicates Formal Protest to Zoot-Suit Fights," *Atlanta Constitution,* June 10, 1943.

150. "Mexicans and Negroes Victimized," *Amsterdam News,* June 19, 1943.

151. Smith, *Great Black Way,* 86–89.

152. "Mexicans and Negroes Victimized."

153. Rudy Leyvas interview in *Zoot Suit Riots.*

154. Smith, *Great Black Way,* 87.

155. Bob Rodriguez interview, February 14, 2000.

156. Rudy Sanchez to Eduardo Quevedo, June 6, 1943, Eduardo Quevedo Papers, box 1, folder 11.

157. Manuel Reyes to Alice McGrath, June 16, 1943, Alice McGrath Collection, folder "biographical file."

158. McWilliams, *North from Mexico,* 257–58.

6. RACE RIOTS ACROSS THE UNITED STATES

1. "Race Riots Sweep Nation: 16 Dead, over 300 Hurt in Michigan, Texas, Mississippi," *Pittsburgh Courier,* June 26, 1943.

2. "National Race War Feared: Racial Strife Confounds Nation Fighting to Keep Democracy on Top," *Amsterdam News,* June 26, 1943.

3. NAACP to New York mayor Fiorello La Guardia, July 29, 1943, Fiorello La Guardia Papers, microfilm roll 0197.

4. Paul Gilje, *Rioting in America* (Bloomington: Indiana University Press, 1996). On the historiography of riots in the urban United States, see also, for example, Louis H. Masotti and Don Bowen, eds., *Riots and Rebellion: Civil Violence in the Urban Community* (Beverly Hills: Sage, 1968); Rodney Allen and Charles Adair, eds., *Violence and Riots in Urban America* (Worthington, Ohio: Charles A. Jones, 1969); Saul Bernstein, *Alternatives to Violence: Alienated Youth and Riots, Race, and Poverty* (New York: Association Press, 1967); Joseph Boskin, *Urban Racial Violence in the Twentieth Century* (London: Glencoe Press, 1976); Johnson, "Gender, Race, and Rumours," 253. In surveying riot studies in U.S. historiography, Johnson charts a first wave of scholarship in the 1970s that focused on the long-term structural problems in urban areas leading to riots, and a second wave in the 1980s and 1990s that more closely examined the social composition and motivations of urban rioters.

5. For a typology of U.S. race riots, see, for example, Allen D. Grimshaw, "Lawlessness and Violence in America and Their Special Manifestations in Changing Negro-White Relationships," in Grimshaw, ed., *Racial Violence in the United States* (Chicago: Aldine, 1969), 23–26. Grimshaw identifies charges of black assaults on white women as a common cause of "southern style race riots" and cites competition over housing, labor, and public facilities as a frequent cause in "northern style race riots." While typology is useful for charting the multitude of factors contributing to urban riots, most riots during World War II, as this chapter's focus on the race riots in the summer of 1943 illustrates, were caused by multiple elements and did not easily fit into such a classification.

6. Meyer, "Zoot Suiters—A New Youth Movement."

7. "Zooters Escape San Diego Mob," *Los Angeles Times,* June 10, 1943.

8. Stephen J. Pitti, *The Devil in Silicon Valley: Northern California, Race, and Mexican Americans* (Princeton: Princeton University Press, 2003), 125–26.

9. "Baltimore Acts to Break Up Zoot Suit Gang," *Chicago Daily Tribune,* June 10, 1943.

10. *Washington Post,* June 12, 1943.

11. "Band Members, Mistaken for Zoot-Suiters, Beaten," *Houston Chronicle,* June 10, 1943; "Krupa Musicians Beaten in Subway," *Washington Post,* June 11, 1943; "Four Zoot-Suiters Beaten," *Washington Post,* June 13, 1943; "Blame Hearst Press for Build-up of Zoot-Suit Riots into Race War," *People's Voice,* June 19, 1943; *Los Angeles Times,* June 13, 1943.

12. "Blame Hearst Press for Build-up of Zoot-Suit Riots into Race War."

13. Lipsitz, *Rainbow at Midnight,* 65. On wildcat and hate strikes during the war, see ibid., 69–92. On wartime labor unrest more generally, see, for example, Nelson Lichtenstein, *Labor's War at Home* (Cambridge: Cambridge University Press, 1982).

14. Lipsitz, *Rainbow at Midnight,* 82.

15. On the riots at the Alabama Dry-dock and Shipbuilding Company in Mobile, see ibid., 26; Johnson, "Gender, Race, and Rumours," 263; James Burran, "Racial Violence in the South during World War II" (Ph.D. thesis, University of Tennessee, 1977), 104–28.

16. "Alabama White Dailies Blast Riots at Mobile Shipyard as Axis Aids," *People's Voice,* June 5, 1943.

17. "Mission to Mobile," An Investigation of Race Relations in the Shipyards of the Alabama Dry-dock and Shipbuilding Company, by James E. Jackson, Jr., Educational Director, Southern Negro Youth Congress, Birmingham, Alabama, Papers of the National Negro Congress, box 35.

18. Johnson, "Gender, Race, and Rumours, 262–63."

19. Jackson, "Mission to Mobile."

20. Lipsitz, *Rainbow at Midnight,* 26; Johnson, "Gender, Race, and Rumours, 263; Burran, "Racial Violence in the South," 113.

21. Jackson, "Mission to Mobile."

22. Ibid.

23. Ibid.; "Alabama White Dailies Blast Riots"; "Rumor 2 Dead after Riot in Mobile Plant," *Amsterdam News,* June 5, 1943.

24. "Alabama White Dailies Blast Riots."

25. Jackson, "Mission to Mobile."

26. Ibid.

27. "Mob Destruction Sweeping Nation," *Amsterdam News,* June 26, 1943.

28. Lipsitz, *Rainbow at Midnight,* 81.

29. Johnson, "Gender, Race, and Rumours," 257.

30. "Mob Destruction Sweeping Nation"; "Attack Story of Woman False, Is Growing Belief," *Pittsburgh Courier,* June 26, 1943; "Axis Influence Blamed as Cause of Texas Outrage," *Pittsburgh Courier,* Texas Edition, June 26, 1943; Johnson, "Gender, Race, and Rumours," 257–58.

31. *Houston Chronicle,* June 18, 1943.

32. "Military Court to Probe Beaumont Mob Violence," *Houston Chronicle,* June 17, 1943.

33. "Attack Story of Woman False, Is Growing Belief."

34. "Mob Destruction Sweeping Nation."

35. "Attack Story of Woman False, Is Growing Belief."

36. "Mob Destruction Sweeping Nation."

37. Ibid.

38. For more on the riot in Beaumont, see "Beaumont Is Quiet after Night of Rioting," *Houston* Chronicle, June 16, 1943; Johnson, "Gender, Race, and Rumours," 257–61; Lipsitz, *Rainbow at Midnight,* 81–82; Burran, "Racial Violence in the South," 171–77.

39. The Southern Negro Youth Congress, for example, noted the Mobile riot as part of "a general strikewave conspiracy which the conscious associates and followers of Axis strategists are endeavoring to let loose upon our country in order to paralyze production, undermine morale, destroy national unity and forestall the execution of the military decisions of the allied high command." See Jackson, "Mission to Mobile." In Beaumont, the chief of police attributed the riot to fifth-column sympathizers who initiated rumors of a black uprising to provoke the town's white residents to violence. In support of his assertions, the chief blamed the German-descended population that worked in the war plants of central and East Texas. See "Mob Destruction Sweeping Nation." Although no evidence supports these claims, it is more than likely that Axis powers did capitalize on propaganda that broadcast the inability of the United States to maintain social control in its own cities.

40. "Not Axis, But Evil Whites Started Riots," *Amsterdam News,* June 26, 1943.

41. Himes, *If He Hollers Let Him Go,* 180–81.

42. On the Detroit riot, see, for example, Dominic J. Capeci Jr. and Martha Wilkerson, *Layered Violence: The Detroit Rioters of 1943* (Jackson: University Press of Mississippi, 1991); Dominic J. Capeci Jr., *Race Relations in Wartime Detroit* (Philadelphia: Temple University Press, 1984); B. J. Widick, *Detroit: City of Race and Class Violence* (Detroit: Wayne State University Press, 1989); Arthur M. Lee and Norman Humphrey, *Race Riot* (New York: Dryden Press, 1943); Richard Walter Thomas, "From Peasant to Proletarian: The Formation and Organization of the Black Industrial Working Class in Detroit, 1915–1945" (Ph.D. thesis, University of Michigan, 1976).

43. On the Sojourner Truth housing incident, see, for example, "Fear New Rioting If Troops Go," *Amsterdam News,* July 3, 1943; Thurgood Marshall,

"The Gestapo in Detroit," *The Crisis,* August 1943, reprinted in Boskin, *Urban Racial Violence in the Twentieth Century,* 56–61; Lipsitz, *Rainbow at Midnight,* 69–70.

44. Johnson, "Gender, Race, and Rumours," 263–64; Terry Ann Knopf, *Rumors, Race, and Riots* (New Brunswick: Transaction Books, 1975), 55–59.

45. Marshall, "The Gestapo in Detroit."

46. Johnson, "Gender, Race, and Rumours," 264–65; Knopf, *Rumors, Race, and Riots,* 57–58.

47. "People's Voice Receives Eye Witness Account of Detroit Riot," *People's Voice,* July 3, 1943.

48. Johnson, "Gender, Race, and Rumours," 264; Knopf, *Rumors, Race, and Riots,* 57.

49. "People's Voice Receives Eye Witness Account of Detroit Riot."

50. "To-Hell-with-Democracy Is Riot Theme; FDR Orders Troops in Detroit," *People's Voice,* June 26, 1943.

51. "Four Detroit Rioters Who Shot Aged Man 'For Fun' Arrested," *People's Voice,* August 7, 1943; "White Youths Admit Killing Detroit Negro in Race Riot June 21," *Sacramento Bee,* July 31, 1943, in Carey McWilliams Papers, collection 1243, box 31, folder "Race Riots–Detroit."

52. "People's Voice Receives Eye Witness Account of Detroit Riot."

53. Marshall, "The Gestapo in Detroit."

54. On the debate over police behavior in the Detroit riot, see, for example, ibid.; Capeci and Wilkerson, *Layered Violence,* 18–21.

55. "To-Hell-with-Democracy Is Riot Theme"; "Fear New Rioting If Troops Go," *Amsterdam News,* July 3, 1943.

56. For analysis of arrest records during the Detroit riot, see Capeci and Wilkerson, *Layered Violence,* 214–23; Johnson, "Gender, Race, and Rumours," 265.

57. Capeci and Wilkerson, *Layered Violence,* 20; "Race Riots Sweep Nation."

58. "'Fact-Finding' Report on Detroit Riot Whitewashes Police; Blames Negroes," *People's Voice,* August 21, 1943. Also see "Final Detroit Report Blames Negroes for Riot," news clipping dated August 12, 1943, in Carey McWilliams Papers, collection 1243, box 31, folder "Race-Riot Detroit"; "Riot Blame Put on Negroes; Detroit Tense," *PM,* July 28, 1943, in ibid.

59. Capeci and Wilkerson, *Layered Violence,* 21–22.

60. Ibid., chapter 3, "Faces in the Crowd."

61. Francis Biddle, U.S. Attorney General, to Lester B. Granger, Executive Secretary, National Urban League, August 12, 1943, Papers of the National Negro Congress, box 73.

62. "FBI Chief Lays Rioting at Door of Hoodlums," *People's Voice,* August 14, 1943.

63. "'Fact-Finding' Report on Detroit Riot Whitewashes Police; Blames Negroes." Also see "Final Detroit Report Blames Negroes For Riot"; "Riot Blame Put on Negroes; Detroit Tense."

64. "'Fact-Finding' Report on Detroit Riot Whitewashes Police; Blames Negroes."

65. National Negro Congress to President Franklin D. Roosevelt, July 1943, Papers of the National Negro Congress, box 75. The same letter was sent to Detroit mayor Edward Jeffries, Director of the Office of Civilian Defense James Landis, Chairman of the President's Committee on Fair Employment Practices Msgr. [sic] Haas; Senators F. Van Nuys, Ernest McFarland, Robert Wagner, and James Mead; and congressmen representing New York City and Detroit.

66. Ibid.

67. Report of Emergency Conference Meeting on Detroit Klan Riots, June 29, 1943, ibid.

68. Martin Popper to "Dear Sir," July 1, 1943, ibid.

69. Program of Action on Nation-Wide Race Riots Adopted by Conference of National Organizations, ibid.

70. Ibid.

71. "Axis Influence Blamed as Cause of Texas Outrage."

72. "'Won't Happen Here!' Says La Guardia," *Amsterdam News,* June 26, 1943.

73. "Detroit Can't Happen Here Rally Planned," *Amsterdam News,* July 10, 1943.

74. "A New Yorkers Pledge," undated news clipping, Fiorello La Guardia Papers, microfilm roll, 0197.

75. For more on these incidents, see Capeci, *Harlem Riot of 1943,* 136–37; Cheryl Greenberg, "The Politics of Disorder: Reexamining Harlem's Riots of 1935 and 1943," *Journal of Urban History* 18, no. 4 (August 1992): 423.

76. For more on the Harlem riot, see, for example, Capeci, *Harlem Riot of 1943;* Greenberg, "The Politics of Disorder," 395–441; Greenberg, *Or Does It Explode?*

77. "Harlem Riot Damages Hit $5,000,000 Mark," *Amsterdam News,* August 7, 1943.

78. Report No. D-3, August 21, 1943, Research Division, Bureau of Special Services, Office of War Information, Harlem Riots of 1943 Report (hereafter HRR), folder 1, collection MG 193, Schomburg Center for Research in Black Culture, Los Angeles.

79. "Elmer Carter Hits Harlem Outbreaks," *Amsterdam News,* August 7, 1943.

80. Ralph Ellison, *Invisible Man* (New York: Vintage Books, 1995), 541–42.

81. Report No. D-3, August 21, 1943, Research Division, Bureau of Special Services, Office of War Information, HRR; "Rumors of Soldier's Killing Caused Frenzied Mob to Riot," *Amsterdam News,* August 7, 1943; "Known Facts of Sunday Night's and Monday Morning's Disturbances," *People's Voice,* August, 7, 1943; "Harlem Riot Damages Hit $5,000,000 Mark," *Amsterdam News,* August 7, 1943. For narratives of the riot, see also Capeci, *Harlem Riot of 1943,* 99–101; Johnson, "Gender, Race, and Rumours," 267–68.

82. "Known Facts of Sunday Night's and Monday Morning's Disturbances"; "Racial Element Not Present in New York Riots; Leaders Act Quickly to Restore Law and Order," *People's Voice,* August 7, 1943; "Nothing Solved—But Much Needed (an Editorial)," *Amsterdam News,* August 7, 1943.

83. Preliminary Report on Reactions to the Harlem Riot, Special Memo 76, Research Division and Surveys Division, Bureau of Special Services, Office of War Information, August 6, 1943, HRR; "Lift Curfew: Police Alert," *Amsterdam News,* August 7, 1943.

84. Report No. D-3, August 21, 1943, Research Division, Bureau of Special Services, Office of War Information, HRR; Preliminary Report on Reactions to the Harlem Riot, Special Memo 76, Research Division and Surveys Division, Bureau of Special Services, Office of War Information, August 6, 1943, ibid.

85. Preliminary Report on Reactions to the Harlem Riot, Special Memo 76, Research Division and Surveys Division, Bureau of Special Services, Office of War Information, August 6, 1943, HRR; "Riots Express Resentment against Existing Social Ills," *People's Voice,* August 7, 1943.

86. Greenberg, "The Politics of Disorder," 395–441. Greenberg's analysis is critical because it recognizes that nonwhite communities were influenced by internal as well as external political developments. For more on the argument that riot violence stems from socioeconomic deprivation and frustration, see, for example, Allen Grimshaw, "Factors Contributing to Colour Violence in the United States and Great Britain," in Grimshaw, *Racial Violence in the United States,* 254–69; Stanley Lieberson and Arnold Silverman, "The Precipitants and Underlying Conditions of Race Riots," *American Sociological Review* 30 (December 1965): 887–98; Ted Gurr, "Urban Disorder: Perspectives from the Comparative Study of Civil Strife," in Grimshaw, ed., *Racial Violence in the United States,,* 371–83.

87. "Harlem's OPA Branch Making Progress in Adjusting Local Prices," *Amsterdam News,* September 18, 1943.

88. Walter Davenport, "Harlem . . . Dense and Dangerous," *Colliers,* September 23, 1944, quoted in Greenberg, "The Politics of Disorder," 432–33.

89. Report No. D-3, August 21, 1943, Research Division, Bureau of Special Services, Office of War Information, HRR.

90. Ibid.

91. Ibid.

92. "1935 Riot Causes Started '43 Riot," *Amsterdam News,* August 7, 1943.

93. Wilfred H. Kerr, letter titled "Hoodlums Didn't Start Riots; Twas Jim Crow," printed in "Readers Comment on Recent Rioting," *Amsterdam News,* August 14, 1943.

94. Memo, Chief Inspector to Police Commissioner, August 31, 1943, Fiorello La Guardia Papers, microfilm roll 0197.

95. "75 Women Nabbed for Taking Goods," *Amsterdam News,* August 14, 1943.

96. Report No. D-3, August 21, 1943, Research Division, Bureau of Special Services, Office of War Information, HRR.

97. "Aftermath of Harlem Riots," *Amsterdam News,* August 21, 1943.

98. Memo, Chief Inspector to Police Commissioner, August 31, 1943.

99. "Negro, White Leaders Ask for Restoration of Peace," *People's Voice,* August 7, 1943 (statements by Congressman Marcantonio, Judge Steven Jackson of the Children's Court, Justice Hubert T. Delaney of the Children's Court,

and Edward S. Lewis, executive secretary of the New York Urban League, respectively).

100. "Known Facts of Sunday Night's and Monday Morning's Disturbances"; "Racial Element Not Present in New York Riots."

101. "Racial Element Not Present in New York Riots"; "Nothing Solved—But Much Needed (an Editorial)." Domenic J. Capeci Jr. also credits the prompt and evenhanded response by the NYPD and Mayor La Guardia for preventing more damage and ending the rioting relatively quickly. See Capeci, *Harlem Riots of 1943.*

102. "Nothing Solved—But Much Needed (an Editorial)."

103. *New York Times,* August 3, 1943, quoted in Allen D. Grimshaw, "The Harlem Disturbances of 1935 and 1943: Deviant Cases?" in Grimshaw, *Racial Violence in the United States,* 117–18.

104. Harold Orlansky, "Harlem Riot: A Study in Mass Frustration," *Social Analysis Report No. 1* (New York, 1943), quoted in Grimshaw, "The Harlem Disturbances of 1935 and 1943," 118.

105. Statement by the City-Wide Citizens Committee on Harlem, *People's Voice,* August 7, 1943; "City-Wide Council of Races Formed to Probe, Wipe Out Riot Causes," *People's Voice,* August 28, 1943.

106. "This Is Our Common Destiny," *People's Voice,* August 7, 1943.

107. Statement of Walter White, Executive Secretary of the NAACP, in "Negro, White Leaders Ask for Restoration of Peace."

108. "Harlem Looks to the Future," *People's Voice,* August 14, 1943.

109. Statement of Joseph Curran and Saul Mills, Greater New York Industrial Council, in "Negro, White Leaders Ask for Restoration of Peace."

110. "Riots Express Resentment against Existing Social Ills."

111. "Harlem Looks to the Future."

112. "Mayor Has 'Cure' for Harlem—But!" *Amsterdam News,* September 11, 1943.

113. For a useful comparison of the two riots, see Greenberg, "The Politics of Disorder," 395–441.

114. Ibid.; "1935 Riot Causes Started '43 Riot"; "Causes of Harlem's Two Riots Known; Awaits Action by City Heads," *Amsterdam News,* September 18, 1943.

115. "Causes of Harlem's Two Riots Known."

116. Theodore H. Hernades, letter titled "Hoodlumism Started Disturbances," printed in "Readers Comment on Recent Rioting."

117. F.I., letter titled "That Wasn't a Riot; Twas Mass Stealing," printed in "Readers Comment on Recent Rioting."

118. Preliminary Report on Reactions to the Harlem Riot, Special Memo 76, Research Division and Surveys Division, Bureau of Special Services, Office of War Information, August 6, 1943, HRR.

119. Report No. D-3, August 21, 1943, Research Division, Bureau of Special Services, Office of War Information, HRR.

120. Ibid.

121. Ibid.

122. Ibid.

123. Ibid.

124. Ibid.

125. Ibid.

126. "New Trial for Youth Who Told Cop Bronx Needed Riot," *Amsterdam News,* September 18, 1943.

127. Langston Hughes, "Beaumont to Detroit, 1943," *Common Ground* (Winter 1943): 104, quoted in Capeci, *Harlem Riot of 1943,* 75–76.

128. Adam Clayton Powell, Sr., "Riots and Ruins," manuscript, n.d. (1945?), Schomburg typescript collection, box 33, quoted in Greenberg, "The Politics of Disorder," 427–28.

129. NAACP to Mayor Fiorello La Guardia, July 29, 1943.

EPILOGUE

1. "Mexicans, Negroes Victimized," *Amsterdam News,* June 19, 1943.

2. For an analysis of the changing meaning and context of the zoot suit since World War II, see, for example, Susan Marie Green, "Zoot Suiters: Past and Present" (Ph.D. thesis, University of Minnesota, 1997).

3. See, for example, Madrid-Barela, "In Search of the Authentic Pachuco," 31–60; Pagán, *Murder at the Sleepy Lagoon,* 213–18.

4. See, for example, Ramírez, "Crimes of Fashion"; Spickard, "Not Just the Quiet People."

5. On low riders and their connection to the zoot as a cultural symbol, see, for example, Luis Plascencia, "Low Riding in the Southwest: Cultural Symbols in the Mexican Community," in García et al., *History, Culture and Society,* 141–75. For more on low-rider culture, see, for example, Denise Sandoval, "Cruising through Low Rider Culture : Chicana/o Identity in the Marketing of *Low Rider* Magazine," in Alicia Gaspar de Alba, ed., *Velvet Barrios: Popular Culture and Chicana/o Sexualities* (New York: Palgrave Macmillan, 2003); Brenda Jo Bright, "Remappings: Los Angeles Low Riders," in Brenda Jo Bright and Liza Bakewell, eds., *Looking High and Low: Art and Cultural Identity* (Tucson: University of Arizona Press, 1995), 89–123.

6. Robin D. G. Kelley, "The Riddle of the Zoot: Malcolm Little and Black Cultural Politics during World War II," in Kelley, *Race Rebels,* 161–81; Daniels, "Los Angeles Zoot."

7. For studies that consider the relational, comparative, or international character of culture and politics during the Civil Rights Movement, see, for example, Laura Pulido, *Black, Brown, Yellow, and Left: Radical Activism in Los Angeles* (Berkeley: University of California Press, 2006); Oropeza, *¡Raza Sí! ¡Guerra No!*; George Mariscal, *Brown-Eyed Children of the Sun: Lessons from the Chicano Movement, 1965–1975* (Albuquerque: University of New Mexico Press, 2005).

8. Rod Hernandez, "Between Black, Brown & Beige: Latino Poets and the Legacy of Bob Kaufman," *Callaloo* 25, no. 1 (Winter 2002): 190–96.

9. On the varied politics of Chicano movement poetry, see, for example, Ramón Gutiérrez, "Community, Patriarchy, and Individualism: The Politics of Chicano History and the Dream of Equality," *American Quarterly* 45, no. 1

(March 1993): 44–72. On Chicana/o Movement feminism more generally, see, for example, Alma M. García, "The Development of a Chicana Feminist Discourse, 1970–1980," in Ellen Carol DuBois and Vicki L. Ruiz, eds., *Unequal Sisters: A Multicultural Reader in U.S. Women's History* (New York: Routledge, 1990), 418–31.

10. George Lipsitz, "Not Just Another Social Movement: Poster Art and the Movimiento Chicano," in *American Studies in a Moment of Danger* (Minneapolis: University of Minnesota Press, 2001), 176.

11. Ibid., 176–77.

12. For an excellent synopsis of immigration in the United States since the 1960s, see David Gutiérrez, "Demography and the Shifting Boundaries of 'Community': Reflections on 'U.S. Latinos' and the Evolution of Latino Studies," in David Gutiérrez, ed., *The Columbia History of Latinos in the United States since 1960* (New York: Columbia University Press, 2004), 1–42.

13. On the globalization of capital and its repercussions for studies of U.S. culture, see the excellent essay by George Lipsitz, "In the Midnight Hour: American Studies in a Moment of Danger," in *American Studies in a Moment of Danger*, 3–30. On culture and globalization more generally, see Arjun Appadurai, "Disjuncture and Difference in the Global Cultural Economy," in Patrick Williams and Laura Chrisman, eds., *Colonial Discourse and Post-colonial Theory: A Reader* (New York: Columbia University Press, 1994); Lisa Lowe and David Lloyd, eds., *The Politics of Culture in the Shadow of Capital* (Durham, NC: Duke University Press, 1997). On urban youth culture and the deindustrialization of U.S. cities, see, for example, Robin D. G. Kelley, "Kickin' Reality, Kickin' Ballistics: 'Gangsta Rap' and Postindustrial Los Angeles," in *Race Rebels,* 183–227; Tricia Rose, *Black Noise: Rap Music and Black Popular Culture in Contemporary America* (Hanover, OH: Wesleyan University Press, 1994). On globalization and the postindustrial city more generally, see, for example, Saskia Sassen, *The Global City: New York, London, Tokyo* (Princeton, NJ: Princeton University Press, 2001).

14. On Chicana/o and Latina/o hip-hop, see, for example, Pancho McFarland, "Here Is Something You Can't Understand . . . : Chicano Rap and the Critique of Globalization," in Arturo Aldama and Naomi Quiñonez, eds., *Decolonial Voices: Chicana and Chicano Cultural Studies in the 21st Century* (Bloomington: Indiana University Press, 2002), 297–315; Raquel Z. Rivera, *New York Ricans from the Hip Hop Zone* (New York: Palgrave Macmillan, 2003); Juan Flores, *From Bomba to Hip-Hop: Puerto Rican Culture and Latino Identity* (New York: Columbia University Press, 2000).

Bibliography

PRIMARY SOURCES

Archival Collections and Government Documents

Bass, Charlotta. Collection. Southern California Library for Social Studies and Research, Los Angeles.

Black Newspapers Collection. Schomburg Center for Research in Black Culture. New York Public Library.

Bowron, Fletcher. Collection, 1934–1970. The Huntington Library, San Marino, CA.

California Legislature. Joint Fact-Finding Committee on Un-American Activities, 1945.

Corona, Bert. Papers. Department of Special Collections, Stanford University, Stanford, CA.

Ford, John Anson. Collection. The Huntington Library, San Marino, CA.

Harlem Neighborhood Association Papers. Schomburg Center for Research in Black Culture, New York Public Library.

Harlem Riots of 1943, Report. Schomburg Center for Research in Black Culture. New York Public Library.

Kenny, Robert. Collection, 1823–1975. Southern California Library for Social Studies and Research, Los Angeles.

La Guardia, Fiorello. Papers. Municipal Archives, New York City.

Lane, Layle. Papers. Schomburg Center for Research in Black Culture, New York Public Library.

McGrath, Alice. Collection. Department of Special Collections, University of California, Los Angeles.

———. Papers. Department of Special Collections, University of California, Los Angeles.

McWilliams, Carey. Papers. Department of Special Collections, University of California, Los Angeles.

Mexican American Collection, Chicano/Chicana Experience. Department of Special Collections, California State University, Long Beach.

Papers of the National Association for the Advancement of Colored People. Part 15, Segregation and Discrimination, Complaints and Responses, 1940–1955, series A. Legal Dept., NAACP, Bethesda, MD.

Papers of the National Negro Congress. Schomburg Center for Research in Black Culture, New York Public Library.

Quevedo, Eduardo. Papers. Department of Special Collections, Stanford University.

Records of the Commandant's Office, General Correspondence, 1924–1955. Records of Shore Establishments and Naval Districts, 181, Eleventh Naval District. National Archives and Records Administration, Pacific Region, Laguna Niguel, CA.

Rosie the Riveter Revisited: Women and the World War II Work Experience. Interviews of Rose Echeverria Mulligan, Mary Luna, Margarita Salazar, Beatrice Morales Clifton, Margarita Salazar (McSweyn), Adele Hernandez Milligan, J. K., Videll Drake. Department of Special Collections, California State University, Long Beach.

Ruiz, Manuel. Papers. Department of Special Collections, Stanford University.

Sleepy Lagoon Defense Committee Archive. Collection 107. Department of Special Collections, University of California, Los Angeles.

United States Bureau of the Census, Sixteenth Census of the United States 1940.

Oral Histories

Pseudonyms are marked with an asterisk.

Author interviews

Alcoser, Joe. San Diego, CA. 1998.

Alvarez, Antonio. San Diego, CA. February 25, 1994.

Galindo, Ramón. Austin, TX. June 27, 2000.

Hernandez, Maria.* Los Angeles. February 14, 2000.

Perkins, Perry.* San Diego, CA. December 20, 2001.

Rivas, Lupe.* Los Angeles. January 13, 2000.

Rodriguez, Bob.* Los Angeles. February 14, 2000.

Department of Special Collections, University of California, Los Angeles

"John Anson Ford and Los Angeles County Government," John Anson Ford Oral History. Interviewed by L. Craig Cunningham, 1967. Collection 300/50.

"Law and Social Conscience." Ben Margolis Oral History. Interviewed by Michael Batter, July 9, 1984. Collection 300/250

"The Education of Alice McGrath." Alice McGrath Oral History. Interviewed

by Michael Balter, December 28, 1984; January 20 and 21, 1985. Collection 300/269.
"In All Things Honorable." Carey McWilliams Oral History. Interviewed by Joel Gardner, July 13, 1978. Collection 300/195.

SECONDARY SOURCES

Acuña, Rodolfo. *Occupied America: A History of Chicanos*. 3rd ed. New York: Harper and Row, 1988.

Adler, Patricia Rae. "The 1943 Zoot-Suit Riots: Brief Episode in a Long Conflict." In Servin, *An Awakened Minority*, 142–58.

Aldama, Arturo J., and Naomi Quiñonez, editors. *Decolonial Voices: Chicana and Chicano Cultural Studies in the 21st Century*. Bloomington: Indiana University Press, 2002.

Allen, Rodney F., and Charles Adair, editors. *Violence and Riots in Urban America*. Worthington, OH: Charles A. Jones, 1969.

Alund, Aleksandra, and Raoul Granqvist, editors. *Negotiating Identities: Essays on Immigration and Culture in Present-Day Europe*. Amsterdam: Rodopi, 1995.

Amit-Talai, Vared, and Helena Wulff, editors. *Youth Cultures: A Cross-Cultural Perspective*. London: Routledge, 1995.

Anderson, Benedict. *Imagined Communities*. London: Verso, 1983.

Anderson, Jervis. *This Was Harlem: A Cultural Portrait, 1900–1950*. New York: Farrar, Strauss and Giroux, 1982.

Anderson, Karen. *Wartime Women: Sex Roles, Family Relations, and the Status of Women during World War II*. Westport, CT: Greenwood Press, 1981.

Aparicio, Frances, and Candida Jaquez, editors. *Musical Migrations*. Vol. 1, *Transnationalism and Cultural Hybridity in Latin/o America*. New York: Palgrave Macmillan, 2003.

Appadurai, Arjun. "Disjuncture and Difference in the Global Cultural Economy." In Williams and Chrisman, *Colonial Discourse and Post-colonial Theory*, 324–39.

Austin, Joe. *Taking the Train: How Graffiti Became a Crisis in New York City*. New York: Columbia University Press, 2001.

Austin, Joe, and Michael Nevin Willard, editors. *Generations of Youth: Youth Cultures and History in Twentieth-Century America*. New York: New York University Press, 1998.

Back, Les. "X Amount of Sat Siri Akal! Apache Indian, Reggae Music, and Intermezzo Culture." In Alund and Granqvist, *Negotiating Identities*, 139–66.

Bailey, Beth. *The First Strange Place: The Alchemy of Race and Sex in World War II Hawaii*. New York: Free Press, 1992.

Bakare-Yusuf, Bibi. "The Economy of Violence: Black Bodies and the Unspeakable Terror." In Price and Shildrick, *Feminist Theory and the Body*, 311–23.

Baker, Houston, Jr. *Modernism and the Harlem Renaissance*. Chicago: University of Chicago Press, 1987.

Banay, Ralph S. "A Psychiatrist Looks at the Zoot Suit." *Probation* 22, no. 3 (1944): 81–85.

Barajas, Frank. "The Defense Committees of Sleepy Lagoon: A Convergent Struggle against Fascism, 1942–1944." *Aztlan* 31, no. 1 (Spring 2006): 33–62.

Barkan, Elazar. *The Retreat of Scientific Racism: Changing Concepts of Race in Britain and the U.S. between the World Wars.* Cambridge: Cambridge University Press, 1992.

Bass, Charlotta. *Forty Years.* Los Angeles: Charlotta Bass, 1960.

Bernstein, Saul. *Alternatives to Violence: Alienated Youth and Riots, Race, and Poverty.* New York: Association Press, 1967.

Bhabba, Homi. *The Location of Culture.* London: Routledge, 1994.

Black Public Sphere Collective, The, editors. *The Black Public Sphere: A Public Culture Book.* Chicago: University of Chicago Press, 1995.

Blum, John Morton. *United Against: American Culture and Society during World War II.* Colorado Springs: U.S. Air Force Academy, 1983.

———. *V Was for Victory: Politics and Culture during World War II.* New York: Harcourt Brace Jovanovich, 1976.

Blumberg, Barbara. *The New Deal and the Unemployed: The View from New York City.* Lewisburg, PA: Bucknell University Press, 1979.

Bonefeld, Werner, editor. *Revolutionary Writing: Common Sense Essays in Post-political Politics.* Brooklyn: Autonomedia, 2003.

Boskin, Joseph. *Urban Racial Violence in the Twentieth Century.* London: Glencoe Press, 1976.

Brandt, Nat. *Harlem at War: The Black Experience in WWII.* Syracuse: Syracuse University Press, 1996.

Bright, Brenda Jo. "Remappings: Los Angeles Low Riders." In Bright and Bakewell, *Looking High and Low*, 89–123.

Bright, Brenda Jo, and Liza Bakewell, editors. *Looking High and Low: Art and Cultural Identity.* Tucson: University of Arizona Press, 1995.

Bryant, Clora, et al., editors. *Central Avenue Sounds: Jazz in Los Angeles.* Berkeley: University of California Press, 1998.

Buckley, Gail. *American Patriots: The Story of Blacks in the Military from the Revolution to Desert Storm.* New York: Random House, 2001.

Burran, James. "Racial Violence in the South during World War II." Ph.D. thesis, University of Tennessee, 1977.

Butler, Judith. *Gender Trouble: Feminism and the Subversion of Identity.* New York: Routledge, 1990.

Calavita, Kitty. *Inside the State: The Bracero Program, Immigration, and the I.N.S.* New York: Routledge, 1992.

Calhoun, Craig, editor. *Habermas and the Public Sphere.* Cambridge: MIT Press, 1992.

Callahan, Manuel. "Zapatismo beyond Chiapas." In Solnit, *Globalize Liberation*, 217–28.

Calloway, Cab. *The New Cab Calloway's Hipsters' Dictionary.* New York: 1944. Reprint as appendix to Calloway and Rollins, *Of Minnie the Moocher and Me.*

Calloway, Cab, and Bryant Rollins. *Of Minnie the Moocher and Me.* New York: Thomas Y. Crowell, 1976.

Camarillo, Albert. *Chicanos in a Changing Society: From Mexican Pueblos to American Barrios in Santa Barbara and Southern California, 1848–1930.* Cambridge, MA: Harvard University Press, 1979.

Campbell, D'Ann. *Women at War with America: Private Lives in a Patriotic Era.* Cambridge, MA: Harvard University Press, 1984.

Capeci, Dominic J., Jr. *The Harlem Riot of 1943.* Philadelphia: Temple University Press, 1977.

———. *Race Relations in Wartime Detroit.* Philadelphia: Temple University Press, 1984.

Capeci, Dominic J., Jr. and Martha Wilkerson. *Layered Violence: The Detroit Rioters of 1943.* Jackson: University Press of Mississippi, 1991.

Castillo, Richard Griswold del. "The Los Angeles 'Zoot Suit Riots' Revisited: Mexican and Latin American Perspectives." *Mexican Studies–Estudios Mexicanos* 16, no. 2 (Summer 2000): 367–78.

Castles, Stephen, and Alastair Davidson. *Citizenship and Migration: Globalization and the Politics of Belonging.* New York: Routledge, 2000.

Certeau, Michel de. *The Practice of Everyday Life.* Berkeley: University of California Press, 1984.

Chambers, Ross. *Room for Maneuver: Reading the Oppositional in Narrative.* Chicago: University of Chicago Press, 1991.

Chavez, Ernesto. *Mi Raza Primero! Nationalism, Identity, and Insurgency in the Chicano Movement in Los Angeles, 1966–1978.* Berkeley: University of California Press, 2002.

Chibnall, Steve. "Whistle and Zoot: The Changing Meaning of a Suit of Clothes." *History Workshop Journal* 20 (Autumn 1985): 56–81.

Clark, Kenneth, and James Barker. "The Zoot Effect in Personality: A Race Riot Participant." *Journal of Abnormal and Social Psychology* 40, no. 1 (January 1945): 143–48.

Clarke, John, Stuart Hall, Tony Jefferson, and Brian Roberts. "Subcultures, Cultures, and Class." In Hall and Jefferson, *Resistance through Rituals*, 9–74.

Cohen, Lizabeth. *A Consumer's Republic: The Politics of Mass Consumption in Postwar America.* New York: Knopf, 2003.

Cosgrove, Stuart. "The Zoot Suit and Style Warfare." *History Workshop Journal* 18 (Autumn 1984): 77–91.

Cronon, William, George Miles, and Jay Gitlin, editors. *Under an Open Sky: Rethinking America's Western Past.* New York: W. W. Norton, 1992.

Dalfiume, Richard M. *Desegregation of the U.S. Armed Forces: Fighting on Two Fronts, 1939–1953.* Columbia: University of Missouri Press, 1969.

Daniels, Douglas Henry. "Los Angeles Zoot: Race 'Riot,' the Pachuco, and Black Music Culture." *Journal of African American History* 87, no. 1 (Winter 2002): 98–118.

Daniels, Roger. *Concentration Camps, U.S.A.: Japanese Americans and World War II.* New York: Holt, Rinehart and Winston, 1970.

———. *Prisoners without Trial: Japanese Americans in World War II.* New York: Hill and Wang, 1993.

Davis, Mike. *City of Quartz: Excavating the Future of Los Angeles.* London: Verso, 1990.

De Genova, Nicholas, ed., *Racial Transformations: Latinos and Asians Remaking the United States.* Durham, NC: Duke University Press, 2006.

de Graaf, Lawrence. "The City of Black Angels: Emergence of the Los Angeles Ghetto, 1890–1930." *Pacific Historical Review* 39 (1970): 323–52.

de Leon, Juana Ponce, editor. *Our Word Is Our Weapon: Selected Writings, Subcomandante Insurgente Marcos.* New York: Seven Stories Press, 2001.

Delgado, Celeste Fraser, and Jose Esteban Muñoz, editors. *Everynight Life: Culture and Life in Latin/o America.* Durham, NC: Duke University Press, 1997.

Desmond, Jane C. "Embodying Difference: Issues in Dance and Cultural Studies." In Delgado and Muñoz, *Everynight Life,* 33–64.

Donnan, Hastings, and Thomas Wilson. *Borders: Frontiers of Identity, Nation, and State.* New York: Berg, 2001.

Donnan, Hastings, and Thomas M. Wilson, editors. *Border Identities: Nation and State at International Frontiers.* Cambridge: Cambridge University Press, 1998.

Dorner, Jane. *Fashion in the Forties and Fifties.* New Rochelle, NY: Arlington, 1975.

Dreyfus, Hubert L., and Paul Rabinow. *Michel Foucault: Beyond Structuralism and Hermeneutics.* Chicago: University of Chicago Press, 1982.

DuBois, Ellen Carol, and Vicki L. Ruiz, editors. *Unequal Sisters: A Multicultural Reader in U.S. Women's History.* New York: Routledge, 1990.

Ellison, Ralph. *Invisible Man.* New York: Random House, 1982.

Enstad, Nan. *Ladies of Labor, Girls of Adventure: Working Women, Popular Culture, and Labor Politics at the Turn of the Century.* New York: Columbia University Press, 1999.

Epstein, Jonathon S., editor. *Youth Culture: Identity in a Postmodern World.* Malden, MA: Blackwell, 1998.

Erenberg, Lewis A., and Susan Hirsch, editors. *The War in American Culture: Society and Consciousness in World War II.* Chicago: University of Chicago Press, 1996.

Escobar, Edward. *Race, Police, and the Making of a Political Identity: Mexican Americans and the Los Angeles Police Department, 1900–1945.* Berkeley: University of California Press, 1999.

Escobedo, Elizabeth Rachel. "Mexican American Home Front: The Politics of Gender, Culture, and Community in World War II Los Angeles." Ph.D. thesis, University of Washington, 2004.

España-Maram, Linda. "Brown 'Hordes' in McIntosh Suits: Filipinos, Taxi Dance Halls, and Performing the Immigrant Body in Los Angeles, 1930s–1940s." In Austin and Willard, *Generations of Youth,* 118–35.

Esteva, Gustavo. "Regenerating People's Space." *Alternatives* 12 (1987): 125–52.

———. "The Zapatistas and People's Power." *Capital and Class* 68 (Summer 1999): 153–82.

Esteva, Gustavo, and Madhu Suri Prakash. *Grassroots Post-modernism: Remaking the Soil Of Cultures.* London: Zed Books, 1998.

Farber, David, editor. *The Sixties: From Memory to History.* Chapel Hill: University of North Carolina Press, 1994.

Flores, Juan. *From Bomba to Hip-Hop: Puerto Rican Culture and Latino Identity.* New York: Columbia University Press, 2000.

Fogelson, Robert M. *The Fragmented Metropolis: Los Angeles, 1850–1930.* Cambridge: Harvard University Press, 1967.

Foley, Neil. "Becoming Hispanic: Mexican Americans and the Faustian Pact with Whiteness." In Foley, *Reflexiones 1997*, 53–70.

———, editor. *Reflexiones 1997: New Directions in Mexican American Studies.* Austin: University of Texas Press, 1997.

———. *The White Scourge: Mexicans, Blacks, and Poor Whites in Texas Cotton Culture.* Berkeley: University of California Press, 1997.

Fornan, Johan, and Goran Bolin. *Youth Culture in Late Modernity.* London: Sage, 1995.

Foucault, Michel. *Power/Knowledge: Selected Interviews and Other Writings, 1972-1977.* New York: Pantheon Books, 1972.

———. *Discipline and Punish: The Birth of the Prison.* New York: Pantheon Books, 1977.

Franklin, John Hope, and Alfred A. Moss Jr. *From Slavery to Freedom: A History of Negro Americans,* 6th ed. New York: Knopf, 1988.

Fraser, Nancy. "Rethinking the Public Sphere: A Contribution to the Critique of Actually Existing Democracy." In Calhoun, *Habermas and the Public Sphere,* 109–42.

Fredrickson, George. *White Supremacy: A Comparative Study in American and South African History.* Oxford: Oxford University Press, 1981.

Freeman, Joshua. *Working Class New York: Life and Labor since World War II.* New York: New Press, 2000.

Fregoso, Rosa Linda. "Homegirls, Cholas, and Pachucas in Cinema: Taking Over the Public Sphere." *California History* 74, no. 3 (Fall 1995): 317–27.

Gaines, Kevin. *Uplifting the Race: Black Leadership, Politics, and Culture in the Twentieth Century.* Chapel Hill: University of North Carolina Press, 1996.

Galtung, Johan. "Cultural Violence." In Steger and Lind, *Violence and Its Alternatives,* 39–53.

García, Alma. "The Development of Chicana Feminist Discourse, 1970–1980." In DuBois and Ruiz, *Unequal Sisters,* 418–31.

García, Mario T. *Mexican Americans: Leadership, Ideology, and Identity, 1930–1960.* New Haven: Yale University Press, 1989.

García, Mario T., et al., editors. *History, Culture, and Society: Chicano Studies in the 1980s.* Ypsilanti, MI: Bilingual Press, 1983.

García, Matt. *A World of Its Own: Race, Labor, and Citrus in the Making of Greater Los Angeles, 1900–1970.* Chapel Hill: University of North Carolina Press, 2001.

Gaspar de Alba, Alicia, editor. *Velvet Barrios: Popular Culture and Chicana/o Sexualities.* New York: Palgrave Macmillan, 2003.

Gelder, Keith, and Sarah Thornton, editors. *The Subcultures Reader.* London: Routledge, 1997.

Gerstle, Gary. *American Crucible: Race and Nation in the Twentieth Century.* Princeton, NJ: Princeton University Press, 2001.

Gilje, Paul. *Rioting in America.* Bloomington: Indiana University Press, 1996.

Gillespie, Dizzy, with Al Fraser. *To Be or Not—to Bop: Memoirs.* New York: De Capo Press, 1985.

Gilroy, Paul. *Small Acts: Thoughts on the Politics of Black Cultures.* London: Serpent's Tail Press, 1993.

———. *"There Ain't No Black in the Union Jack": The Cultural Politics of Race and Nation.* Chicago: University of Chicago Press, 1991.

Gioia, Ted. *West Coast Jazz: Modern Jazz in California, 1945–1960.* Oxford: Oxford University Press, 1992.

Goldberg, David Theo, editor. *Multiculturalism: A Critical Reader.* Oxford: Blackwell, 1995.

Gonzales, Jorge. "Cultural Fronts: Towards a Dialogical Understanding of Contemporary Cultures." In Lull, *Culture in the Age of Communication,* 106–31.

Gould, Stephen J. *The Mismeasure of Man.* New York: Norton, 1981.

Graham, Hugh, and Ted Gurr, editors. *The History of Violence in America: Historical and Comparative Perspectives.* New York: Bantam Books, 1969.

Gramsci, Antonio. *Selections from the Prison Notebooks.* New York: International Publishers, 1971.

Green, Susan Marie. "Zoot Suiters: Past and Present." Ph.D. thesis, University of Minnesota, 1997.

Greenberg, Cheryl. *Or Does It Explode? Black Harlem in the Great Depression.* New York: Oxford University Press, 1991.

———. "The Politics of Disorder: Reexamining Harlem's Riots of 1935 and 1943." *Journal of Urban History* 18, no. 4 (August 1992): 395–441.

Gregory, Steven. *Black Corona: Race and the Politics of Place in an Urban Community.* Princeton, NJ: Princeton University Press, 1998.

Griffith, Beatrice. *American Me: Fierce and Tender Stories of the Mexican-Americans of the Southwest.* New York: Pennant Books, 1954.

———. "Who Are the Pachucos?" *Pacific Spectator* (Summer 1947).

Grimshaw, Allen. "Factors Contributing to Colour Violence in the United States and Great Britain." In Grimshaw, *Racial Violence in the United States,* 254–69.

———. "The Harlem Disturbances of 1935 and 1943: Deviant Cases?" In Grimshaw, *Racial Violence in the United States,* 117–19.

———. "Lawlessness and Violence in America and Their Special Manifestations in Changing Negro-White Relationships." In Grimshaw, *Racial Violence in the United States,* 14–28.

———, editor. *Racial Violence in the United States.* Chicago: Aldine, 1969.

Gupta, Akhil, and James Ferguson. "Culture, Power, Place: Ethnography at the End of an Era." In Gupta and Ferguson, *Culture, Power, Place,* 1–29.

Gupta, Akhil, and James Ferguson, editors. *Culture, Power, Place: Explorations in Critical Anthropology*. Durham, NC: Duke University Press, 1997.

Gurr, Ted. "Urban Disorder: Perspectives from the Comparative Study of Civil Strife." In Grimshaw, *Racial Violence in the United States*, 371–83.

Gutiérrez, David. "Demography and the Shifting Boundaries of 'Community': Reflections on 'U.S. Latinos' and the Evolution of Latino Studies." In Gutiérrez, *The Columbia History of Latinos in the United States since 1960*, 1–42.

———. "Migration, Emergent Ethnicities, and the 'Third Space': The Shifting Politics of Nationalism in Greater Mexico." *Journal of American History* 86, no. 2 (September 1999): 481–517.

———. *Walls and Mirrors: Mexican Americans, Mexican Immigrants, and the Politics of Ethnicity*. Berkeley: University of California Press, 1995.

———, editor. *The Columbia History of Latinos in the United States since 1960*. New York: Columbia University Press, 2004.

Gutiérrez, Ramón. "Community, Patriarchy and Individualism: The Politics of Chicano History and the Dream of Equality." *American Quarterly* 45, no.1 (March 1993): 44–72.

———. "Ethnic Studies: Its Evolution in American Colleges and Universities." In Goldberg, *Multiculturalism*, 157–67.

Halberstam, Judith. *Female Masculinity*. Durham, NC: Duke University Press, 1998.

Hall, Stuart. "Cultural Identity and Diaspora." In Williams and Chrisman, *Colonial Discourse and Post-colonial Theory*, 392–403.

———. "Gramsci's Relevance for the Study of Race and Ethnicity." In Morley and Chen, *Stuart Hall*, 411–40.

———. "Old and New Identities, Old and New Ethnicities." In King, *Culture, Globalization, and the World System*, 41–68.

———. "What Is This 'Black' in Black Popular Culture?" In Morley and Chen, *Stuart Hall*, 465–75.

Hall, Stuart, and Tony Jefferson, editors. *Resistance through Rituals: Youth Subcultures in Post-War Britain*. London: Routledge, 1996.

Harroway, Donna. *Simians, Cyborgs, and Women: The Reinvention of Nature*. New York: Routledge, 1991.

Hartman, Susan. *The Home Front and Beyond: American Women in the 1940's*. Boston: Twayne, 1982.

Hayashi, Brian Masaru. *Democratizing the Enemy: The Japanese American Internment*. Princeton, NJ: Princeton University Press, 2004.

Hebdige, Dick. *Subculture: The Meaning of Style*. London: Routledge, 1994.

Hernandez, Rod. "Between Black, Brown & Beige: Latino Poets and the Legacy of Bob Kaufman." *Callaloo* 25, no. 1 (Winter 2002): 190–96.

Himes, Chester. *If He Hollers Let Him Go*. London: Falcon Press, 1947. Reprint, New York: Thunder's Mouth Press, 2002.

Hirsch, Arnold R. *Making the Second Ghetto: Race and Housing in Chicago, 1940–1960*. Cambridge: Cambridge University Press, 1983.

Hoffman, Abraham. *Unwanted Mexican Americans in the Great Depression: Repatriation Pressures, 1929–1939*. Tucson: University of Arizona Press, 1974.

Holloway, John. *Change the World without Taking Power: The Meaning of Revolution Today.* London: Pluto Press, 2002.

———. "In the Beginning Was the Scream." In Bonefeld, *Revolutionary Writing,* 15–22.

Holloway, John, and Eloina Pelaez, editors. *Zapatista! Reinventing Revolution in Mexico.* London: Pluto Press, 1998.

Holsinger, M. Paul, and Mary Anne Schofield, editors. *Visions of War: World War II in Popular Literature and Culture.* Bowling Green, OH: Bowling Green State University Popular Press, 1992.

Honey, Maureen. *Bitter Fruit: African American Women in World War II.* Columbia: University of Missouri Press, 1999.

Huggins, Nathan. *Harlem Renaissance.* New York: Oxford University Press, 1971.

Jew, Victor. "Getting the Measure of Tomorrow: Chinese and Chicano Americans under the Racial Gaze, 1934–1935 and 1942–1944." In De Genova, *Racial Transformations,* 62–90.

Johnson, Gaye. "A Sifting of Centuries: Afro-Chicano Interaction and Popular Musical Culture in California, 1960–2000." In Aldama and Quiñonez, *Decolonial Voices,* 316–29.

Johnson, Marilynn S. "Gender, Race, and Rumours: Re-examining the 1943 Race Riots." *Gender & History* 10, no. 2 (August 1998): 252–77.

Johnson, Susan Lee. "A Memory to Sweet Soldiers: The Significance of Gender in the History of the American West." *Western Historical Quarterly* 24, no. 4 (November 1993): 495–518.

Jones, Solomon James. *The Government Riots of Los Angeles, June 1943.* San Francisco: R and E Research Associates, 1973.

Kelley, Robin D. G. *Race Rebels: Culture, Politics, and the Black Working Class.* New York: Free Press, 1994.

Kessner, Thomas. *Fiorello H. La Guardia and the Making of Modern New York.* New York: McGraw-Hill, 1989.

King, Anthony D., editor. *Culture, Globalization, and the World System.* Binghamton: Department of Art and Art History, State University of New York, 1991.

Knopf, Terry Ann. *Rumors, Race, and Riots.* New Brunswick, NJ: Transaction Books, 1975.

Larson, Edward J. *Sex, Race, and Science: Eugenics in the Deep South.* Baltimore: Johns Hopkins University Press, 1995.

Lears, T. J. Jackson. "The Concept of Cultural Hegemony: Problems and Possibilities." *American Historical Review* 90 (1985): 567–93.

Lee, Arthur M., and Norman Humphrey. *Race Riot.* New York: Dryden Press, 1943.

Leonard, Kevin Allen. "Brothers under the Skin? African Americans, Mexican Americans, and World War II in California." In Lotchin, *The Way We Really Were,* 187–214.

Lichtenstein, Nelson. *Labor's War at Home.* Cambridge: Cambridge University Press, 1982.

Lieberson, Stanley, and Arnold Silverman. "The Precipitants and Underlying

Conditions of Race Riots." *American Sociological Review* 30 (December 1965): 887–98.

Lipsitz, George. *American Studies in a Moment of Danger*. Minneapolis: University of Minnesota Press, 2001.

———. *Rainbow at Midnight: Labor Culture in the 1940s*. Urbana: University of Illinois Press, 1994.

———. *Time Passages: Collective Memory and American Popular Culture*. Minneapolis: University of Minnesota Press, 1990.

———. "Who'll Stop the Rain? Youth Culture, Rock 'n' Roll and Social Crisis." In Farber, *The Sixties*, 206–34.

Lopez, Ian Haney. *Racism on Trial: The Chicano Fight for Justice*. Cambridge: Belknap Press, 2003.

———. "The Social Construction of Race: Some Observations on Illusion, Fabrication, and Choice." *Harvard Civil Rights–Civil Liberties Law Review* 29 (Winter 1994): 1–62.

Lotchin, Roger W., editor. *The Way We Really Were: The Golden State in the Second Great War*. Urbana: University of Illinois Press, 2000.

Lott, Eric. "Double V, Double-Time: Bebop's Politics of Style." *Callaloo*, no. 36 (Summer 1988): 597–605.

Lowe, Lisa. *Immigrant Acts: On Asian American Cultural Politics*. Durham, NC: Duke University Press, 1996.

Lowe, Lisa, and David Lloyd, editors. *The Politics of Culture in the Shadow of Capital*. Durham, NC: Duke University Press, 1997.

Lugo, Alejandro, and Bill Maurer, editors. *Gender Matters: Rereading Michelle Z. Rosaldo*. Ann Arbor: University of Michigan Press, 2000.

Lull, James, editor. *Culture in the Age of Communication*. New York: Routledge, 2000.

Macías, Anthony. "Bringing Music to the People: Race, Urban Culture, and Municipal Politics in Postwar Los Angeles." *American Quarterly* 56, no. 3 (September 2004): 693–717.

———. *Mexican American Mojo: Popular Music, Dance, and Urban Culture in Los Angeles, 1938–1968*. Durham, NC: Duke University Press, forthcoming.

———. "Rock con Raza, Raza con Jazz: Latinos/as and Post–World War II Popular American Music." In Aparicio and Jaquez, *Musical Migrations*, Vol. 1, 183–97.

Madrid-Barela, Arturo. "In Search of the Authentic Pachuco: An Interpretive Essay." *Aztlan* 4, no. 1 (Spring 1973): 31–60.

Maira, Sunaina. "Imperial Feelings: Youth Culture, Citizenship, and Globalization." In Suárez-Orozco and Qin-Hilliard, editors. *Globalization*, 266–86.

Maira, Sunaina, and Elisabeth Soep, editors. *Youthscapes: Popular Culture, National Ideologies, Global Markets*. Philadelphia: University of Pennsylvania Press, 2004.

Malbon, Ben. "Clubbing: Consumption, Identity and the Spatial Practices of Every-Night Life." In Skelton and Valentine, *Cool Places*, 203–34.

Malcolm X. *The Autobiography of Malcolm X, as Told to Alex Haley*. New York: Ballantine Books, 1973.

Mariscal, George. *Brown-Eyed Children of the Sun: Lessons from the Chicano Movement, 1965–1975*. Albuquerque: University of New Mexico Press, 2005.

Martin, Randy. *Critical Moves: Dance Studies in Theory and Politics*. Durham, NC: Duke University Press, 1998.

Masotti, Louis, and Don Bowen, editors. *Riots and Rebellion: Civil Violence in the Urban Community*. Beverly Hills: Sage, 1968.

Matsumoto, Valerie. *Farming the Home Place: A Japanese American Community in California, 1919–1982*. Ithaca: Cornell University Press, 1993.

Mazón, Mauricio. *The Zoot-Suit Riots: The Psychology of Symbolic Annihilation*. Austin: University of Texas Press, 1984.

McFarland, Pancho. "Here Is Something You Can't Understand . . . : Chicano Rap and the Critique of Globalization." In Aldama and Quiñonez, *Decolonial Voices*, 297–315.

McKinnon, Catriona, and Iain Hamsher-Monk, editors. *The Demands of Citizenship*. New York: Continuum, 2000.

McMillan, Neil. *Dark Journey: Black Mississippians in the Age of Jim Crow*. Urbana: University of Illinois Press, 1989.

McWilliams, Carey. *North from Mexico: The Spanish-Speaking People of the United States*. Philadelphia: J. B. Lippincott, 1968.

Midnight Notes Collective. *Auroras of the Zapatistas: Local and Global Struggles of the Fourth World War*. Brooklyn: Autonomedia, 2001.

Miller, David. *Citizenship and National Identity*. Cambridge: Polity Press, 2000.

Mintz, Steven. *Huck's Raft: A History of American Childhood*. Cambridge, MA: Belknap Press of Harvard University Press, 2004.

Molina, Natalia. *Fit to Be Citizens? Public Health and Race in Los Angeles, 1879–1939*. Berkeley: University of California Press, 2006.

Montejano, David. *Anglos and Mexicans in the Making of Texas, 1836–1986*. Austin: University of Texas Press, 1987.

Moore, Christopher. *Fighting for America: Black Soldiers—The Unsung Heroes of World War II*. New York: One World/Ballantine, 2004.

Moore, Joan W. *Homeboys: Gangs, Drugs, and Prison in the Barrios of Los Angeles*. Philadelphia: Temple University Press, 1978.

Morin, Raul. *Among the Valiant: Mexican Americans in World War II and Korea*. Alhambra, CA: Borden, 1963.

Morley, David, and Kuan-Hsing Chen, editors. *Stuart Hall: Critical Dialogues in Cultural Studies*. New York: Routledge, 1996.

Muller, Eric. *Free to Die for Their Country: The Story of the Japanese American Draft Resisters in World War II*. Chicago: University of Chicago Press, 2001.

Muñoz, Carlos. *The Chicano Movement: Youth, Identity, Power*. New York: Verso, 2003.

Nalty, Bernard C. *Strength for the Fight: A History of Black Americans in the Military*. New York: Free Press, 1986.

Nash, Gerald. *The American West Transformed: The Impact of the Second World War*. Bloomington: Indiana University Press, 1985.

———. *World War II and the West: Reshaping the Economy.* Lincoln: University of Nebraska Press, 1990.

Odum, Howard. *Race and Rumors of Race: Challenge to American Crisis.* Chapel Hill: University of North Carolina Press, 1943.

Omi, Michael, and Howard Winant. *Racial Formation in the United States: From the 1960s to the 1980s.* New York: Routledge, 1994.

Oropeza, Lorena. *¡Raza Si! ¡Guerra No! Chicano Protest and Patriotism during the Viet Nam War Era.* Berkeley: University of California Press, 2005.

Osofsky, Gilbert. *Harlem: The Making of a Ghetto.* New York: Harper and Row, 1971.

Otis, Johnny. *Upside Your Head! Rhythm and Blues on Central Avenue.* Hanover, OH: Wesleyan University Press, 1993.

Pagán, Eduardo Obregón. *Murder at the Sleepy Lagoon: Zoot Suits, Race, and Riot in Wartime L.A.* Chapel Hill: University of North Carolina Press, 2003.

Paz, Octavio. *The Labyrinth of Solitude.* New York: Grove Press, 1985.

Peña, Manuel. *The Texas-Mexican Conjunto.* Austin: University of Texas Press, 1985.

Pepper, Art and Laurie. *Straight Life: The Story of Art Pepper.* New York: Da Capo Press, 1994.

Perez, Emma. *The Decolonial Imaginary: Writing Chicanas into History.* Bloomington: Indiana University Press, 1999.

Perks, Robert, and Alisdair Thomson, editors. *The Oral History Reader.* London: Routledge, 1997.

Pitti, Stephen J. *The Devil in Silicon Valley: Northern California, Race, and Mexican Americans.* Princeton, NJ: Princeton University Press, 2003.

Plascencia, Luis. "Low Riding in the Southwest: Cultural Symbols in the Mexican Community." In García et al., *History, Culture, and Society,* 141–75.

Polenberg, Richard. *America at War: The Home Front, 1941–1945.* Englewood Cliffs, NJ: Prentice-Hall, 1972.

Price, Janet, and Margrit Shildrick, editors. *Feminist Theory and the Body: A Reader.* New York: Routledge, 1999.

Pulido, Laura. *Black, Brown, Yellow, and Left: Radical Activism in Los Angeles.* Berkeley: University of California Press, 2006.

Ramírez, Catherine S. "Crimes of Fashion: The Pachuca and Chicana Style Politics." *Meridians: Feminism, Race, Transnationalism* 2, no. 2 (2002): 1–35.

———. *The Woman in the Zoot Suit: Mexican American Women, Nationalism, and Citizenship.* Durham, NC: Duke University Press, forthcoming.

Ramos-Zayas, Ana Y. "Delinquent Citizenship, National Performances: Racialization, Surveillance, and the Politics of 'Worthiness' in Puerto Rican Chicago." *Latino Studies* 2 (2004): 26–44.

Reed, Merl E. *Seedtime for the Modern Civil Rights Movement: The President's Committee on Fair Employment Practice, 1941–1946.* Baton Rouge: Louisiana State University Press, 1991.

Reisler, Mark. *By the Sweat of Their Brow: Mexican Immigrant Labor in the U.S., 1900–1940.* Westport, CT: Greenwood Press, 1976.

Rivas-Rodriguez, Maggie, editor. *Mexican Americans and World War II.* Austin: University of Texas Press, 2005.

Rivera, Raquel. *New York Ricans from the Hip Hop Zone*. New York: Palgrave Macmillan, 2003.

Robinson, Greg. *By Order of the President: FDR and the Internment of Japanese Americans*. Cambridge, MA: Harvard University Press, 2003.

Romo, Ricardo. *East Los Angeles: History of a Barrio*. Austin: University of Texas Press, 1983.

Rose, Tricia. *Black Noise: Rap Music and Black Popular Culture in Contemporary America*. Hanover, CT: Wesleyan University Press, 1994.

Ruiz, Vicki. *Cannery Women, Cannery Lives: Mexican Women, Unionization, and the California Food Processing Industry, 1930–1950*. Albuquerque: University of New Mexico Press, 1987.

———. *From Out of the Shadows: Mexican Women in Twentieth-Century America*. New York: Oxford University Press, 1998.

Sánchez, George. *Becoming Mexican American: Ethnicity, Culture and Identity in Chicano Los Angeles, 1900–1945*. Oxford: Oxford University Press, 1993.

Sandoval, Denise. "Cruising through Low Rider Culture: Chicana/o Identity in the Marketing of Low Rider Magazine." In Gaspar de Alba, *Velvet Barrios*, 179–96.

Sassen, Saskia. *The Global City: New York, London, Tokyo*. Princeton, NJ: Princeton University Press, 2001.

Scott, James. *Domination and the Arts of Resistance: Hidden Transcripts*. New Haven: Yale University Press, 1990.

Scott, Joan. *Gender and the Politics of History*. New York: Columbia University Press, 1988.

Serna, Laura Isabel. "The Zoot Suiter and the Fifi: Transnational Origins of Chicano Resistance." Paper presented at the Mexican American History Workshop, University of Houston, May 6–7, 2005.

Servin, Manuel P., editor. *An Awakened Minority: The Mexican-Americans*. Beverly Hills: Glencoe Press, 1970.

Shah, Nayan. *Contagious Divides: Epidemics and Race in San Francisco's Chinatown*. Berkeley: University of California Press, 2001.

Shimakawa, Karen. *National Abjection: The Asian American Body Onstage*. Durham, NC: Duke University Press, 2002.

Sides, Josh. *L.A. City Limits: African American Los Angeles from the Great Depression to the Present*. Berkeley: University of California Press, 2003.

Simpson, Caroline Chung. *An Absent Presence: Japanese Americans in Postwar American Culture, 1945–1960*. Durham, NC: Duke University Press, 2001.

Skelton, Tracey, and Gill Valentine, editors. *Cool Places: Geographies of Youth Cultures*. London: Routledge, 1998.

Smith, R. J. *The Great Black Way: L.A. in the 1940s and the Lost African American Renaissance*. New York: PublicAffairs, 2006.

Soja, Edward. *Postmodern Geographies: The Reassertion of Space in Critical Social Theory*. London: Verso, 1989.

Solnit, David, editor. *Globalize Liberation: How to Uproot the System and Build a Better World*. San Francisco: City Lights Books, 2004.

Solomon, Larry J. *Roots of Justice: Stories of Organizing in Communities of Color*. Berkeley: Chardon Press, 1998.

Spickard, Paul. "Not Just the Quiet People: The Nisei Underclass." *Pacific Historical Review* 68 (1999): 78–94.

Starr, Kevin. *Embattled Dreams: California in War and Peace, 1940–1950.* Oxford: Oxford University Press, 2002.

Steger, Manfred B., and Nancy S. Lind, editors. *Violence and Its Alternatives: An Interdisciplinary Reader.* New York: St. Martin's Press, 1999.

Suárez-Orozco, Marcelo, and Desirée Baolian Qin-Hilliard, editors. *Globalization: Culture and Education in the New Millennium.* Berkeley: University of California Press, 2004.

Takaki, Ronald. *Double Victory: A Multicultural History of America in World War II.* New York: Little, Brown, 2000.

Thomas, Richard Walter. *From Peasant to Proletarian: The Formation and Organization of the Black Industrial Working Class in Detroit, 1915–1945.* Ph.D. thesis, University of Michigan, 1976.

Thompson, E. P. *The Making of the English Working Class.* New York: Vintage Books, 1966.

Trend, David. *Radical Democracy: Identity, Citizenship, and the State.* New York: Routledge: 1996.

Tuck, Ruth D. "Behind the Zoot-Suit Riots." *Survey Graphics: Magazine of Social Interpretation* 32 (July 1943): 313–16, 335–36.

Turner, Ralph H., and Samuel J. Surace. "Zoot Suiters and Mexicans: Symbols in Crowd Behavior." *American Journal of Sociology* 62 (1956): 14–20.

Tyler, Bruce M. "Black Jive and White Repression." *Journal of Ethnic Studies* 16, no. 4 (Winter 1989): 31–66.

———. "Zoot-Suit Culture and the Black Press." *Journal of American Culture* 17, no. 2 (Summer 1994): 21–34.

U.S. Latinos and Latinas in World War II Oral History Project, Department of Journalism, University of Texas, Austin. *Narratives: Stories of U.S. Latinos and Latinas in World War II* 1, no. 1 (1999).

Vandenberg, Andrew, editor. *Citizenship and Democracy in a Global Era.* New York: St. Martin's Press, 2000.

Viesca, Victor. "The Battle of Los Angeles: The Cultural Politics of Chicana/o Music in the Greater Eastside." *American Quarterly* 56, no. 3 (September 2004): 719–39.

———. "Elegua in East Los Angeles: The Son Jarocho and the Afro-Mexican Dimension in Contemporary Chicana/o Music." Paper presented at Caribbean Soundscapes: A Conference on Caribbean Music and Culture, New Orleans, March 13, 2004.

———. "Straight Out the Barrio: Ozomatli and the Importance of Place in the Formation of Chicano/a Popular Culture in Los Angeles." *Cultural Values* 4, no. 4 (October 2000): 445–73.

Vigil, James Diego. *Barrio Gangs: Street Life and Identity in Southern California.* Austin: University of Texas Press, 1988.

———. *Rainbow of Gangs: Street Culture in the Mega City.* Austin: University of Texas Press, 2002.

Wall, Cheryl A. *Women of the Harlem Renaissance.* Bloomington: Indiana University Press, 1995.

Warner, Michael. "Publics and Counterpublics." *Public Culture* 14, no. 1 (2002): 49–89.

Watson, Jon. "Crossing the Colour Lines in the City of Angels: The NAACP and the Zoot-Suit Riot of 1943." *University of Sussex Journal of Contemporary History* 4 (2002).

Weatherford, Doris. *American Women and World War II.* New York: Facts on File, 1990.

Weglyn, Michi. *Years of Infamy: The Untold Story of America's Concentration Camps.* Seattle: University of Washington Press, 1996.

West, Elliot, and Paula Petrik, editors. *Small Worlds: Children and Adolescents in America, 1850–1950.* Lawrence: University Press of Kansas, 1992.

White, Shane, and Graham White. *Stylin': African American Expressive Culture from Its Beginnings to the Zoot-Suit.* Ithaca, NY: Cornell University Press, 1998.

Widener, Daniel. "Perhaps the Japanese Are to Be Thanked? Asia, Asian Americans, and the Construction of Black California." *positions* 11, no. 1 (2003): 135–81.

Widick, B. J. *Detroit: City of Race and Class Violence.* Detroit: Wayne State University Press, 1989.

Williams, Patrick, and Laura Chrisman, editors. *Colonial Discourse and Post-colonial Theory: A Reader.* New York: Columbia University Press, 1994.

Willis, Paul. *Learning to Labor: How Working Class Kids Get Working Class Jobs.* New York: Columbia University Press, 1981.

Winkler, Alan. *Home Front USA: America during World War II.* Arlington Heights, IL: Harlan Davidson, 1986.

Wintz, Cary D., editor. *The Harlem Renaissance, 1920–1940.* New York: Garland, 1996.

Woodward, C. Vann. *The Strange Career of Jim Crow.* New York: Oxford University Press, 1966.

Wynn, Neil. *The Afro-American and the Second World War.* London: Elek, 1976.

Index

Italicized page numbers refer to illustrations.

AMERICAN CROSSROADS

Edited by Earl Lewis, George Lipsitz, Peggy Pascoe, George Sánchez, and Dana Takagi